WILLS, ADMINISTRATION AND TAXATION: A PRACTICAL GUIDE

EIGHTH EDITION

By

J. S. BARLOW, M.A. (Cantab.) LL.M. (London)

Solicitor; Deputy Director of Academic Studies, College of Law, York

L. C. KING, LL.B. (Bristol), Dip. Crim. (Cantab.)

Solicitor (hons); Principal Lecturer, College of Law, Store Street

A. G. KING, M.A.

Solicitor (hons); Head of Education, Clifford Chance, London; formerly Senior Lecturer, College of Law, Lancaster Gate

First edition 1983
Second edition 1986
Third edition 1988
Fourth edition 1990
Fifth edition 1992
Sixth edition 1994
Reprinted 1994
Seventh edition 1997
Eighth edition 2003

Published by Sweet & Maxwell Ltd
100 Avenue Road, Swiss Cottage, London NW3 3PF
Typeset by MFK Mendip, Frome, Somerset
Printed in England by TJ International Ltd, Padstow, Cornwall

No natural forests were destroyed to make this product; only farmed
timber was used and replanted

A CIP catalogue record
for this book is available
from the British Library

(www.sweetandmaxwell.co.uk)

ISBN 0 421 79960-9

Preface

This book was originally written principally for students. However, many practitioners have found it to be an invaluable first source of reference. The eighth edition has been written with this in mind. We have tried to keep the text reasonably concise while covering all the points which are likely to be needed by most practitioners.

The book states the law as at April 9, 2003.

J. S. Barlow
L. C. King
A. G. King

Acknowledgments

The publishers and authors wish to thank the following bodies for permission to reprint material from the following sources:

Butterworth & Co (Publishers) Ltd: *Encyclopaedia of Forms and Precedents* (4th ed.).
Capital Taxes Office: *IHT Form 200.* Crown copyright.
Laserform Copyright material reproduced with the permission of Laserform International Limited.

Contents

Table of Cases

Table of Statutes

NB: With the passing of the Finance Act 1986, the Capital Transfer Tax Act 1984 is now known as the Inheritance Tax Act 1984. References in this table are to the name of the Act as it appears in the text.

Table of Statutory Instruments

1.   Introduction: What to do After Death

When a person dies there are a number of practical steps which must be taken. For example, the death must be registered, the funeral arranged and the property of the deceased must be made safe. These matters are usually dealt with by members of the deceased's family or by friends.

The question then arises "Who is to be entitled to the deceased's assets?" It is at this point that a solicitor is most likely to be consulted. It is often assumed that the disposition of property depends entirely on whether or not a deceased made a valid will but in fact the disposition of many substantial assets is not affected by the presence or absence of a will. For example, if a deceased owned a house as a joint tenant with another person that property will pass automatically to the survivor as a result of the right of survivorship; if the deceased had taken out insurance policies for the benefit of other people the proceeds of such policies will frequently be paid directly to those people; if the terms of the deceased's employment provide for payment of a lump sum on death it is common for the trustees of the scheme to be given a discretion to pay the lump sum to the person or persons they consider appropriate (the employee is entitled to inform the trustees of his or her wishes as to the destination of the lump sum but the trustees have an overriding discretion). These matters are discussed in Chapter 21.

The disposition of other assets does, however, depend on whether or not there is a valid will. If there is no valid will the disposition of property will be determined by the intestacy rules (explained in Chapter 3). If there is a will it is necessary to discover whether or not it is valid. This requires a consideration of whether or not the testator had sufficient mental capacity at the time the will was made and whether the appropriate formalities were complied with (see Chapter 2). It is quite possible for a will successfully to dispose of some but not all of the deceased's assets. This may be because the will does not deal with all of the deceased's property or because some of the gifts fail (see Chapters 16 & 17). In such cases the disposition of the property is governed partly by the will and partly by the intestacy rules.

It may be difficult to discover whether or not a will exists. If one cannot be found amongst the deceased's papers it is advisable to contact any solicitors consulted by the deceased to discover whether or not a will was deposited with them and to contact the deceased's bank to discover whether or not the deceased had a safe deposit box which might contain it. There is a procedure whereby wills can be deposited during a person's lifetime at the Principal Registry of the Family Division but this is little used. However, it would obviously be worth contacting the Registry if a will is proving difficult to find (there are similar provisions for Scotland and Northern Ireland).

It is necessary for someone to undertake the task of finding the will and checking whether or not it is valid. It is also necessary for someone to collect in the assets of the deceased, pay the debts and other liabilities of the deceased and then transfer the remaining assets to the persons entitled. In order to collect in the assets a person dealing with the estate will often have to *prove* that he or she has authority to deal with the deceased's assets. This is done by producing a grant of representation obtained from the Probate Registry by the person(s) entitled to administer the estate.

Similarly there may be problems when it comes to transferring property of the deceased to the persons entitled. In the case of chattels it will often be sufficient to hand them to the person entitled; many assets (for example, land) are, however, held in the name of the deceased and must somehow be transferred into the name of the new owner if the new owner is to be able to deal with them. A grant of representation enables the person entitled to act on behalf of the estate of the deceased person to transfer property into the name of the new owner.

If the deceased by will appointed someone to administer his estate, that person is called an executor and obtains a grant of representation called a grant of probate which merely *confirms* that person's authority to act in connection with the estate. If no executor was appointed or if the appointed executor is not willing or able to act the Non-Contentious Probate Rules 1987 set out an order for determining who is entitled to act; such a person is called an administrator and must obtain a grant of letters of administration which *confers* authority to act. Executors and administrators can both be referred to as "the personal representatives" of the deceased.

It will often be necessary to obtain a grant of representation in connection with the administration before assets can be collected in or transferred to beneficiaries. The procedure is explained in Chapter 10.

Acting as executor or administrator is a time consuming task. It is also one that carries with it duties and obligations and if those duties are not properly carried out there may be personal liability (this is discussed in Chapter 11). Readers may wonder why anyone is ever willing to act as a personal representative. There are a variety of reasons. Solicitors, banks and trust corporations will be willing to act as executors provided the will authorises them to charge for their services; beneficiaries will usually be willing to act since until someone accepts office it may be impossible to distribute the assets; friends or relatives of the deceased appointed as executors may be willing to accept office as a mark of their respect for the deceased and as a way of helping the bereaved.

2.   Is There a Valid Will?

A. Formalities

1. INTRODUCTION

The formalities required for a valid will are set out in s.9 of the Wills Act   **2.001**
1837, as substituted by s.17 of the Administration of Justice Act 1982. A
will which fails to comply with these formalities is invalid and cannot be
admitted to probate.
   The substituted s.9 provides that:

> "No will shall be valid unless—
>
> (a) it is in writing, and signed by the testator, or by some other
> person in his presence and by his direction; and
> (b) it appears that the testator intended by his signature to give
> effect to the will; and
> (c) the signature is made or acknowledged by the testator in the
> presence of two or more witnesses present at the same time;
> and
> (d) each witness either—
> > (i) attests and signs the will; or
> > (ii) acknowledges his signature,
> >   in the presence of the testator (but not necessarily in the
> >   presence of any other witness), but no form of attestation
> >   shall be necessary."

Different formalities are required in the case of a statutory will of a
mental patient and a privileged testator may make a valid will informally
(see paras 2.011–2.012 below).

2. "IN WRITING"

A will must be "in writing". The writing may be the handwriting of the   **2.002**
testator or any other person or it may be typewriting or any form of
printing or (presumably) produced by a photographic process. The
writing may be in ink, pencil or produced by any other means which make
it visible. However, using a combination of ink and pencil writing raises a
rebuttable presumption that the parts in pencil are deliberative only and
they will be excluded from probate in the absence of evidence that the
testator intended them to be final.
   A will may be made on any material and may be written in any language
(or even in code provided that evidence is available from which the code
may be deciphered).
   In practice most wills are either prepared by a solicitor and typed on

paper or are handwritten by the testator on a will form which contains printed clauses for the standard parts of the will. Downloading from the internet is becoming increasingly popular.

3. THE SIGNATURE

Signature of the testator

2.003   Any mark made by the testator is a valid signature provided the testator *intended* it to be his signature. Testators should be encouraged to sign with their usual signatures so as to avoid any doubt as to the validity of the signature.

The following have been held to be signatures:

(a) a mark made by a rubber stamp with the testator's name on it (*In the Goods of Jenkins* (1863));

(b) the thumb print of an illiterate (*In the Estate of Finn* (1935));

(c) a set of initials (*In the Goods of Savoy* (1851)).

The signature need not consist of a name at all. Thus in *In the Estate of Cook* (1960) a document ending with the words "your loving mother" was admitted to probate on the basis that the testatrix in writing them had intended to refer back to her name which appeared earlier in the document.

The mark relied on as a signature must be complete in the sense that the testator completed as much as he *intended* to be his signature. For example, in *Re Colling* (1972) the testator started to sign his name in the presence of two witnesses one of whom left before he had finished writing. The will was held not to be properly executed since the signature was not completed in the presence of two witnesses. In *In the Goods of Chalcraft* (1948) the testatrix started to sign her name and wrote "E. Chal" before she became too weak to continue. This was held to be a valid signature on the basis that she had decided to end the signature at that point and so the signature was complete.

Signature by another person

2.004   The signature of some person other than the testator is valid provided it is made "in his presence and by his direction". The testator must be present both mentally and physically when the signature is made (see para.2.006 for the meaning of "presence").

The person signing at the testator's direction may be any person including one of the witnesses and may sign either with his own name or with the testator's name. (It is best for the person signing to sign his own name and write that he is signing on behalf of the testator, in his presence and by his direction.)

4. THE TESTATOR INTENDED BY HIS SIGNATURE TO GIVE EFFECT TO HIS WILL

2.005   The original s.9 required that the signature should be "at the foot or end" of the will. This led to a number of cases where probate was refused because the position of the signature did not comply exactly with this description. The Wills Act Amendment Act 1852 was then passed to extend the meaning of "foot or end". However, the excessively complicated wording of that Act forced the courts to make some very narrow distinctions. The substituted s.9 now no longer requires that the signature should be at the foot or end of the will. It is sufficient that "it appears that the testator intended by his signature to give effect to the will".

The exact scope of this requirement will have to be decided upon by the court. In *Wood v Smith* (1991) the court accepted that the signature could be at the top. In the same case the court also held that a signature at the top was valid even though written before the rest of the will. This will only, however, be so if the signature and writing of the will were "all part of one transaction". A signature in the margin of a will would probably satisfy the requirement and so probably would a signature on a separate page attached to the beginning or end of the will. A handwritten will which happened to include the testator's name (for example by starting with words such as "This is the will of me John Smith ...") might, however, still be refused probate on the basis that the words were not intended as a validating *signature* at all but merely as a description of the testator.

The practice (resulting from the wording of the Wills Act Amendment Act 1852) of admitting part of a document to probate but of refusing to admit the parts which appear physically after the signature in certain circumstances, would seem no longer to be possible. This is because the substituted section contemplates that the signature validates all or none of the will.

A signature on an envelope containing an otherwise unsigned will is valid if it was intended to give effect to the will. However, if the signature was written for some other reason (for example, to *identify* the will) the will is not validly signed.

5. SIGNATURE MADE OR ACKNOWLEDGED IN THE PRESENCE OF AT LEAST TWO WITNESSES

The substituted s.9 (like its predecessor) requires that the testator's **2.006** signature is "made or acknowledged by the testator in the presence of two or more witnesses present at the same time". A signature is made in the presence of witnesses, if they see the testator in the act of signing. The witnesses are not required to look at the signature itself nor need they know that the document is a will. It is not necessary to prove that the witnesses actually saw the act of signing; it is sufficient to show they were in such a position that they *could* have seen.

An acknowledgement of signature can be made by words or by conduct. There is an acknowledgement if the testator, or someone else in his presence, asks the witnesses to sign a document and they see his signature on it. The witnesses need not know that the document is a will. However, they must see the signature or at least have an opportunity of doing so. If the *signature* is covered up there is, therefore, no valid acknowledgement (however, the fact that the rest of the will is covered up does not prevent the acknowledgement being valid). The acknowledgement must be made to two or more witnesses present *at the same time.* A will is not, therefore, valid if an acknowledgement is made by the testator to each witness in the absence of the other.

6. WITNESSES

Attestation

2.007   The substituted s.9 requires that each witness must attest and sign the will or acknowledge his signature in the presence of the testator. They must do so *after* the testator has signed or acknowledged. It is not essential that they should sign in each other's presence although, as we have already seen, they must both be present when the testator signs or acknowledges his signature.

Couser v Couser (1996) provides useful guidance on the meaning of "presence" and "acknowledgment". The testator and first witness had both signed the will before the second witness arrived. The testator informally acknowledged his signature by asking the second witness to sign. The first witness had got up to make coffee and was some distance away although in the same room. She gave no formal acknowledgment of her signature but, throughout the period in which the second witness was signing, kept up a discussion with the testator as to whether or not his will would be valid. The judge held that the second witness had signed in the presence of the first witness because the second witness was clearly in such a position that she could have seen. He also held that her continued discussion of the will amounted to an acknowledgment of her own signature. Thus, the two witnesses had signed or acknowledged after the testator had acknowledged his signature in the presence of both the witnesses.

The signatures of the witnesses must "attest" the will, that is the signature must be placed on the will with the intention of validating the testator's signature and not, for example, for the purpose of merely identifying the will. The signatures may appear anywhere on the will and need not be next to or after the testator's signature.

The testator must be mentally and physically present when the witnesses sign. The testator is not mentally present if, for example, he lapses into a coma before the witnesses have finished signing. The testator need not have actually seen the witnesses sign: he is regarded as physically present if he could have seen them had he chosen to look. (Thus, in *Casson v Dade* (1781) the testatrix signed in her solicitor's office in the presence of two witnesses and then retired to her carriage which was waiting in the street outside. There was no evidence that she saw the witnesses sign but, if she had turned her head, she could have seen them through the windows of the carriage and the office. The will was admitted to probate.)

Capacity of witnesses

2.008   No particular rules are laid down as to who may act as a witness. The sole test is whether the witnesses were capable of attesting at the time when they signed. A minor may therefore witness a will although a very young child may not since he would not be capable of understanding the significance of what he was doing. A blind person cannot act as a witness since he cannot have the opportunity to see the signature, similarly a person who is very drunk or of unsound mind would be incapable of attesting.

In choosing witnesses a solicitor should bear in mind that they may be required to give evidence as to due execution. The persons chosen should therefore not be very old or likely to be hard to trace. A beneficiary of the will or a beneficiary's spouse should not be chosen since, although his signature is perfectly valid, he will usually lose his legacy if he witnesses (Wills Act 1837, s.15, see Chapter 16 below). A charging clause is no longer a legacy for these purposes (see Trustee Act 2000, s.28) and so a solicitor can witness a will containing a professional charging clause and appointing as executor the solicitor or a firm in which he is a partner.

7. ATTESTATION CLAUSES

An attestation clause recites that the proper formalities have been **2.009** complied with. A simple clause might read "Signed by the said [Testator] in our joint presence and then by us in his presence" and would be written next to the testator's signature and immediately above the witnesses' signatures. The value of such a clause is that it raises a presumption of due execution.

If there is no attestation clause the registrar, before admitting the will to probate, must require an affidavit of due execution from a witness or if this is not convenient from any other person who was present at execution (Non-Contentious Probate Rules 1987, r.12(1)). If such an affidavit cannot be obtained, other evidence (such as an affidavit to show that the signature on the will is in the handwriting of the deceased) will be required (r.12(2)). Rule 12(3) of the Non-Contentious Probate Rules provides that a registrar may accept a will for proof without evidence if he is satisfied that the distribution of the estate is not thereby affected. In other cases where there is no evidence the court may apply the maxim *omnia praesumuntur rite ac solemniter esse acta* and admit the will to probate if it appears to have been signed and witnessed but this will usually require a hearing before a judge and will, therefore, lead to delay and added expense.

Where the will has been signed by another person at the direction of the testator or where the testator is blind or illiterate special forms of attestation clauses are desirable. The clause should make it clear that the testator had knowledge of the contents of the will at the time of execution.

A will does not have to be dated although it is desirable that it should be to avoid uncertainty as to which of several testamentary documents is the last will. In *Corbett v Newey* (1996), a will was held to be invalid where the testatrix had handed her executed will to her solicitors with a blank next to the date. Her intention was that the will was not to come into effect until certain lifetime gifts had been completed. She wanted her solicitors to date the will when the gifts were complete. However, the court held that the will was invalid because it had not been intended to have immediate effect it is not possible to execute a will conditionally.

8. ARRANGEMENTS FOR EXECUTION

2.010   In an increasingly litigious climate it is important for solicitors to take care over the arrangements for execution of wills. In *Esterhuizen v Allied Dunbar* (1998), a will drafting company was held liable in negligence to a disappointed beneficiary where a will was invalid as a result of having been witnessed by only one person. Longmore J. said:

> "It is in my judgement not enough just to leave written instructions with the testator. In ordinary circumstances just to leave written instructions and to do no more will not only be contrary to good practice but also in my view negligent."

For their own protection solicitors should have in writing an offer in the following terms:

- the client can visit the solicitor's office for execution;
- if the client prefers, the solicitor will visit the client's house with a member of staff;
- if the client prefers, the client can make his/her own arrangements.

In *Gray v Richards Butler (Supervision of Execution of a Will)* (2000) a will was invalid because the two witnesses had not been present at the time that the testator signed or acknowledged the will. The case was decided before *Esterhuizen* but was not reported until a later date. Lloyd J. took a different approach to Longmore J. in *Esterhuizen* and found that the solicitor had not been negligent in failing to offer to supervise the will. He commented that the solicitor's written instructions were "most comprehensive" and that his conduct did not fall short of that required of the "reasonably competent solicitor". It was in his opinion necessary "to bear in mind the very clear terms of the attestation provision of the will".

There was a clear assumption in *Gray* that a solicitor has a duty to examine a will returned post execution. On the particular facts the court accepted that there was nothing about the will which should have aroused the solicitor's suspicion. It follows though that a solicitor who fails to offer to inspect a will may well be negligent if the will turns out to be wrongly executed.

When a solicitor is asked to prepare a will for a client it is best, in order to avoid problems, to adopt the following procedure wherever possible:

(a) The will is prepared by the solicitor from the client's instructions and explained to him.

(b) The client attends at the solicitor's office and, in the presence of two witnesses, places his signature at the end of the will next to a suitable attestation clause.

    (i) The witnesses must not be beneficiaries or spouses of beneficiaries.

    (ii) The solicitor must not be a witness if there is a charging clause in favour of him or his firm (if he is a partner).

    (iii) Even if the solicitor is not a witness he should be present to ensure that the correct procedure is adopted.

(c) The witnesses sign in the presence of the testator (as required by law) and of each other (not required, but useful so that either witness can give evidence as to the other's signature if necessary).

(d) A number of cases have held that, where a will is written on more than one piece of paper, there must be physical contact between the pages at the time of attestation if the will is to be valid. It is doubtful whether this rule survives the enactment of the substituted s.9. However, for the avoidance of doubt as to what has been attested and to prevent accidental loss of parts of the will, all the pages should be securely fastened together.

(e) It is good office practice to keep an attendance note explaining what was done and referring to the addresses of the witnesses so that they can be contacted if necessary to prove due execution.

(f) A copy of the will should be kept and the solicitor should insert on it the names of the testator and witnesses and date of execution. (Such a copy may be admissible to probate if the original is lost, see para.2.038.)

If the client wishes to execute the will at home, the solicitor should offer to supervise execution and have a written record that the offer was made and rejected. The solicitor can make a separate charge for the supervision provided this was made clear in the terms of engagement. The will must be accompanied by very clear instructions. (In particular the client should be warned not to allow anyone who is or whose spouse is a beneficiary to witness, should be told where to sign, should be told to sign his usual signature in ink and should be told to sign in the presence of the witnesses and before they sign.) There must also be an offer to inspect the will after execution.

If a will is to be executed in hospital the solicitor should bear in mind that in many hospitals medical staff are normally prohibited from witnessing wills by the hospital authorities. If this rule applies it is safer to take witnesses to the hospital than to rely on finding witnesses there (other patients are not suitable since there may be doubt about their capacity and they are likely to be hard to trace if needed to give evidence).

If there is any possibility that the capacity of the testator to make a will may be challenged at a later date it is advisable to try to get a doctor to witness the will and/or to make a written statement as to the testator's mental state on the relevant day. (See para.2.026.)

9. PRIVILEGED WILLS

The form of the will
A will can be made informally by a testator who has privileged status. The **2.011** will can be made in any form including a mere oral statement. Such a will is known as a nuncupative will. The only requirement is that the statement made should show an intention to dispose of property in the event of death even if the person making it does not know that he is making a will. Such a will is valid even though made by a minor provided he has privileged status.

Privileged status

2.012   The right to make a privileged will extends to any soldier on actual military service or mariner or seaman being at sea.

"Soldier" includes a member of the R.A.F. and naval or marine personnel serving on land. The exact extent of "actual military service" is open to some doubt. Broadly speaking the term may be said to include activities closely connected with warfare, whether or not war has been declared and whether or not the testator has actually arrived at the scene of the fighting. In *Re Jones* (1976) a soldier serving in Northern Ireland was held to have privileged status. Similarly the term "being at sea" cannot be defined precisely. A seaman on leave who is not in receipt of instructions to join any particular ship is not "at sea" *Re Rapley (Deceased)* (1983). However, a mariner is treated as being at sea for this purpose when he is still on land but under orders to join his ship.

It is the circumstances in which the will was made which are relevant in deciding whether a person had privileged status, not the circumstances in which death occurred.

10. INCORPORATION OF DOCUMENTS

2.013   A properly-drawn will should be contained in one document so as to avoid doubt as to its contents. If changes are to be made later they may be included in a codicil (see paras 2.039–2.041 below). However, if desired an unexecuted document can be incorporated into a will by referring to it in the will. The document is then admitted to probate as part of the will.

An unexecuted document is incorporated if:

(a) it is in existence at the time of execution of the will (or of a codicil republishing the will); and

(b) it is *referred to* in the will as being in existence at the time of execution; and

(c) it is clearly identified in the will.

Document in existence

2.014   Whether a document is in existence at the time of execution is a question of fact. The person who seeks to have it admitted to probate must prove its existence at that time.

Referred to as in existence

2.015   The document must be referred to in the will as in existence at the time of execution. Thus a will which says "I leave £100 to each of the persons named in the list *now* to be found in my desk" satisfies this condition (and the list will be validly incorporated provided it can be shown that it was in fact in existence when the will or confirming codicil was executed). A will which says "I leave £100 to each of the persons named in a list which *I will write* before my death" does not satisfy this condition. Even if the list was made before execution, it will not be admitted to probate as the will refers to its coming into existence at a later date. There are some marginal cases where the wording of the will does not make it clear whether or not the document is extant at the time of execution. In such cases the court will refuse to incorporate the unexecuted document. For example, in *University College of North Wales v Taylor* (1908) probate was refused where the will referred to "any memorandum amongst my papers".

If the will is republished by a codicil an unexecuted document will be incorporated if it is in existence at the time of execution of the codicil and is referred to as being in existence in either the will (which is republished and so speaks from the date of the codicil) or the codicil. *In the Goods of Smart* (1902) demonstrates that this is so but on the facts of that case probate of the unexecuted document was refused because the will referred to its coming into existence in the future.

The document must be identified

The unexecuted document is only incorporated if it is identified by the will. The identification must be sufficient to indicate, without ambiguity, what document is referred to. **2.016**

Practical considerations

Incorporation of documents by reference should be avoided unless absolutely necessary both because of the danger of drafting the will in a way which does not properly incorporate them and because of the danger that the document referred to might be lost before the testator dies. **2.017**

A properly drafted will should make clear whether or not a document referred to is being incorporated. If it does not, the registrar is likely to require any such document to be produced and may call for affidavit evidence as to whether or not the document is incorporated (Non-Contentious Probate Rules 1987, r.14(3)).

Once a document has been incorporated into a will it is treated as an ordinary part of the will and must be filed at the probate registry with the rest of the will. Wills are a matter of public record so that the whole of the will, including the unexecuted document incorporated by reference, is available to the public. There is no point, therefore, in putting sensitive information into a document to be incorporated into the will, with the intention of keeping that information secret.

B. Capacity

1. Age

Persons under the age of 18 cannot make a valid will (Wills Act 1837, s.7 as amended by the Family Law Reform Act 1969, s.3(1)(a)) unless they have privileged status. Privileged status is enjoyed by soldiers on actual military service and mariners and seamen at sea (Wills Act 1837, s.11). **2.018**

On the death of a minor (other than one who has made a privileged will) his estate will be administered under the intestacy rules.

Persons aged 16 and over can, however, make a valid statutory nomination of certain assets provided the nomination is in writing and witnessed by at least one person. For a fuller discussion of nominations see Chapter 21.

2. THE MENTAL STATE OF THE TESTATOR

Testamentary capacity

2.019   According to *Banks v Goodfellow* (1870) a testator only has testamentary capacity if he has "a sound and disposing mind and memory". This requires the testator to understand three things:

(a) *The nature of the act and its effects.* It is not necessary for the testator to understand the precise legal machinery involved in the will so long as he understands its broad effects.

(b) *The extent of the property of which he is disposing.* The testator is not expected to be able to produce a detailed list of every item of property owned. It is sufficient if he has a broad recollection of its extent.

(c) *The claims to which he ought to give effect.* This means that the testator must be able to bring to mind the persons who are "fitting objects of the testator's bounty" (*per* Sir J. Hannen in *Boughton v Knight* (1873)). It does not of course mean that having done so he must dispose of his property to those people. It is sufficient that he is capable of considering them. In *Battan Singh v Armirchand* (1948) a testator who was very ill in the last stages of consumption left his property to certain creditors stating that he had no living relatives. In fact he had three nephews of whom, the evidence showed, he was very fond. The court said that he clearly lacked testamentary capacity having forgotten the moral claims of his nephews.

The time at which testamentary capacity is to be judged

2.020   The general rule is that the testator must have the testamentary capacity at the time the will is signed and witnessed. However, under the rule in *Parker v Felgate* a will may be valid even though the testator has lost testamentary capacity by the time the will is executed provided:

(a) the testator had testamentary capacity at the time he gave a solicitor instructions to prepare a will; and
(b) the will is prepared in accordance with those instructions; and
(c) at the time the will is executed the testator remembers having given instructions for a will to be prepared and believes that the will has been prepared in accordance with those instructions. It is immaterial that the testator does not remember precisely what the instructions were or cannot understand the will if it is read to him.

This principle has been extended to a will prepared by a solicitor on the basis of his client's own draft (*In the Estate of Wallace, Solicitor of the Duchy of Cornwall v Batten* (1952)). However, because of the possibility of abuse, this principle will be applied with caution, if at all, where instructions are relayed to a solicitor through an intermediary (*Battan Singh v Armirchand*).

Capacity does not have to be perfect

2.021   It is important to remember that the only issue is whether or not the testator fulfils the *Banks v Goodfellow* test. It is perfectly possible for a person to be a mental patient for the purposes of the Mental Health Act (incapable of managing his own affairs) and yet be capable of making a valid will.

Ewing v Bennet (2001) and *Barrett v Kaspryyk* (2000) show that a testator need not have unclouded mental faculties.

In *Ewing v Bennet* the testatrix executed her will in early November. There was medical evidence that by December she was in the early stages of Alzheimer's disease. The manageress of the sheltered accommodation where the testatrix lived said that she was forgetful and confused but not seriously affected by senile dementia. The solicitor who took instructions for the will had been concerned that there might be an Inheritance Act claim because the testatrix wished to leave nothing to one daughter (on the basis that she had received substantial amounts in the testatrix's lifetime). He had, therefore, had several meetings with the testatrix and had very full attendance notes. He was satisfied that she fulfilled the *Banks v Goodfellow* test. The Court of Appeal agreed with the trial judge. It appeared that the testatrix's capacity was impaired *to some extent* at the time she executed the will. However, she retained testamentary capacity.

In *Barrett v Kaspryyk* the testatrix was suffering from terminal cancer and was in hospital on heavy medication when she made her will. Her son contended that, as a result of the cocktail of drugs she was taking, she lacked capacity.

Park J. rejected the son's claim. There was strong medical evidence from those who had attended the testatrix in hospital and from the "very experienced legal executive" who had taken instructions that she had not lost her capacity. The son's own expert admitted that it was not a "foregone conclusion" that she would have been incapable.

In both cases the court attached weight to the evidence of the solicitor and legal executive who had taken instructions. Both had clear, contemporaneous attendance notes.

The burden of proof

Just as the person propounding a will must *prove* that it was properly **2.022** signed and witnessed so must he prove that at the time of execution the testator had testamentary capacity. If the burden of proof is not discharged the will is not admitted to probate. *Vaughan v Vaughan* (2002) is a good illustration of the principle. The testatrix was aged 82 and in poor health having had several strokes. In a period of a few weeks before her death she was taken by different members of her family to the family solicitor three times and made three wills each in different terms. The family solicitor refused to prepare any further wills without medical evidence as to capacity.

Four days before she died, the testatrix was taken by her son, John, to see another solicitor. She executed a further will which gave John substantial benefits. The other three children challenged this will on various grounds including lack of testamentary capacity.

Behrens J. found that there was grave suspicion of incapacity. He **2.023** accepted that there was some evidence on both sides. However, it *was for John to prove capacity* and he had not done so.

"I do not know if [Mrs Vaughan] had the capacity to make the will. In the circumstances of this case the burden of proving testamentary capacity or on removing my suspicions remains with John Vaughan. In my judgment, John Vaughan does not come within a measurable distance of satisfying me of the righteousness of the transactions and removing those suspicions, or indeed of establishing testamentary capacity."

There are two important presumptions which must be considered:

(a) *Will rational.* If the will appears rational on the face of it there is a presumption that the testator had testamentary capacity; the will is therefore admitted to probate unless anyone attacking it can produce sufficient evidence to rebut the presumption. If the presumption is rebutted, it is then up to the propounder to prove testamentary capacity.

(b) *Mental states continue.* Mental states are presumed to continue; thus, if a person who normally suffers from mental illness makes a will, it is presumed that he lacked testamentary capacity. It is then up to the propounder of the will to rebut the presumption by proving that the will was made in a lucid interval.

In *Richards v Allan* (2001) an elderly testatrix was discharged from hospital and shortly afterwards made a will at the suggestion of a friend and in favour of the friend.

The friend's brother-in-law, a solicitor, prepared the will on the basis of instructions relayed by the friend (not, of course, best practice).

The friend arranged for the testatrix to sign the will at a time when the testatrix's sister (who shared the house) was absent. The testatrix was visited by her doctor in the morning and by a friend in the evening. Both said that they found her confused. The friend contended that the will had been validly executed between the two visits and indeed the two witnesses said that they had observed nothing strange in the testatrix's behaviour.

The will was found invalid on the basis of (1) lack of capacity and (2) lack of knowledge and approval.

Anthony Mann Q.C. referred to the presumption that mental states continue. The testatrix's confusion was a serious and continuing problem resulting from her diabetes and her medication. *It was not credible that the will had been executed in a lucid interval between two periods of confusion.*

In *Brown v Deacy* (2002) the court said that "convincing proof" of a lucid interval is required.

2.024   Wherever possible objective medical evidence should be obtained. It is dangerous to rely on the opinions of friends or family who may be partial but also may be genuinely unaware of deterioration in the mental abilities of someone they have known well for many years. In a recent unreported case *In the Estate of Ellen Wilkes (Deceased)* (2000) a consultant physician specialising in the care of the elderly gave expert evidence. He warned against the acceptance at face value of statements, whether by medical practitioners or others, indicating that the testatrix was mentally well at the relevant times, without some form of objective diagnostic analysis (such as a Mini Mental State Examination).

In the absence of such a test, comments about the testatrix's apparent mental ability are purely subjective. In the consultant's opinion they should be viewed with caution since a person may appear to have intact mental functions despite severe deficits in reality. It is common to encounter elderly people who seem quite well, but do badly in simple objective tests. In the case of a Mini Mental State Examination, he would expect at least 25 out of 30 points for a person with capacity to make a will, but it would be perfectly possible to have a good interaction with a person who only scored 10 points.

Solicitors often feel embarrassed about raising the question of mental capacity with clients. It is best to approach the matter on the basis of avoiding any possibility of an unnecessary challenge at a later date. The Association of Contentious Trusts and Probate Specialists has published a checklist for solicitors to work through when there are any doubts about mental capacity. It is available on their website *www.ACTAPS.com.*

Insane delusions

An insane delusion is a belief in the existence of something in which no rational person could believe and which could not be eradicated from the testator's mind by reasoned argument (*Dew v Clark and Clark* (1826)). A person suffering from such a delusion can make a valid will provided the delusion is on a subject in no way connected with the will (for example, a belief that the testator is pursued by evil spirits). However, if the delusion affects the testator's judgment, either generally or on one point which affects the dispositions made, the testator does not have testamentary capacity. If the delusion affects the whole will (as in *Dew v Clark and Clark* where the testator had an irrational dislike of his daughter as a result of which he left her nothing in his will) probate will be refused to the whole will. If the delusion affects only part of the will then only that part will be excluded from probate (as in *In the Estate of Bohrmann* (1938) where one clause of a codicil was omitted from probate).   **2.025**

Practical precautions

A solicitor who has any doubts as to the capacity of a client proposing to make a will or any suspicion that lack of capacity may later be alleged, should try to avoid future problems by obtaining medical advice. It is desirable that a medical practitioner examine the testator, preferably at the time the will is signed since the severity of certain mental conditions, for example, senility, vary markedly over relatively short periods of time. Doctors and nurses will normally refuse to witness wills. In such a case ask the doctor or nurse caring for the testator to make a statement as to the mental condition of the testator. A full and careful attendance note should be made by the solicitor or member of his staff who is present. If possible the note should be made contemporaneously.   **2.026**

It is important that solicitors try to comply with the so-called "Golden Rule" set out in full in Chapter 13. In addition to trying to obtain medical approval, the rule requires solicitors to:

- discuss any earlier will with the client (and the reasons for changing it); and

- take the instructions in the absence of anyone who may stand to benefit or who may have influence over the testator.

It is not always possible to interview clients alone as they will sometimes insist that a companion remains with them. However, practitioners should make sure that they have a clear attendance note establishing that it was the client's wish that the third party remained.

Statutory wills

2.027   Section 96(1)(e) of the Mental Health Act 1983 (replacing the Mental Health Act 1959, s.103A as amended) gives the Court of Protection power to make a will on behalf of an adult mental patient. The will is made by an "authorised person" who signs the patient's name and his own name; it is witnessed in the usual way and then sealed with the official seal of the Court of Protection.

A mental patient is a person who is incapable by reason of mental disorder of managing and administering his property and affairs (s.94).

A statutory will can make any provision which could be made by the patient if he had capacity except that it cannot dispose of immovable property situate outside England and Wales. The Court seeks to make the will which the patient would have made, acting reasonably and on competent legal advice, had he or she enjoyed a brief lucid interval. In *Re C. (Spinster and Mental Patient)* (1991) the patient had never been rational. It was held that, in those circumstances, the court should make a will putting itself in the position of the patient and assuming that she would, if rational, have acted "decently in accordance with contemporary standards of morality".

Another example of the use of the procedure was *Re D.(J.)* (1982). The testatrix made a will leaving her house to one of her daughters (who lived with her) and residue to be divided between her other children. The daughter then remarried, the testatrix sold her house, bought a house near her daughter but in fact moved in with the daughter and never used the new house as her home. (The sale of the original house caused the gift of it to her daughter to fail (see "ademption", paras 16.014–16.019).) The daughter and her husband paid for the testatrix's maintenance out of their own pockets for a considerable time until the Court of Protection ordered a payment to them out of the mother's property. The daughter applied to the Court of Protection for the execution of a codicil to her mother's will on the ground that her mother had become senile. The deputy master ordered a legacy of £10,000 to the daughter. The daughter appealed contending that she was entitled to more. The High Court held that the test to be applied was what provision this patient would have made in her will had she not been suffering from mental disorder. A judge has a complete discretion in reviewing the master's order (that is, a judge can vary an order without finding that the master has erred in principle) and on the facts of this case ordered a legacy of £15,000 to the daughter with a substitutional gift to the daughter's husband, if the daughter predeceased her mother.

Procedure
A draft will must be approved by the Court of Protection. It is then **2.028**
executed on behalf of the patient and a certified copy is returned to the
court for sealing. In *Re Hughes (Deceased)* (1999) it was established that it
is irrelevant if the sealing occurs after the death of the patient.

The sealing merely confirms that the statutory will, as executed,
conforms to its authorisation. It is not analogous to the signing of the will
by a mentally capable testator.

A statutory will cannot be made for a minor. Where a minor receives a
large damages award, legal advisers should consider what will happen to
the funds if the minor dies intestate. It is preferable that such sums should
be settled on the minor for life rather than held for the minor absolutely.
Bouette v Rose (2000) is an example of the unsatisfactory operation of the
intestacy rules. The property passed equally to the child's mother who
had cared for her throughout her life and to the child's father who had had
no contact with her. Fortunately the mother's application under the
Inheritance (Provision for Family and Dependants) Act as a person
maintained by the deceased was successful.

C. Knowledge and Approval

1. PRESUMPTION

A testator must know and approve the contents of the will. (This does not **2.029**
apply to an adult mental patient who need not know and approve the
contents of a statutory will.) If a testator signs a will having no knowledge
of the contents, the will is invalid. The time at which knowledge and
approval is required is the time of execution of the will. However,
knowledge and approval (like testamentary capacity) is established if the
testator knew and approved of instructions given to a solicitor to draw up
a will (*Parker v Felgate* above).

The burden of proof of knowledge and approval lies on the person
propounding the will; however, there is normally a rebuttable
presumption that a testator who executes a will (particularly if he has read
the will or has had the will read over to him) does so with knowledge and
approval of the contents. This presumption does not arise:

(a) *In the case of a blind or illiterate testator or where another person
signs on behalf of the testator.* In such cases the registrar will require
evidence that the testator had actual knowledge of the contents (Non-
Contentious Probate Rules 1987, r.13). It is advisable in such a case that
the attestation clause should include a statement that the will was read
over to and approved by the testator. If it does not, affidavit evidence will
be required from the witnesses or from some other person present.
or

(b) *Where there are suspicious circumstances.* If there is evidence of
suspicious circumstances, the will is not admitted to probate unless the
propounder can prove that the testator did know and approve the
contents. The most obvious example of a suspicious circumstance is

where the will is prepared by a major beneficiary or close relative of a major beneficiary. In *Wintle v Nye* (1959) the House of Lords expressed the view that: "It is not the law that in no circumstances can a solicitor or other person who has prepared a will for a testator take a benefit under it. But that fact creates a suspicion that must be removed by the person propounding the will. In all cases the court must be vigilant and jealous. The degree of suspicion will vary with the circumstances of the case. It may be slight and easily dispelled. It may, on the other hand, be so grave that it can hardly be removed" *per* Viscount Simmonds. In *Wintle v Nye* it was held that the gift to the draftsman was not admissible to probate for want of knowledge and approval but that the rest of the will could stand. (Solicitors are subject to special rules of professional conduct in relation to receiving legacies from clients; these are dealt with in para.2.033.)

2.030   In *Fuller v Strum* (2002) the Court of Appeal considered a will prepared by a major beneficiary. It stated the general principle that the court's suspicion ought generally to be excited where a party prepares a will under which he takes a benefit. The court should not pronounce in favour of that will unless the suspicion is removed. *Prima facie*, if the person with the burden of proof gives no evidence, the issue will be decided against him. However, the onus imposed on the party propounding the will is normally discharged by proof of capacity and the fact that the testator executed the will. *Additional evidence is not always required where a beneficiary prepares a will.* The preparation of the will is merely a suspicious circumstance of more or less weight depending upon the circumstances.

The circumstances of a particular case may raise such grave suspicion that it can hardly be removed. *Fuller v Strum* was not such a case. The will was short and simple and the testator had had an opportunity to read it.

The Court of Appeal expressly approved the "properly objective" approach of Lloyd J. in *Hart v Dabbs* (2001). The major beneficiary had been instrumental in the preparation of the will. He was arrested on suspicion of murdering the testator but later released for lack of evidence. The will was held valid on the basis that it was a short, simple document and there was no reason to doubt the testator's knowledge and approval: "so long as he read the document he would have had no difficulty taking in its provisions even if someone else prepared it".

2. MISTAKE

2.031 A mistake may mean that the testator had no knowledge or approval of the will as a whole (for example, where he executes the wrong will) or of part only of the will (as in *Wintle v Nye*). If a testator includes words in his will having intended to write other words, the words mistakenly included will be omitted from probate; similarly if a testator includes words in his will but does not know or approve them those words will be omitted from probate. An example of the latter type of mistake occurred in *Re Phelan* (1972). The testator bought three printed will forms and, thinking that every holding of shares had to be dealt with in a separate will, executed three wills in favour of X, each will disposing of a separate shareholding. Each will was executed on the same day and each contained a printed revocation clause. Stirling J. held that as the words of revocation were clearly included in the wills by inadvertence and misunderstanding they could be omitted from probate.

The probate court will not interfere, however, where a testator deliberately selects certain words and includes them in the will, even if it is clearly shown that the testator was mistaken as to their legal effect. Thus in *Collins v Elstone* (1893) a testatrix deliberately included a revocation clause under the misapprehension that it would revoke only a small part of her earlier will. The court held that the revocation clause could not be omitted from the will. The rule is the same where a draftsman prepares a will on behalf of a testator and deliberately selects words being mistaken as to their legal effect; those words will be admitted to probate (*Re Horrocks* (1939)).

The probate court has always had power to omit words from probate. Prior to the Administration of Justice Act 1982 it did not have any power to insert words even where it was obvious that words had been omitted accidentally. However, s.20 of that Act alters this rule to a limited extent. It provides that if a court is satisfied that a will is so expressed that it fails to carry out the testator's intentions in consequence of:

    (a) a clerical error, or
    (b) a failure to understand his instructions,

it may order that the will be rectified so as to carry out his intentions. The remedy is discretionary. See *Grattan v McNaughton* (2001). After the expiry of six months from the date of the grant of representation an application for rectification cannot be made except with leave from the court. It is possible to make applications out of time and the recent case of *Chittock v Stevens* (2000) decided that such applications will be governed by the same guiding principles as applications under the Inheritance (Provision for Family and Dependants) Act, s.4. Personal representatives who distribute after that date will not be liable on the ground that they should have taken into account the possibility of an out-of-time application being made.

If, therefore, a typing error is made in a will, the probate court can order **2.032** that words included by mistake be omitted and that words omitted by mistake be inserted. Similarly if a solicitor misunderstands his instructions the court can order that the mistake be rectified. In *Wordingham v Royal Exchange Trust Co.* (1991) the draftsman omitted a clause containing a power of appointment which it had been intended to include in the will. This was held to be a clerical error and so rectification was ordered. However, it would appear that the Act has not altered the rule that if the testator or draftsman is mistaken as to the legal effect of words deliberately selected for inclusion in the will the court cannot interfere.

An application for rectification may be made to a registrar, unless a probate action has been commenced.

The application must be supported by an affidavit, setting out the grounds of the application, together with such evidence as can be adduced as to the testator's intentions and as to whichever of the following matters are in issue:

(a) the respects in which the testator's intentions were not understood, or

(b) the nature of any alleged clerical error.

Unless otherwise directed, notice of the application shall be given to every person having an interest under the will whose interest might be prejudiced by the rectification applied for and any comments in writing by any such person shall be exhibited to the affidavit in support of the application. (Non-Contentious Probate Rules 1987, r.55.)

Virtually all the recent cases on rectification refer with approval to the judgment of Chadwick J., as he then was, in *Re Segelman (Deceased)* (1996) in which he said:

"... although the standard of proof required in a claim for rectification made under s.20(1) of the 1982 Act is that the court should be satisfied on the balance of probabilities, the probability that a Will which the Testator has executed in circumstances of some formality reflects his intentions is usually of such weight that convincing evidence to the contrary is necessary."

A disappointed beneficiary may sometimes have a choice of remedy available; typically the beneficiary may have a possible negligence action against the solicitor who drafted the will as well as a possible action for rectification. In *Walker v Medlicott* (1999) the Court of Appeal stated that, where possible, a plaintiff must mitigate his damage by bringing proceedings for rectification of the will first. Only if that remedy is unavailable or unlikely to be successful should the plaintiff consider the negligence action. *Horsefall v Haywards* (2000) was an example of a case where rectification would not have been appropriate. The proceeds of sale of the estate assets had been transmitted to Canada and it appeared very unlikely that the beneficiaries would be able to recover them even if the rectification application was successful.

3. SPECIAL RULES RELATING TO SOLICITORS

2.033   As we saw in para.2.029 above if a will is prepared by a major beneficiary or close relative of a major beneficiary the propounder of the will must prove that the testator knew and approved the contents of the will. If the propounder can do this then, unless there is evidence of fraud or undue influence (see para.4) the will is admitted to probate. However, solicitors are subject to special rules of conduct laid down by the Council of the Law Society as a result of a case in 1973. In that case two solicitors in partnership were struck off the roll on the grounds, *inter alia*, that they or their respective families had been given substantial benefits under two wills prepared in their office, neither client having received independent advice. The Law Society's ruling is as follows:

"Where a client intends to make a gift *inter vivos* or by will to his solicitor, or to the solicitor's partner, or a member of staff or to the families of any of them and the gift is of a significant amount, either in itself or having regard to the size of the client's estate and the reasonable expectations of prospective beneficiaries, the solicitor must advise the client to be independently advised as to that gift and if the client declines, must refuse to act.

The following points should be noted:

(1) If the client declines to be independently advised, the solicitor must refuse to act for him in drawing the will, or any other document by which the gift is to be made. It is not sufficient merely to have the will or other document witnessed by an independent solicitor.

(2) A solicitor must also ensure that members of his staff do not embody in any will or document a gift to themselves without the approval of the solicitor. If the member of staff seeks the solicitor's approval, the same rule as to independent advice applies.

(3) Where a client wishes to leave a legacy which is not of a significant amount to his solicitor, there is no need for independent advice. However, the solicitor should satisfy himself that the client does not feel obliged to make such a gift.

(4) Occasionally, a testator may wish to leave all or a substantial part of his estate to a solicitor to be dealt with in accordance with the testator's wishes as communicated to the solicitor either orally or in a document, or as a secret trust. The Council consider that where a solicitor in such circumstances will not benefit personally and financially, there is no need to ensure the testator receives independent advice. However, solicitors should preserve the instructions from which the will was drawn and should also see that the terms of such secret trust are embodied in a written document signed or initialled by the testator.

(5) Where the donor or testator is a relative of the solicitor and wishes to make a gift or leave a legacy to the solicitor, the solicitor must consider whether in these circumstances independent advice is essential. The same principle will apply if the intended recipient is a partner of the solicitor, or a member of his staff and the donor or testator is a relative of the intended recipient."

D. Force, Fear, Fraud or Undue Influence

1. INTRODUCTION

If a will is made as a result of force, fear, fraud or undue influence it will   **2.034** not be regarded as the act of the testator and will be refused probate. A person who alleges that a will was made as a result of one of these factors must *prove* it. There are no presumptions to assist in discharging the burden of proof.

2. FORCE OR FEAR

2.035   There is little authority on this but obviously if it can be shown that a testator made a will only because he was being injured or threatened with injury the will cannot be admitted to probate.

3. FRAUD AND UNDUE INFLUENCE

2.036   Fraud is something which misleads a testator. Examples of fraud are making false representations as to the character of others to induce the testator to make or to revoke gifts or to exclude persons from a proposed will. Another example would be obtaining a gift from a testator as a result of pretending to be lawfully married to him. As Lord Langdale said in *Giles v Giles* (1836) it is clear that "a legacy given to a person in a character which the legatee does not fill, and by the fraudulent assumption of which character the testator has been deceived, will not take effect". See also *In the Estate of Posner* (1953).

Undue influence is something which overpowers the volition of the testator without convincing the judgment; a testator may be persuaded but not coerced. It is often difficult to draw the line between zealous persuasion and undue influence; so long as the testator retained real freedom of choice a court will not interfere but, if it can be shown that the testator merely surrendered to intolerable pressure, this will amount to undue influence. The court will more readily find undue influence where a testator was weak (whether mentally or physically). In the case of *inter vivos* gifts there is a presumption of undue influence where a donee stands in a fiduciary relationship to a donor, for example, father and child, doctor and patient, solicitor and client, but there is no such presumption in the case of testamentary gifts. This is because many of the relationships which give rise to the presumption *inter vivos* are precisely the relationships which would lead a testator to want to make a gift by will. Thus, if there is no positive evidence of undue influence there is no question of refusing probate (*Parfitt v Lawless* (1872)).

Re Good, Carapeto v Good (2002) is a recent example of the difficulty of proving undue influence. The court accepted that the circumstances gave rise to a legitimate suspicion of coercion. However, the judge felt that there was insufficient evidence to satisfy him that there had been coercion as opposed to legitimate persuasion. The case also illustrates the danger of making an allegation of undue influence which is not substantiated. The unsuccessful challengers will normally have to pay all the costs on the basis that a person should not have to pay to clear his own name.

2.037   In *Barclays Bank v Etridge and other appeals* (2001) Lord Nicholls, albeit in a different context (the correct procedure to be followed by banks where one party to a marriage is offering the matrimonial home as security for a loan to that party) considered the obligations of solicitors in cases where there may be undue influence. He said that a solicitor has to ensure that the client receives a clear explanation of the nature and consequences of the act in the absence of the person seeking to benefit. It is not necessary for the solicitor to approve of the transaction. However, in a case "where it is glaringly obvious that the wife is being grievously wronged. ... the solicitor should decline to act further".

Killick v Pountney (2000) is an example of a successful allegation of undue influence. The court emphasised the importance of taking instructions from the client in the absence of any person who might benefit from the will or exert influence on the client.

The action which the court will take if fraud or undue influence is proved depends on the effect that the fraud or undue influence produced. If it resulted in the entire will being made in a particular way the entire will is refused probate; if it resulted in a legacy being given to a beneficiary that legacy will fail (*Giles v Giles* (1836); *Kennell v Abbott* (1799)). If a testator was prevented from revoking a will in favour of X and making one in favour of Y the court may allow Y to claim that the property should be held by X on trust for him (*Betts v Doughty* (1879)).

E. Lost Wills

If a will has been lost or accidentally destroyed it is possible to obtain **2.038** probate of a copy or reconstruction provided an order is first obtained. If, however, a will which was known to have been in the testator's possession cannot be found after his death there is a presumption that it was destroyed by the testator with the intention of revoking it (*Eckersley v Platt* (1866)). This presumption will have to be rebutted if an order for the proof of a copy or reconstruction is to be obtained.

The procedure for obtaining an order is set out in the Non-Contentious Probate Rules 1987, r.54. The same procedure is used where probate of an oral will is sought. The order can be made by a district judge or registrar but he can require that the matter be referred to a judge of the Family Division. The application must be supported by an affidavit setting out the grounds of the application, and by such evidence on affidavit as the applicant can adduce as to:

(a) the will's existence after the death of the testator or, where there is no such evidence, the facts on which the applicant relies to rebut the presumption that the will has been revoked by destruction;

(b) in respect of an oral will, the contents of that will; and

(c) in respect of a reconstruction of a will, the accuracy of that reconstruction.

The district judge or registrar may require additional evidence in the circumstances of a particular case as to due execution of the will or as to the accuracy of the copy will, and may direct that notice be given to persons who would be prejudiced by the application.

F. Codicils

1. DEFINITION

2.039   A testamentary instrument which is executed in the same way as a will and which supplements the terms of an existing will (either by adding to it, by amending it or by revoking it in part) is usually referred to as a codicil. A codicil must comply with the same requirements as a will, if it is to be admitted to probate.

2. REPUBLICATION

2.040   The execution of a codicil to a will "republishes" the will provided there is some indication of an intention to republish. Any reference to the earlier will in the codicil is sufficient to amount to an indication of an intention to republish. When a will is republished it takes effect as if executed at the date of the codicil but with the incorporation of any changes made by the codicil.

Republication may affect the construction of a will both in respect of persons and property. In *Re Hardyman, Teesdale v McClintock* (1925) a will made in 1898 gave a legacy to the "wife of my cousin". The wife died with the result that the gift to her lapsed. The testatrix later executed a codicil to her will (which did not refer specifically to the legacy). This republished the will at the date of the codicil. Since the cousin had no wife living at that date the gift in the will took effect as a gift to the first person the cousin married after the date of the codicil.

In *Re Reeves, Reeves v Pawson* (1928) the testator gave his daughter "my present lease" in certain named property. At the time the will was executed the testator owned a short lease of the property. He later took a longer lease of the same property and then executed a codicil which referred to the will. The daughter was held entitled to the new (long) lease which the deceased owned at the date of the codicil.

If a will is altered before its republication and the alteration is not executed the republication has the effect of validating the alteration. However, there is a presumption that unexecuted alterations were made after the execution of the codicil so that evidence will be required to rebut the presumption.

The republication of a will by a codicil executed by independent witnesses has the effect of saving a gift to a witness of the original will (who would otherwise be deprived of the gift under Wills Act 1837, s.15). This remains so even if the beneficiary witnesses a later codicil.

3. REVIVAL

2.041   A *revoked* will can be revived by re-execution of the will or by execution of a codicil to the will showing an intention to revive. A mere reference to the earlier instrument is not sufficient to revive it; there must be words which make it clear that the effect of that document is being confirmed. A will cannot be revived unless it is still in existence. The effect of revival is the same as republication.

The revocation of a will by a codicil is not sufficient to revive an earlier revoked will. Once revoked a will stays revoked unless there is a formal act of revival. For example, a testator makes a will in 1980 and then makes a will in 1981 which revokes the 1980 will. The testator then executes a codicil which revokes the 1981 will. The 1980 will is not thereby revived. The codicil is the only document admissible to probate.

4. REVOCATION

A codicil may expressly revoke an earlier will or codicil in whole or in part. If no express revocation clause is included it will impliedly revoke an earlier instrument to the extent that it is inconsistent with it. Revocation is dealt with in the next section.   **2.042**

G. Revocation

1. INTRODUCTION

The various ways in which wills can be revoked are dealt with in paras 3 to 8 below.   **2.043**

2. MUTUAL WILLS

A will is always revocable during the lifetime of the testator (unless he loses testamentary capacity). A will cannot be made irrevocable. If a testator contracts not to revoke he is still free to do so. However, in that case revocation would be a breach of contract and the testator's estate would be liable to pay damages.

Equity may intervene under the doctrine of mutual wills to impose a trust on a testator's property. This occurs where two or more people make wills in agreed terms and agree that neither will revoke without the consent of the other. If the first to die carries out his part of the agreement equity will regard it as unconscionable for the survivor to deviate from the agreed terms. Therefore, equity will impose a trust on the survivor's property. The survivor remains free to revoke his will but because of the existence of the trust the new dispositions of the property will be ineffective.

The trust is a floating one during the lifetime of the survivor and crystallises on the survivor's death. This means that the survivor is free to deal with the property during his lifetime and raises some concern as to what happens if the survivor gives away or dissipates the joint assets. In *Re Cleaver* (1981), Nourse J. quoted with approval from the judgment of Dixon J. in *Birmingham v Renfrew* (1937) in which he said: "No doubt gifts and settlements, *inter vivos*, if calculated to defeat the intention of the compact, could not be made by the survivor and his right of disposition, *inter vivos* is, therefore not unqualified."

The doctrine of mutual wills applies only where the first party to die does so having carried out the agreement. In *Re Hobley (Deceased)* (1997) the first party to die had executed a codicil revoking one of the gifts in his will. The court said that it could not attempt to assess the importance of the deviation from the original agreement. An apparently minor alteration by one testator might have sentimental importance to the other. The doctrine of mutual wills required any alteration to have been agreed by both parties. Consequently, the second spouse was not bound by the agreement.

2.044   The case of *Re Dale* (1994) confirmed that it was not necessary that the testators agree to leave property to *each other*. Equity will intervene to impose a trust on the property of the survivor where the agreement is that each testator shall leave property to a third party, for example their children. If the surviving testator revokes his will and purports to leave his property (now held on trust for the agreed beneficiary), his will is perfectly valid but his personal representative will take the property subject to a trust in favour of the agreed beneficiaries. Ideally, solicitors should enquire as to the existence of an agreement to leave property in a particular way when taking instructions to change a will and when taking instructions to act in an administration.

In *Goodchild v Goodchild* (1996) the Court of Appeal confirmed the first instance decision that in order for wills to be mutual, there must be clear evidence of mutual intention not to revoke unilaterally. However, the testator's belief that her husband would give effect to what she believed their mutual intentions to be established a moral obligation binding on her husband. The obligation justified a claim by the adult son under the family provision legislation (see para.20.005).

Lack of evidence of agreement that the wills were to be irrevocable unilaterally also caused a claim for mutual wills to fail in *Birch v Curtiss* (2002). It is clearly essential to include a recital of the agreement where it is intended that the doctrine is to apply. However, where wills are **not** intended to be mutual, it is helpful to include a statement that the parties are free to revoke. It may avoid the waste of costs that arises when unnecessary challenges are made to a will. It would have been particularly useful in *Birch v Curtiss* where the court accepted that there was an agreement as to how the surviving husband was to leave his property but no evidence as to whether there was a further agreement not to revoke.

The recent case of *Healey v Brown* (2002) demonstrates the important changes to the doctrine resulting from the (Law of Property (Miscellaneous Provisions) Act 1989 which provides that an agreement to dispose of land or an interest in land is unenforceable unless in writing and signed by both parties.

2.045   A husband and wife had made wills which were mutual and which agreed that the survivor was to leave the matrimonial home (held as beneficial joint tenants) to the wife's niece. After his wife's death the husband transferred the house into the joint names of himself and his son from an earlier marriage. It was held that because the agreement between the spouses related to land and was not signed and in writing, the doctrine of mutual wills could not apply. The court held that equity can intervene to impose a constructive trust where, as here, it is unconscionable to provide no remedy. However, a constructive trust of this type is limited to the property received from the promisor and cannot affect property already held by the promisee (see *Re Goodchild* (1996)). The only way in which property already held can be impressed with a constructive trust is where the original owner has consented (as is the case with mutual wills).

In this case, therefore, the son held the property half for himself absolutely and half for the niece.

3. MARRIAGE

Section 18 of the Wills Act 1837 deals with the effect of marriage on a will. **2.046** A new s.18 was substituted by the Administration of Justice Act 1982. The new section applies to wills executed after December 31, 1982. The somewhat different rules which apply to earlier wills are not considered in this book. The new section provides that the marriage of the testator automatically revokes any will made before marriage. There are, however, three exceptions to this rule:

(1) *Section 18(3)*

"Where it appears from a will that at the time it was made the testator was expecting to be married to a particular person and that he intended that the will should not be revoked by the marriage, the will shall not be revoked by his marriage to that person."

This subsection saves a will from being revoked by marriage provided that two conditions are satisfied.

(a) The testator must have been expecting to be married to a *particular* person at the time of execution. A will made by a testator who expected to marry someone soon after making the will but who had not decided whom to marry would, therefore, be revoked by the subsequent marriage of the testator. It is not, however, required that the testator should be engaged to marry at the time when the will is made.

It must "appear from the will" that the testator is expecting to marry a particular person so that an express statement to that effect should be included. It is probable that in the absence of such a statement a reference to "my fiancée" or "my future wife" in the will would satisfy this requirement.

(b) It must also "appear from the will" that the testator intended that the will should not be revoked by the marriage. There is no guidance in the Act as to how such an intention is to be shown. It is possible that if the will gives substantially all of the testator's estate to the expected spouse this condition might be satisfied. However, it is preferable to include an express statement as to the testator's intention in a professionally drawn will. A suitable clause would be: "I declare that I make this will expecting to be married to [insert name of expected spouse] and that I intend that this will shall not be revoked by my marriage to the said [expected spouse]".

Marriage to any person other than the person whom the testator **2.047** expected to marry at the time of execution will revoke the will.

(2) *Section 18(4)*

"Where it appears from a will that at the time it was made the testator was expecting to be married to a particular person and that he intended that *a disposition in the will* should not be revoked by his marriage to that person:

    (a) that disposition shall take effect notwithstanding the marriage; and

    (b) any other disposition in the will shall take effect also, unless it appears from the will that the testator intended the disposition to be revoked by the marriage."

In a professionally drawn will the testator's intention should be made clear by the use of a suitable declaration. For example, the testator may wish to give £10,000 to X notwithstanding his marriage. A suitable declaration would be "I give £10,000 to X and declare that this gift is to take effect notwithstanding the celebration of my forthcoming marriage with Y".

If the testator wishes any other dispositions to be revoked by the marriage it must "appear from the will" that this is his intention (s.18(4)(b)). If the testator includes a declaration that one disposition is not to be revoked by a marriage and does not make any such declaration in relation to other dispositions, it is arguable that he has shown an intention that those other dispositions *are* to be revoked by marriage. An express declaration to that effect should be included in the will for the sake of certainty. For example: "I declare that all the gifts contained in this will other than the gift to X are to be revoked by the celebration of my forthcoming marriage with Y."

An appointment of executors is not a "disposition" nor are administrative provisions (such as an extension to the statutory power of insurance). Such clauses will, therefore, be revoked by marriage even though the dispositive parts of the will are saved from revocation in whole or in part by s.18(4). However, if the entire will is saved from revocation by s.18(3) it is clear that the non-dispositive clauses remain effective.

(3) Section 18(2)

This provides that the exercise of a power of appointment by will remains effective notwithstanding subsequent marriage. In this case the appointment is saved from revocation whether or not the will is expressed to be made in expectation of marriage and whether or not the testator was expecting to be married when the will was made. The exercise of a power of appointment is not, however, saved from revocation by s.18(2) where the property appointed would pass to the personal representatives of the testator in default of appointment.

4. DIVORCE

2.048   The Administration of Justice Act 1982 inserts a new s.18A into the Wills Act 1837. This provides that if a marriage is dissolved or annulled by the decree of a court the will is to take effect as if any appointment of the former spouse as executor or executor and trustee of the will were omitted. This will usually mean that the deceased will die without an executor so that letters of administration with the will annexed will be required but if any person has been appointed co-executor with the former spouse that person will remain entitled to take a grant of probate.

The new section also provides that on dissolution or annulment of a marriage any devise or bequest to the former spouse lapses. If the will contains no substitutional gift the property given to the former spouse will, therefore, fall into residue or if itself a gift of residue will pass on intestacy.

Section 18A(3) provides that if the gift to the spouse is a gift of a life interest the interest of the remainderman is accelerated so that he takes an immediate interest even if his interest was expressed to be contingent on surviving the life tenant.

The provisions of s.18A are subject to any contrary intention expressed in the will and the lapse of gifts to the former spouse is expressly stated to be without prejudice to any claim under the Inheritance (Provision for Family and Dependants) Act 1975 (as to which see Chapter 20).

It should be noted that s.18A applies only to dissolution or annulment decreed by a court. A separation does not, therefore, in any way change the effect of a married person's will. A person contemplating separation should always consider making a new will. Furthermore, even when a dissolution or annulment is decreed the only effect is to cause gifts to the former spouse to lapse; the will should therefore be reviewed at such time to ensure that it disposes of the property as the testator wishes in view of the changed circumstances.

Re Sinclair (Deceased), Lloyds Bank v Imperial Cancer Research Fund   **2.049**
(1985) revealed a problem with the section as originally drafted. A testator had left property to his wife provided she survived by one month. There was then a gift to the Cancer Research Fund which was expressed to take effect "if my said wife shall predecease me or fail to survive me for one month. . . ." The testator and his wife were divorced and the gift to her, therefore, "lapsed". The testator then died and his former wife survived by more than one month. Clearly the wife could not take but the question arose as to whether the gift to the Fund would take effect or whether there was an intestacy. The Court of Appeal held the word lapse means no more than "fail" so that the divorced beneficiary is not deemed to have died before the testator. The conditional gift to the Fund, therefore, could not take effect. The residuary gift having failed, the property therefore passed under the intestacy rules to the testator's brother. The decision in *Re Sinclair* led to the amendment of will precedents so that substitutional gifts were expressed to take effect "If the gift to my said spouse shall fail *for any reason* . . .". The conditional gift can then take effect.

The Law Reform (Succession) Act 1995 has removed the problems revealed by *Re Sinclair*.

The Act amends s.18A of the Wills Act so that where a marriage has been dissolved or annulled the former spouse shall be treated as having died on the date of the annulment or dissolution. This means that a substitutional gift drafted to take effect "if my spouse predeceases or fails to survive me by [a specified period]", can now take effect where the marriage is dissolved. It is, therefore, unnecessary to include the words "or if this gift fails for any other reason" to cover the possibility of the marriage ending in termination. However, will drafters may prefer to retain these words to cover the possibility of the gift in the will failing for any other unforeseen reason—for example, forfeiture.

The writers had wondered whether they were being unduly cautious in suggesting retaining the words "or fails for any other purpose" to cover the possibility of forfeiture. However, the decision of the Court of Appeal in *Re Jones (Deceased)* (1997) was on exactly this point.

The testatrix was killed by her son, Robert, who was convicted of her manslaughter. Her will left her estate to Robert and if he predeceased her to "such of my nephews ... as shall be living at the date of her death".

The gift to Robert could not take effect. Did the estate pass to the nephews under the terms of the will or did it pass on intestacy?

The Court of Appeal held unanimously that as the event provided for in the will (the predecease of Robert) had not occurred, the gift over could not take effect.

Therefore the estate passed on intestacy.

The decision in *Re DWS* (2001) was similar. The Court of Appeal said that on intestacy the substitutional gift to issue of a deceased class member cannot take effect where a member's interest has been forfeited under the Forfeiture Act. Under the terms of the statutory trusts issue cannot take effect if the parent is "living". The principle will apply in the same way where a class member disclaims an interest.

5. DESTRUCTION

2.050   A will may be revoked by "burning tearing or otherwise destroying the same by the testator or by some person in his presence and by his direction with the intention of revoking the same". (Wills Act 1837, s.20.) Both an act of destruction and an intention to revoke are required for this type of revocation. Neither alone is sufficient.

"Burning tearing or otherwise destroying"

2.051   A physical act of destruction is required so that simply crossing out the wording of the will or the signature of the testator or writing words such as "cancelled" or "revoked" across the will is insufficient to revoke. For example, in *Cheese v Lovejoy* (1877) the testator wrote "all these are cancelled" on the will and crossed out part of it. He then threw the will away but it was found by a servant who preserved it until the testator's death. The will was held to be valid. Although the testator intended to revoke the will he had done nothing which could be regarded as "burning tearing or otherwise destroying" it. Whether destruction has occurred is a question of degree. For example in *In the Estate of Adams (Deceased)* (1990) parts of the will had been heavily scored through with a ball-point pen. This was held to amount to destruction of those parts. The amount of interference with the will was far greater than mere crossing out.

If the testator destroys part of a will this may amount to revocation of the will as a whole if the part destroyed is sufficiently substantial or important (for example, the attestation clause). However, destruction of part may be treated as revocation of only part where the part destroyed is less important. Thus, in *Re Everest* (1975) the testator cut off certain parts of the will containing trusts of residue. It was held that the rest of the will remained valid. In *Hobbs v Knight* (1838) the testator cut out his signature from the will. This was held to be a revocation of the whole will. In deciding how far the revocation extends the court will hear evidence of the testator's intention. In the absence of such evidence the court will decide on the basis of the state of the will after the destruction. If a testator wishes to revoke a will by destruction, he should ensure that the will is totally destroyed. However, since doubts may arise after death as to the testator's true intention at the time of destruction, it is usually preferable to effect the revocation by means of a further testamentary instrument.

Revocation by destruction is only effective if the testator has completed the intended act of destruction. This is illustrated by the curious case of *Doe d. Perkes v Perkes* (1820) where the testator tore a will into four pieces in the presence of a beneficiary with whom he was angry. He was then restrained from further destruction by a third party and, when his anger had subsided, was heard to say "It is a good job it is no worse"; from this the court inferred that the testator had intended more tearing so the act of destruction was incomplete and the will still valid.

If the destruction is carried out by some person other than the testator, it is only effective if done in his presence and by his direction. A destruction in the absence of the testator or without his direction cannot be ratified by the testator so that his only course is to revoke by a further testamentary instrument.

Intention

The testator must *intend* to revoke the will at the time of the destruction. **2.052** Accidental destruction does not, therefore, revoke a will nor does destruction by a testator who thinks the will is invalid (since then his intention is merely to destroy an apparently useless piece of paper).

If a will known to have been in the testator's possession is not found after his death it is presumed that he destroyed it with intention to revoke it. Similarly if a will is found to have been in the testator's possession and is found torn or otherwise destroyed at his death there is a presumption that the testator destroyed it with the intention of revoking it. Either of these presumptions may be rebutted (for example, by evidence that the testator referred to his will shortly before death in such a way as to indicate that he regarded it as valid).

If a will is destroyed but not revoked (because of lack of intention to revoke or because the destruction was done in the absence of the testator), it remains valid. Probate may be obtained of a copy or reconstruction if the terms can be proved with sufficient certainty (see para.2.038).

Conditional revocation

Where a will is destroyed with an intention to revoke, it is a question of **2.053** fact whether the revocation is absolute (and therefore immediately effective) or conditional (and therefore only effective if the condition is satisfied). Extrinsic evidence is admissible to prove whether the revocation was conditional.

A common reason for revoking a will is that the testator wishes to make a new will disposing of his property in a different way. If the testator has left the bulk of his property to X he may decide to revoke his will so as to make a new will leaving it to Y. If this is done primarily so as to exclude X from benefit the court will infer that the revocation of the original will was absolute. If on the other hand it can be shown that the testator wanted to benefit Y but would have preferred X to take rather than those entitled on intestacy, the court will infer that the revocation was conditional on the execution of a valid will leaving the property to Y so that X will take unless a new will has been made. This is often referred to as "the doctrine of dependent relative revocation" since the revocation is dependent on the making of the new will. However, there must be some evidence that the testator's intention to revoke was conditional. For example, in *Re Jones* (1976) the testatrix made a will leaving a smallholding to certain beneficiaries. She later told her bank manager that she wished to leave the smallholding to her nephew because of the beneficiaries' attitude to her and because they had acquired their own property. The testatrix died soon after this conversation and the will was found mutilated after her death (the signatures and the gift of the smallholding having been cut out). The court held that the will was not saved from revocation since the testatrix's intention was to revoke whether or not she was able to make a new will.

The fact that a new will is intended is only one of many things which may lead to the inference that revocation was conditional. For example, in *In the Estate of Southerden* (1925) the testator made a will in favour of his wife. He thought that his wife would take all his property on intestacy and so destroyed the will by burning it. Because of the size of the estate the wife was entitled to only part of the testator's property on intestacy; the court held that the will was destroyed conditionally on the wife taking the whole estate. It therefore remained valid as the condition would not be satisfied by revocation of the will.

In *Re Finnemore (Deceased)* (1991) the deceased made three wills. Each made a gift to C and each contained a revocation clause. C's husband witnessed the second and third wills. On the face of it this meant that C could not take because of the Wills Act 1837, s.15 (see para.16.032). However, the court held that the revocation clauses in the second and third wills were conditional on the validity of the gifts contained in them. There clauses were, therefore, ineffective to revoke the gift in the first will to C. They were, however, effective to revoke the rest of the first and second wills.

6. A TESTAMENTARY INSTRUMENT

2.054   A will may be revoked in whole or in part by a later will or codicil or by "some writing declaring an intention to revoke the same and executed in the manner in which a will is ... executed" (Wills Act 1837, s.20).

The clearest way in which a later will may revoke an earlier one is where it contains an express revocation clause. Such a clause should always be included in a new will which deals with the whole of the testator's property. A common form of wording is "I hereby revoke all former wills and testamentary dispositions heretofore made by me". If a codicil is drawn up great care should be taken with the wording of any revocation clause to ensure that it revokes only those parts of the earlier will which the testator intends to revoke or replace. Similarly, a revocation clause must be carefully drawn where a client has made a will to deal with foreign property. The revocation clause should be limited to revoking wills dealing with property in England and Wales.

Even without express words of revocation a will or codicil revokes an earlier will or codicil to the extent that it is inconsistent with it. Where a client has a will dealing with foreign property any subsequent will should be expressly limited to assets in England and Wales.

The doctrine of conditional revocation may apply to save a will (or part of it) from revocation by a later will or codicil. This applies where the revocation (express or implied) in the later instrument is conditional on the effectiveness of that instrument (see, for example *Re Finnemore (Deceased)* (1991) (see para.2.053)). If the later will starts with a revocation clause but then disposes of the property in a way which is ineffective (for example, because of ambiguity as to the identity of the beneficiary) the court may construe the revocation clause as conditional so that it will not be admitted to probate. In this case, as the court is required to construe the later will or codicil, it will not hear extrinsic evidence as to the testator's intention.

7. REVOCATION BY PRIVILEGED TESTATOR

2.055 A testator who enjoys privileged status may revoke a will informally whether the will was made informally or not. A testator who makes a privileged will while a minor may revoke it while still a minor even if he has lost the privileged status before revoking (Family Law Reform Act 1969, s.3). However, it seems that the revocation cannot then be made by an informal document but only by destruction (if there is a written will capable of destruction) or by a formal, attested document.

8. ALTERATIONS AND OBLITERATIONS

2.056 Section 21 of the Wills Act 1837 provides that "No obliteration, interlineation or other alteration made in any will after the execution thereof shall be valid ... except so far as the words or effect of the will before such alteration shall not be apparent, unless the alteration shall be executed in like manner as hereinbefore is required for the execution of a will ...".

An alteration made before execution with the knowledge and approval of the testator is valid. However, an alteration in a will is presumed to have been made after execution except that an alteration which completes a blank space in the will is presumed to have been made before execution. Either of these presumptions may be rebutted by internal evidence from the will itself or by extrinsic evidence (for example a sworn statement from the draftsman or a witness). Once an alteration is shown to have been made before execution it is admissible to probate as part of the will.

An alteration made after execution of the will which is itself signed by the testator and by at least two witnesses is admitted to probate as it complies with the formalities required by the Wills Act 1837. It follows that an alteration which is witnessed is not valid unless the alteration (or the will as altered) is signed by the testator (see *Re White (Deceased)* (1990)). For the avoidance of doubt, any alteration to a will, even if made before execution, should be attested. It is sufficient if the testator and witnesses of the will put their initials in the margin next to the alteration.

2.057 A slightly different problem arises where words are crossed out or otherwise made more difficult to read without the alteration being attested. If the original wording is "apparent" it is admitted to probate, the crossing out being ignored. Wording is regarded as apparent if it can be read by ordinary means such as close inspection through a magnifying glass or by holding the document up to the light.

Where the original wording is not apparent because it has been scratched out, covered over or otherwise obliterated it is excluded from probate if the obliteration was made by the testator with an intention to revoke. The effect of obliterating words in this way is that they are revoked.

If the obliteration was made by someone other than the testator or by the testator but without intention to revoke, extrinsic evidence (such as evidence from drafts or copies, infra-red photographs or removal of paper stuck over the words) is permitted to prove the original wording.

Where the testator made the obliteration with a conditional intention to revoke, the court will allow the original wording to be proved by extrinsic evidence and admitted to probate if the condition has not been satisfied. The most likely example of such a conditional intention is that the original wording should only be revoked if substituted wording is admissible to probate. (For example, the will originally says "I give to X the sum of £1,000", the testator obliterates "£1,000" and writes "£1,500" instead—clearly the court can infer that X is to get £1,000 if the substitution of £1,500 is not effective.) If the substitution is ineffective because it has not been executed the court will admit extrinsic evidence to prove the original wording. This is really another example of conditional revocation and the same considerations apply as in the case of conditional destruction (see para.2.053 above).

3.   Intestacy

A. Introduction

3.001 There are many advantages to be gained by making a will, but the majority of people die without having made one, either out of ignorance of the courses of action open to them, or out of a reluctance to contemplate their own deaths, or from a mistaken belief that, for them, a will is pointless.

The devolution of certain assets is fixed irrespective of whether there is a will. Thus, property held as joint tenants passes by the right of survivorship and nominated property passes to the nominee. (See Chapter 21.)

The problem where there is no will is to determine who is to share in the other assets of the deceased's estate. The answer is to be found in Pt IV of the Administration of Estates Act 1925, as amended, which lays down who is entitled to an intestate's residuary estate (that is, the deceased's assets after the payment of debts and expenses). The Act specifies the entitlements of the deceased's immediate family; the provisions were based on "the average will" filed with the Probate Registry in the years before 1925, although they have been amended since.

While the intestacy rules ensure that the "next-of-kin" share in the estate the proportions are arbitrary and therefore often unsuitable; inevitably they give no rights to friends or charities who might have benefited had the deceased made a will. (If a relative or dependant feels the intestacy rules do not make adequate financial provision for him, he may be able to bring a claim under the Inheritance (Provisions for Family and Dependants) Act 1975, s.1(1) which provides that the court is not bound to assume that the intestacy rules make reasonable provision for the next-of-kin—see Chapter 20.)

B. Total or Partial Intestacy

3.002 For the rules to apply, the deceased must have died either totally or partially intestate.

The deceased dies totally intestate if he has either made no will at all, has made an invalid will, has revoked any wills that he has made or has made a will which does not effectively dispose of any property.

The deceased dies partially intestate if he has left a valid will which disposes of only part of his estate. This can happen in two ways:

(a) The deceased may have made a valid will which fails to dispose of the whole estate (for example, because it contains no residuary gift). An example of such a will is one leaving money in a building society account to X but not dealing with the rest of the estate; or

(b) The deceased may have made a valid will which dealt with the whole of his estate but the residuary gift may fail in whole or in part (for example, because a residuary beneficiary pre-deceases the testator and no substitutional gift is included in the will).

In general the same rules apply whether the deceased died totally or partially intestate. Where there are differences these will be indicated later.

C. Undisposed of Property is held on a Statutory Trust

1. THE GENERAL RULE

3.003 The Administration of Estates Act 1925, s.33(1) as amended by the Trusts of Land and Appointment of Trustees Act 1996 provides:

> "on the death of a person intestate as to any real or personal estate, such estate shall be held on trust by his personal representatives with the power to sell it."

Section 33(2) provides that:

> "The personal representatives shall pay out of:
> (a) the ready money of the deceased (so far as not disposed of by his will, if any); and
> (b) any net money arising from disposing of any other part of his estate (after payment of costs),
> all … funeral, testamentary and administration expenses, debts and other liabilities … and out of the residue of the said money the personal representatives shall set aside a fund sufficient to provide for any pecuniary legacies bequeathed by the will (if any) of the deceased."

2. PARTIAL INTESTACY

3.004 The statutory trust imposed by s.33 applies to a partial intestacy as well as to a total intestacy. The provisions of the will take precedence over the intestacy rules. Thus, if the undisposed of property was left on an *express* trust (for example, T leaves "residue on trust for sale to A and B in equal shares" and A predeceases T), the express trust prevails over the statutory trust. This may appear to be a minor point but will be important if the *terms* of the express trust differ from s.33 (for example, by directing payment of inheritance tax attributable to lifetime gifts made by the deceased).

D. Order of Entitlement Under the Intestacy Rules

Before considering the detailed rules relating to the entitlements of the **3.005**
beneficiaries it is useful to set out the basic structure of the
Administration of Estates Act provisions.

First, where there is a surviving spouse he or she takes everything
unless the intestate also left certain relatives.

(a) If the intestate also left issue (that is children, grandchildren and
remoter lineal descendants) the spouse and issue share the
estate provided the issue satisfy the requirements of the
statutory trusts.

(b) If the intestate left no surviving issue, but left a surviving parent
or parents, the parent(s) and the spouse share the estate. The
parent(s) take(s) the property absolutely or in equal shares. If no
parent survives, but the intestate left a living brother or sister of
the whole blood (or their issue) they share the assets with the
spouse, provided that they satisfy the requirements of the
statutory trusts.

(The "statutory trusts" are defined at para.3.015 below.)

If the intestate left no surviving spouse, the estate is distributed as
follows:

(a) to issue on the statutory trusts, but if none, then to

(b) parents absolutely (and equally if both are alive), but if none,
then to

(c) brothers and sisters of the whole blood (*i.e.* the children of the
same parents as the deceased) on the statutory trusts, but if
none, then to

(d) brothers and sisters of the half blood (*i.e.* those who share one
parent with the deceased) on the statutory trusts, but if none,
then to

(e) grandparents absolutely and equally if more than one, but if
none, then to

(f) uncles and aunts of the whole blood (*i.e.* brothers and sisters of
the whole blood of one of the parents of the deceased) on the
statutory trusts, but if none, then to

(g) uncles and aunts of the half blood (*i.e.* those with one parent in
common with one of the parents of the deceased) on the
statutory trusts, but if none, then to

(h) the Crown, Duchy of Lancaster or the Duke of Cornwall as
"*bona vacantia*".

Section 46(1)(vi) of the Administration of Estates Act 1925 gives the
Crown a discretion to make provision for dependants of the intestate
whether they are related to the deceased or not. Similarly the Crown may
provide for "other persons for whom the intestate might reasonably have
been expected to make provision".

If the intestate died resident within the Duchy of Lancaster or in
Cornwall, the Duchy or the Duke of Cornwall respectively take the assets
as *bona vacantia* subject to the same discretions.

It should be noted that each category must be considered in the order listed above and only if there is *no one* in a particular category is it necessary to consider the next category. Furthermore, since a blood relationship is vital under the intestacy rules, the *spouse* of a person within one of these categories has no right to share in the estate. Matters relevant to the particular categories are considered below.

E. The Rights of a Surviving Spouse

1. THE SPOUSE'S ENTITLEMENT

3.006   The Law Reform (Succession) Act 1995, s.1, introduces a statutory survivorship period for spouses of intestates dying on or after January 1, 1996. In order to take an interest on intestacy a spouse who survives the intestate must do so for 28 days, before taking an interest.

The spouse's precise entitlement to the deceased's undisposed-of "residuary estate" depends on whether any other close relatives survived the intestate.

For these purposes, a divorced spouse has no rights in the deceased's estate and for deaths occurring on or after January 1, 1970, neither has a *judicially* separated spouse, since he or she is treated as already being dead provided the separation is still continuing (Matrimonial Causes Act 1973, s.18(2)). (This is not the case, however, if there is a magistrates' court separation order in effect (see s.18(3)) although no such separation orders may be made after the Domestic Proceedings and Magistrates' Courts Act 1978.)

A client who consults a solicitor with a view to obtaining a divorce or judicial separation should be asked whether or not he has made a will. If he has not, he should be advised to consider making one since if he dies intestate before the date of the decree absolute, his property will pass to the surviving spouse. (If he has made a will, he should be advised to review it in the light of the changed circumstances.)

Spouse alone surviving

3.007   If the intestate left a surviving spouse but no issue, parents or brothers or sisters of the whole blood (or their issue), the personal representatives hold *the whole of the estate* on trust for sale for the spouse *absolutely*. Remoter relatives such as grandparents or uncles and aunts have no rights to share in the estate.

Spouse and issue surviving

3.008   The estate of an intestate who leaves a surviving spouse and issue is divided between the spouse and the issue. The spouse receives:

   (a) The deceased's "personal chattels" absolutely. "Personal chattels" are defined in Administration of Estates Act 1925, s.55(1)(x). They are "carriages, horses, stable furniture and effects (not used for business purposes), motor cars and accessories (not used for business purposes), garden effects, domestic animals, plate, plated articles, linen, china, glass, books, pictures, prints, furniture, jewellery, articles of household or personal use or ornament, musical and scientific instruments and apparatus, wines, liquors and consumable stores, but do not include any chattels used at the death of the intestate for business purposes nor money or securities for money". To summarise this long definition, personal chattels are items of personal and domestic use and ornament. This has been held to cover a yacht (*Re Chaplin* (1950)) and a collection of watches (*Re Crispins' Will Trusts* (1975)). In the latter case Russell L.J. said that "cherishing ... by eye and hand [could bring the watches] within the definition of articles of personal use".

(b) A "statutory legacy" of £125,000 where death occurs on or after December 1, 1993. The legacy is payable free of tax and costs, together with interest at 6 per cent per annum from death until payment. The costs and interest come from the residue of the estate. In the case of deaths occurring prior to December 1, 1993 lower levels of statutory legacy are payable.

(c) If there is anything left in the estate after (a) and (b), the spouse receives a life interest (*i.e.* a right to the income until death) in one-half of the residue.

The other half of the residue and the interest in remainder in the trust created for the spouse go to the issue on the statutory trusts.

Spouse and parent or brother and sister (or their issue) surviving

Where the intestate leaves a spouse but no issue, the estate is divided as follows if one or more parents of the intestate (or brothers and sisters or their issue) also survive. The spouse receives: **3.009**

(a) The "personal chattels" (defined above) absolutely.

(b) A statutory legacy of £200,000 where death occurs on or after December 1, 1993. Again the legacy is payable free of tax and costs plus 6 per cent per annum interest. In the case of deaths occurring prior to December 1, 1993 lower levels of statutory legacy are payable.

(c) One-half of the residue *absolutely*. In contrast to paragraph 3.8 above, the spouse in this case receives the capital and not merely the income from this part of the estate.

The rest of the estate (that is, the other half of any residue) goes to the parent or parents in equal shares absolutely or, if none, to the brothers and sisters of the whole blood or their issue on the statutory trusts (see below).

2. THE SPECIAL RULES APPLYING TO SPOUSES

Redemption of life interest

Where the intestate is survived by a spouse and issue, the spouse is entitled to a life interest in one-half of the residue of the estate. This means the spouse will receive the income from the trust for sale for life. However, a spouse may prefer to receive a capital sum (particularly if the residue is small and so capable of producing only a small income). **3.010**

Section 47A of the Administration of Estates Act 1925 allows the spouse to elect to convert the life interest into a capital sum. The election must be made within 12 months of the grant of representation (the time limit may be extended at the discretion of the court) in writing to the personal representatives (s.47A(6)). If the sole personal representative is the surviving spouse, the election is made to the Senior Registrar of the Family Division of the High Court. A complex formula for determining the capital value of the interest is laid down in statutory instruments made under the Administration of Justice Act 1977. Provided the issue are *sui juris* the life interest can be valued by agreement between the spouse and issue, thus removing the necessity of complying with the statutory provisions.

The effect of the provision can be seen in the following example. The residue of the intestate's estate, after taking personal chattels and the statutory legacy, is £50,000, and the spouse is entitled to a life interest in £25,000. Instead of receiving the income from this, the spouse can capitalise the interest using the formula and receive, say, £10,000 in cash. The rest of the estate, after deducting the costs of the capitalisation is held on the statutory trusts for the issue.

If the spouse makes this election, no "transfer of value" is made for the purposes of inheritance tax. However, since less of the deceased's estate is treated as passing to the spouse, less of the estate attracts the spouse exemption so more inheritance tax may become payable on the deceased's estate (see Chapter 4).

Acquiring the matrimonial home

3.011   If the intestate and the surviving spouse were joint beneficial tenants of the dwelling-house in which the surviving spouse was resident at the deceased's death, the *jus accrescendi* will automatically vest it in the spouse. If, however, the intestate was the sole owner or held as tenant-in-common, the house or his interest as tenant-in-common in the house will be part of the undisposed of property. The surviving spouse may wish to acquire the house. This can be achieved in a number of ways.

The Second Schedule to the Intestates' Estates Act 1952 gives a surviving spouse the right to *require* the personal representatives to appropriate "any dwelling-house in which the surviving spouse was resident at the time of the intestate's death" in total or partial satisfaction of an absolute and/or capitalised interest in the estate.

If the dwelling-house is worth more than the spouse's absolute entitlement, the personal representative can still be required to appropriate the dwelling-house but the spouse must then pay "equality money" from his or her own resources to make up the difference (Sch.2, para.5(2)). The house is valued at the value at the date of appropriation, not death (*Re Collins* (1975)). If it is a time of rising property values, it is important to advise a client to make such an election quickly.

As with capitalising a life interest, the spouse must exercise the right within 12 months of the grant of representation (again subject to the court's power to extend the time limit) by notice in writing to the personal representatives.

The spouse will frequently be a personal representative of the deceased. If the spouse is one of two or more personal representatives notice must be given to the others. The Schedule does not mention the giving of notice where the spouse is the sole personal representative.

A personal representative is in a fiduciary position as regards the estate **3.012** and like a trustee must not profit from that fiduciary position. The Schedule provides that where the spouse is one of two or more personal representatives the rule that a trustee should not purchase trust property is not to prevent the purchase of a dwelling-house from the estate. The Schedule says nothing of the position where a spouse is a sole personal representative. A spouse who is a sole personal representative and who wishes to exercise the right to take a dwelling-house ought to do one of the following:

(a) secure the appointment of a second personal representative; or
(b) obtain the consent of the other beneficiaries (but this is only appropriate if they are of full age and capacity); or
(c) obtain the consent of the court.

The need for such steps is confirmed by the case of *Kane v Radley-Kane* (1998). The case concerned an appropriation of shares under Administration of Estates Act 1925, s.41 rather than an election to take a dwelling house. However, the court referred to the right of election under the 1952 Act. It emphasised the fact that the right only exists where the spouse is one of two or more personal representatives and that a sole personal representative would have to take additional steps.

During the 12 month period the personal representatives need to obtain the spouse's written consent if they wish to dispose of the house, unless they have to sell it to raise money for the administration when there is no other asset available.

When a spouse chooses to exercise this right, it does not matter whether the deceased held the freehold or merely a leasehold interest in the house (except where the lease has less than two years to run). However, in four circumstances set out in Sch.2, paras 2 and 4(2) to the 1952 Act, the consent of the court is required before the spouse can exercise the right. The consent is required if the house:

(a) forms part of a building, the whole of which is comprised in the residuary estate; or
(b) is held with agricultural land similarly comprised; or
(c) as to the whole or part was used as a hotel or lodging house at the death of the intestate; or
(d) as to part was used for non-domestic purposes at the death of the intestate (which would be the case if part of the house was used as a shop).

In these circumstances, the court must be satisfied that the exercise of the right will not diminish the value of the other residuary assets nor make them more difficult to sell.

If a spouse wishes to avoid an application to the court or if the right of election is unavailable for any other reason (for example, expiry of the 12 months' time limit) it is possible to make use of the ordinary power of appropriation contained in s.41 of the Administration of Estates Act 1925. This power allows personal representatives to appropriate assets in or towards satisfaction of pecuniary legacies or entitlement under the intestacy rules provided the legatee or next-of-kin consents and provided no specific legatees are prejudiced. The power is freely available and the court's consent is not normally required. However, the spouse has no right to insist on such an appropriation and so must seek the agreement of the personal representatives.

As with the right of election under the 1952 Act a spouse who is a sole personal representative must take care not to breach the rule against self-dealing. In *Radley-Kane* the second wife of the intestate acted as the sole administrator, despite the fact that there were children of the intestate, on the basis that the value of the estate was below the limit of her statutory legacy. She appropriated to herself shares in a private company which had been valued for probate purposes at £50,000. Two years after the death she sold the shares for over £1.1m. The court held that the appropriation of assets in satisfaction of a pecuniary legacy due to a personal representative was in clear contravention of the self-dealing rule. The administrator should either have obtained the consent of the beneficiaries or sought directions from the court. The court did, however, accept that an appropriation would be permitted if the assets were equivalent to cash (for example, government stock or quoted shares).

Abolition of hotchpot

3.013   The Law Reform (Succession) Act 1995, s.1(2), abolishes the requirement under the Administration of Estates Act 1925, s.49(1)(aa) that surviving spouses bring benefits received by will into account against entitlement on intestacy. Thus, there is no longer any hotchpot requirement for surviving spouses. This applies in respect of deaths on or after January 1, 1996.

F. The Rights of Issue

1. GENERAL

3.014   As we saw in para.3.005 above, after the surviving spouse the next category of next-of-kin who share in the deceased's estate are the issue. The issue take the appropriate share of the estate on the statutory trusts. If a spouse survives, the issue take one-half of the residuary estate after the statutory legacy has been deducted as well as the interest in remainder in the spouse's one-half. If there is no surviving spouse the issue take the whole residuary estate.

2. THE STATUTORY TRUSTS

The "statutory trusts" are set out in the Administration of Estates Act 1925, s.47. Under this section the property is held equally for the children of the intestate who are either alive or *en ventre sa mère* at the date of the intestate's death. The children who satisfy this requirement have a mere contingent interest unless and until they reach 18 or marry under that age. If an infant child dies unmarried, the property is dealt with as if that child had never existed.

3.015

Thus far, references have been made only to "children" since it is children who are the primary beneficiaries under this heading. However, if a child predeceases the intestate and that child leaves issue at the date of death, those grandchildren or their issue take *per stirpes* the share which their parent would have taken provided those issue reach 18 or marry under that age.

Example 1

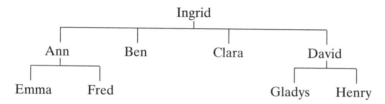

Clara and David predeceased Ingrid who died intestate. Ann, Ben and all the grandchildren are over 18. The estate will be divided into three parts. Ann and Ben each have vested interests in one-third of the estate. Clara has predeceased the intestate without leaving issue and has no entitlement. David has predeceased the intestate but has left issue. David's issue divide his share equally between them so that Gladys and Henry take one-sixth of the estate each. If Henry had also predeceased Ingrid but was survived by children, they would have shared the property to which he was entitled, provided they satisfied the statutory trusts.

Example 2

Ian died intestate; all the children survived Ian. Andrew and Charles have vested interests immediately on the death of the intestate. If they die before receiving their share of the deceased's property, their share will pass to their estates. Barbara and Dorothy have only contingent interests and therefore if either dies without attaining the age of 18 or marrying, her share of the estate will be divided amongst Ian's other children.

Example 3

3.016   Irene dies intestate, survived by her husband Henry, her two children and her father Peter. Henry, therefore, receives the personal chattels, the £125,000 statutory legacy (plus interest) and a life interest in one-half of the residue. The other half of the residue is held on the statutory trusts for the two children. If either dies unmarried and before reaching the age of 18, the property will be held for the other on the statutory trusts. If both die unmarried and before reaching 18, the estate is dealt with as if they had never existed. Henry will be entitled to a statutory legacy of £200,000 (plus interest) and the residue of the estate will be shared equally by him with Peter, Irene's father.

The fact that persons who fail to reach the age of 18 or marry earlier are dealt with as if they had never existed means that property may pass to someone (Peter, in this example) who appeared to have no entitlement at the moment of death. Furthermore if Henry and Peter had survived Irene but both died before Charlotte and Charles, Henry and Peter's estates could both have benefited. This is because the property is distributed as it would have been at the date of Irene's death had neither Charlotte nor Charles existed.

3. HOTCHPOT

Abolition of hotchpot

3.017   The Law Reform (Succession) Act 1995, s.1(2) abolishes the requirement under the Administration of Estates Act 1925, ss.47(1)(iii) and 49(a) that children and issue bring lifetime advances and benefits received by will into account against entitlement on intestacy. Thus, there is no longer any hotchpot requirement for children or issue. This applies in resect of deaths on or after January 1, 1996.

4. ADOPTED, LEGITIMATE AND ILLEGITIMATE CHILDREN

Adopted children

3.018   For the purposes of entitlement under an intestacy arising on or after January 1, 1976, ss.39 and 46(4) of the Children Act 1975 provide that an adopted child is the legitimate child of its adoptive parent or parents. (This rule applies if the adoption order was made by a court in the United Kingdom, the Isle of Man or the Channel Islands. The same rule applies to certain foreign adoptions.) The child is thus debarred from claiming on the intestacy of its natural parents and is treated as a child of the adopting parents. Such a child is therefore entitled to take on the intestacy of adoptive grandparents and brothers and sisters.

Legitimated children
Sections 5(1)–(4) and 10(1) of the Legitimacy Act 1976 provide that a **3.019**
legitimated child is entitled to share in a deceased's intestacy as if it had
been born legitimate.

Children whose parents were not married at the time of their birth
In the case of deaths occurring before the coming into force of the Family **3.020**
Law Reform Act 1987, an illegitimate relationship was not recognised for
the purposes of distribution of property on intestacy subject to two
limited exceptions.

In respect of deaths occurring after April 4, 1988, the distribution of
assets on intestacy (and otherwise) is to be determined without regard to
whether or not the parents of a particular person were married to each
other.

Section 20 of the 1987 Act removes the protection which existed under
the old law for personal representatives who distributed property in
ignorance of the existence of illegitimate claimants. *Prima facie*, it
appears, therefore, that personal representatives should undertake
investigations to discover whether or not there are hitherto unknown
relatives of the deceased alive whose parents were not married.
Presumably, however, the protection against claimants of the estate
available generally to personal representatives under the Trustee Act
1925, s.27 and the *Benjamin Order* procedure (see Chapter 14) extends to
cover the claims of persons whose parents were not married. Moreover,
s.18(2) of the Family Law Reform Act makes special provision for the
administration of an intestate's estate. It provides that where the parents
of a child who dies intestate were not married to each other at the time of
that child's birth there is a presumption that the child has not been
survived by *his father or by any person related to him only through his
father*. Thus, personal representatives will be able in the absence of
evidence to the contrary to distribute on the basis that no such persons are
alive.

Examples
(1) X, whose parents have not married, dies intestate without a spouse
or issue. He is known to be survived by his mother but nothing is known of
his father or of his father's relatives.

X's mother will take the whole estate since the personal representatives
are entitled to presume that the father and the father's relatives have
predeceased X.

(2) As above, X, whose parents did not marry, has died intestate
without a spouse or issue. However, his mother is dead and the only
relative on his mother's side still living is her brother of the whole blood
(X's maternal uncle). Nothing is known of X's father or of any of the
father's relatives except that the father's brother of the whole blood is
known to be alive (X's paternal uncle). X's estate will be divided between
the two uncles. X's personal representatives are entitled to presume that
the father and father's relatives other than the brother have predeceased
X.

G. The Rights of Others

3.021 It should be noted that the other relatives who take on the statutory trusts (that is brothers and sisters of the whole and half blood and uncles and aunts of the whole or half blood) must fulfil the same requirements as issue; that is, they must be living at the intestate's death and reach 18 or marry earlier. A person who predeceases the intestate can be replaced *per stirpes* by his own issue provided they reach the age of 18 or marry earlier.

There has never been any hotchpot requirement for other relatives.

4.   Inheritance Tax

A. Introduction

1. Definitions

Inheritance tax is, *prima facie*, payable where there is a *chargeable* **4.001**
transfer. A chargeable transfer is defined as "any *transfer of value* which is
made to an individual but is not ... an exempt transfer" (Inheritance Tax
Act 1984, s.2(1)). A transfer of value is defined as "a *disposition* made by a
person ... as a result of which the value of his estate immediately after the
transfer is less than it would be but for the disposition. ..." The amount by
which the value of the transferor's estate is less as a result of the
disposition is the *value transferred* on which inheritance tax is *prima facie*
payable.

Transfers of value occur *inter vivos* as a result of gifts of property or
sales at an undervalue. Section 4 of the Inheritance Tax Act 1984 provides
that a deceased person is to be treated as if he had made a transfer of value
immediately before his death the value of which is equal to the value of his
whole estate immediately before death. The "estate" is the aggregate of
all the property to which a deceased person was beneficially entitled
immediately before death (s.5). In fact the charge on death is by far the
most important type of charge as most *inter vivos* transfers are exempt or
potentially exempt (in the latter case they become exempt if the donor
survives seven years).

The structure of inheritance tax is rather complicated as the outline
above will show. This is largely because the tax is a modification of capital
transfer tax. Capital transfer tax was a tax on death estates and on *inter
vivos* transfers (with far less extensive exemptions than apply to
inheritance tax). The Act which is now called the Inheritance Tax Act
1984 was formerly the Capital Transfer Tax Act 1984. That Act in its
unamended form continues to apply to certain transactions entered into
before March 18, 1986. References in documents (for example, wills)
made before that date to capital transfer tax are now to be taken as
references to inheritance tax.

2. Occasions of charge to inheritance tax

There are three categories of transfer which can give rise to inheritance **4.002**
tax (exemptions or reliefs may be available to extinguish or reduce a
charge—these are dealt with later).

(a) *A transfer on death*. Such a transfer is taxed at the full rates of tax.

(b) *A potentially exempt transfer*. This is an *inter vivos* transfer of value made on or after March 18, 1986 made by an individual whereby property becomes comprised in the estate of another individual or in an accumulation and maintenance settlement or a disabled trust (the taxation of settlements and trusts is dealt with in Chapter 7). Such a transfer can arise when the transferor omits to exercise a right (such as by failing to sue on a debt). In addition a transfer of value made on or after March 17, 1987 by an individual into a settlement with an interest in possession (that is, broadly speaking, where an individual creates a life interest in property by making an *inter vivos* gift—see Chapter 7) is a potentially exempt transfer as is the surrender or sale of an interest in possession in such a settlement.

A potentially exempt transfer becomes fully exempt if the transferor survives seven years after the transfer. If he dies within seven years the transfer becomes chargeable at the rates in force at the date of death (see below for the calculation of tax and the reduction where the transferor survives more than three years).

(c) *A chargeable transfer* made before death. This type of transfer is immediately taxable but at only half the rates which apply on death. If the transferor dies within seven years the transferee becomes taxable at the full rates in force at the date of the death.

Most transfers made *inter vivos* are now potentially exempt so that few transfers are immediately taxable as chargeable transfers. The main categories of chargeable transfers made before death are:

(a) Transfers to settlements without an interest in possession (see Chapter 7—a "settlement without an interest in possession" is a discretionary trust or an accumulation trust other than one which satisfies the definition of an accumulation and maintenance settlement).

(b) Chargeable events within settlements without an interest in possession (see Chapter 7).

(c) Transfers under which no property becomes comprised in the estate of another by virtue of the transfer. This occurs where one person buys a service for another. One of the commonest examples is where a grandparent pays school fees for his grandchild. The grandparent's estate is reduced in value so (assuming no exemption is available) there is a transfer of value. However, as the grandchild's estate is not increased it is not within the definition of a potentially exempt transfer.

B. Excluded Property

4.003 Excluded property does not form part of the owner's estate on death for inheritance tax purposes so that, in effect, it is exempt from tax. As far as lifetime transfers are concerned the position is slightly more complicated. A transfer of excluded property *inter vivos* is not a chargeable or potentially exempt transfer unless the transfer causes a reduction in value of non-excluded property in which case there is, to the extent of that reduction, a chargeable or potentially exempt transfer as the case may be.

There are three categories of excluded property:

    (a) Reversionary interests in settled property unless:
          (i) acquired for money or money's worth, or
          (ii) vested in the settlor or settlor's spouse, or
          (iii) expectant on a lease for life at a nominal rent;
    (b) Most types of property situate outside the United Kingdom and owned by a person domiciled outside the United Kingdom and some types of property situate in the United Kingdom but owned by a person not domiciled in the United Kingdom;
    (c) Settled property situate outside the United Kingdom provided the settlor was domiciled outside the United Kingdom when the settlement was made.

C. The Calculation of Tax

1. TWO RATES OF TAX

In respect of transfers made before March 15, 1988 the rates of tax were **4.004** "progressive", that is to say, the rate of tax increased as the total of taxable gifts made by the transferor increased. However, in respect of transfers made on or after that date there are currently only two rates of tax. There is a nil rate band (£255,000 in 2003/2004) and, once that has been exhausted, tax is charged on the balance of the estate at the rate of 40 per cent.

2. CUMULATION

In order to establish whether or not the nil rate band has been exhausted **4.005** in respect of a particular chargeable transfer, it is necessary to take into account all previous chargeable transfers made by the transferor within the seven years before the present transfer (Inheritance Tax Act 1984, s.7(1)). This is called the principle of cumulation. The present transfer is added to all the previous transfers in the last seven years and the tax is then calculated as if the present transfer were the highest part of a single transfer equal to all the transfers (including the present one) made within the last seven years. It is therefore taxed at 40 per cent to the extent that it exceeds the nil rate band.

    The full rate of 40 per cent applies where the transfer is made on death or was made before death but death follows within *three* years. If the transfer is a chargeable transfer made before death the tax charged at the time of the transfer is at half the full rates (Inheritance Tax Act 1984, s.7(2)). If the transfer is a potentially exempt transfer or a chargeable transfer and death occurs within seven years (but not less than three years) of the transfer the tax is charged on the value of the transfer (at the date it was made) at the following percentage of the full rates in force at the time of death:

    (a) where the transfer is made more than three years but not more than four years before the death, 80 per cent;
    (b) where the transfer is made more than four years but not more

than five years before the death, 60 per cent;
  (c) where the transfer is made more than five but not more than six years before the death, 40 per cent;
  (d) where the transfer is made more than six but not more than seven years before the death, 20 per cent;
      (Inheritance Tax Act 1984, s.7(4)).

In the case of a *chargeable* transfer made before death the reduction in the rates mentioned above will be available only to the extent that it does not reduce the amount of tax due on that transfer below the amount originally paid on the *inter vivos* transfer. Thus, no refund of tax is allowed.

Examples
(1) A makes a potentially exempt transfer to B, an individual, of £285,000. A has made no previous chargeable transfers. The potentially exempt transfer is treated initially as one which will prove to be exempt. No inheritance tax is payable at the time of the transfer. (For the purposes of this illustration and the following ones in this section exemptions and reliefs are ignored.)

If A dies within three years of the transfer, the potentially exempt transfer becomes chargeable and tax will become payable at the full rates in force at the date of death. Thus, assuming that the 2003/04 rates are still in force at the time of the transferor's death the first £255,000 will be taxed at nil per cent and the remaining £30,000 will be taxed at 40 per cent; a total of £12,000 will be payable.

If A dies more than three years after but within seven years of the transfer, the potentially exempt transfer becomes chargeable but at only a percentage of the full rate in force at the date of the death. Thus, assuming that the 2003/04 rates are still in force at the time of the transferor's death and A's death was within four years of the transfer, tax will be charged at 80 per cent of the full rate, that is:

$$\frac{80}{100} \times £12,000 = £9,600$$

(2) Before death A makes a chargeable transfer to a settlement with no interest in possession of £285,000. A has made no other chargeable transfers. As explained in the previous example tax calculated at the full rate on such a transfer would be £12,000. Since this is a lifetime transfer tax is payable at half that rate so £6,000 will be payable.

(3) Having made the chargeable transfer of £285,000 referred to in the previous example, A dies three years six months later when the table of rates provides for (say) £265,000 to be taxed at a nil rate and the balance at 40 per cent. The recalculation of tax on the transfer will give a tax figure of:

£	£	Rate %		Amount £
0 –	265,000	0	=	Nil
265,000 –	285,000	40	=	8,000

Only 80 per cent of that tax figure of £8,000 is payable since death occurred more than three years after the transfer. Thus,

$$\text{Tax payable on death } \frac{80}{100} \times £8,000 = £6,400$$

Credit must be given for any tax already paid. Thus,

	£
Tax payable on death	6,400
Less: Lifetime tax paid	(6,000)
Extra tax now payable	400

If the table of rates on A's death provides for (say) £275,000 to be taxed **4.006** at a nil rate and the balance at 40 per cent the recalculation would give a tax figure of:

£	£	Rate %		£
0 –	275,000	0	=	Nil
275 –	285,000	40	=	4,000

Only 80 per cent of that tax figure of £4,000 is payable since death occurred more than three years after the transfer. Thus,

$$\text{Tax payable on death } \frac{80}{100} \times £4,000 = £3,200$$

More than £3,200 in tax was paid *inter vivos*. No reclaim is, however, permitted so there will simply be no extra tax payable on death.

As we explained briefly above when deciding which rates of tax are to be charged on a particular chargeable transfer it is necessary to take into account all previous chargeable transfers made within seven years before the present transfer. An illustration may be helpful. For the purposes of this illustration exemptions and reliefs have been ignored.

Example
A has made no previous chargeable transfers.

May 20, 2003	A transfers £100,000 to X, an individual
May 20, 2004	A transfers £260,000 to Y, a discretionary trust
May 20, 2009	A transfers £125,000 to X, an individual
Dec 20, 2010	A dies, owning £120,000 of assets

Since the 2003 transfer is potentially exempt, it is assumed that it will prove to be an exempt transfer until either seven years expires or the transferor dies within that period. Therefore, no tax is payable in 2003 and the transfer is not cumulated with the chargeable transfer to Y made in 2004. On May 20, 2010 the 2003 transfer actually becomes exempt.

The transfer to Y in 2004 is a chargeable transfer made before death and as such is taxed at half the full rates of tax. Tax will be calculated as follows:

Amount transferred £	Full rate	Half rate	Tax payable at half rate £
0 – 255,000	nil	nil	nil
255 – 260,000	40%	20%	1,000
			1,000

Therefore £2,000 will be payable in 2004.

The 2009 transfer is potentially exempt and so no tax is paid at the time of the transfer.

On A's death in 2010 tax on the 2004 transfer will be recalculated at the full rates in force in tax year 2010/11. Since death has occurred more than six years after the transfer only 20 per cent of the full rates of tax is payable. If this is less than the £1,000 already paid no refund is available.

As a result of A's death within seven years of the 2009 transfer it becomes chargeable. In fact death has occurred within three years of the transfer and so tax will be calculated at the full rates in force in tax year 2010/11. As £260,000 of chargeable transfers have already been made the rates appropriate to a transfer from £260,000–£385,000 will be used. Finally the tax due on the transfer on death will be calculated at the full rates for tax year 2010/11. As £385,000 of chargeable transfers have already been made the rates appropriate to a transfer from £385,000 to £505,000 will be used.

3. GROSSING-UP

The basic principle

4.007   Where inheritance tax is paid by the donor (as it may be in the case of a chargeable transfer made before death), the loss to the donor resulting from the transfer is the value of the gift *plus* the inheritance tax on it. It is on this gross figure that inheritance tax is payable. In such a case the value of the *net* gift is known but in order to calculate the gross loss to the estate it is necessary to "gross up" the net gift. Inheritance tax is then calculated on the gross loss to the donor.

Example

A has made chargeable transfers which have exhausted his nil rate band. He now makes a chargeable transfer to a discretionary trust of £10,000 and agrees to pay the inheritance tax attributable to the transfer.

The tax payable is calculated by "grossing up" the gift of £10,000 that is by treating the £10,000 as a net amount the tax on which has been notionally deducted. The whole transfer falls within the 40 per cent tax band but as it is a transfer made *before* death tax will be charged at one-half the full rate, that is at 20 per cent. Thus, it can be seen that the gift is 80 per cent of the gross amount transferred.

$$\text{net} = \frac{80}{100} \times \text{gross}$$

The gross figure can, therefore, be found by multiplying the net amount by 100 and dividing it by 80.

$$\text{gross} = \text{net} \times \frac{100}{80}$$

$$i.e. \ £10,000 \times \frac{100}{80} = £12,500$$

The difference between the gross and net amounts is the amount of the tax, *i.e.* £12,500 – £10,000 = £2,500.

Where inheritance tax is paid by the donee the gross loss to the donor is known and no grossing-up calculation is necessary.

Example
A has made chargeable transfers which have exhausted his nil rate band. He now makes a chargeable transfer to a discretionary trust of £10,000; the donee is to pay the inheritance tax attributable to the transfer.

The gross loss to the donor is £10,000. The transfer falls within the 40 per cent band but as it is a transfer made before death, the tax will be charged at one-half the full rate, that is at 20 per cent. The inheritance tax is, therefore:

$$£10,000 \times \frac{20}{100} = £2,000$$

It will be observed that in the first example the donee receives £10,000 and the donor loses £12,500 whereas in the second example the donee receives £8,000 and the donor loses £10,000. In the case of *inter vivos* transfers it is, therefore, important for the donor to consider carefully the amount he can afford to transfer and the amount he wishes the donee to receive. Where the gift consists of an asset rather than cash, the problem may be particularly serious as neither donor nor donee may have sufficient cash available to pay the inheritance tax. However, if the *donee* is paying the tax it is possible in respect of certain types of property to elect to pay the tax by instalments (see para.4.048 below) and this will mitigate the problem.

Grossing-up is required on an *inter vivos* gift whenever the *donor* pays the tax. The parties may agree that the donee will pay but if the donee fails to do so and the donor in fact pays, grossing-up is required.

Grossing-up is not normally required on the transfer of property forming part of the estate on death. The reason for this is that the tax on death is on the full value of the estate (subject to exemptions) not on the loss to the donor's estate. In very limited circumstances grossing-up is required to calculate the tax on death (see paras 4.050–4.055 below).

Where a potentially exempt or a chargeable transfer has been made and death occurs within seven years, tax may be payable as a result of the death. This is primarily the liability of the donee. As the donee will be paying the tax the gift to the donee is a gross gift and no grossing-up is required.

Gifts involving more than one tax band
If a transferor makes a transfer of value part of which is taxed at nil per **4.008** cent and part of which is taxed at 40 per cent, only the part falling within

the 40 per cent tax band needs to be grossed up. (In respect of transfers made before March 15, 1988 when there were several different rates of tax the calculation was more complicated.)

4. GIFTS WITHIN SEVEN YEARS OF DEATH—CHANGES IN VALUE

4.009 The object of charging the full rates or a proportion of the full rates of tax on death within seven years of a transfer is to prevent donors who know they are about to die from saving tax by making *inter vivos* transfers. It is, therefore, considered appropriate that relief from the extra tax should be given in certain cases where the value of the property transferred has declined between the transfer and the death. The rules which provide this relief are, in detail, very complex but their broad effect is to allow a decline in value of an asset to be deducted from the amount liable to the extra tax where the donee still owns the asset at the donor's death. Where the asset has been sold before the donor's death by the donee (or his spouse) at a loss in a qualifying sale (which broadly means in a genuine commercial transaction) the decline in value between the date of the gift and the date of sale may be deducted from the amount liable to extra tax. Special rules apply to certain types of property (including land and shares) and no relief is given where the asset was tangible movable property which had a predictable useful life of 50 years or less immediately before the transfer to the donee.

5. GIFTS WITHIN SEVEN YEARS OF DEATH—CHANGES OF RATE

4.010 When a potentially exempt transfer or chargeable transfer become taxable as the result of death within seven years, the rate of tax chargeable will be the rate in force at the date the gift was made except to the extent that rates have been reduced (Sch.2). This is quite a useful tax planning tool since it means that a transferor who fears that rates of tax may rise can make a gift now and guarantee that no increases in the rate of tax will affect the transfer. The transfer will, however, get the benefit of any reductions in rate—a rare example of having your tax cake and eating it.

6. GIFTS WITH A RESERVATION

4.011 The Finance Act 1986 contains special provisions in respect of property subject to a reservation. Property is regarded as subject to a reservation where an individual transfers property by way of gift and *either* the donee does not bona fide assume possession and enjoyment within the relevant period *or* at any time in the relevant period the property is not enjoyed to the entire, or virtually the entire, exclusion of the donor. The relevant period is the period ending with the date of death of the deceased and beginning seven years earlier or at the date of the gift if it was made within seven years of the death.

If a donor dies and there is property which is regarded as subject to a reservation at the date of his death, the property is treated for the purpose of inheritance tax as if it was part of his estate on death.

If property ceases to be subject to a reservation within the "relevant period" the donor is treated as making a potentially exempt transfer at that date. This means that tax will be payable on the property which was subject to a reservation if the donor dies within seven years of the property ceasing to be subject to a reservation.

There is clearly the possibility of double charges to tax on the same property.

Example
A transferor gives a country cottage to his son in 2003 stipulating that he retains the right to spend holidays there for three months in the summer for the next three years. He dies in 2008. The initial transfer in 2003 is a PET (arguably the value transferred is reduced because of the transferor's entitlement to occupation). The termination of the right to holidays after three years in 2006 is a PET equal in value of the right to occupation. Because this is a "deemed" PET it cannot be reduced by annual exemptions. When the transferor dies in 2008 both PETs become chargeable.

Had the transferor died before his right of occupation ceased, the continued reservation of benefit would mean that the entire value of the cottage would have been included in the transferor's estate.

There are Inheritance Tax (Double Charges Relief) Regulations 1987 which provide a measure of relief in such cases. They require alternative calculations to be made. It is necessary to consult the Rules carefully since the procedure varies according to the types of transfer involved.

Section 102(5) provides that the reservation of benefit rules have no application where there is a disposal to a spouse which is exempt under IHTA 1984, s.18. In *I.R.C. v Eversden* (2002) a wife transferred 95 per cent of the matrimonial home to a trust in 1988 and retained 5 per cent.

Her husband was the life tenant of the trust and after his death the property was to be held for a class of discretionary beneficiaries, which included the settlor, for 80 years and then for the settlor's daughter and her issue. The trustees had power to acquire property for the use and enjoyment of the beneficiaries.

The husband occupied the matrimonial home as life tenant of the trust with the settlor until he died in 1992. Because he died with a life interest in the property, it was included in his estate for IHT purposes at its then value of £147,000.

Simplifying the facts slightly the settlor was in sole occupation of the house until she died. The Revenue argued that as a result of the reservation of benefit rules the whole of the trust fund was included in the settlor's estate. The estate argued that the reservation of rules did not apply because there had been an exempt transfer.

After "anxious consideration" Lightman J. agreed with the taxpayers. If a gift is exempt *at the time it is made*, the reservation of benefit rules cannot have any application at a later date. He went on to say:

> "The duration of the proprietary interest gifted to the spouse is irrelevant even as it is irrelevant how long the spouse retains the proprietary interest and whether the spouse gifts the proprietary interest on to someone else eg the children of the donor and donee."

The case has attracted a lot of attention as there are clear opportunities for saving tax. Unsurprisingly the Revenue has appealed and has expressed the intention of obtaining a change in the legislation if it loses the appeal.

D. Valuation of Property

1. GENERAL RULES

4.012 On a lifetime transfer the loss to the donor or on death the value of the estate will depend on the valuation of particular items of property.

Section 160 of the Inheritance Tax Act 1984 provides that "... the value at any time of any property shall for the purposes of inheritance tax be the price which the property might reasonably be expected to fetch if sold in the open market at that time; but that price shall not be assumed to be reduced on the grounds that the whole property is to be placed on the market at one and the same time". The market value of any property is a question of fact. If property is actually sold within a short period after death on the open market the price received will be evidence (though not conclusive evidence) of the market value at the date of death.

The qualification which prohibits the assumption that all the property is to be sold at the same time will not affect valuation in most cases but would be relevant in valuing a large holding of shares in a private company (or even in a public company if the holding was a significant proportion of the share capital).

2. VALUATION ON DEATH

4.013 The transfer of value on death is a transfer of all property owned by the deceased *immediately before his death.* However, the Inheritance Tax Act 1984, s.171(1) provides that "changes in the value of [the] estate which have occurred by reason of the death ... shall be taken into account as if they had occurred before the death". The effect of this provision is to take into account changes in the market value of property which *result* from the death. Sometimes this will lead to an increase in the value of the estate, sometimes to a decrease.

For example, if the deceased is the managing director of a private company and owns a majority shareholding in it the value of the shares may well decline because of his death. Such a decline is likely to occur wherever the goodwill of the company is dependent on the personal ability of the deceased and is particularly likely in cases where the deceased has no successor able and willing to continue to run the company's business.

An example of an increase in the value of property resulting from the death of the owner is where the deceased owned a life insurance policy on his own life payable to his estate. Clearly, the value of the policy will increase as a result of the death from the surrender value of the policy to its capital value.

It is important to remember that the transfer on death is a transfer of the deceased's "estate", that is property to which the deceased was beneficially entitled (Inheritance Tax Act, s.5). Thus, any item not in the deceased's beneficial enjoyment will not be part of the estate and will not attract inheritance tax. Insurance policies must be looked at closely to see whether or not they are part of the estate. Where a policy on the deceased's life is owned beneficially by a third party it does not form part of the deceased's estate and so no inheritance tax is payable on the proceeds of the policy on his death. Examples of policies not beneficially owned by the deceased are policies taken out under the Married Women's Property Act or written in trust for a third party.

Section 171 only allows changes in the *market* value of property to be taken into account, it does not allow changes in the value of the property *to the deceased* to be taken into account. For this reason the deceased's share in joint property (which passes to the remaining joint tenant by survivorship) is fully taxable. Although it is true that the value to the deceased's *estate* of the joint property is nil once the deceased is dead, this does not affect the market value of the *property*.

3. SPECIAL VALUATION RULES

Quoted shares
Quoted stocks and shares are normally valued by taking the lower of the two prices quoted in the Stock Exchange Daily Official List for the relevant day and adding to it one-quarter of the difference between the lower and higher prices there quoted (for example, if the Daily List shows 200p/205p the value will be 201.25p for inheritance tax purposes) or if it produces a lower figure by taking a figure halfway between the lowest and highest prices at which bargains were struck on the relevant day. The "relevant day" is the day of death or the last or next trading day before or after death. "Quoted" means listed on a recognised stock exchange (Inheritance Tax Act 1984, s.272). **4.014**

Unquoted shares
In the case of shares not listed on the Stock Exchange, although recent bargains will be taken as a starting point, other factors may lead to a different value being adopted (SP 18/80). **4.015**

The valuation of unquoted shares is factually very difficult but will take into account: the dividend record of the company, the retained earnings (especially where earnings have been retained with a view to increasing the share value), the profitability of the company even if profits have not been used to pay dividends (this is especially relevant where profits have been used to pay high director's fees to a controlling shareholder) and the value of the assets owned by the company (this is especially relevant where the company is likely to be wound up or taken over).

Three special rules apply to the valuation of unquoted shares:

(a) A reduction in value resulting from the death cannot be taken into account if it arises from the fact that the rights attached to the shares are varied as a result of the death (for example, because the articles of the company provide that the shares are then to lose their right to dividend or to vote). (Inheritance Tax Act 1984, s.171(2)).

(b) If the shares are subject to pre-emption rights the market value is to be assessed on the basis that the pre-emption rights do not apply to the hypothetical sale on the open market at the time of death but that they will apply to the hypothetical purchaser (in other words the value is the price which a purchaser would pay knowing that he would be subject to the pre-emption rights in the future). This was established in *I.R.C. v Crossman* (1937) an estate duty case decided on legislation which was in this respect similar to the inheritance tax legislation.

(c) The value on death is calculated on the assumption that a prospective purchaser would have all the information which a prudent prospective purchaser might reasonably require if he were purchasing from a willing vendor by private treaty and at arm's length (Inheritance Tax Act 1984, s.168(1)).

Other assets subject to restrictions on sale
The *Crossman* principle referred to above has been extended to other assets sold subject to restrictions. For example in *Alexander v I.R.C.* (1991) a flat which had been purchased by the deceased under the "Right to Buy" scheme was subject to an obligation to repay the discount if sold within five years of its purchase. The deceased died one year after purchase. The Court of Appeal held that the property was to be valued on the basis of the amount a purchaser would pay to stand in the shoes of the deceased, *i.e.* to obtain the property subject to the obligation of repaying the discount if the property was sold within five years.

There has been a series of cases on the correct valuation of non-assignable agricultural tenancies, *e.g. Baird's Executors v I.R.C.* (1991), *Walton v I.R.C.* (1996). It has been accepted that such tenancies have a value and therefore the question of deciding on the value is simply a matter of evidence. The Court of Appeal in *Walton* confirmed that there are no hard and fast valuation rules. It is incorrect to proceed on the basis that the landlord is a "special purchaser" if in fact the freeholder is not interested in acquiring the tenancy. The taxpayer should be careful in such a case to gather adequate information on the value of the property. In the absence of such evidence from the taxpayer the view of the Revenue will go unchallenged.

Sale within one or four years of death
4.016 If quoted shares are sold within one year of death or an interest in land within four years of death for less than the value at death a reduction of the tax may be claimed in certain circumstances. (See para.12.013.)

Commorientes
4.017 Section 184 of the Law of Property Act 1925 provides that where two or more people die in circumstances such that it is uncertain which of them survived, for the purposes of succession to property the deaths are deemed to occur in the order of seniority so that the elder is deemed to die first. Consequently if the elder has left property to the younger, the younger will inherit that property which will then pass under the terms of the will or intestacy of the younger. (For a detailed discussion of this rule and a limited exception to it, see Chapter 16.)

However, for inheritance tax purposes, s.4(2) of the Inheritance Tax Act 1984 provides that "where it cannot be known which of two or more persons who have died survived the other or others they shall be assumed to have died at the same instant". Therefore, where two or more persons die and the order of deaths cannot be known a double charge to tax is avoided. If the elder person has left property to the younger it will be taxed as part of the elder's estate (unless an exemption is available) but the younger will not be deemed to have survived for tax purposes and so the property will not be taxed as part of his estate.

Example
A and her son B are killed in a car accident. A's will leaves everything to B. B's will leaves everything to X. It is uncertain whether A or B died first; therefore for the purposes of succession to property the deaths are deemed to occur in order of seniority and A's property passes to B. B's property (including that which has been inherited from A) then passes to X. For the purposes of inheritance tax, A and B are deemed to die at the same instant. Thus, when calculating inheritance tax payable on B's estate, B's estate is deemed not to include the property received from A.

If A and B in the above example are husband and wife, the whole of A's estate will be exempt as it is passing to a spouse. B's estate is deemed not to include the property inherited from A. A's property is, therefore, not charged to inheritance tax. This is an extremely beneficial result but since it is impossible to guarantee dying in circumstances where s.4(2) would apply, it is difficult to use the provision for effective tax planning. However, when drafting wills for spouses, it is possible to provide that a survivorship clause is not to apply if the order of death of the spouses is uncertain. This ensures that the benefit of the spouse exemption is retained if deaths occur *commorientes*.

4. RELATED PROPERTY

Certain assets are more valuable when owned in conjunction with other **4.018** assets of the same type than when owned individually. For example, a share in a company owned as part of a majority shareholding in the company will be more valuable than a share owned as part of a minority shareholding. There is a possibility that spouses might try to avoid inheritance tax by using the spouse exemption to split the ownership of such items between themselves. In order to prevent this special rules applying to the valuation of "related property" exist. Section 161(2) of the Inheritance Tax Act 1984 provides that property is related to other property owned by the transferor's spouse at the time of the transfer. Property is also related to property which was transferred by the transferor by an exempt transfer to a charity, political party or certain national bodies (as defined by Inheritance Tax Act 1984, Sch.3), and is owned by the charity, etc., at the time of the transfer or has been owned by it within five years before the transfer. This provision is designed to prevent abuse where a person makes an exempt transfer to a charity of property from which he can benefit or which he controls.

On a transfer of related property the transferred property and the property related to it are valued as one asset. Tax is then paid on the proportion of the total which is transferred.

Example
A owns 40 per cent of the shares in a private company and A's spouse owns another 30 per cent. If A dies and makes a chargeable transfer of the shares his estate will be taxed not on a 40 per cent holding but on four-sevenths of a 70 per cent holding. This figure is likely to be considerably higher than the value of a 40 per cent holding since a 70 per cent holding gives control of the company.

All property held by spouses is related but in most cases the value will not be affected (for example, if each spouse owns a motor car neither car will be more highly valued as the values of the two properties are factually entirely independent). Apart from shares in private companies, the most likely types of property which may be more highly valued because of the related property rule are collections of chattels and property held as beneficial joint tenants or as tenants-in-common.

When property is valued as related property on death, it is that value which is taxed (unless an exemption applies). However, if that property is sold within three years of death by the personal representatives or a person in whom the property concerned vested immediately after the death in an arm's length sale it can be revalued as if there had been no related property (Inheritance Tax Act 1984, s.176). This may result in a repayment of tax. Such a revaluation is not permitted where the sale is made in conjunction with a sale of the related property.

5. APPORTIONMENT OF INCOME ATTRIBUTABLE TO A PERIOD FALLING PARTLY BEFORE AND PARTLY AFTER DEATH

4.019 In order to calculate the value of the estate for inheritance tax purposes it is necessary to include any income which accrued prior to death even if it is not paid until after death. The pre-death portion of such income is chargeable to inheritance tax and must be shown on the Inland Revenue Account (if one is required) while the post-death portion is not chargeable to inheritance tax and will not be shown on an Inland Revenue Account. Income which is *paid* before death and which relates to a period falling wholly or partly *after* death is not apportioned. It is all treated as a capital asset of the estate. A direction in the will that no apportionments of income should be made, while relevant for the purposes of distribution amongst beneficiaries, is entirely irrelevant for the purposes of inheritance tax.

The following examples illustrate the way in which types of income may have to be apportioned when calculating the value of the estate for inheritance tax.

Examples

4.020 (a) *Interest.* Interest which has accrued *up to* the date of death on assets such as money in a building society account or deposit bank account is treated as capital and is chargeable to inheritance tax. Interest on such assets which accrues *from* the date of death is treated as income and is not chargeable to inheritance tax.

(b) *Rent.* If rent is payable in advance and the due date for payment falls *before* death the whole of the rent is treated as capital irrespective of when it is paid. Thus, even if it is paid after death the whole amount due must be included as an asset on the Inland Revenue Account and is chargeable to inheritance tax.

If the rent is payable in arrear for a period which falls partly before and partly after death it is necessary to apportion the rent. The pre-death portion is included as an asset on the Inland Revenue Account and is chargeable to inheritance tax, the post-death portion is not.

(c) *Dividends.* Shares may be valued "cum div." or "ex div.". If they are valued "cum div." this means that the share price has been calculated on the basis that a purchaser buying the stocks or shares would be entitled to the *whole* of the next dividend. The share price is, therefore, increased to compensate the vendor for the loss of that part of the year's interest or dividend that has already accrued. For inheritance tax purposes if the probate valuation is made "cum div." that value is entered on the Inland Revenue Account and no further reference need be made to the dividend, since the value of the dividend or interest is included in the share price.

As the date for payment of interest or of a dividend approaches companies close their transfer books. This means that if shares are sold after that date the next interest payment or dividend will be sent to the *old* registered owner. If shares are valued after this date they will be valued "ex div.". This means that the basic share price is reduced to compensate the purchaser for the fact that if he buys he will receive no benefit from the next dividend payment. For inheritance tax purposes if the probate valuation is made "ex div." the ex div. price is entered on the Inland Revenue Account but so is the whole of the dividend payment which will be paid to the estate by the company.

We will see in Chapter 6 that for income tax purposes if a dividend is declared after death or interest paid after death for a period which falls partly before and partly after death the whole of such a receipt will be treated as income and will, therefore, be liable to income tax. This could lead to an element of double taxation since the receipt would already have been apportioned and a part of it made chargeable to inheritance tax. There is, therefore, a limited income tax relief (Income and Corporation Taxes Act 1988, s.699 as amended) whereby residuary income is treated as reduced, for the purposes of income tax liability in excess of the basic rate only, by an amount equal to the inheritance tax liability on that income, grossed up at the basic rate.

(d) *Government securities.* A holder of securities receives interest rather than dividends. Just as the price of company shares can be quoted "cum" or "ex div." so the price of securities can be quoted "cum interest" (that is with the right to receive accrued interest) or "ex interest" (that is without the right to receive any of the next interest payment). For inheritance tax purposes if the valuation is "cum interest" that value is entered on the Inland Revenue Account and no further reference is made to the interest. If the valuation is "ex interest" the capital value of the security and the whole of the next interest payment payable to the estate are included as separate items.

6. LIABILITIES

4.021   Liabilities are taken into account in valuing a transferor's estate to the extent that they were incurred for consideration in money or money's worth or imposed by law (Inheritance Tax Act 1984, s.5) and provided there is no right to reimbursement (Inheritance Tax Act 1984, s.162(1)). In the case of death, the value of the estate for tax purposes is the net amount after deducting debts (and other liabilities incurred for consideration) and liabilities imposed by law (such as a liability to pay the community charge and a liability to pay damages in tort). Reasonable funeral expenses may also be deducted (Inheritance Tax Act 1984, s.172).

A mortgage or other liability which is an incumbrance on particular property is taken as reducing the value of that property (rather than the estate generally) so far as that is possible. At first sight this rule might seem unimportant since the whole net value of the estate is taxable anyway but it is relevant where exemptions, such as the spouse exemption (see para.4.023 below), are available.

For example, an estate consists of a house worth £100,000 and £100,000 cash. The house is subject to a mortgage of £10,000. The value of the estate on death is, therefore, £190,000 for tax purposes. If the house is given to the spouse of the deceased and the cash to children an asset worth £90,000 will pass to the spouse and will be exempt (since the mortgage reduces the value of the property given to the spouse). The remaining £100,000 will be regarded as passing to non-exempt beneficiaries and, therefore, chargeable to inheritance tax. If the mortgage reduced the value of the estate generally, an asset worth £100,000 would have passed to the spouse (and been exempt) leaving £90,000 to be regarded as passing to the non-exempt beneficiaries (and chargeable to inheritance tax).

Incidental costs of transferring assets are ignored in calculating the value transferred unless they are incurred by the transferee in which case they reduce the value transferred. This rule has no application to transfers on death because the transfer on death (which takes place for tax purposes the moment before death) is an automatic transfer on which no incidental costs can arise.

Where an estate includes property situated outside the United Kingdom, an allowance is made against that property for any expense incurred in administering or realising the property which is shown to be attributable to the situation of the property. The allowance cannot exceed 5 per cent of the value of the property.

The Finance Act 1986, s.103 introduced special provisions to prevent deduction being made for a debt where consideration has been provided directly or indirectly by the deceased. For example father gives son £200,000. Son lends it back to father. On father's death the debt due to son will be non-deductible under s.103.

The so-called "loan" or nil rate band debt scheme involves a surviving spouse incurring a liability which reduces the value of the estate on death. Section 103 may cause problems.

Example 1
First spouse to die (H) gives a nil rate band legacy to a discretionary trust for children and residue to his wife (W). The estate is £400,000 of which the matrimonial home is £300,000. Instead of the executors using liquid funds to pay the legacy, they transfer all the assets to the spouse and accept an IOU which they then give to the trustees of the nil rate band settlement. W has the use of all the assets and when she dies there is a liability which reduces the value of her estate. The Revenue has accepted that the scheme works when "properly drafted". The will must give the trustees power to accept the debt in lieu of cash and should relieve them from liability if there are insufficient funds to pay off the debt when W dies.

Example 2
The facts are as above but some time before H's death W gave H a substantial gift as part of an equalisation of estates exercise. If W now incurs a debt in connection with H's estate, the Revenue may argue that the debt is non-deductible. They have been asked whether or not s.103 would apply in this context and declined to say that it did not.

One solution in such a case is to leave the residue to W for life so that it is the trustees of the settlement who incur the debt not the spouse. Another possibility is for the executors to charge the assets transferred to W with the debt so that she does not incur the debt. However, s.103 problems will still arise if the house is sold and the executors advance funds to W for the purchase of a replacement property.

A liability to pay an insurance company a sum from the death estate in return for a payment from the company is not deductible unless the policy proceeds form part of the death estate.

E. Exemptions

1. INTRODUCTION

Certain transfers are exempt from inheritance tax as a result of the **4.022** Inheritance Tax Act 1984, ss.18–29 and other parts of the inheritance tax legislation. An exempt transfer is not liable to tax nor is it included in the cumulative total of the transferor (so that it does not affect the rate of tax on later transfers). All the exemptions will be considered in this chapter although they are not all relevant on death. The exemptions which are relevant only to transfers made *before* death are included since lifetime gifts are sometimes a suitable (and from the tax point of view beneficial) alternative to disposing of property by will.

2. THE SPOUSE EXEMPTION

This exemption is available *inter vivos* and on death. Inheritance Tax Act **4.023** 1984, s.18 provides that a transfer of value is exempt "to the extent that the value transferred is attributable to property which becomes comprised in the estate of the transferor's spouse. ..." This means that gifts to the transferor's spouse, before death or on death, are completely exempt. The exemption is lost if the gift does not take effect immediately so that a gift by a testator "to A for life, remainder to my spouse" is not an exempt transfer. However, the spouse exemption is not lost if the gift is conditional and the condition is satisfied within 12 months of the transfer. Thus, if property is left to a spouse, provided he survives for a period of up to 12 months, the spouse exemption will be available provided that the spouse survives the specified period. However, there are other considerations which make a survivorship period exceeding six months inadvisable. Such a gift will be treated as creating a settlement without an interest in possession (see Chapter 7) and will result in an immediate chargeable transfer from the deceased to the settlement.

The spouse exemption is available even though the gift to the spouse is not absolute, provided the spouse takes an immediate interest. The exemption applies, therefore, if T makes a gift "to my spouse for life remainder to X".

For inheritance tax purposes (unlike income tax and capital gains tax) "spouse" has a normal meaning so that the exemption is available even though the parties are separated.

The spouse exemption is only available in full if the spouse is domiciled in the United Kingdom. If the spouse is domiciled elsewhere only the first £55,000 of transfers to him or her are exempt.

In *Executor of Holland deceased v IRC* (2003) the special commissioners held that the spouse exemption was limited to married couples and was not available to cohabitees. This was not contrary to the Human Rights Act. Cohabitees are not analogous to married couples and in any event the difference in treatment was objectively and reasonably justifiable. Married persons have mutual rights and obligations relating to maintenance during their lives and after their deaths. These interlocking property rights and obligations justify the special tax treatment of spouses.

3. GIFTS TO CHARITIES, ETC.

4.024   Transfers of value are exempt "to the extent that the values transferred ... are attributable to property which is given to charities". (Inheritance Tax Act 1984, s.23.) There is now no limit to the amount which is exempt under this provision. As with the spouse exemption the gift must be immediate and, if conditional, any condition must be satisfied within 12 months. In addition a gift to a charity must normally be absolute if the exemption is to be available.

Transfers of value to exempt political parties are entitled to relief in the same way as transfers to charity. A political party qualifies for exemption if it had two members elected to the House of Commons at the last general election or one member if the party's candidates generally got at least 150,000 votes.

Transfers of value to certain national bodies are entitled to relief in the same way as transfers to charities. The Inheritance Tax Act 1984, Sch.13 contains a list of the national bodies to which this rule applies; they include, for example, national museums and art galleries, universities and their libraries, local authorities and government departments.

Transfers of value to non-profit-making bodies (other than charities, political parties and national bodies) are also exempt if the property transferred is within certain specified categories (which may broadly be described as covering scenic, historic or scientifically important land, buildings, books, papers or objects) and the Treasury direct that an exemption is to be available.

Transfers to charities, etc., are only exempt if the money or other property given is to be used exclusively for the purposes of a charity, political party, national or non-profit-making body. The exemptions are not available if "the property or any part of it *may* become applicable for (other) purposes. ..." (Inheritance Tax Act 1984, ss.24(3), 25(2), 26(7)).

4. THE "ANNUAL" EXEMPTION

This exemption is only available on transfers made *before* death. Section 19 of the Inheritance Tax Act 1984 provides for an annual exemption of £3,000. This exemption applies to the first £3,000 of transfers in each tax year (April 6 to April 5 inclusive). This exemption is available in addition to other exemptions so that a transferor can give as much property as he likes to his spouse and still have the annual exemption available for gifts to others.   **4.025**

To the extent that the annual exemption is not used in a particular year the unused part may be carried forward for one year but no longer. For example, a transferor who made no transfer last year will be entitled to a £6,000 exemption this year. To ensure that the carry forward is limited to one year the exemption of the current year must be used first and only after the whole of that exemption is exhausted can anything brought forward from the previous year be used.

For example, if A transfers nothing in year one, £6,000 of relief will be available in year two. If only £4,000 is transferred in year two this will use up the whole of year two's exemption and £1,000 from year one. Thus, in year three only an exemption of £3,000 will be available.

If more than one transfer is made in a tax year, the annual exemption must be allocated to the first chargeable transfer made in that tax year. If more than one transfer is made on the same day the exemption is apportioned *pro rata* irrespective of the order in which the gifts are made.

The annual exemption must be allocated to the *first* transfer in a tax year even though that transfer would otherwise be potentially exempt. This means that it is more tax efficient to make a lifetime chargeable transfer earlier in the tax year than a potentially exempt transfer.

Example
Alan has never made any transfers of value. In the tax year 2003/04 he gives £206,000 to Beth and then £306,000 to a discretionary trust. He survives seven years.

The annual exemption must be allocated to the first transfer which is therefore exempt as to £6,000 and potentially exempt as to £200,000; the second transfer is a lifetime chargeable transfer of £306,000. As Alan survives seven years the potentially exempt transfer becomes fully exempt and Alan derives no benefit from the annual exemption.

In addition to the annual exemption, outright *inter vivos* gifts worth up to £250 per donee are exempt (Inheritance Tax Act 1984, s.20). This exemption does not apply to the first part of a gift which exceeds £250.

(For example, a donor who gives three people £250 each does not pay any tax and does not use up any of the £3,000 exemption but, if £600 is given to one donee, £600 of the £3,000 exemption is used up.)

5. NORMAL EXPENDITURE OUT OF INCOME

4.026　The relief for normal expenditure is only available *inter vivos*. The Inheritance Tax Act 1984, s.21 provides that a transfer of value is exempt to the extent that:

(a) It is made as part of the normal expenditure of the transferor. (It is a question of fact whether this requirement is satisfied. The Revenue will treat expenditure as normal if it is made under a legal obligation (for example, a deed of covenant) or if similar expenditure is in fact incurred on a regular basis.)

(b) It is (taking one year with another) made out of income; and

(c) It is such that the transferor's usual standard of living is not affected by it.

Bennett v I.R.C. (1995) shows how useful this exemption can be in tax planning.

Mrs Bennett was an elderly widow and the life tenant of a trust which had always produced a very modest income (£300 p.a. approx.). In 1987 the income of the trust increased enormously as a result of the sale of trust assets. Mrs Bennett instructed her trustees to continue to pay her £300 p.a. and to use the surplus income, for which she had no need, to her sons. The trustees paid £9,300 in 1989 to each of the three sons and £60,000 the following year. She then died. The Revenue contended that the transfers were failed potentially exempt transfers. The personal representatives contended that they were exempt as normal expenditure out of income.

The court agreed that the transfers were exempt. It said that "normal expenditure" required a demonstration of a settled pattern of giving. This could be demonstrated by a pattern of giving over a period of time or by the individual assuming a commitment. "There is no fixed minimum period during which the expenditure should have occurred ... if the prior commitment or resolution can be shown, a single payment implementing the commitment or resolution may be sufficient ... the amount of expenditure need not be fixed in amount nor indeed the individual recipient be the same. As regards quantum, it is sufficient that a formula or standard has been adopted by application of which the payment (which may be of a fluctuating amount) can be identified. ..."

6. GIFTS IN CONSIDERATION OF MARRIAGE

4.027　This exemption is only available *inter vivos*. The Inheritance Tax Act 1984, s.22 provides that a gift in consideration of marriage is exempt to the extent of:

(a) £5,000 if made by a parent of one of the parties to the marriage,

(b) £2,500 if made by a remoter ancestor of one of the parties or by a party to the prospective marriage,

(c) £1,000 in any other case.

The limits apply to each marriage, not to each donee (so that a parent cannot give £5,000 to his child and £1,000 to his future child-in-law and obtain exemption for £6,000).

7. FAMILY MAINTENANCE

This exemption is only available *inter vivos*. The Inheritance Tax Act **4.028**
1984, s.11 provides that a disposition is not a transfer of value (and so is
exempt) if it is made by one party to a marriage in favour of the other
party or of a child of either party and is for the maintenance of the other
party or for the maintenance, education or training of the child. In the
case of a disposition in favour of a spouse there would usually be an
exemption anyway (see para.4.023 above) but the family maintenance
exemption applies to ex-spouses and to spouses domiciled outside the
United Kingdom whereas the normal spouse exemption does not. The
exemption for maintenance, etc., of children is normally available only to
the parents (including adoptive and step-parents) but where the child is
not in the care of its parents it extends to others maintaining the children
in certain circumstances.

The Inheritance Tax Act 1984, s.11(3) provides that dispositions in
favour of dependent relatives other than spouses and children are exempt
to the extent that they are "reasonable provision for care or
maintenance".

8. CUMULATIVE EFFECT OF EXEMPTIONS

The exemptions referred to above (other than the small gifts exemption) **4.029**
are cumulative with each other. After the exemptions have been claimed
the transferor is entitled to a certain amount (£255,000 for Tax Year
2003/04) taxed at a nil rate. For example, a transferor who has made no
previous gifts and who wishes to benefit his child who is about to be
married as much as possible without a potential liability to inheritance tax
if he dies within seven years could give the following:

	£
Annual exemption from last year	3,000
Annual exemption for this year	3,000
Marriage exemption	5,000
Nil rate	255,000
	266,000

The transferor's spouse could make similar provision immediately and
both could give further sums of £3,000 annually. Seven years after these
gifts the potentially exempt transfer of £250,000 will prove to be exempt
and the transferor will be free to make further transfers up to the limit of
the then nil rate band without any liability to inheritance tax.

9. MISCELLANEOUS

An exemption is available for the whole value of the estate of a person **4.030**
who dies as a result of active or other warlike service and who is a member
of the armed forces or a civilian accompanying armed forces (Inheritance
Tax Act 1984, s.154).

"Conditional" exemption is available on death and on certain *inter
vivos* transfers in respect of assets designated by the Treasury as being of

national, scientific, historic or artistic interest (Inheritance Tax Act 1984, ss.33–35 as amended by Finance Act 1985, s.26). Claims must be made within 2 years of the transfer of value or such longer period as the Board may allow (s.30(3BA)) inserted by Finance Act 1998). The exemption is only available if suitable undertakings are given. The taxpayer must undertake to take reasonable steps to preserve the asset, to secure reasonable access to the public and to keep objects permanently in the United Kingdom. There had been concern that proper access for the public was not always available. Finance Act 1998, therefore, provided that access by prior appointment is not sufficient. There must be extended access and also greater disclosure of information about items. See Inheritance Tax Act 1984, s.31(4FA) and (4FB). The exemption is "conditional" on these undertakings. Tax becomes payable if an undertaking is broken or if there is a disposal and similar undertakings are not given. Tax will normally become payable in any event if the asset is sold.

F. Reliefs

1. INTRODUCTION

4.031 A relief does not give complete exemption from inheritance tax but does lead to a reduction in the inheritance tax payable.

A variety of reliefs are available such as quick succession relief under s.161 of the Inheritance Tax Act 1984 (where a *death* occurs within five years of a chargeable transfer), relief on the value of growing timber under the Inheritance Tax Act 1984, ss.125–130 (where within two years of a death an election claiming relief is made) and most importantly reliefs for business and agricultural property under Inheritance Tax Act 1984, ss.103–114 and ss.115–124A. These reliefs have become even more important as a result of the availability of 100 per cent relief.

Quick succession relief and timber relief are only available on death, not on transfers made before death.

The reliefs on business and on agricultural property are available on transfers *inter vivos* and on death. They take effect by means of a percentage reduction in the value transferred. A reduction in the value transferred will have the effect of reducing the tax payable. The relief will prevent any charge to tax arising, where it brings the value transferred within the nil rate band.

The object of these reliefs is to ease the burden of taxation on businesses and agricultural land. To ensure that taxpayers cannot take unfair advantage of them there are rules requiring a minimum period of ownership before the relief becomes available. Further mitigation of the hardship of paying tax out of business and agricultural property (which might otherwise lead to the forced sale of such property) is provided by the instalment option (as to which see para.4.048).

2. AGRICULTURAL RELIEF

4.032 Agricultural relief is available in respect of "agricultural property". Agricultural property is defined by the Inheritance Tax Act 1984, s.115(2) and includes agricultural land and pasture and certain land and buildings occupied *in association with it* including farm-houses, farm buildings and cottages as are of a character appropriate to the property.

The definition has been extended (in the case of transfers made on or after April 6, 1995) to include land used for short term coppice.

Farm cottages must have been occupied for the purposes of agriculture. However an ESC dated February 13, 1995 extends the relief to cottages by retired farm employees or their surviving spouses in certain circumstances.

There have been a number of cases where the Revenue has declined to allow relief on farm houses because they have not been occupied for the requisite period or have not been occupied *with* the land. *Starke v I.R.C.* was an example of a house which was not occupied *with* land. The house was situate with some substantial outbuildings and one or two small areas of enclosed land but failed to qualify for relief. *Harrold v I.R.C.* is an example of a house which was not occupied for the requisite period. The taxpayer had bought a farm and started working it but could not live in the farmhouse which was in a dilapidated state until essential repairs were carried out. The special commissioners found that despite the taxpayer's care for the property and work on it, he was not in occupation until he actually moved in.

It is frequently difficult in practice to determine whether or not a farmhouse is of a character appropriate to the property. *Lloyds TSB as personal representative of Antrobus (Deceased) v I.R.C.* (2002) summarised the relevant principles as follows:

1. one should consider whether the house is appropriate by reference to its size, content and layout with the farm buildings and the particular area of farm-land being farmed;
2. one should consider whether the house is proportionate in size and nature to the requirements of the farming activities conducted on the agricultural land or pasture in question;
3. although one cannot describe a farmhouse which satisfies the "character appropriate" test, one knows one when one sees it;
4. one should ask whether the educated rural layman would regard the property as a house with land or a farm;
5. one should consider the historical dimension and ask how long the house in question has been associated with the agricultural property and whether there was a history of agricultural production.

Applying these tests the house in question was "of a character appropriate to the property".

Executors of Higginson v I.R.C. (2002) confirmed that there is no single test. In that case the house was of such value that it was the predominant element of the unit. It was a house with farmland going with it (and not vice versa).

The Revenue considers that a milk quota comprises a separate asset distinct from the land. It will not, therefore, qualify for agricultural property relief but may qualify for business property relief. See *Cottle v Coldicotte* (1995 S.T.C.(Sco.) 239).

Agricultural relief takes the form of a percentage reduction in the "agricultural value" of the property which is defined as "the value of the property if the property were subject to a perpetual covenant prohibiting its use otherwise than as agricultural property" (s.115(3)). The effect of this definition is that relief is available to the extent of the value of a farm or other agricultural property *as a farm* but any other value attached to it, such as development value, is not relieved (although business property relief may be available on that value—see below).

In the case of charges to tax arising on or after March 10, 1992, the reduction in value is either 100 per cent or 50 per cent.

4.033   The percentage reduction in the agricultural value of the property is 100 per cent where the transferor had the right to vacant possession immediately before the transfer or the right to obtain it within 12 months after the transfer (s.116(2)). (100 per cent relief is also available in certain other cases where the transferor has been beneficially entitled to the property since before March 10, 1981 but in this case there is an upper limit of £250,000 on the value which can be reduced by 100 per cent.)

ESC F17 has extended 100 per cent relief to cases where the transferor's interest in the property immediately before the transfer either:

(1) carried the right to vacant possession within 24 months of the date of the transfer; or
(2) is notwithstanding the terms of the tenancy valued at an amount broadly equivalent to vacant possession value.

Illustrations of (1) include *Gladstone v Bower* arrangements. An illustration of (2) would be the type of arrangement in *I.R.C. v Gray* (1994). In this case Lady Fox had granted a tenancy to a partnership in which she was entitled to 97.5 per cent of the profits. The Revenue successfully contended that as she would have been able to offer the reversion and the partnership for sale together, they should be valued as one unit.

However agricultural land subject to such arrangements will now qualify for 100 per cent relief.

In other cases the relief is 50 per cent (s.116(2)). Where land is owned by joint tenants or tenants in common each of them is deemed to have a right to vacant possession if the interests of all of them together carry that right (s.116(6)). It is obviously desirable to have the right to vacant possession. A landowner who is thinking of granting a *Gladstone v Bowers* tenancy should not grant it for more than a year and a day so that the right to vacant possession within 12 months exists virtually from the very beginning of the tenancy.

The right to agricultural relief only applies if certain requirements are satisfied. First, the transferor must have *occupied* the land for the purposes of agriculture "throughout the period of two years ending with the date of the transfer" or it must have been *owned* by him throughout the period of seven years ending with the date of the transfer and was occupied by him *or another* for the purposes of agriculture throughout that period (s.117). This means that a farmer who buys his own farm qualifies for relief (at 100 per cent) after two years if he continues to occupy it up to the time of transfer. A person who buys a farm and puts in a tenant qualifies for relief (at 50 per cent) only after seven years. A tenant who purchases his farm qualifies for relief (at 100 per cent) immediately if he has been in occupation for two years. Any break in the periods of ownership or occupation is fatal to the availability of the relief.

Section 94 of the Finance Act 1997 extends agricultural property relief to former farm land dedicated under the Government's Habitat scheme. The scheme, which is designed to protect the environment and maintain the countryside, takes land out of farming for 20 years. Until the Finance Act changes this meant that the land was not eligible for relief because it could not fulfil the requirement that land must have been occupied for agriculture for a minimum of two years if owner occupied or seven years if occupied by someone else.

Special rules apply in relation to the occupation requirement where a farmer moves from one farm to another (s.118), where a farm is owned by the spouse of a former owner or where there is a transfer within two years of a previous transfer provided one transfer is on death (section 120).

A transfer of shares in a company which owns agricultural property is eligible for relief to the extent that the value of the shares reflects the agricultural value of land and provided the shareholder is in control of the company. Occupation by the company is deemed to be occupation by the controlling shareholder (s.119).

Clawback of relief on inter vivos transfers
Where a transfer is made before death, whether chargeable or potentially exempt, and the transferor dies within seven years, the relief is available only if the property originally given or qualifying property representing it has remained as agricultural property in the ownership of the transferee from the date of transfer to the date of death of the transferor. If the transferee dies before the transferor within the seven-year period, relief is only available on the death of the transferee if the same conditions are satisfied. This is more fully discussed in connection with business property relief.

4.033

If only a proportion of the property originally given or qualifying property representing it remains in the ownership of the transferee at the date of death, relief is available on the proportion of the property owned at that date (s.124A).

Clawback is discussed more fully in connection with business property relief.

It is important to note that where a transferor dies on or after March 10, 1992, having made a transfer of value within the seven years before that date, relief (if available) will be at the appropriate new rate.

3. BUSINESS PROPERTY RELIEF

This relief is available in respect of "relevant business property". The relief is a reduction in the value transferred by a particular percentage depending on what type of property is being transferred (Inheritance Tax

4.034

Act 1984, s.104). Relevant business property is property falling into one of the following six categories:

(a) Property consisting of a business or an interest in a business (this includes the interest of a sole proprietor or of a partner in a business) (s.105(1)(a));

(b) Unquoted securities which alone or with other shares owned by the transferor or with related property gave the transferor control of the company (s.105(b)). A person has control if he controls more than 50 per cent of the votes exercisable in general meeting.

In deciding whether or not one person has control it is not possible to ignore votes attaching to shares held by another person who lacks capacity: *Walding v I.R.C.* (1996).

It is sufficient for the transferor to control a majority of shares *immediately before* the transfer. A company may buy back and cancel some shares with the result that after the cancellation a shareholder may have more than 50 per cent of the remaining shares. A transfer by the shareholders at that point will attract 100 per cent relief even if more shares are issued shortly afterwards.

It is not necessary for the transfer to cause the transferor to lose control. The transfer of one share from an 80 per cent shareholding will attract 100 per cent relief on the transfer of that one share.

(c) Shareholdings in unlisted companies (s.105(1)(bb)).

In the three cases above the relief is 100 per cent

(d) Shareholdings in listed companies which alone or with other shares owned by the transferor or with related property gave the transferor control immediately before the transfer. Again control is exercising more than 50 per cent of the votes in general meeting. Temporary control will suffice. Relief is available until the size of the holding dips below the crucial point. Where a persons intends to make a number of gifts of shares from such a holding, it is desirable to make the smaller gifts first to try to ensure that control is maintained for as long as possible.

(e) Land or buildings, machinery or plant used immediately before the transfer wholly or mainly for the purposes of a company controlled by the transferor or of a partnership of which he was a member.

(f) Land or buildings, machinery or plant used immediately before the transfer for the purposes of a business carried on by the transferor and which was settled property in which the transferor had an interest in possession.

In the three cases above, the relief is 50 per cent

In the case of tax charges arising before March 10, 1992, the division was into slightly different categories and the relief was at the rate of 50 per cent or 30 per cent.

"Business"

The term "business" includes a profession or vocation but does not **4.035**
include a business carried on otherwise than for gain (s.103(3)). It
includes an interest at Lloyds and the interest of market makers on the
London International Financial Futures and Options Exchange (LIFFE).
(Inheritance Tax (Market Makers) Regulations 1993). Agriculture is
regarded as a type of business so that business property relief may be
available to the extent that agricultural relief cannot be claimed (that is
business property relief is available for any non-agricultural value of
agricultural property).

Businesses which consist of dealing in securities, stocks, shares, land or
buildings or of holding investments are specifically excluded from relief
(s.105(3)).

Some commercial landlords have attempted to argue that they are
entitled to relief because they are in active management of the land rather
than mere passive landlords. On the whole, such arguments have met with
little success. See *Powell v I.R.C.* (1997), *Martin (Executors of Moore) v
I.R.C.* (1995) and *Burkinyoung v I.R.C.* (1995).

There have been a number of cases involving the availability of relief
on static caravan sites. In *Hall v I.R.C.* (1997) the greater part of the
income came from rents and standing charges and it was held that the
business was "mainly" that of making or holding investment. In *Furness v
I.R.C.* (1999) the taxpayer obtained relief where net profit from caravan
sales exceeded that from net rents. In *Weston v I.R.C.* (2000) the High
Court confirmed that the question of whether or not a business consisted
wholly or mainly of making or holding investments was a question of fact
for the Special Commissioners.

In *Farmer v I.R.C.* (1999) the special commissioner concluded that a
business which comprised farming and letting of former farm buildings
was one business consisting mainly of farming. The case is interesting
because the net profit from lettings exceeded that from farming but that
was not conclusive. Relevant was the amount of time spent on the various
activities, the allocation of capital employed between the activities and
the fact that farming turnover often exceeded turnover from rents.

Business property relief is given on the net value of business property
(s.110). This is the value after deducting liabilities incurred for the
purposes of the business (for other inheritance tax purposes in the case of
death liabilities are deducted from *the whole estate* unless charged on
particular property).

In order to qualify for relief certain requirements must be satisfied.
First, the transferor must have owned the relevant business property
throughout the period of two years before the transfer (s.107(1)).
Property which replaces other relevant business property qualifies for
relief even though not owned for two years provided that the aggregate
period of ownership exceeds two years in the five years before the
transfer. Until the new property has been owned for two years the relief is
limited to the value of the original property (s.107(2)).

Where a transfer of value of relevant business property is followed by
another transfer of the same property, the second owner need not own the
property for two years before becoming entitled to the relief provided

that the relief was available on the first transfer and one of the transfers was a transfer on death (s.109(1)). A person who received property on the death of his *spouse* may aggregate the spouse's period of ownership with his own so as to make up a two-year period of ownership (s.108).

When a business (or other relevant business property) has been owned for two years business property relief is available on its full value at the time of the transfer (at the appropriate percentage). It is not, therefore, necessary to show that particular assets of the business have been owned for two years. However, the value of an asset is excluded from relief if it has not been used wholly or mainly for the purpose of the business throughout the two years before the transfer or throughout the period since it was acquired if later.

Excepted assets. In order to prevent taxpayers "parking" private assets in a business and then seeking to obtain business property relief on them, Section 112 provides that relief is not available on "excepted assets". There are assets which were neither:

(a) used wholly or mainly for the purposes of the business concerned throughout the whole of the previous two years, nor
(b) required at the time of the transfer for future use.

These are alternative requirements. An asset which fulfils either one of the requirements will not be an excepted asset. However, (b) is not available where relief is claimed on an asset used by a company controlled by the transferor or by a partnership of which he is a member.

Clawback of relief on inter vivos transfers

4.036 As with agricultural relief, where a transfer is made before death, whether chargeable or potentially exempt, and the transferor dies within seven years the relief is available only if the property originally given or qualifying property representing it has remained as relevant business property in the ownership of the transferee from the date of the transfer to the date of death of the transferor. If the transferee dies before the transferor within the seven-year period, relief is only available on the death of the transferee if the same conditions are satisfied.

The property must remain relevant business property in the hands of the donee. This may be beyond the control of the donee. For example, a donor with a controlling holding may give a donee 20 per cent of the shares in an unquoted trading company, thus qualifying for 100 per cent relief. A year later the donor may sell the assets of a trading company and decide to keep the cash in the company using the company as an investment company. If the transfer becomes chargeable, the donee will have no relief available because the shares are no longer in a trading company and no longer qualify as relevant business property.

If only a proportion of the property originally given or qualifying property representing it remains in the ownership of the transferee at the date of death, relief is available on the proportion of the property owned at that date (s.113A).

In the case of both agricultural and business property relief it is sufficient if "property representing" the original property is in the hands of the donee at the relevant date.

There are some rather strange limitations:

(a) The *whole* of the consideration must have been applied on acquiring the replacement property.

(b) The replacement property must be acquired within three years *after* the disposal of the original property. Note that there is no provision as with roll over relief for the replacement property to be obtained *before* the disposal.

(c) The provision applies only to the first replacement and not to subsequent ones.

It is important to note that where a transferor dies on or after March 10, 1992, having made a transfer of value within the seven years before that date, relief (if available) will be at the appropriate new rate.

The December 1994 Tax Bulletin gives guidance on two matters relating to agricultural and business property relief;

(1) If agricultural property is replaced with business property (or vice versa) shortly before the owner's death, the periods of ownership can be amalgamated.

(2) Where the donee of agricultural property has sold the gifted property and replaced it with business property, agricultural property relief is denied by section 124A(1). Consequently section 114(1) does not exclude *business* property relief if the conditions for relief are satisfied. In the reverse situation, a farming business acquired by the donee can be relevant business property for the purposes of section 113B(3)(c).

4. TIMBER

A relief is available on the value of growing timber for transfers made on **4.037** death but not for *inter vivos* transfers (Inheritance Act 1984, ss.125–130). The relief is only available if a written election is made within two years of death. Where an election is made no tax is payable on the value of the timber provided that the deceased was either beneficially entitled to the land on which the timber is growing for five years before his death or acquired it otherwise than for consideration in money or money's worth within the five years.

The relief for timber is merely a conditional relief since tax becomes payable on a later sale or *inter vivos* gift of the timber. The tax is payable at the deceased's death rate and treating the value as the highest part of the value of his estate. Tax is paid on the value of the timber at the date of the later disposal, not on its value at the date of death, and is payable by the person entitled to the proceeds of sale or who would be so entitled if the disposal had been a sale.

The effect of this relief is that no tax is payable on timber until it is sold or given away *inter vivos*; the tax payable is calculated by reference to the estate of the last person to die owning it.

Timber relief is not available where the woodlands qualify for agricultural property relief (short rotation coppice) and commercial woodlands will often qualify for business property relief.

5. Quick succession relief

4.038   Where a person dies within five years of a transfer to him (whether *inter vivos* or on death) a relief commonly called quick succession relief is available (Inheritance Tax Act 1984, s.141). The relief takes the form of a reduction in the amount of tax payable on death equal to a percentage of the tax paid on the *net* amount of the increase in the value of the deceased's estate caused by the transfer within five years.

The percentage relief is:

100 % if the death is within one year;
80 % if more than one but not more than two years;
60 % if more than two but not more than three years;
40 % if more than three years but not more than four years; and
20 % if more than four years but not more than five years.

Example
A dies and leaves B £12,500 worth of property. A's estate pays £2,500 in tax. B dies three years and three months later. The reduction of tax on B's death is 40 per cent of the tax on the net amount of the increase in B's estate. This can be calculated in the following way:

$$\frac{\text{net amount}}{\text{gross amount}} \times \text{tax} \times \% = \text{reduction}$$

i.e. in this case

$$\frac{£10,000}{£12,500} \times £2,500 \times \frac{40}{100} = £800$$

The reduction produced by quick succession relief is available whether or not the deceased still owned the property transferred to him within the five years before death. Where the amount of quick succession relief is more than the amount of tax to which the deceased would otherwise have been liable, no tax will be payable on the death (although no reclaim of the excess relief from the Revenue is possible—the excess may be carried forward to be set off against the liability of the deceased's beneficiary on his death if it is within five years of the original transfer to the deceased).

G. Liability for Inheritance Tax on Death

1. Introduction

4.039   The inheritance tax legislation includes rules to determine who is liable to account to the Inland Revenue for inheritance tax due as a result of death.

Where inheritance tax is payable on an estate no grant of representation can be obtained until the amount due is paid to the Revenue. The Revenue is concerned with getting the money and section 200(1) sets out four categories of people who are concurrently "accountable" or "liable" to the Revenue for the inheritance tax due on death. The Revenue is not concerned with who actually bears the burden of inheritance tax and it may be that the person who is accountable to the

Revenue for the tax (for example, the personal representative of the deceased) has a right to recover the money paid from individual beneficiaries. The question of where the burden of inheritance tax eventually falls to be dealt with at paras 4.042–4.046 below.

Since inheritance tax must normally be paid before the grant of representation is obtained the persons accountable to the Revenue (for example, the personal representatives) frequently encounter difficulty in realising assets of the estate to raise cash to pay the amount due. (See Chapter 12). It is common for them to borrow money from a bank in order to discharge their liability.

2. THE FOUR CATEGORIES OF PERSONS ACCOUNTABLE FOR INHERITANCE TAX ON DEATH ARE SET OUT IN SECTION 200(1):

(a) The personal representatives of the deceased are accountable for **4.040** the inheritance tax attributable to any free estate of the deceased. "Free estate" includes property held by the deceased as co-owner (whether as joint tenant or tenant-in-common), property disposed of by *donatio mortis causa* and property disposed of by nomination.

The liability of ordinary personal representatives for inheritance tax is limited to the value of assets which they received or would have received but for their own neglect or default (s.204(1)).

The term personal representative includes an executor *de son tort, i.e.* a person who has made himself liable as executor by intermeddling in the estate (see Chapter 8). The liability for inheritance tax of such a person is limited to the value of assets that have come into his hands, *I.R.C. v Stype Investments* (1982).

(b) The trustees of a settlement are accountable for inheritance tax attributable to property comprised in the settlement immediately before the death.

Their liability is limited to the value of assets which they received or disposed of or which they have become liable to account for to the beneficiaries and to the extent of any other property available in their hands for the payment of tax or which might have been available but for their own neglect or default (s.204(2)).

(c) Any person in whom property is vested (whether beneficially or not) or who is entitled to an interest in possession is accountable for the inheritance tax attributable to such property.

This category includes beneficiaries under a will, persons entitled to property under the intestacy rules, a beneficiary with an interest in possession in property settled after death and a purchaser. A purchaser for money or money's worth of property is not, however, liable where the property is not subject to an Inland Revenue charge (see below, para.4.061).

Liability of such persons is limited to the value of the property (or any property which represents it) (s.204(3)).

(d) Where property was settled prior to death a beneficiary for whose benefit settled property or income therefrom is applied thereafter is accountable for the inheritance tax attributable to such property.

A beneficiary of a discretionary trust would be an example of such a person. Liability is limited to the amount of the property or income received (less any income tax) (s.204(5)).

Where a person makes a gift before death and reserves a benefit in the property, that property will be treated in certain circumstances as part of the donor's estate on death. Where it is so treated, the personal representatives of the deceased are liable for the tax on that property only if the tax remains unpaid 12 months after the end of the month of death. Their liability is limited to the value of assets which they received or would have received but for their own neglect or default.

3. LIABILITY FOR ADDITIONAL TAX ON LIFETIME GIFTS

4.041   Where death occurs within seven years of a potentially exempt transfer, inheritance tax may become payable. Where death occurs within seven years of a chargeable transfer extra tax may become payable. In such circumstances the following are liable for the tax or extra tax:

(a) The personal representatives of the transferor (but only to a limited extent—see below);
(b) Any person the value of whose estate is increased by the transfer;
(c) So far as the tax is attributable to the value of any property, any person in whom the property is vested (whether beneficially or otherwise) at any time after the transfer, or who at any such time is beneficially entitled to an interest in possession in the property;
(d) Where by the chargeable transfer any property becomes comprised in a settlement, any person for whose benefit any of the property or income from it is applied.

A person liable as a trustee is liable only to the extent of property which he has actually received or disposed of or has become liable to account for to the beneficiaries and to the extent of any other property available in his hands for the payment of tax or which might have been so available but for his own neglect or default.

A person liable for tax as a person in whom property is vested or as a person entitled to a beneficial interest in possession in property is liable only to the extent of that property.

A person liable for tax as a person for whose benefit property or income has been applied is liable only to the extent of that property or income (less any income tax).

The personal representatives of the transferor are liable only to the extent that as a result of the limitations of liability relevant to the other categories no one falling within any of the other categories is liable *or* the tax remains unpaid 12 months after the end of the month in which the death of the transferor occurred. In such a case their liability is limited to the value of assets which they received or would have received but for their own neglect or default.

In a case where potentially exempt or chargeable transfers were made within seven years of death and inheritance tax is due, personal representatives would be wise to refrain from completely distributing the assets of the estate until satisfied that the tax has been paid. If they do not, they may find themselves personally liable for unpaid tax. (The same point applies where they may be liable for tax in respect of property given *inter vivos* subject to a reservation of benefit—see para.4.040 above.) In cases where a solicitor acting as a personal representative incurs such a liability in the course of his private practice, the liability will be indemnified from the Solicitors' Indemnity Fund but only to the extent that funds are otherwise unavailable. See *Law Society's Gazette*, March 7, 1990 (also see para.14.006).

H. Burden (or Incidence) of Inheritance Tax

1. INTRODUCTION

When inheritance tax is due on death the beneficiaries of the estate will be **4.042** very concerned to discover on which part of the estate the burden of the tax will fall since this may affect the size of their entitlement. The following example illustrates this.

Example
T leaves a house to A, a pecuniary legacy to B, jewellery to C and the residue of the estate to D. There is substantial inheritance tax to pay. The personal representatives are liable for the inheritance tax and before obtaining a grant of representation must send a cheque for the amount of tax due to the Capital Taxes Office. The personal representatives are likely to borrow the money from the bank and the question then arises as to how the burden of repaying the loan is to be borne. If the entire burden falls on residue, D's benefit from the estate will be much reduced; whereas, if the burden is divided proportionately amongst the beneficiares, D will receive rather more but the benefits received by A, B and C will be reduced.
   A testator may include an express direction in the will as to whether or not assets are to bear their own tax. In the absence of such a direction there are statutory rules.

2. EXPRESS DIRECTION IN THE WILL AS TO BURDEN

The testator may state in the will that certain gifts are to be "free of **4.043** inheritance tax" while others are to bear their own; if such a direction is included it is conclusive and the inheritance tax payable on gifts made "free of tax" will be a testamentary expense paid from the property available to pay other debts of the estate (primarily undisposed of property and residue). Any professionally drawn will should include an express direction as to the burden of inheritance tax since this not only avoids future disputes but leads the testator to consider whether the proposed disposition of property is satisfactory having regard to the burden of inheritance tax. (However, as we shall see in para.4.052, a direction that an exempt share of residue is to bear inheritance tax attributable to a non-exempt share of residue must be disregarded.)

3. No express direction in will

4.044 In order to remove uncertainties which had arisen, Inheritance Tax Act 1984, s.211 makes express provision for the burden of inheritance tax in relation to deaths occurring on or after July 25, 1983.

Section 211 provides that where personal representatives are liable for inheritance tax on the value transferred by a chargeable transfer made on death the tax shall be treated as part of the general testamentary and administration expenses of the estate but only so far as it is attributable to the value of property in the United Kingdom which:

(a) vests in the deceased's personal representatives; and
(b) was not, immediately before the death, comprised in a settlement.

The provision is subject to any contrary intention shown by the deceased in his will. As we shall see in Chapter 15, expenses of the estate (and debts) are paid primarily from undisposed-of property and, if none, from the residue of the estate. Thus, where under s.211(1) inheritance tax is to be treated as a general testamentary and administration expense the burden of it falls primarily on the undisposed-of property and on the residue. Section 211(3) provides that "where any amount of tax paid by personal representatives on the value transferred by a chargeable transfer made on death does not fall to be borne as part of the general testamentary and administration expenses of the estate, that amount shall, where occasion requires, be repaid to them by the person in whom the property to the value of which the tax is attributable is vested".

The effect of s.211(3) is that whenever personal representatives are liable to pay inheritance tax (as they are on all of the deceased's free estate and on settled land which devolves on them) they have a right to recover it from the particular beneficiary taking the property to which it relates *unless* the tax is a general, testamentary and administration expense under s.211(1); (that is *unless* the property to which the inheritance tax is attributable was situate in the United Kingdom, vested in the personal representatives and was not comprised in a Settled Land Act settlement immediately before the death). As a result of s.211(3) the personal representatives can recover from the particular beneficiary concerned (subject to contrary intention) inheritance tax attributable to:

(a) non-United Kingdom property,
(b) property not vesting in the personal representatives (that is, joint property passing by survivorship, property subject to a nomination or to a *donatio mortis causa*),
(c) property which was immediately before the death comprised in a Settled Land Act settlement.

(The personal representatives will only have accounted for inheritance tax in respect of trust property where the property was settled land devolving on them. They are not *liable* for inheritance tax in respect of other types of trust property and so will not generally be involved in the payment or recovery of inheritance tax relating to it.)

4. PRACTICAL PROBLEMS

In practice where personal representatives have accounted to the Inland **4.045** Revenue for inheritance tax for which they were liable they may encounter difficulties in obtaining repayment for the residuary estate from the person in whom the property is vested. The personal representatives should take all possible steps to minimise such difficulties.

If a pecuniary legacy has been left to a legatee and the will declares that the legatee is to bear the burden of inheritance tax attributable to it the personal representatives should deduct an appropriate amount and pay the net legacy to the legatee. Obviously if an asset is left, rather than cash, no deduction can be made. However, the personal representatives should not vest the asset in the beneficiary until arrangements have been made for reimbursement of the amount due.

If the beneficiary has got possession of the asset (for example, because the property has passed by survivorship) there is nothing the personal representatives can do to prevent problems arising unless other assets due to the beneficiary under the will or intestacy rules are in the hands of the personal representatives. If the personal representatives have got possession of other assets due to the beneficiary they should ensure that all repayments of inheritance tax due to the residuary estate are made before they part with the assets.

Personal representatives have power under s.212 to sell, mortgage or charge property *whether or not it is vested in them* to raise money for tax for which they are liable. It would obviously be difficult to do this where the property is not vested in them but the fact that they have such a sanction may persuade the person in whom it is vested to pay them the amount due.

5. APPORTIONING THE BURDEN OF INHERITANCE TAX

Where the burden of inheritance tax due is to be divided amongst **4.046** different people, it is necessary to apportion the inheritance tax amongst the various assets comprised in the estate. This can be done in one of two ways.

Either calculate an average rate of inheritance tax for the estate and apply that rate to the assets each beneficiary is to receive; *or* (more simply) allocate a proportionate part of the total inheritance tax to each beneficiary. The result of the two methods will be identical.

Example
A dies having made no chargeable *inter vivos* transfers. Her estate comprises:

	£
realty	255,000
personalty	100,000
	355,000

Her will directs that realty is to bear its own tax and is to pass to B, that a pecuniary legacy of £30,000 bearing its own tax is to pass to C, and that residue is to pass to D. No exemptions apply.

The tax on her estate is calculated as follows:

Band		Rate	Tax
£	£	%	£
0 – 255,000		nil	nil
255 – 355,000		40	40,000
	Total inheritance tax bill		40,000

The tax must then be apportioned.

Using method 1:

Calculate estate rate

i.e.
$$\frac{\text{Total tax}}{\text{Value of estate}} \times 100$$

$$\frac{£40,000}{£355,000} \times 100 = 11.2676\%$$

This rate can then be applied to the property bearing its own tax passing to each beneficiary:

B's share of tax burden $\dfrac{11.2676}{100} \times £255,000 = £28,732.39$

C's share of tax burden $\dfrac{11.2676}{100} \times £30,000 = £3,380.29$

The rate will also be applied to the residue passing to D. The residue amounts to £70,000 that is the personalty of £100,000 less the £30,000 legacy.

D's share of tax burden $\dfrac{11.2676}{100} \times £70,000 = £7,887.32$

The total tax payable on the whole estate is £40,000.

Using method 2:

Allocate a proportion of the total inheritance tax to each beneficiary:

i.e.
$$\text{total tax} \times \frac{\text{beneficiary's share of estate}}{\text{total estate}}$$

B's share of tax burden $£40,000 \times \dfrac{255,000}{355,000} = £28,732.39$

C's share of tax burden $£40,000 \times \dfrac{30,000}{355,000} = £3,380.29$

D's share of tax burden $£40,000 \times \dfrac{70,000}{355,000} = £7,887.32$

The total tax payable on the whole estate is £40,000.

I. Time for Payment

1. GENERAL POSITION

The tax on a transfer on death is payable six months after the end of the **4.047** month in which death occurred. The tax on a chargeable transfer made before death is payable six months after the end of the month in which the transfer is made or, if the transfer is made after April 5, and before October 1, at the end of April in the next year. Where tax or extra tax is payable on a lifetime transfer because of the death of the donor it is payable six months after the end of the month of death.

Where tax is paid after the date on which it should have been paid interest is chargeable on it. The rate of interest is prescribed by statutory instrument.

2. INSTALMENT OPTION

The inheritance tax on certain types of property may be paid by **4.048** instalments over a 10-year period in certain circumstances (Inheritance Tax Act, ss.227–228).

Transfer on death

- (a) Land of any description (this term is not further defined but clearly freehold and leasehold interests are included).
- (b) Shares or securities in a company giving the deceased control of the company immediately before death.
- (c) Unquoted shares or securities which did not give the deceased control provided that the Revenue are satisfied that the payment of the tax in one sum would cause undue hardship.
- (d) Unquoted shares or securities which did not give the deceased control where at least 20 per cent of the tax payable on the death by the person paying the tax on those shares is either tax on those shares or on those shares and other instalment option property.
- (e) Unquoted shares which did not give the deceased control and the value of which exceeds £20,000 at the time of death provided that either:
    - (i) they are at least 10 per cent (by nominal value) of all the shares in the company or
    - (ii) they are ordinary shares and are at least 10 per cent (by nominal value) of all the ordinary shares in the company.
- (f) A business or an interest in a business including a profession or vocation. Liabilities incurred for the purposes of the business must be deducted in computing what is the value of the business for this purpose (normally liabilities are deducted from the whole rather than from particular assets unless the assets are charged with payment of the liabilities).

"Unquoted" means not quoted on a recognised stock exchange

(Finance (No. 2) Act 1992, Sch.14, paras 5 and 6) and shares are regarded as "unquoted" for the purposes of (c), (d) and (e) above even if they are quoted on the Unlisted Securities Market (Finance (No. 2) Act 1992). A person has control for this purpose if he (with the benefit of any shares or securities which are related property) has voting control on all questions affecting the company as a whole (Inheritance Tax Act 1984, s.269).

In cases where business property relief or agricultural property is available at 100 per cent the instalment option will be irrelevant.

Lifetime transfers
Inheritance tax on chargeable transfers made before death may be paid by instalments in respect of the same types of property as in the case of transfers on death. However, this relief is only available where the inheritance tax is *paid by the donee*. In the case of tax payable on the value transferred by a potentially exempt transfer which proves to be chargeable (or extra tax payable where the transferee dies within seven years of a chargeable transfer), the instalment option is available only to the extent that one of the following conditions is fulfilled:—

    (a) the transferee owns the qualifying property throughout the period from transfer until the death of the transferor (or, if earlier, of the transferee); or,

    (b) in the case of property eligible for business or agricultural relief, the transferee has disposed of the original property but has applied the proceeds in acquiring replacement property; or

    (c) in the case of unquoted shares the shares must remain unquoted up to the date of death of the transferor (or, if earlier, of the transferee).

The instalment option is also available on transfers on the termination of an interest in possession in settled property and when tax becomes payable in the case of settlements without an interest in possession. In the case of woodlands tax can always be paid by instalments even if paid by the donor.

Procedure for payment by instalments
4.049 The payment of tax by instalments is only possible where the person paying the tax gives notice in writing to the Revenue that he wishes to pay in that way. (On death notice is given in the Inland Revenue Account— see paras 10.034–10.043.) Where the election is made tax is payable in 10 equal annual instalments. The first instalment is due on the date on which the tax would be due if not paid by instalments (in the case of death six months after the end of the month of death).

The taxpayer may pay off all remaining instalments at any time within the 10 years and must do so if the assets are sold. In the case of tax paid by instalments on non-agricultural land, not comprised in a business, interest on the whole of the outstanding tax is payable and is added to each instalment. In the case of tax paid by instalments on shares (other than shares in investment companies), business or interests in businesses interest is only payable to the extent that an instalment of tax is overdue.

It is common for personal representatives to choose to exercise the option initially even if they feel they may wish to pay off the outstanding amount in one lump sum at a later stage. The reason for considering a temporary exercise of the option is that it reduces the amount of inheritance tax falling due for payment six months after the end of the month of the death and so keeps to a minimum the amount of money which may have to be borrowed to pay the inheritance tax due. Once the personal representatives have obtained the grant of representation, they are able to realise assets of the estate and may then decide (particularly if interest is payable on the amount outstanding) to use the money to pay off any outstanding inheritance tax.

Personal representatives should remember that they remain personally liable for the inheritance tax on the death estate until it has been paid in full. Thus, if they transfer property on which the instalment option has been claimed to beneficiaries, they should consider what steps, if any, they can take to ensure that full payment is made. This may well mean retaining assets as security.

The case of *Howarth's Executors v I.R.C.* (1997) indicates the perils which can exist for the unwary. The deceased's will was proved by her son, H, and his wife, who were both beneficiaries, and by S, an employee of a firm of solicitors, who was not a beneficiary.

The executors elected to pay tax in instalments. The deceased's assets were transferred to the two beneficiaries. Initially instalments were paid by H but these ceased and H was eventually declared bankrupt. The Revenue served notices of outstanding tax and interest of £8,084.71 on the three executors.

The Special Commissioner held that, although H was primarily liable for the payment of tax, the co-executor, S, remained personally liable. He had joined in the election to pay by instalments and had then consented to transfer all the assets to the beneficiaries. In so doing he had taken an obvious risk.

J. Partially Exempt Transfers

1. INTRODUCTION

The transfer of value on death is for inheritance tax purposes one transfer **4.050** of the whole of the deceased's estate. This transfer may be fully taxable, fully exempt or it may be partly taxable and partly exempt (for example, because part but not all of the property is given to a spouse, charity, political party or exempt body). If it is partly taxable and partly exempt Inheritance Tax Act 1984, s.38 contains rules for calculating the amount of inheritance tax and as to the burden of tax. These rules can give rise to rather complicated arithmetical computations. Details of the method of calculation vary according to the type of dispositions made. The two types of calculation are dealt with in the next two sub-paragraphs.

2. "SPECIFIC" GIFTS NOT BEARING THEIR OWN TAX TO NON-EXEMPT BENEFICIARY RESIDUE TO EXEMPT BENEFICIARY

For this purpose any gift is "specific" if it is not a gift of residue (s.42). If a **4.051** specific gift is not exempt, the tax in respect of it will normally be paid from residue (see paras 4.039–4.041). The specific legatee is treated as having received an amount *net* of tax and, therefore, the net gift must be grossed up at the death rate to calculate the amount of the tax borne by residue.

Example
A has made *inter vivos* chargeable transfers which have exhausted his nil rate band and has died with a death estate of £50,000. On his death he gives £12,000 to his son and *does not provide that this gift is subject to tax*; he gives the residue to his (*i.e.* A's) wife. Since the gift of £12,000 is not made to bear its own tax the tax will come out of exempt residue so grossing-up is required.

£12,000 grossed up at the death rates with a cumulative total which has exhausted his nil rate band is:

$$£12,000 \times \frac{100}{60} = £20,000$$

The tax is the difference between the gross and net gifts.

$$£20,000 - £12,000 = £8,000$$

The estate is therefore divided as follows:

	£	£
Tax		8,000
Gift to Son		12,000
Residue	50,000	
	(20,000)	
		30,000
		50,000

3. RESIDUE PARTLY TO EXEMPT AND PARTLY TO NON-EXEMPT BENEFICIARIES

Section 41 states that "notwithstanding the terms of any disposition" none of the tax attributable to residue shall fall on an exempt share of residue.

Thus, if residue is left "to pay debts and tax and then to be divided between" an exempt and a non-exempt beneficiary, the share of the non-exempt beneficiary is diminished by tax while the share of the exempt beneficiary is not.

Example
A dies with a nil cumulative total leaving an estate of £600,000 to be divided equally between son and spouse. The half of the estate passing to the son bears its own tax.

£	£
0–255,000 = nil	
255–300,000 =	18,000

The half passing to the spouse bears no tax.

The case of *Re Benham* (1995) caused problems for practitioners. For a discussion of the problems raised by *Benham* see para.4.46 below.

4. SPECIFIC GIFTS NOT BEARING THEIR OWN TAX TO NON-EXEMPT BENEFICI-
ARIES RESIDUE PARTLY TO EXEMPT PARTLY TO NON-EXEMPT BENEFICIARIES

In this situation the tax on the "specific" gifts is borne by the whole of the **4.052**
residue unless the will provides otherwise. The tax on the non-exempt
part of residue *must* however be borne by that part of the residue only.
This is because Inheritance Tax Act 1984, s.41 provides that exempt
residue is not to bear the tax on any other part of *residue.*
   To calculate the tax it is necessary to gross up the specific gift (or gifts)
not bearing its own tax as if it were cumulated with any chargeable
lifetime transfers but was the only taxable part of the estate on death. This
figure is then added to any other parts of the estate which are in fact
taxable (*i.e.* specific gifts bearing their own tax and non-exempt residue)
to calculate an "assumed rate" of tax. The specific gift not bearing its own
tax is then grossed up again at the assumed rate and the tax on the estate is
tax on that figure plus tax on any other non-exempt parts of the estate (*e.g.*
residue).

Example
A dies leaving an estate of £380,000. She has made no lifetime transfers
and leaves £270,000 to her daughter, residue to be divided between her
husband and her sister. The will contains no directions as to the burden of
inheritance tax.

(a) Gross up the gift to the daughter as if it were the only taxable gift
    on death. On this assumption £255,000 is within the nil rate band
    so only £15,000 has to be grossed up at 40 per cent. £15,000
    grossed up at 40 per cent is £25,000. The gross legacy is therefore
    £255,000 + £25,000 = £280,000
(b) Calculate the other taxable parts of the estate. Only half of the
    residue is taxable, the other half is going to the husband (and so
    is exempt):
(c) Add the grossed-up legacy and the taxable half of residue to give
    the taxable estate:

	£
Value of estate	380,000
Less grossed up legacy	(280,000)
"Residue"	100,000
Taxable half of residue	50,000
Taxable estate	
Taxable half of residue	50,000
Grossed up legacy	280,000
Taxable estate	330,000

(d) Calculate an assumed rate. This is the rate of tax which would be
    charged on an estate of £330,000. The tax would be £30,000 and

the assumed rate would therefore be:

$$\frac{£30,000}{£330,000} \times 100 = 9.09\%$$

(e) Gross up the specific gift not bearing its own tax at the assumed rate:

$$£270,000 \times \frac{100}{100 - 9.09}$$

$$= £270,000 \times \frac{100}{90.71}$$

$$= £297,651.85$$

(f) Tax is now payable on the grossed-up specific gift and half the residue, *i.e.*:

	£
Value of estate	380,000
Less legacy with	
tax thereon	(297,651.85)
"Residue"	82,348.15
Half residue	41,174.07

Tax is therefore payable on:

	£
Taxable half of residue	41,174.07
Legacy with tax	
thereon	297,651.85
Taxable estate	338,825.92

Tax is therefore £33,530.37.

The portion of the £33,530.37 attributable to the specific legacy is borne by the residue as a whole. The balance of the residue is then split into two equal parts and the portion of the £33,530.37 attributable to the non-exempt residue is borne entirely from the non-exempt part of residue. In apportioning the inheritance tax bill either of the two methods explained in para.4.046 can be used.

5. SECTION 41 AND *RE BENHAM'S WILL TRUSTS* (1995)

4.053   The deceased left the residue of the estate to pay debts and then to pay to those beneficiaries "as are living at my death and who are listed in List A and List B ... in such proportions as will bring about the result that the aforesaid beneficiaries named in List A shall receive 3.2 times as much as the aforesaid beneficiaries named in List B ...".

Some of the beneficiaries were charities and some were not.

The deputy judge hearing the case held that "the plain intention of the testatrix is that at the end of the day each beneficiary whether charitable or non-charitable should receive the same as the other beneficiaries ...".

He found that this was to be achieved by grossing up the shares of the non-charitable legatees so that *after payment of tax* charitable and non-charitable legatees ended up with the same amount.

The effect was that more of the estate had to be allocated initially to the non-exempt beneficiaries so that after the payment of tax they retained the same net amount that the exempt beneficiaries received. The Revenue received more tax than it would have had the initial division been equal. The exempt beneficiaries received less.

It was not clear whether the case was to be interpreted as of very limited importance turning on the particular words used by the testatrix which demonstrated an intention that residue was to be divided unequally or whether it was to be interpreted as of general application wherever residue was left to be divided "equally" between exempt and non-exempt beneficiaries. There was uncertainty and practitioners and charities were unhappy.

There was an exchange of correspondence between the CTO and the British Heart Foundation. The charity was concerned that the decision would result in a reduction in the amount of property passing to exempt beneficiaries (see *Tax Journal*, September 5, 1996, p. 3 and *Private Client Business* 1996, no. 5, p. 295).

The CTO's response stated that in their view *Benham* is a decision "primarily concerned with ascertaining the intention of the testatrix and ... does not directly involve the Inland Revenue". It confirmed that the decision followed from the particular facts of the case and that "if the Will is drafted in 'common form' with a direction to ascertain residue after payment of funeral and testamentary expenses and debts followed by a bequest of that residue, then it is focusing on the ascertainment and division of disposable residue rather than on what each beneficiary is to receive. Accordingly a will so drafted would not appear to involve *Benham*-style grossing up computations."

The decision in *Re Ratcliffe, Holmes v McMullan* (1999) has alleviated the problems caused by *Re Benham*. In *Re Ratcliffe* the testatrix left her residue after payment of debts, funeral and testamentary expenses to be divided equally between exempt and non-exempt beneficiaries. Blackburne J. was of the view that, on a true construction of the will, the testatrix intended to divide her residue equally before payment of tax between the beneficiaries. The non-exempt beneficiaries then had to pay tax from their share without grossing-up.

He accepted that a will could direct that residue be divided unequally between exempt and non-exempt beneficiaries so that after payment of tax they were each left with the same amount. However, he said that "much clearer wording would be needed than the common form wording actually used". He said that he did not regard *Re Benham* as laying down any principle and, accordingly, did not feel bound to follow it.

There are two problems for practitioners:

    (1) How to draft a will in the light of *Benham* and *Ratcliffe*?
    (2) How to deal with the administration of an estate where the will

contains a standard gift of residue dividing it between exempt and non-exempt beneficiaries?

Will drafting

4.054   This is relatively simple. Ask the testator whether he wants his residue to be divided equally between the exempt and non-exempt beneficiaries. Explain that the result will be that the non-exempt beneficiary will "end up" with less because his share will be reduced by inheritance tax.

The alternative is that the residue is divided unequally. The result is that the initial share of the non-exempt beneficiary is bigger leaving the two shares of equal size once the tax has been deducted. Obviously more of the estate will be lost in tax since more of it is being given to a non-exempt beneficiary. It is permissible to point out to the testator that the calculation of the gifts after his death will be *extremely* complex.

Once the testator has decided on the type of gifts he wants the will must be drafted to give clear effect to his wishes. There are many suitable precedents; the following is taken from Butterworths' Will Probate and Administration Service Form 1A, 22.1.

My trustee shall hold the Trust Fund ON TRUST

(a) as to one share absolutely for my Wife (Husband) (*or give name if not already defined as such*) if she (he) survives me for 28 days.

(b) as to another share (or as to the whole if the preceding gift fails) absolutely for such of my children as are alive at my death (and reach the age of [18]) and if more than one in equal shares PROVIDED that if any child of mine [is already dead or] dies before me [or before reaching that age] but leaves a child or children alive at the death of the survivor of my child and me who reach the age of [18] or marry under that age then such child or children shall take absolutely and if more than one in equal shares so much of the Trust Fund as that child of mine would have taken on attaining a vested interest

AND the shares given by (a) and (b) above shall be such shares as before [after] the deduction of any inheritance tax attributable to them respectively are of equal [or are of values bearing to one another the proportions [2:1] the larger share being that given by [a] [b]].

Administration of an estate

It is necessary to construe the will to determine the testator's intention. If the will contains a common form residuary gift directing division of residue after payment of debts and inheritance tax, it would seem safe in the light of *Re Ratcliffe* to divide the residue equally before payment of tax. However, if there is any ambiguity or unusual wording, the correct construction may not be uncertain. In such a case it would be desirable to get the agreement of the beneficiaries to the method of division but they may not be united. Probably the only thing to be done in such a case is to point out the cost of litigation if the parties are unable to agree.

6. PARTLY EXEMPT TRANSFERS AND AGRICULTURAL AND BUSINESS PRO-
PERTY RELIEF

Prior to the Finance Act 1986 anomalous results sometimes arose where a **4.055** partly exempt transfer included property qualifying for agricultural or business property relief. The Finance Act 1986 therefore included provisions designed to ensure that the reliefs are available in a consistent manner. Where there is a specific gift of property qualifying for relief the relief attaches to that property irrespective of whether the specific beneficiary is an exempt or non-exempt beneficiary. In other cases, that is where such property is part of the residue of the estate, the relief is allocated *pro rata* to the property transferred (s.39A).

Example
A dies with an estate of £1m including a business worth £500,000 qualifying for 100 per cent relief. A has a nil cumulative total. A leaves £200,000 to son and residue to spouse. Since the business has not been left specifically to anyone the benefit of the relief must be apportioned *pro rata* amongst the gifts.

Thus, the value for tax purposes of the legacy to the son will be:

$$200,000 \times \frac{500,000}{1,000,000} = £100,000$$

The value of the residue passing to the spouse will be:

$$800,000 \times \frac{500,000}{1,000,000} = £400,000$$

It is clearly beneficial from an inheritance tax point of view to leave property attracting relief to a non-exempt beneficiary and property not eligible for relief to a spouse. However, there may be good non-tax reasons for wanting to leave the property qualifying for relief to the spouse. In such a case it is possible to use s.39A to obtain some relief for the non-exempt beneficiary. The section provides that where property eligible for relief is not specifically bequeathed the benefit of the relief is apportioned *pro rata* through the estate.

Example
T has an estate of £1 million which includes £500,000 of property qualifying for relief at 100 per cent. He leaves a pecuniary legacy of £400,000 to his son and residue to his wife.

As the property attracting relief has not been specifically bequeathed the benefit must be apportioned *pro rata* between the exempt and chargeable parts of the estate.

Each part of the estate is multiplied by the chargeable value transferred (£500,000 after relief) and divided by the value of the estate before relief (£1 million). Thus the value attributable to the son's share of the estate is reduced as follows:

$$400,000 \times \frac{500,000}{1,000,000} = £200,000$$

The value attributed to the wife's share of the estate is reduced as follows:

$$600,000 \times \frac{500,000}{1,000,000} = £300,000$$

The effect of s.39A can cause problems where the testator has used a formula clause to pass a legacy to a non exempt beneficiary "equal to the maximum amount that can pass without payment of inheritence tax". If the residuary estate includes property eligible for relief, the amount passing under such a gift will be increased. If this is not what the testator wants, the will should either leave the property eligible for relief to a specific beneficiary or impose a "cap" on the amount that can pass under the gift, for example "the legacy is not to exceed the value of the nil rate band in force at my death".

K. Some Particular Problems

1. INTER-RELATIONSHIP OF INHERITANCE TAX AND CAPITAL GAINS TAX

4.056   Capital gains tax, like inheritance tax, is a tax charged on movements of capital assets. It is not payable on death (except in certain circumstances in respect of settled property). However, a lifetime transfer may give rise to capital gains tax liability, as well as to inheritance tax liability. Such liability must be taken into account when deciding between lifetime gifts and gifts on death. To ensure that one tax is not paid on the amount of the other tax two rules apply:

(a) Capital gains tax paid by the transferor is not treated as a loss to the transferor's estate for inheritance tax purposes.
(b) Capital gains tax paid by the transferee reduces the value transferred to inheritance tax purposes.

Example
A makes a chargeable *inter vivos* transfer to B of an asset acquired for £10,000; the current value of the asset is £20,000. It will be assumed that capital gains tax is £4,000 (*i.e.* 40 per cent of the £10,000 gain—this will in fact be the amount of tax if there are no exemptions available and if A is a higher rate taxpayer). We will assume that the rate of inheritance tax is half of 40 per cent. This would be the appropriate rate if the transferor had used up his annual exemption and nil rate band. Remember that the value transferred is grossed up where the transferor pays the inheritance tax.

(a) If transferor pays both taxes:
  (i) Capital gains tax (£4,000) is not a loss to the transferor's estate.
  (ii) Inheritance tax is payable on the grossed-up gift.
      Gross gift for inheritance tax purposes

$$£20,000 \times \frac{100}{80} = £25,000$$

      inheritance tax = £5,000

  (iii) Total cost to transferor CGT   £4,000
                            Gift   £20,000
                            IHT   £5,000
                                                    £29,000

           Amount added to cumulative total   £25,000
           Benefit to transferee   £20,000

(b) If transferee pays both taxes:
   (i) Capital gains tax (£4,000) reduces value transferred to £16,000

   (ii) Inheritance tax is payable on gift (not grossed up) less £4,000 (the capital gains tax)
   Inheritance tax   £16,000 × 20% = £3,200

   (iii) Total cost to transferor   £20,000

   Amount added to cumulative total   £16,000
   Net benefit to transferee   £12,800

(c) If transferor pays inheritance tax and transferee pays capital gains tax:
   (i) Capital gains tax (£4,000) reduces value transferred.
   (ii) Inheritance tax is payable on grossed up amount of gift less capital gains tax:

$$£16,000 \times \frac{100}{80} = £20,000$$

   Inheritance tax:

$$£20,000 \times \frac{20}{100} = £4,000$$

   (iii) Total cost to transferor Gift   £20,000
                                 IHT   £4,000
                                          ─────────────
                                                          £24,000

   Amount added to cumulative total   £20,000
   Benefit to transferee   £16,000

(d) If transferee pays inheritance tax and transferor pays capital gains tax:
   (i) Capital gains tax (£4,000) not a loss to transferor's estate
   (ii) Inheritance tax payable on gift (not grossed up)
                                £20,000 × 20% = £4,000

   (iii) Total cost to transferor   £24,000

   Amount added to cumulative total   £20,000
   Benefit to transferee   £16,000

Note:
The amount added to the cumulative total (*i.e.* the amount on which inheritance tax is paid) is always less (by £4,000 in this example) than the real loss to the transferor when capital gains tax is taken into account. This is because saying that capital gains tax is not a loss to the transferor's estate when he pays it and saying that capital gains tax paid by the transferee is treated as reducing the value transferred is really the same thing expressed in a different way.

Where capital gains tax hold-over relief is claimed on a gift (see **4.057** para.5.014) a different rule applies to deal with the overlap between the two taxes. The amount of inheritance tax paid on the transfer of value is deducted in computing the donee's chargeable gain on a later disposal by him. Where the donor dies within seven years of the gift the inheritance tax may have to be recalculated. In such a case the transferor's estate is entitled to a refund of capital gains tax paid, if appropriate. However, the deduction is only permitted to the extent that it will wipe out the chargeable gain and so cannot give rise to an allowable loss.

Example
A buys a business asset for £18,000 and makes a chargeable *inter vivos* transfer of it to B, when it is worth £20,000. Hold-over relief is claimed. We will assume that the rate of inheritance tax is half of 40 per cent. This would be the appropriate rate if the transferor had used up his annual exemption and the nil rate band. We will ignore the possibility of business property relief for the purpose of this calculation. If A pays the inheritance tax it will be £5,000 (with grossing-up), if B pays it will be £4,000 (without grossing-up).

   B then sells the business asset for £22,500. Assuming that there are no incidental costs of disposal and that no indexation relief is available, the gain according to normal capital gains tax principles would be £4,500 (£22,500 – £18,000 = £4,500) since B is allowed to deduct A's acquisition cost from his disposal consideration. However, as hold-over relief was claimed the amount of inheritance tax paid on the original transfer can be deducted in computing the gain for capital gains tax purposes.

(a) Chargeable gain where B (the donee) paid the inheritance tax:

	£
Gain	4,500
Less	(4,000*)
Reduced gain	500

*Note:
The whole of the inheritance tax is deducted, thus leaving a chargeable gain of £500 on which capital gains tax will be payable unless there is an exemption available (for example the annual exemption).

(b) Chargeable gain where A (the donor) paid the inheritance tax:

	£
Gain	4,500
Less	(5,000)
Reduced gain	Nil**

**Note:
A deduction is permitted only to the extent that it is necessary to extinguish a gain. It is not allowed to produce a loss.

In the above example had the transfer been potentially exempt, no inheritance tax would have been payable at the time of the transfer. Therefore if B had sold the business asset for £22,500 before A's death capital gains tax would have been payable on the full gain of £4,500. If B was a higher rate taxpayer capital gains tax would be calculated as follows:

$$\frac{40}{100} \times £4,500 = £1,800$$

However, if A then died, say, four-and-a-half years after the transfer to B, inheritance tax would become payable at 60 per cent of the full rate. Assuming that B paid the inheritance tax there would be no grossing-up and the inheritance tax would be 60 per cent of the full rate of 40 per cent (assuming the rates remain identical to the current rates):

$$\frac{60}{100} \times \frac{40}{100} \times £20,000 = £4,800$$

The £4,800 of inheritance tax now due would be deducted from the gain of £4,500 and would extinguish it. Thus the capital gains tax could be reclaimed.

2. ANTI-AVOIDANCE PROVISIONS

Taxpayers are entitled to arrange their financial affairs so as to avoid paying tax unnecessarily. However, such arrangements may be attacked by the Inland Revenue either under the special inheritance tax provisions relating to "associated operations" rules or under general principles laid down by the House of Lords in *Furniss v Dawson* (1984).   **4.058**

Associated operations

Section 268 of the Inheritance Tax Act 1984 provides that where a transfer of value is made by "associated operations" carried out at different times it shall be treated as made at the time of the last of them. "Associated operations" are defined very widely as being "any two or more operations which affect the same property ... or any two operations of which one is effected with reference to the other or with a view to enabling or facilitating the other to be effected whether effected by the same or different people and whether or not they are simultaneous".   **4.059**

The object of these provisions is to prevent donors avoiding inheritance tax by making artificial arrangements; for example, by fragmenting transfers of value in order to get the benefit of successive annual exemptions.

There is uncertainty as to the circumstances in which the Revenue would seek to use these provisions. Obviously many individuals wish to arrange their financial affairs so as to provide the maximum benefit for members of their family and so as to avoid unnecessary tax; this may well involve arrangements which *could* be regarded as associated. In particular, it is common, where one spouse is much wealthier than the other, for the wealthier spouse to make use of the spouse exemption to transfer assets to the poorer spouse. This enables the poorer spouse to make transfers to the issue of the couple which will attract lifetime exemptions and/or prove to be fully exempt if the donor survives seven years. When the associated operations provisions were discussed in Parliament in 1975 the Chief Secretary to the Treasury said that transfers between spouses would only be attacked in blatant cases where a transfer was made *on condition* that the recipient would at once use the money to make gifts to others. Thus, spouses appear to be free to equalise their estates but a certain amount of caution should be used.

Furniss v Dawson

4.060   The House of Lords in *Furniss v Dawson* stated that where a taxpayer achieves a purpose either by using a preordained series or transactions or a single composite transaction and steps are inserted which have no commercial purpose apart from the avoidance of a liability to tax the inserted steps are to be disregarded for tax purposes.

The extent to which this principle will be applied in the area of personal taxation is uncertain but certainly taxpayers should be cautious about embarking on artificial schemes designed to achieve tax advantages.

In view of the House of Commons statement on the Revenue's approach to associated operations it is unlikely that transfers between spouses will be attacked under *Furniss v Dawson*.

L. Certificates of Discharge

4.061   If the Inland Revenue is satisfied that the tax attributable to a chargeable transfer has been or will be paid they can (and, if the transfer is one made on death, must) give a certificate to that effect (s.239(1)). The effect is to discharge all persons (unless there was fraud or non-disclosure of material facts) from liability for any further claim for tax. It also extinguishes any Inland Revenue charge on property for that tax.

It is also possible to obtain a more limited certificate which extinguishes an Inland Revenue charge on property which is to be purchased but which does not discharge any accountable person.

An Inland Revenue charge for unpaid inheritance tax attaches to property other than United Kingdom personal property beneficially owned by the deceased before death which vests in the personal representatives.

Where property subject to an Inland Revenue charge is disposed of that property ceases to be subject to the charge (although the property representing it becomes subject to the charge) if:

(a) in the case of land the charge was not registered; or
(b) in the case of United Kingdom personalty the purchaser had no notice of the facts giving rise to the charge.

It frequently happens that adjustments have to be made to the value of the estate during the administration (for example, because estimated figures are finalised). In such a case the personal representatives must submit a corrective account to the Inland Revenue giving full information of all changes in value. Until the personal representatives have obtained a certificate of discharge they cannot safely complete the distribution of the assets comprised in the estate since further tax may become due as a result of adjustments to the value of the estate.

A certificate of discharge does not affect any further tax which becomes payable as a result of the discovery of additional assets or as a result of increases in the amount of property passing to non-exempt beneficiaries after a variation or disclaimer (see Chapter 19). In such a case the personal representatives should apply for a further certificate after the additional tax has been paid.

Where personal representatives have paid all the inheritance tax due other than that outstanding on instalment option property it is possible to obtain a limited certificate expressed to be a full discharge save and except the inheritance tax due on the instalment option property.

5.   Capital Gains Tax

A. Introduction

5.001 The *death* of an individual does not give rise to a liability to capital gains tax (save in very limited circumstances where there is settled property). However, capital gains tax may have to be considered in connection with all or any of the following:

(a) disposals made by the deceased up to the date of death;
(b) disposals made by the personal representatives after the date of death during the period of administration; and
(c) disposals made by beneficiaries of assets they have received from the estate.

Before considering these three situations, a brief outline of the capital gains tax system contained in the Taxation of Chargeable Gains Act 1992, is necessary. All references are to that Act unless otherwise stated.

B. Capital Gains Tax Generally

5.002 Capital gains tax is payable when a *chargeable person* makes a disposal of *chargeable assets* giving rise to a *chargeable gain* unless an *exemption or relief* applies. The tax is charged on a "current year basis" by reference to gains made in a "tax year", from April 6 to the following April 5 (officially called a "year of assessment").

1. TAXABLE PERSON

5.003 Every person who is resident or ordinarily resident in the United Kingdom is potentially liable to capital gains tax. This includes the personal representatives of a deceased person, who are treated as a continuing body of persons with the same residence or ordinary residence as the deceased.

2. DISPOSALS

5.004 The Act does not provide an exhaustive definition of the term but it is clear that a sale or gift amounts to a "disposal". Furthermore s.21(2) provides that the term "disposal" covers part disposals. Thus the sale of part of a plot of land is a disposal as is the grant of a lease or an easement. In addition, there are statutory provisions by which certain transactions are treated as disposals (such as the total loss or destruction of an asset or the granting of an option).

In most situations the date of disposal is self-evident. However, if an asset is disposed of under a contract, the date of disposal is the date of the contract, not the date on which the asset is eventually transferred (s.28(1)). If a contract is conditional the operative date is the date on which the condition is satisfied (s.28(2)).

3. CHARGEABLE ASSETS

The definition of *assets* for capital gains tax purposes is set out in s.21(1)   **5.005**
which provides that:

"All forms of property shall be assets for the purposes of this Act, whether situated in the United Kingdom or not, including:

    (a) options, debts and incorporeal property generally, and
    (b) any currency other than sterling, and
    (c) any form of property created by the person disposing of it or otherwise coming to be owned without being acquired" (such as goodwill in a business).

All *assets* are *chargeable assets* subject to a few exceptions including sterling and motor cars.

4. CHARGEABLE GAINS

The basic rule
A gain arises if the "consideration for disposal" exceeds the "allowable   **5.006**
deductions" provided for in the Act.

The "consideration for disposal" is the sale price if the asset is sold in an arm's length transaction or the market value if there is a gift or a gift element. The market value is the price which the asset might reasonably be expected to fetch on a sale in the open market. Section 272(2) provides that no reduction in the value can be made by assuming that the assets would be placed on the market at the same time.

Once the "consideration for disposal" has been calculated, the allowable expenditure is deducted to calculate the chargeable gains. The allowable expenditure is defined by s.38(1) and falls into three categories:

    (a) Initial expenditure, which is the original purchase price (or market value if the asset was acquired by way of gift) plus incidental costs incurred in acquiring the asset, such as solicitors' fees and stamp duty. If the asset was not acquired by the taxpayer from anyone else (because, for example, it is the goodwill of a business he has set up) the initial expenditure is that wholly and exclusively incurred in providing the asset.

    (b) Subsequent expenditure, which is expenditure wholly and exclusively incurred for the purpose of enhancing the value of the asset (the expenditure being reflected in the state or nature of the asset at the time of disposal) and expenditure incurred in establishing preserving or defending title to, or a right over, the asset.

    (c) Incidental costs of disposal such as solicitors' fees, estate agents' fees, the cost of advertising, etc.

There must be excluded from the calculation any sum that is charged to income tax (such as portions of premiums on certain leases which are taxable under Income and Corporation Taxes Act 1988, Sch.A) or any expense that is deductible for income tax purposes (such as the cost of *repairs* to an asset as opposed to the cost of improvements).

With regard to the allowable deductions, special rules apply if part only of an asset is disposed of since it would clearly be unfair for the taxpayer to be able to deduct expenditure laid out on the whole asset against the sale price of only part. In these circumstances s.42(2) provides that the allowable expenditure to be deducted from the sale price (or market value if appropriate) of the part sold or given away is found by multiplying the total expenditure on the whole asset by:

$$\frac{A}{A + B}$$

where A is the consideration received for the part disposed of and B is the market value of the part retained.

Example
Terence buys a plot of land for £40,000 (his only allowable expenditure). He sells part for £45,000; the value of the remainder is £15,000. From the £45,000 sale proceeds he can deduct:

$$£40,000 \times \frac{£45,000}{£45,000 + £15,000}$$

$$i.e. \qquad £40,000 \times \frac{£45,000}{£60,000}$$

$$= £30,000$$

He therefore has a gain of £15,000.

The indexation allowance
5.007 The system of capital gains taxation as originally enacted took no account of inflation, with the result that taxpayers suffered tax on the apparent gain arising as a result of inflation, rather than on the real increase in the asset's value.

This defect was partially remedied by the introduction of an "indexation allowance" which increased the deductions available in respect of initial and subsequent expenditure (ss.53 and 54). The effect was to "index link" allowable expenditure so that only "real" profits were potentially taxable on a subsequent disposal. The allowance has been abolished for gains arising on assets acquired in or after April 1998 by individuals, personal representatives and trustees. The allowance is, therefore, still available for gains on assets acquired before April 1998 but only for the period ending with that month. The allowance will, therefore, be of less and less importance over time.

To calculate the allowance each item of initial and subsequent expenditure is multiplied by a decimal fraction (rounded to three decimal places) produced from the following formula:

$$\frac{RD - RI}{RI}$$

where RD is the retail prices index for the month of the disposal and RI represents the retail prices index for March 1982 or, if later, the month in which the expenditure was incurred. If several items of expenditure were incurred at different times they must be indexed separately. If the figure for RD is smaller than that for RI, no allowance is available (so that gains are not increased if the Retail Prices Index goes down).

Special rules for assets held on April 6, 1965 and March 31, 1982
Capital gains tax came into force on April 6, 1965 and tax has never been levied on gains arising before that date. In March 1988 it was announced that the base date for capital gains tax would be altered. In respect of disposals made on or after April 6, 1988 no tax is levied on gains arising prior to March 31, 1982. Taxpayers are treated as having disposed of assets on March 31, 1982 and as having acquired them at market value at that date.

5.008

Example
A acquires an asset in 1980 for £2,000; on March 31, 1982 it is worth £8,000; on September 1, 1992 he disposes of the asset for £9,000. Ignoring exemptions and the availability of any indexation allowance for the purposes of this example he will be treated as making a chargeable gain of £1,000 (£9,000 – £8,000).

Special provisions ensure that the amount of a gain or loss is not increased by the new base date.

When calculating the indexation allowance available for an asset owned on March 31, 1982, s.55(1) provides that the asset is deemed to have been sold and immediately re-acquired at its market value on that date.

Losses
If deducting the allowable expenditure from the sale proceeds or market value of the asset shows that the taxpayer has made a loss, it may be set off against all gains made during the current tax year. If this year's gains are insufficient to absorb the whole loss, it may be carried forward and set off against all future gains as they arise. The losses can be carried forward indefinitely until such gains arise (s.2(2)). Losses must be deducted before taper relief (see below) is taken into account.

5.009

It is important to note that in the tax year in which the loss arises, it must be set against that year's gains to reduce them as far as is possible. This is so even if the loss would reduce the gains below the annual exemption limit (currently £7,900—see para.5.014). However, if there are unabsorbed losses which are carried forward, in the future years they are used only to the extent necessary to reduce the gains of those later years to the amount of the annual exemption (s.3(5)).

Example
During the tax year 2003/04, X sells two assets; one gives rise to a gain of £6,000 and the other disposal shows a loss of £8,000. The loss must be set

against the gain reducing it to nil and leaving £2,000 unabsorbed loss that can be carried forward to 2004/05.

If X in this later year sells an asset making a gain of £8,200, only £500 of the loss brought forward is used to reduce the gain to £7,900, leaving £1,500 of the unabsorbed loss to be carried forward to 2005/06.

A loss is only allowable in circumstances where, if a gain had been made on the disposal of the asset it would have been a *chargeable* gain. Thus the sale of a private motor car at a loss does not give rise to an allowable loss.

Indexation allowances and losses

5.010   The indexation allowance is not available to create or increase a loss.

Taper Relief

5.011   Taper relief came into effect on April 6, 1998 and gives relief on chargeable gains after allowable losses have been taken into account.

To attract the relief, the asset which has been disposed must have been owned for the minimum qualifying period. That period is one year for "business assets" and three years otherwise.

The relief is available to individuals, personal representatives and trustees.

The relief is given by reducing the percentage of the gain which is chargeable. For business assets, from April 6, 2002 only 50 per cent of the gain is chargeable once the asset has been owned for one year. This is reduced to only 25 per cent for assets owned for two or more years.

The relief available for other assets is on a different sliding scale. Once the asset has been owned for three years, only 95 per cent of the gain is chargeable. This percentage is reduced by 5 per cent for each year of ownership until, after 10 years of ownership, the maximum relief (60 per cent of the gain being chargeable) is reached.

"Business assets" are defined in Sch.A1 and there is a distinction between shares and other assets.

Shares will be "business assets" if the company is a "qualifying company", that is a trading company (or the holding company of a trading group) and the taxpayer is an individual, personal representative or trustee. From April 6, 2000 all shareholdings in unquoted trading companies, investments in listed trading companies carrying 5 per cent of the voting rights and all shareholdings in listed trading companies held by officers or employees attract the relief. Prior to that the definition was more restricted. The old rules remain relevant where a taxpayer owned shares prior to April 6, 2000. If such shares are sold, the gains will have to be apportioned to determine the amount of taper available.

For assets other than shares in tax year 2003/04, the asset must be used in a trade carried on by the owner (an individual, personal representative or trustee) or by a "qualifying company". For disposals on or after April 6, 2004 assets used wholly or partly for a business carried on by individuals, trustees of settlements, personal representatives or certain partnerships will qualify as business assets irrespective of whether the owner of the assets is involved in carrying on the business concerned.

5. EXEMPTIONS AND RELIEFS

Certain exemptions and reliefs are available. In some cases they extinguish, and in others they reduce, the taxpayer's liability.   **5.012**

Exemptions

The main exemptions are: **5.013**

(a) The taxpayer's only or main residence together with gardens and grounds up to, normally, 0·5 of a hectare (s.222). The property must normally have been the taxpayer's main residence throughout his period of ownership and not have been bought with a view to making a gain on the disposal (s.224(3)). Certain periods of absence are disregarded including:

    (i) a period of absence not exceeding three years; and

    (ii) any period of absence during which the taxpayer was employed, or held an office, all the duties of which were performed outside the United Kingdom; and

    (iii) a period of absence, not exceeding four years, throughout which the taxpayer was prevented from residing as a result of the situation of his place of work or as a result of his employer requiring him to reside elsewhere, the condition being reasonably imposed to secure the effective performance of his duties.

(The last 36 months of ownership will be disregarded in any event; the taxpayer may still claim full relief whether or not the property was occupied as his main residence during that period—s.223(1).) If the taxpayer occupies more than one residence, he can choose which is to be treated as his main residence. By concession, "relief is also given where personal representatives dispose of a house which before and after the deceased's death has been used as their only or main residence by individuals who under the will or intestacy are entitled to the whole or substantially the whole of the proceeds of the house either absolutely or for life" (Inland Revenue Concession D5).

(b) Items of tangible movable property having a predictable useful life not exceeding 50 years (s.45), such as most yachts;

(c) Chattels where the *consideration* for disposal does not exceed £6,000 (s.262). Marginal relief exists if the consideration exceeds £6,000;

(d) National savings certificates and premium bonds (s.121).

Others include:

(a) Damages for personal injuries and betting winnings (s.51);

(b) Interests under trusts, unless the interest was acquired for money or money's worth (s.76);

(c) Gains made on the disposal of certain government securities (s.115(1));

(d) Decorations for valour unless acquired for consideration in money or money's worth (s.268);

(e) Foreign currency purchased for personal use abroad (s.269);

(f) Life assurance policies and deferred annuity contracts (s.210);

(g) Works of art in certain circumstances (s.258).

Reliefs

5.014 If the assets disposed of do not come within any of the categories in para.5.013, there may be relief from liability to tax as a result of one of the following:

(a) the first £7,900 of gains arising on the disposals made during the current tax year (s.3). Married couples are taxed independently on their capital gains and have separate annual exemptions.

(b) Gains on disposal of business assets by a taxpayer who has attained the age of 50 or has retired on ill-health grounds below that age. Following the introduction of taper relief, this relief has been withdrawn on a phased basis. It will no longer be available from the tax year 2003/04 onwards.

In respect of disposals taking place on or after April 6, 1995 gains made on the disposal of shares in an approved Venture Capital Trust are exempt. The shares disposed of must not have been acquired in excess of the permitted maximum. A qualified exemption for shares acquired under the Enterprise Investment Scheme is also available.

Deferments

5.015 The final group of reliefs are those which have the effect of deferring the payment of tax.

When a transfer is made by way of gift or sale at under-value, the donor and donee may in certain circumstances elect to "hold over" any gain so that the donee is treated as acquiring the asset at the donor's acquisition value. When an owner sells certain types of assets, he may elect to "roll over" any gain into new assets purchased so that the acquisition cost is reduced by the amount of the rolled-over gain. If an election is made either to hold over or roll over a gain, the whole of the gain must be held or rolled over. It is not possible to elect to hold or roll over a portion of a gain allowing the balance to be covered by the annual exemption.

While tax can eventually become payable on the "held-over" or "rolled-over" gain, it will not be payable until some time in the future. These reliefs may offer advantages beyond the mere postponement of the payment of tax but the possible advantages differ depending on whether the gain is "held over" on a gift or "rolled over" on a sale.

Hold over Relief

5.016 Considering "held-over" gains first, the advantages are that:

(a) when tax is paid by the donee in the future it will be paid with money that may have been reduced in value by inflation, and

(b) if the donee dies while owning the property the gain will be effectively extinguished (see para.5.021).

There is, however, the disadvantage that the donor will lose the benefit of his annual exemption.

The circumstances in which the "hold-over" relief applies include:

(a) *Transfers between spouses.* If a gift is made from one spouse to the other, the asset is treated as having been acquired for a consideration giving rise to neither a gain nor a loss, so that any gain is *automatically* "held over" into the hands of the new owner (s.58).

(b) *Gifts to charities.* The donor is treated as having made the disposal for a consideration which gives rise to neither a gain nor a loss (s.257). Gains made by charities are normally exempt (s.256).

(c) *Business assets.* Where a taxpayer disposes (otherwise than under a bargain at arm's length) of "business assets" a joint election can be made by the transferor and transferee (or by the transferor alone if the disposal is to the trustees of a settlement) that any gain be held over (s.165). The donee receives no credit for the donor's accrued taper relief. Business assets are, broadly, assets used for the purposes of a trade, profession or vocation carried on by the transferor or his personal company. The term also covers shares, provided the shares are in an unquoted company or in the transferor's personal company.

(d) *Transfers chargeable to inheritance tax.* Where a disposal is made which is chargeable to inheritance tax or would be but for the existence of the annual exemption, a joint election can be made by the transferor and transferee (or by the transferor alone if the disposal is to the trustees of a settlement) that any gain be held over. The relief is available only to disposals which are initially chargeable to inheritance tax, and not to those which are initially potentially exempt but which become chargeable as a result of the death of the transferor within the seven years. Chapter 7 deals more fully with chargeable transfers but they are broadly transfers to and from settlements without an interest in possession. Note that a transfer is technically chargeable to inheritance tax even though it is within the transferor's nil rate band (s.262(a)).

(e) *Transfers exempt from inheritance tax.* Where a disposal is made which is exempt from inheritance tax because it is a transfer either to a political party, for the public benefit, to a maintenance fund for historic buildings or of property designated by the Treasury as of outstanding national interest, a joint election can be made by the transferor and transferee (or by the transferor alone if the transfer is to the trustees of a settlement) that the gain be held over (s.260(2)(b)).

(f) *Transfers from an accumulation and maintenance trust.* Where a beneficiary becomes absolutely entitled to assets from an accumulation and maintenance trust the trustees and beneficiary may jointly elect that any gain be held over. Chapter 7 deals more fully with accumulation and maintenance trusts. Hold-over relief is available only where the trust retains the status of an accumulation and maintenance trust at the time that the beneficiary becomes absolutely entitled to the assets (s.260(2) (d)).

The roll-over relief which is available on the sale of assets offers the same advantages and suffers the same disadvantages as hold-over relief. It enjoys a further advantage in that when the tax becomes payable (because the asset has been sold in circumstances when the accrued gain cannot be rolled over) the taxpayer may be able to use a relief not previously available to him to reduce or cancel his gain.

Roll-over Relief.

5.017   The "roll-over" relief applies:

(a) *On the replacement of business assets.* When a trader sells certain business assets (including land, buildings, plant and machinery) and reinvests the proceeds of sale in new business assets within certain time limits, any gain realised on the sale can be "rolled over" into the new asset. The effect of this is to reduce the trader's acquisition price of the asset by the "rolled-over" gain (ss.152–159).

(b) *On the incorporation of a business.* If the taxpayer transfers an unincorporated business (and all assets other than cash) as a going concern to a company in exchange for shares, the gain realised on the disposal to the company can be "rolled over" into the newly acquired shares. The effect is that the shares (subject to certain conditions) are treated as having been acquired for the same value as the assets transferred instead of at market value at the date of the disposal (ss.162 & 162A).

(c) *Deferral relief under the Enterprise Investment scheme (s.150C).* This deferral relief allows an investor to defer a CGT charge on a gain arising on the disposal of a qualifying EIS investment where the gain is rolled over into another qualifying investment within the qualifying time.
There are a number of conditions which must be satisfied for the investment to be a "qualifying investment". However, the key ones are that the investment must be wholly in cash to subscribe for ordinary, non-preferential shares in a company which qualifies for the purposes of EIS income tax relief and the shares must be issued to fund a "qualifying business activity".

(d) *Reinvestment in a Venture Capital Trust.* Gains on any disposals can be deferred by matching it against a qualifying investment in a Venture Capital Trust made within a period of 12 months before or 12 months after the chargeable gain (Sch.5C (2)).

6. THE RATES OF TAX

5.018   Once all relevant exemptions and reliefs have been deducted from the gain, tax is levied on the remaining chargeable gains. The rates of capital gains tax are equivalent to the rates of income tax which would apply if gains were treated as the top slice of income. Accordingly, and depending on the level of an individual's income, a taxpayer is taxed at rates equivalent to the starting rate (10 per cent), the basic rate of income tax

(22 per cent) or the higher rate of income tax (40 per cent) or partly one and partly the other.

Example
For tax year 2003/04 A has taxable income (after reliefs) of £22,000 and gains, after allowing for the annual exemption, of £11,000. The gains must be treated as the top slice of A's income. The basic rate limit of £30,500 will be exceeded. Thus the first £8,500 of the gains will be taxed at 22 per cent and the remaining £2,500 at 40 per cent.

7. THE DATE FOR PAYMENT OF TAX

Capital gains tax due from individuals and trustees tax is payable on a current year basis on January 31 following the year of assessment (TMA 1970, s.59B). Interest is charged on tax remaining unpaid after the due date.   **5.019**

If the sale price is paid by instalments over a period exceeding 18 months, the tax can be paid over a similar period (subject to a maximum of 8 years) if undue hardship would otherwise be caused (s.280).

Where hold-over relief is not available on a disposal by way of gift (or deemed disposal under s.71(1) or s.72—see Chapter 7) tax on certain assets can be paid in 10 equal yearly instalments (s.281). An election must be made in writing by the person paying the tax. Payment by instalments is possible only where hold-over relief is *not available* and not where it is available but the taxpayer chooses not to claim it.

The relevant assets are land or an interest in land, any shares or securities which immediately before the disposal gave the person disposing of the shares control of the company, any shares not giving control and not listed on a recognised stock exchange.

C. The Capital Gains Tax Liability of the Deceased

Prior to the date of death, the deceased may have made disposals which gave rise to capital gains tax liability. If this liability has not been discharged prior to the death, the personal representatives must discharge it on the deceased's behalf. The personal representatives calculate tax in accordance with the principles outlined above and will be able to claim, on behalf of the deceased, the benefit of any exemptions or reliefs the deceased could have claimed. Once these exemptions and reliefs have been claimed, the personal representatives will pay tax on behalf of the deceased at the appropriate rate(s).   **5.020**

The deceased may have unrelieved losses in the tax year of death. Section 62(2) provides that such losses can be carried back and set against the gains realised by the deceased in the three tax years preceding the tax year of death, taking later years first. If tax was paid in any of those earlier years, a rebate will be claimed.

If there are still unrelieved losses, these cannot be taken over by the personal representatives to set off against gains they make.

If the deceased made a disposal by way of a *donatio mortis causa*, no chargeable gain arises (s.62(5)).

D. The Capital Gains Tax Liability of the Personal Representatives

1. THE POSITION ON DEATH

5.021 There is no disposal of assets on death. Section 62(1)(a) provides that the assets of which a deceased person was competent to dispose shall be deemed to be *acquired* on his death by the personal representatives for a consideration equal to their market value at the date of the death. Since there is a deemed acquisition but no deemed disposal, no capital gains tax liability arises as a result of the death. The same rule applies to a person who held property jointly with the deceased.

If the value of a deceased's assets have been ascertained for inheritance tax purposes s.274 requires that value to be the asset's value for capital gains tax purposes. This will then determine the acquisition cost of the personal representatives and of the legatee, if the asset is transferred to a legatee.

This method of valuation can be beneficial to taxpayers where, for example, an asset owned by the deceased receives a high inheritance tax value as a result of the related property rules. However, s.274 only has this result if the inheritance tax value has actually been *ascertained*. The Revenue stated in its April 1995 Tax Bulletin that a value is not ascertained where:

(a) assets attract the spouse exemption or 100 per cent business or agricultural property relief;

(b) the CTO is of the view that the estate will be clearly within the nil rate band;

(c) the shares are in a company with excepted assets but little or no inheritance tax is at stake.

The fact that inheritance *reliefs* are available will not reduce the capital gains tax valuation.

If quoted shares and securities are sold within 12 months from the date of death, at less than market value at the date of death, the personal representatives can elect that, for inheritance tax purposes, the sale price be substituted for the probate value. (See below, Chapter 12.) If the reduced value is taken for inheritance tax purposes, it becomes the acquisition price of the personal representatives for capital gains tax purposes as well. The personal representatives cannot keep the original acquisition value for capital gains tax purposes once they have elected for the inheritance tax reduction. If land or an interest in land is sold within four years of death at less than market value at the date of death, the personal representatives can elect that the sale price be substituted for the probate value. It is not clear whether the reduced value becomes the acquisition value for capital gains tax purposes.

2. DISPOSALS BY THE PERSONAL REPRESENTATIVES

In the course of administering the estate, the personal representatives **5.022**
may have to sell assets. If they do so, they will be liable to capital gains tax
on any gains realised after deduction of any losses they incur on their
disposals. The calculation of liability has been outlined in paras 5.002–
5.018. Personal representatives will be chargeable to capital gains tax at a
rate of 34 per cent. They never pay capital gains tax at the lower or higher
rates. The fact that personal representatives never pay a higher rate of tax
means that it may be beneficial for them rather than legatees to sell assets
of the estate which the legatee does not want to keep *in specie*. The
indexation allowance and taper relief are available to personal
representatives in exactly the same way that they are available to
individuals.

In addition to the normal deductions for incidental selling expenses,
personal representatives are entitled to deduct a proportion of the costs
of valuing the estate for probate purposes (*I.R.C. v Richards' Executors*
(1971)). The Inland Revenue publishes a scale of permitted deductions
(SP 7/81). However, the personal representatives are free to claim more
than the scale deduction where they can show that the actual cost was
higher.

The rights of personal representatives to claim exemptions and relief
are limited. In the tax year of death, and the two following tax years, the
personal representatives can claim the annual exemption currently £7,900
(s.3(7)). Thereafter all the gains they realise (other than on assets within
para.5.013) are taxable. The only or main residence exemption cannot
apply to personal representatives since a continuing body of persons
cannot have a residence. However, by concession (ESC D5), if before and
after the death, the residence has been used as their only or main
residence by individuals who, under the will or intestacy, are entitled to
the whole or substantially the whole of the proceeds of sale of the house
either absolutely or for life, the exemption can be claimed (see above,
para.5.013).

If the personal representatives have made losses on their disposals but
have no, or insufficient, gains to set them against, these unabsorbed losses
cannot be passed on to the beneficiaries.

Where personal representatives are proposing to sell an asset which has
fallen in value since death and have no gains against which the loss can be
set, it may be preferable for them to consider vesting the asset in a
beneficiary and allowing the beneficiary to sell. Even if the beneficiary has
no gains in the current tax year, the loss can be carried forward
indefinitely (see para.5.009 above).

3. TRANSFERS TO LEGATEES

For capital gains tax purposes, s.64(2) defines the term "legatee" as **5.023**
including "any person taking under a testamentary disposition or on an
intestacy or partial intestacy, whether he takes beneficially or as trustee,
and a person taking a *donatio mortis causa* shall be treated ... as a legatee
and his acquisition as made at the time of the donor's death".

Section 62(4) provides that when the personal representatives transfer an asset to a legatee under the terms of a will, or the intestacy rules, no chargeable gain accrues to the personal representatives. The personal representatives' acquisition is treated as the legatee's acquisition. The position is the same if the personal representatives appropriate an asset in or towards satisfaction of a pecuniary legacy or a share in residue. Therefore, such transfers cannot give rise to capital gains tax liability if the asset has risen in value since the date of death and neither can the personal representatives have the benefit of a loss where the asset has fallen in value since the date of death.

If the personal representatives vest assets in trustees (even if they themselves are the trustees) the trustees are treated in the same way as legatees and so acquire the asset at market value at the date of death. When the beneficiaries of the trust become absolutely entitled to the trust assets there will be a charge to capital gains tax if the assets have risen in value since the death.

When the personal representatives are deciding which assets to sell and which to vest in beneficiaries, they should take into account their own and the beneficiaries' present and future tax liability. The rate payable by beneficiaries will often be the higher rate (40 per cent) instead of the 34 per cent rate payable by the PRs.

Personal representatives should be particularly careful when dealing with charities. If the personal representatives sell an asset which shows a capital gain, tax will be paid at the rate of 34 per cent. If the asset is transferred to the charity who then make the sale, the gain is exempt (s.256). It is possible for the personal representatives to appropriate an asset to a charity and then sell on behalf of the charity as a bare trustee. The s.256 exemption will then be available. It is important to have a clear record of the appropriation and the instruction to sell.

E. The Capital Gains Tax Liability of Beneficiaries

5.024   As has already been explained, the legatees, whether they are entitled under a will or the intestacy rules, whether they receive a specific legacy, an asset in satisfaction of a pecuniary legacy or a residuary legacy or whether they are beneficially entitled or are merely entitled as trustees, receive the property at market value at the date of the death.

This means they take the asset with the benefit of any unrealised losses that may have accrued since the death and subject to any unrealised gains that have arisen since that date. They cannot, however, take over any unrelieved losses which the personal representatives realised.

Insofar as indexation allowance is relevant, the beneficiaries acquire the assets at their value at the date of death, together with the benefit of any indexation allowance allowed to the personal representatives. The legatee's entitlement to taper relief runs back to the date of death.

On subsequent disposals by beneficiaries the gain or the loss must be calculated on the basis of the market value at the date of death, increased by any indexation allowance available. A beneficiary who purchases an asset from the personal representatives takes as a purchaser not a legatee. Thus the personal representatives will be liable for any gain between date of death and sale.

F. Reporting Requirements for Chargeable Gains

For tax returns for tax year 2003/04 onwards it is not necessary for individuals, trustees and personal representatives (in the tax year following death and the following two tax years) to complete the Capital Gains pages of a tax return where the total of disposal proceeds does not exceed four times the annual exemption which applies to individuals provided:

- Either the gains do not exceed their annual exemption; or
- There are no allowable losses to be deducted from chargeable gains and there is no CGT liability after any available taper has been deducted.

Disposals of assets from spouse to spouse will not count towards the four times annual exemption limit if they are treated as giving rise to neither a gain nor a loss under TCGA, s.58(1) because they are "living together".

For earlier tax years there was a more limited concession.

6. Income Tax

6.001 In the illustrations given in this chapter, it is assumed (except where the contrary is stated) that basic rate tax will remain at starting rate 10 per cent and higher rate 40 per cent for all future tax years.

A. Introduction

6.002 Many people regard income tax as the bane of their lives and would be distressed to discover that the Inland Revenue can pursue them beyond the grave.

When a person dies, income tax must be considered in respect of three different periods:

> (1) the period up to death,
> (2) the administration period, and
> (3) the period after the completion of administration.

The purpose of this chapter is to consider the rules that apply to these different periods but before looking at the detailed rules, a brief explanation of the types of receipt on which income tax is levied and the methods of calculating the tax is necessary.

B. Income Tax Generally

6.003 A detailed discussion of the income tax system is beyond the scope of this book. Instead we intend merely to make some simple basic points to put the particular rules relevant on death into context.

It is necessary when considering income tax to ask the following questions:

> (1) What is income?
> (2) What income is taxable?
> (3) In what year of assessment will income be taxed?
> (4) How is the tax liability calculated?
> (5) What are the rates of tax?
> (6) When is the tax payable?

1. WHAT IS INCOME?

6.004 The first problem that arises is to define the kind of receipt which attracts the charge to income tax. Most people would probably not be able to define income but no doubt would hope to recognise it when they receive it.

As there is no statutory definition of "income", over the years, lawyers have attempted to define the nebulous concept of "income" which is subject to tax. In the case of *London County Council v Att.-Gen.* (1901) Lord MacNaughten said "income tax, if I may be pardoned for saying so, is a tax on income". As a definition this is of little assistance. However, more precise guidelines have developed and it can now be said that the tax is paid on profits of an income nature, as opposed to profits arising on the disposal of a capital asset (although there are cases where capital receipts can be treated as income, such as certain premiums on leases). The distinction between these two types of receipt is, broadly speaking, that to be of an income nature, the receipt should be recurrent.

2. WHAT INCOME IS TAXABLE?

If the receipt is of an income nature, it is necessary to determine into **6.005** which of the four Schedules to the Income and Corporation Taxes Act 1988 ("the Taxes Act") it falls. The Schedules govern the method of calculating the tax on income receipts and the date on which the tax is paid. The Schedules, and the Cases into which they are subdivided, cover all the types of taxable income, *i.e.*:

Schedule A		–profits from a business of letting land
Schedule D	Cases I & II	–trading and professional income
	Case III	–pure income profits (such as annuities, annual payments and interest)
	Cases IV & V	–income from securities and possessions out of the UK
	Case VI	–miscellaneous income
Schedule E		–employment income
Schedule F		–dividends

Note
Schedule B, which applied to woodlands, was abolished as from April 6, 1988. Schedule C, which applied to income from government securities, was abolished as from April 6, 1996.

A few types of income are exempt (for example, scholarship income) and so are tax-free.
Each Schedule and Case (apart from those dealing with pure income) lays down rules as to the expenses which can be deducted to determine net income. The tax year in which the income will be taxed is determined by the basis of assessment relevant to the particular Schedule.

3. WHAT IS THE RELEVANT YEAR OF ASSESSMENT?

Tax is calculated by reference to years of assessment (commonly called **6.006** "tax years"). A new tax year commences on April 6 each year.

The Taxes Act lays down two main bases of assessment—the current year basis and the actual year basis. The former requires that an individual pays tax on the profits made in the accounting period which ends in the tax year and applies to Sch.D Cases I & II income. The latter requires that tax is assessed in each year on the income of that tax year (this applies for example, to Sch.E).

4. How is the tax liability calculated?

General

6.007   Three steps are necessary:

> (a) calculate "statutory income"
> (b) deduct "charges on income" to produce "total income"
> (c) deduct "personal reliefs" to produce "taxable income".

What is "statutory income"?

6.008   The taxpayer's "statutory income" is found by adding together his receipts (after deducting allowable expenses) from all sources, taking into account the relevant basis of assessment. Statutory income includes sums received gross (such as trading income) and the grossed up amounts of sums which are received net of tax.

It is necessary to gross up sums received net of tax since income tax is calculated on the basis of a person's gross income (credit is given for the tax paid or credit given). Examples of sums which are received net are salaries paid net of tax under the P.A.Y.E. system, payments made by trustees to beneficiaries and dividend income.

To gross up a net sum where basic rate tax (BRT) has been deducted, simply multiply the sum actually received by

$$\frac{100}{100 - BRT}$$

The reason why this calculation works is that if the basic rate of tax is 22 per cent and £78 is received net of basic rate tax, then £78 is 78 per cent of the gross figure (22 per cent of the gross figure having already been deducted). To calculate 100 per cent of the receipt simply divide by 78 to find 1 per cent and then multiply by 100 to find 100 per cent.

Example
A beneficiary of a trust fund receives £3,900. Basic rate tax of 22 per cent has already been deducted. When calculating the beneficiary's statutory income the interest is grossed up to £5,000.

$$£3,900 \times \frac{100}{100 - 22} = £5,000$$

£5,000 is included in the taxpayer's income tax return as part of gross income. However, it must be remembered that in the above example £1,100 in tax has already been paid. This sum is a "tax credit" so that, when calculating what tax (if any) is due to the Revenue, an allowance must be made for the £1,100 already paid on behalf of the taxpayer by the trustees.

If the taxpayer is only liable to basic rate tax on the receipt no additional tax need be sent to the Revenue since the "right" amount of tax has already been paid. If the taxpayer pays higher rate tax, additional tax will have to be sent.

If the taxpayer from whom income tax has been deducted is not liable to even basic rate tax (because of his entitlement to personal reliefs and charges), he can normally reclaim, from the Revenue, the basic rate tax already paid on his behalf.

Savings income
Interest on accounts with banks and building societies and interest paid by local authorities is treated somewhat differently. The payer deducts 20 per cent at source. If the taxpayer is a higher rate taxpayer the interest received is grossed up at 20 per cent to calculate the 40 per cent tax on it and is treated as the top slice of the taxpayer's income. The taxpayer is then given credit for the tax already paid. However, a basic rate payer is not liable to pay the difference between the 20 per cent paid and the basic rate as the basic rate is deemed to have been paid. A person who is liable to pay less than 20 per cent (*i.e.* a person with unused personal allowance and/or whose taxable income does not exceed the "starting rate" band) can claim back the tax deducted at source. A person who expects to be in this position may arrange to receive the income gross from the payer.

Example
Peter is entitled to 5 per cent interest on £20,000 invested in a Building Society. He is a higher rate taxpayer. Peter will receive £1,000 less 20 per cent deducted by the Building Society. He will gross up this sum and pay tax at 40 per cent but will be able to deduct the tax paid.

$$£800 \times \frac{100}{80} = £1,000$$

Tax @ 40% = £400, less tax credit £200 = £200.

Dividends
Dividends are dealt with rather differently because the tax credit is **6.009** irrecoverable. The shareholder receives a net dividend together with a tax credit equal to one ninth of the net amount of the dividend. He is then liable to tax on the dividend plus the tax credit. However, if he is liable to the starting or basic rate of tax the tax credit (even though it is only 10 per cent of the gross amount) is deemed to pay the whole of the tax liability (the "Schedule F ordinary rate"). Higher rate taxpayers will pay tax on the grossed up dividend at the rate of 32.5 per cent (the "Schedule F upper rate").

Example
Rita receives a dividend of £900. To this must be added the tax credit of £100. The sum of £1,000 forms part of her statutory income (under Sch.F).

However if she is a basic rate taxpayer the tax credit is deemed to satisfy the basic rate (if she were a higher rate taxpayer she would have to pay 32.5 per cent of the gross sum (£350) but would get credit for the sum paid by the company (£100). She would, therefore, now owe the Revenue £250.).

What are "charges on income"?

6.010   Charges on income are "amounts which fall to be deducted in computing total income" (Taxes Management Act 1970, s.8(8)). The amounts which are deductible are payments under charitable covenants satisfying certain conditions and interest payments on qualifying loans (such as loans for the purchase of an interest in or to make a capital contribution to a partnership). They are deducted from "statutory" income when calculating a person's "total" income because the payer is regarded as having alienated a portion of income so that it ceases to be the payer's income and becomes the payee's. If the payment is an "annual payment" (*e.g.* a Gift Aid payment), the payer must deduct basic rate tax from the payment and pay it to the Revenue on behalf of the payee.

What is "taxable income"?

6.011   From "total income" the taxpayer deducts any allowable losses then certain personal reliefs to leave taxable income. The reliefs which may be deducted include the personal allowance. This is available to any "individual". The personal representatives of a deceased person are not an individual for this purpose and so do not get a personal allowance. Individuals over 65 with relatively small incomes get an increased personal allowance as do blind persons. The effect of these allowances is to reduce the sum on which tax is paid with the result that the taxpayer saves the highest rate of tax which would otherwise be payable on the amount of the allowance.

Married couples (this is split between the couple if either so chooses, otherwise it goes to the husband unless they both choose that it should go to the wife) are entitled to further reliefs but restricted to 10 per cent. Unless neither party was born before April 6, 1935 10 per cent of the amount of this relief should be deducted from the final tax bill once it has been calculated.

5. WHAT ARE THE RATES?

6.012   Once "taxable income" has been ascertained, the rates of tax are calculated on it. For the tax year 2003/04 these are a starting rate of 10 per cent on the first £1,960 of taxable income, a basic rate of 22 per cent on the next portion of taxable income up to a limit of £30,500 and a higher rate of 40 per cent on any taxable income in excess of £30,500. This structure is complicated by the rates of tax applicable to particular types of income. Dividends taxable under Sch.F attract a non-refundable credit of 10 per cent (which is irrecoverable even by non-taxpayers). That results in a "Schedule F ordinary rate" of 10 per cent for starting or basic rate taxpayers. A "Schedule F upper rate" of 32.5 per cent is payable by higher rate taxpayers. Certain investment income (*e.g.* interest) is taxed at the "lower rate" of 20 per cent (which is treated as satisfying the basic rate liability arising). (The bands and the personal reliefs will in future tax years rise according to the rate of inflation, unless Parliament decides otherwise.) These rates are applied to all types of income, both earned income and investment income. Investment income is everything which is not earned income.

An example of a simple calculation of a taxpayer's liability may be helpful.

Example

Alec, who is single and aged 30, has the following income on which he is liable to tax in the year 2003/04.

(a) £40,500 from his solicitor's practice (calculated according to the current year basis)
(b) £15,000 gross director's fees from XYZ Ltd, from which the company has deducted £950 under the P.A.Y.E. system. This is the correct amount of tax taking into account the starting and basic rates on the fees left once the personal relief and the charge on income mentioned below have been deducted.
(c) £7,800 from a trust fund paid to him net of basic rate tax.

He has paid £5,000 interest on a £50,000 loan to buy an interest in the firm of solicitors. His tax liability will be calculated as follows:

	£
Statutory income	
Practice receipts	40,000
Salary (gross)	15,000
Income from trust fund	
$\left(\text{grossed up } 7,800 \times \dfrac{100}{78}\right)$	10,000
	65,000
Less	
Charge on income	(5,000)
Total income	60,000
Less	
Personal relief	(4,615)
Taxable income	£55,385

His tax liability is:	£
On the first £1,960 tax at 10%	196
On the next £28,540 tax at 22%	6,279
On the balance of £24,885 tax at 40%	9,954
	16,429

The total tax bill is therefore £16,429 of which £3,150 has already been paid (£2,200 by the trustees of the trust fund and £950 by XYZ Ltd). Therefore, the Revenue will require £13,279 direct from Alec.

6. WHEN IS THE TAX PAYABLE?

6.013   The due date for the payment of tax is January 31 following the year of assessment. However, there are two interim payments due on January 31 in the year of assessment and July 31 immediately following that year. Sch.E tax is deducted before the employee receives it under the P.A.Y.E. system.

C. Income of the Deceased

We will now examine the particular rules which are relevant on death.

1. INTRODUCTION

6.014   It is the responsibility of personal representatives to deal with the income tax affairs both of the deceased and of the estate during the administration period, to ensure that a full declaration of income, arising before and after the death, is made and that tax, at the appropriate rates, is paid. When performing this duty the personal representatives must make returns both in respect of the income of the deceased up to the date of death and in respect of the administration period.

2. INCOME OF THE DECEASED

6.015   The personal representatives must ascertain the statutory income of the deceased for the tax year of death. Only income received or receivable before death is included. Income receivable after death is income of the estate (see para.6.016 below). They will calculate his tax liability in the usual way by deducting any charges on income payable before the death together with a *full* year's personal reliefs, regardless of the date of death.

Once the deceased's taxable income has been calculated, the appropriate rates of tax are applied and any extra tax due is paid or a rebate claimed where relevant.

Example
Betty, unmarried, died on May 6, 2003 aged 59 and her personal representatives find her share of the profits from a solicitor's practice taxable in the tax year 2003/04 is £30,000. They also find she was entitled to a dividend of £900 from A Ltd (declared on May 1, 2003) and that a dividend of £385 on shares which she owned in B Ltd was declared on June 1, 1997. Only the profits and the dividend from A Ltd are treated as the deceased's income; the dividend from B Ltd is treated as income of the estate (see para.6.016 below). The tax calculation will be as follows:

	£
Statutory income	
Profits	30,000
Grossed up dividend	
$\left(£900 \times \dfrac{100}{90}\right)$	1,000
Total income	31,000
Less	
Personal relief	(4,615)
Taxable income	26,385

This taxable income of £26,385 must be divided into non-savings income and savings income. The non-savings income is taxed first and gets the benefit of the personal relief and lower rates of tax. The savings income is taxed as the highest part of the taxable income.

The tax on the non-savings income (that is, the profits from her solicitor's practice only) is

Rate	Amount
%	£
0–1,960 @ 10	196
1,960–25,385 @ 22	5,154
	5,350

The savings income of £1,000 is taxed next and is treated as the highest part of her income but as her income does not exceed the threshold for higher rate tax the dividend is only liable to tax at the Sch.F ordinary rate of 10 per cent. She has a tax credit for 10 per cent so no further tax is due on the dividend. Her personal representatives will only have to pay £5,350.

3. Distinguishing income of the deceased from income of the estate

The personal representatives must differentiate between the deceased's **6.016** income and that of the administration period and this is done by ascertaining when the particular receipt arose. This causes few problems when considering salary or profits from a trade or profession since these sources of income will normally cease with the death. However, other types of income which continue to arise after the death, such as rent, interest or dividends, will cause greater problems since they are often attributable to a period which falls partly before and partly after the death.

Income which is *due* before the death is part of the deceased's income (for example, a dividend on shares due and payable on a date before death) even if paid after death. Income which is *due* after the death is income of the estate (for example a dividend due and payable after death or interest which becomes due and payable on a date after the death). The Apportionment Act 1870 (see below, para.16.053), which provides for the apportionment of income on a day-to-day basis for the purposes of distribution, does not apply for income tax purposes (*I.R.C. v Henderson's Executors* (1931)). As we saw in para.4.019 a limited income tax relief is available where income received after death has been apportioned for inheritance tax purposes and some of that income has been included as an asset of the estate at death attracting inheritance tax (Taxes Act 1988, s.699, as amended).

4. PRACTICAL PROBLEMS

6.017   The income tax liability of the deceased may take a considerable length of time to finalise. This is particularly likely to be the case where the deceased was a sole trader or a partner as there may be delays in preparing the accounts on which the tax liability is to be calculated. There may be additional tax due to the Inland Revenue or there may be repayments of tax due to the deceased as the result, for example, of excessive P.A.Y.E. tax paid by an employer on the taxpayer's behalf. In a press release of April 4, 1996, the Inland Revenue announced their willingness to issue self assessment tax returns before the end of the tax year at the request of personal representatives. The Revenue will then give early confirmation if they decide not to enquire into the return.

The personal representatives are normally required to submit an Inland Revenue Account at the latest within 12 months of the death detailing the assets and liabilities of the deceased and showing the amount of inheritance tax due to the Inland Revenue calculated on the basis of the net value of the estate. At the same time they are required to send a cheque for any inheritance tax due. The value of the estate cannot be accurately determined until all the assets and liabilities are ascertained so any delay in finalising the income tax position of the deceased will prevent the final calculation and payment of inheritance tax due.

Personal representatives are usually anxious to pay inheritance tax promptly, partly because interest starts to run after six months from the end of the month of death but more importantly because they cannot get a grant of representation and therefore cannot start administering the estate until the inheritance tax due has been paid. To prevent delays, personal representatives will frequently estimate the income tax liability of the deceased and pay inheritance tax due on the basis of that estimated figure. When they obtain the final income tax figure, they can if necessary submit a corrective account and make any adjustments to the inheritance tax which prove necessary.

D. Income Arising after Death

6.018   As regards the income received by the estate during the "administration period" different rules apply. This period starts with the day after the date of death and continues until the completion of the administration of the estate (Taxes Act 1988, s.695). It is generally accepted that completion of the administration occurs on the date the residue is ascertained for distribution. Personal representatives cannot claim any personal reliefs since these are only available to individuals. They can deduct interest on a loan (but not an overdraft) to pay inheritance tax when calculating the taxable income of the estate income but only in so far as the loan is to pay tax on personalty vesting in the personal representatives to which the deceased was beneficially entitled, Taxes Act 1988, s.364. Further, this interest is only deductible for one year. Other expenses incurred by the personal representative in administering the estate are not deductible.

The personal representatives pay only basic rate tax on the taxable income of the estate regardless of the amount and type of income. They do not pay tax at the higher rate. Savings income will be received with a tax credit of 20 per cent and dividends with a non-refundable tax credit of 10 per cent so there will be no further liability to tax. If taxed income is paid to a beneficiary, the PRs must supply a certificate of deduction of tax showing the amount of tax and the applicable rate (Taxes Act 1988, s.700(5)). The personal representatives will pay the administration expenses from the estate's income taxed at the rate or rates appropriate to its source or sources.

The range of rates which the estate's income may attract coupled with the absence of a statutory rule determining the source of income from which the expenses are paid gives the personal representatives a range of options.

Taxes Act 1988 s.701 (3A)(a) allows the differing types of income to be divided between the beneficiaries as is just and reasonable taking their different interests into account.

As to the expenses, the order which the Revenue will accept (and which is probably the most beneficial) is as follows:

(a) dividend income (which attract a non-refundable credit); then
(b) income attracting the lower rate of tax (such as interest); then
(c) income attracting the basic rate of tax.

To the extent that income is paid to beneficiaries, further rules are relevant. These differ depending on the beneficiaries' interests in the estate and firstly we will look at the treatment of payments to non-residuary beneficiaries.

1. NON-RESIDUARY LEGATEES

Non-residuary legatees may be entitled to a specific legacy or to a pecuniary or general legacy.   **6.019**

Specific legatees
The subject-matter of a specific legacy may earn income from the date of   **6.020**
death (for example, a house let and producing rental income). A beneficiary only becomes liable to pay tax after the personal representatives have made an assent of the asset to the beneficiary. The liability of the legatee relates back to the date of death so the assessments for intervening tax years will be reopened and tax will be reassessed for the years in which the income arose.

A specific legatee of shares will have the benefit of the 20 per cent tax credit. The legatee will be liable to further tax to the extent that the dividend, treated as the highest part of the taxpayer's income, exceeds the threshold for higher rate tax.

Pecuniary and general legatees

6.021 Such legatees may be entitled to be paid interest on the value of their legacies (see Chapter 16). The question of their liability to income tax on such interest then arises. In many circumstances income tax is chargeable on income even if not accepted but in the case of interest, tax is only payable on sums actually received. Thus, if a beneficiary disclaims entitlement to interest payable to him on a pecuniary or general legacy or the personal representatives cannot pay it, he is not liable to tax—*Dewar v I.R.C.* (1935) (unless a sum has been specifically set aside to pay the legacy in which case tax must be paid even if the legatee fails to draw the interest—*Spens v I.R.C.* (1970)).

If interest is paid to the beneficiary it is taxed as Sch.D, Case III income in his hands (normally as income of the year of receipt, Taxes Act 1988, ss.64, 66 and 67). Payment will be made gross (*i.e.* without deduction of any tax).

2. RESIDUARY LEGATEES

6.022 These rules are themselves sub-divided into those which relate to beneficiaries with limited interests and those which relate to beneficiaries with absolute interests in the residue.

Limited interest legatee

6.023 A legatee has a limited interest in residue if he or she is entitled to income but not to capital. An example of such a beneficiary is a person who has a life interest in residue. All sums received by the legatee will be liable to income tax in the year of receipt. The personal representatives will deduct basic rate tax from the income and pay it to the revenue on behalf of the beneficiary. In the case of savings income the personal representatives will themselves have received the income with a tax credit and so will not have to make any further deduction. Their tax credit will be passed on to the beneficiary. The beneficiary is liable to tax on income received in a particular tax year (before April 6, 1995 a more complex provision applied). The beneficiary will gross up the income to calculate the tax on it and then deduct the tax credits.

Example
Martha is entitled to income for life from her mother's estate. The personal representatives receive various items of income and pay the income to Martha in tax year 2003–04. Martha is a higher rate taxpayer.

	Receipts £		Net amounts £
Rent received gross	5,000 (less BRT deducted by PRs)		= 3,900 (net)
Dividends received net	4,500 (plus tax credit £500)		= 4,500 (net)
Bank interest	1,600 (plus tax credit £400)		= 1,600 (net)

Net	Gross
£3,900 × $\frac{100}{78}$	= £5,000
£4,500 + £1,500	= £5,000
£1,600 × $\frac{100}{80}$	= £2,000
Statutory income	= £12,000
Tax @ 40%	£4,800

Less tax credits
£1,100
£500
£400
£2,000

Tax to pay   £2,800

If payments of income are delayed (so that most of the income is paid to the beneficiary late in the administration) the amount of higher rate tax may be increased. If payment of the income can be spread more evenly the beneficiary may remain below the higher rate threshold. Personal representatives should, if practicable, discuss with the beneficiary the strategy for making payments.

Absolute interest beneficiaries (Taxes Act 1988, s.696)
A beneficiary who is entitled to all or part of the capital of the residue in his own right has an absolute interest.   **6.024**

Such a beneficiary is entitled to both income and capital; income tax is, of course, only payable on income receipts. Therefore, when a beneficiary receives a cash sum from the estate it is necessary to distinguish income from capital receipts.

In order to do this the personal representatives must calculate the "residuary income" of the estate in respect of each tax year. Section 697 of the Taxes Act defines "residuary income" as (broadly) all income less certain charges (including annuities) and management expenses properly chargeable to income. There is no definition of "management expenses properly chargeable to income". However in *Carver v Duncan* (1985), a case on management expenses "properly" chargeable to income for the purposes of liability to additional rate income tax under the Taxes Act 1988, s.832(1) and s.686, it was said that "properly means properly under the general law and not properly under the terms of the particular trust instrument". (Examples of expenses properly chargeable to income would be repairs.) Net residuary income is income received gross less basic rate of tax and savings income received after deduction of 20 per cent tax. Expenses should be set against savings income before income received gross.

Payments made to a residuary beneficiary are treated as his income up to the limit of the residuary income for the tax year in question. The beneficiary must gross up payments received and include the gross amount in his statutory income. He will be given a tax credit for the basic rate tax paid on his behalf by the personal representatives, the lower rate paid on any savings income and a tax credit for any dividends received. Any payments made to the beneficiary in excess of the residuary income are treated as capital and as such are not included in the beneficiary's statutory income.

The rules apply to the payment of any "sums" so the personal representatives cannot specify that a particular payment is capital. The Revenue apparently considers that for these purposes the payment of "any sum" includes a transfer of assets. Thus, the Revenue will treat any asset transferred as an income receipt up to the limit of the beneficiary's income entitlement no matter what the nature of the asset.

Any residuary income which has not been paid to the beneficiary during the administration period is deemed to be paid immediately before the end of the administration period.

Again, so far as is practicable, the personal representatives should discuss with the beneficiary the strategy for making payments. It may be possible for the beneficiary to avoid paying higher rate tax on the estate income in certain tax years if payments can be staggered suitably.

Additional requirements

The Finance Act 1995 introduced a new requirement for personal representatives in relation to residuary beneficiaries. Personal representatives are now required, if so requested by residuary beneficiaries, to provide a written statement setting out the amounts of income paid to the residuary beneficiary in any year of assessment and the amount of tax and the rates which the amounts are deemed to have borne. This requirement was inserted into ICTA 1988 as a new s.700(5).

Inland Revenue Helpsheets

6.025   The Revenue have produced a series of Helpsheets designed to aid personal representatives fulfil their responsibilities as regards income tax.

These Helpsheets are available from the Revenue's website at *www.inlandrevenue.gov.uk.*

7.   Taxation of Trusts and Settlements

A. Introduction

Where property is held on trust the legal and beneficial interests are often **7.001** held by different people and the Revenue find it convenient and, in some cases necessary, to impose liability on both the trustee and the beneficiary. Where the beneficial interest in property is divided between several people, either at a particular time or successively, special rules are required to ensure that the creation of the settlement cannot be used as a means of saving tax.

Tax definitions of "settlements" for inheritance tax, capital gains tax, and income tax are different and will be considered separately later in this chapter. The definitions for tax purposes are not the same as for other purposes and in particular do not distinguish between trusts for sale and strict settlements.

Settlements may be created *inter vivos*, by the intestacy rules or by will. There are many different types of settlement; we will concentrate mainly on two very common types in this chapter.

These are:

(a) A settlement "to A for life remainder to B" (that is a settlement where property is vested in trustees to pay the income from the property to A until A dies and then to vest the property absolutely in B). For inheritance tax purposes this is a settlement "with an interest in possession".

(b) An "accumulation and maintenance settlement". This type of settlement gives the trustees a power to use income for the maintenance of the beneficiaries, and requires them to add any income not so used to capital (*i.e.* to accumulate income). For inheritance tax purposes this is a settlement "without an interest in possession".

We will deal with each tax separately for the sake of clarity but it is important to realise that in deciding whether or not to create a settlement each tax must be taken into account. Furthermore the non-tax consequences of creating a settlement should always be regarded as the first consideration. A gift is unwise, even if it saves tax, if it leaves the settlor or his dependants with insufficient income or capital for their needs.

B. Settlements and Inheritance Tax

DEFINITIONS

7.002   For inheritance tax purposes the term "settlement" is defined, by s.43(2) of the Inheritance Tax Act 1984, as:

> "... any disposition or dispositions of property ... whereby the property is for the time being—
>
> (a) held in trust for persons in succession or for any person subject to a contingency; or
>
> (b) held by trustees on trust to accumulate the whole or part of any income of the property or with power to make payments out of that income at the discretion of the trustees or some other person, with or without power to accumulate surplus income; or
>
> (c) charged or burdened (otherwise than for full consideration. ...) with the payment of any annuity or other periodical payment payable for a life or any other limited or terminable period. ..."

Section 43(3) adds to the definition a lease for life or lives or for a period ascertainable only by reference to a death which is not granted for full consideration.

It should be noted that a settlement is "any disposition or dispositions of property ... whereby the property is *for the time being*" held in one of the various ways listed in the definition. Whether or not property is settled must, therefore, be considered each time that a potential charge to tax arises. Property ceases to be settled once it ceases to be held in one of the various ways listed in the definition even though it may still be held by trustees (for example where they have not yet vested it in a beneficiary who has become absolutely entitled). A bare trust (that is a trust where the beneficiary is entitled to require the transfer of the legal title to himself) is not a settlement for inheritance tax purposes—the beneficiary of such a trust is treated as an absolute owner. A statutory trust for sale imposed where property is held by co-owners is not a settlement for inheritance tax purposes. The co-owners are treated as absolute owners.

Examples of inheritance tax settlements include:

(a) Trustees are holding property for "A for life remainder to B" (successive interest, see s.43(2)(a) above).

(b) Trustees are holding property for "A if he reaches 25" (subject to a contingency, see s.43(2)(a) above).

(c) Trustees are holding property "to accumulate the income therefrom for 10 years and then to pay capital to A" (trust to accumulate until the 10 year period expires, see s.43(2)(b) above).

(d) Trustees are holding property "to pay the income therefrom for 10 years from [date] to such of my children as they shall in their absolute discretion from time to time appoint and thereafter to pay the capital to A" (discretion to pay income until the 10 year period expires, see s.43(2)(b) above).

(e) Property is being held by someone subject to the payment of an annuity to someone else and full consideration was not given for the annuity. For example the will of a testator leaves Blackacre "to my son charged with the payment to X of an annuity of £1,000 per annum for the rest of X's life." In this case there will be a settlement of Blackacre from the death of the testator until the death of X (see s.43(2)(c) above).

C. Inheritance Tax—Settlements with Interest in Possession

1. SIGNIFICANCE OF INTEREST IN POSSESSION

It is extremely important to decide whether or not a trust has an interest in possession. This is because a trust in which there is an interest in possession is treated quite differently for inheritance tax purposes from a trust in which there is no interest in possession.   **7.003**

Section 49(1) of the Inheritance Tax Act 1984 provides that "A person beneficially entitled to an interest in possession in settled property shall be treated ... as beneficially entitled to the property in which the interest subsists". This means that a person with an interest in possession is treated for inheritance tax purposes as the owner of the trust assets. Where a person is entitled to part of the income from settled property he is treated as owning a corresponding part of the property. Special rules apply where one or more beneficiary (for example, an annuitant) is entitled to a fixed amount of income rather than a proportion of the whole or where one or more beneficiary is entitled to the use and enjoyment of property rather than the income from it. These rules are not further considered.

As we shall see at paras 7.012–7.028 below, where there is no interest in possession no one person is treated as beneficially entitled to the settled property. Instead inheritance tax is charged on the value of the trust assets periodically over the lifetime of the trust.

The term "interest in possession" is not defined in the legislation. In most cases it is clear whether or not there is an interest in possession. If a beneficiary has an immediate right to receive income or otherwise to use and enjoy trust property then he has such an interest. Thus the life tenant of a settlement usually has an interest in possession. It is also clear that no one has such an interest in the case of an ordinary discretionary trust since no one has a *right* to income. There are, however, some marginal cases where the position is less clear.

For example in *Pearson v I.R.C.* (1980) a trust fund was held for three beneficiaries (all adults) who were entitled to the property subject to powers of appointment and a power to accumulate; they would each receive one-third of the income unless the trustees exercised the power to accumulate or the power of appointment. The House of Lords by a majority of three to two (and overruling the decisions at first instance and in the Court of Appeal) held that there was no interest in possession. The majority held that an interest in possession is one giving "*a present right to present enjoyment*" and that on these facts there was no such right since the beneficiaries would not receive the income to the extent that the power to accumulate was exercised.

2. AREAS OF UNCERTAINTY

7.004   There are a number of situations where it may not be immediately apparent whether or not an interest in possession exists.

Administrative and dispositive powers

7.005   In theory, a beneficiary with an interest in possession is entitled to trust income as it arises. However, trustees will always have power to pay management expenses of the trust from that income leaving only the balance for the beneficiary. In *Pearson*, Viscount Dilhorne said that there was a distinction between powers which were merely administrative and powers which were dispositive in their nature. A beneficiary with an interest in possession is entitled to all the net income of the trust once the expenses of the trust have been paid. If the trustees have power to withhold that net income from a beneficiary, there is no interest in possession. The difficulty lies in identifying expenses which are merely administrative. Management expenses clearly fall into that category but what if trustees have power to pay items which would be normally be paid from capital (for example, CGT) from income? There are cases where it will be difficult to draw the line.

Power to allow beneficiaries of a discretionary trust to occupy a dwelling house

7.006   The mere existence of such a power is of no importance. However, if the trustees exercise the power, the Revenue may well argue that an interest in possession has been created. The Revenue's view is set out in SP 10/79:

> "... if the power is drawn in terms wide enough to cover the creation of an exclusive or joint residence, albeit revocable, for a definite or indefinite period, and is exercised with the intention of providing a particular beneficiary with a permanent home, the Revenue will normally regard the exercise of the power as creating an interest in possession."

The statement may not stand up to judicial scrutiny but challenging the Revenue is an expensive business.

The statement continues with the following:

> "no interest in possession arises on the creation of a lease for a term or a periodic tenancy for less than full consideration"

It is, therefore, open to trustees to grant a lease to a member of the class at less than a market rent and avoid an allegation of an interest in possession.

(Note that principal private dwelling house relief will be available to the trustees under TCGA 1991, s.225 where a beneficiary occupies a trust asset whether as of right or as the result of the exercise of a trustees' discretion. See *Sansom v Peay* (1976).)

Will expressing wish that a beneficiary be allowed to reside in a dwelling house

Provided the will expresses a mere wish and confers no rights on the beneficiary, there is no interest in possession. However, testators frequently try to protect the position of the beneficiary by directing that the trustees *must* allow the beneficiary to occupy the property. If the beneficiary has a right to occupy, there is an interest in possession.   **7.007**

In *I.R.C. v Lloyds Private Banking* (1998) a wife left her half share in the matrimonial home on trust directing that while her husband:

— was alive,
— wanted to reside in the property,
— kept it in repair, and
— indemnified the trustees against rates, taxes and other outgoings,

her trustees would not:

— make any objection to such residence,
— disturb or restrict it in any way,
— take any steps to enforce the trust for sale on which the property is held,
— obtain any rent or profit from the property.

Subject to this, the property was held for her daughter absolutely.

The husband was held to have an interest in possession in the property. The terms of the gift elevated him to the status of a sole occupier of the whole property, free from the possibility of a claim that he compensate the daughter for her exclusion or that an application be made to court for sale.

In *Faulkner (Trustee of Adams, deceased) v I.R.C.* (2001) a testator directed in his will that H and his wife, W, (or the survivor of them) should be permitted to live in a house which formed part of T's estate for as long as they so wished.

The Special Commissioner agreed with the Revenue that there was an interest in possession. The will did not give any dispositive powers to the trustees to decide whether or not H and W should occupy the property. The trustees had no discretion to refuse any request by H and W that they be permitted to occupy the property. It followed that the will created a settlement in favour of H and W and that H (the survivor of the couple) had an interest in possession at the date of his death.

Co-owner in exclusive occupation

The Revenue has sometimes suggested that where one co-owner is in sole occupation, that co-owner may have an interest in possession in the whole property. In *Woodhall v CIR* (2000) such an argument failed. The testator left his house on trust for sale with a direction that the sale should be postponed so long as any of his children wished to live there. Until sale the trustees were to permit "*all or any of them to occupy*".   **7.008**

All three of the testator's children lived there for a time but two moved out in the 1950s. The third child (Eric) occupied the property until his death.

The Revenue argued that Eric had had an interest in possession in the whole. Eric's executors argued that he had not had an interest in possession at all because he had had no right to exclusive possession. The Special Commissioner found that Eric and the other surviving child each had an interest in possession, being able to claim to occupy the property jointly. The trustees could not exclude them. Eric's estate, therefore, included half of the value of the property.

Comments of Lightman J. in *I.R.C. v Eversden* (2002) suggest that Trusts of Land and Appointment of Trustees Act 1996, s.12 and s.13 may have altered the rights of co-owners.

Prior to the Act beneficial co-owners of land had a *right* of occupation pending sale. After 1997 where land is held on a trust of land, a beneficiary with an immediate interest (such as a co-owner) has a statutory right to occupy *provided* the following conditions are satisfied:

— the purposes of the trust include making land available for his occupation, and
— the land is held by the trustees so as to be available.

There is no right to occupy where the land is either unavailable or unsuitable. Thus, although a co-owner does not have an absolute right of occupation, it seems that where the conditions are fulfilled, a co-owner can insist on occupation.

Section 13 deals with the situation where two or more beneficiaries are entitled to occupy under s.12 (usually the case with co-ownership). Section 13(1) provides that in such cases *the trustees can exclude or restrict the entitlement of one or more but not all.* Any exclusion or restriction must not be unreasonable (s.13(2)).

Where trustees restrict or exclude a beneficiary's right to occupy, they can require the beneficiary in occupation to make payments to the excluded beneficiary.

However, s.13(7) provides that where a person is in occupation the trustees may not (unless the person in occupation or the court consents):

— exercise their powers so as to prevent that person from continuing to occupy the land, or
— in a manner likely to result in such a person ceasing to occupy the land.

Consider the position of a surviving spouse in continuing occupation of the matrimonial home with children as co-owners. The trustees cannot restrict his occupation. This may mean that the spouse has an interest in possession in the whole property.

Similarly if one co-owner agrees with another that one of them will have exclusive possession and the other will not receive any payment, it seems that the beneficiary in occupation has an interest in possession in the whole. The beneficiary who gave up his right to occupy may well have made a potentially exempt transfer of the value of his half share.

3. TAX ARISING ON CREATION OF SETTLEMENT WITH INTEREST IN POSSESSION

A transfer to any type of settlement is a transfer of value by the settlor. Assuming that no exemptions apply, the transfer will be either potentially exempt or chargeable.

A settlor who makes an *inter vivos* transfer to a settlement with an interest in possession on or after March 17, 1987, is treated as making a potentially exempt transfer. Thus, no inheritance tax is payable unless the settlor dies within seven years of the transfer. If the settlor does die within that period the transfer becomes chargeable at the full rates in force at the date of death (subject to the possibility of tapering relief).

Example
On November 5, 2003, S gives £265,000 to trustees to hold on trust for A for life, remainder to B. For the purposes of this example, it is assumed that no exemptions or reliefs apply. S's cumulative total is nil. S dies on February 5, 2005.

No tax is payable on creation. However, on February 5, 2004 the transfer becomes chargeable. The first £255,000 will be taxed at the nil rate; the remaining £10,000 will be taxed at 40 per cent.

As we saw above, a person with an interest in possession in settled property (for example, a life tenant) is deemed to own the trust assets beneficially. Therefore, if a settlor creates a settlement *inter vivos* in which he is the first life tenant there will be no charge to tax. This is because before the creation he *actually* owns the property beneficially; after the creation he is *deemed* to own it beneficially, so for tax purposes the value of his estate has not gone down. Similarly, if the settlor's spouse is the first life tenant, the creation of the settlement (whether *inter vivos* or on death) will not give rise to tax because the spouse exemption will apply.

If the transfer to the settlement is made on the death of the settlor the property to be transferred to the trust will be taxed as part of the settlor's death estate before being transferred to the trustees of the settlement.

A trust with an interest in possession could be used as a preliminary to the creation of a trust without an interest in possession in an attempt to avoid inheritance tax at the settlor's rates were it not for the existence of anti-avoidance provisions contained in the Finance (No. 2) Act 1987.

4. CHARGEABLE EVENTS AFTER CREATION OF SETTLEMENT WITH INTEREST IN POSSESSION

Since a person with an interest in possession is treated as owning the trust property (or a proportion of it if he is entitled to part only of the income) it follows that a termination of an interest in possession is taxable as a disposition *of the trust property* by that person. Tax may thus become chargeable: **7.009**

    (a) on the death of the person entitled to the interest;

    (b) on an actual disposal of the interest (for example, the beneficiary gives his interest away, surrenders it or sells it); or

    (c) on the termination of the interest in any other way (for example, where the interest is determinable at a particular date or on the happening of a particular event, tax will be payable on that day or when that event occurs).

Since the termination of the interest is treated as a transfer of the trust property by the person entitled to the interest, the rate of tax will depend on that person's cumulative total and on whether the termination is on death or during his lifetime.

Example
Trustees are holding a fund of £100,000 on trust for A for life remainder to B. A dies having made chargeable lifetime transfers of £130,000, all in the seven years preceding his death, and owning £150,000 worth of unsettled property on his death. The estate on death is £250,000 (*i.e.* the trust fund and the £150,000 owned by A). This is cumulated with the £130,000 chargeable lifetime transfers so the tax on the death estate of £250,000 is calculated at the rates appropriate for a transfer between £130,000 and £280,000. The tax is, therefore, £10,000 (that is £25,000 at 40 per cent). This tax will normally be paid by the trustees of the settlement and the personal representatives in the same proportions that the trust property and the unsettled property bear to the whole estate on death. In this case the trustees will pay three fifths of the tax and the personal representatives two fifths.

Where a person with an interest in possession sells his interest, tax may be payable even though the sale is for the full value of the interest. This is because the life tenant is treated as owning the trust property absolutely for inheritance tax purposes. However, for the purpose of sale a life interest is valued actuarially taking into account the age and expectation of life of the life tenant. This value will always be less than the value of the settled property itself so that there is bound to be a reduction in the value of the life tenant's estate. The reduction will be the difference between the value of the trust property and the price paid for the life interest.

Example
7.010   A is the life tenant of a trust fund worth £180,000. The actuarial value of A's life interest is £40,000 and he sells it for that amount. A is treated as making a transfer of value of £140,000. This transfer is a potentially exempt transfer. No tax is payable initially. Tax will be payable if the transferor dies within seven years.

Where an interest in possession comes to an end and at that time the life tenant becomes beneficially entitled to the trust property there is no tax to pay. This is because before the interest ends he is treated as owning the trust property, after it ends he actually owns it so that for tax purposes there is no loss to his (or anyone else's) estate.

Example
Trust property is held on trust to pay the income to A until 25 and thereafter to A absolutely. When A reaches 25, no tax will be payable.

The same rule applies where the life tenant becomes entitled to another interest in possession in the same property.

Example
Trust property is held on trust for A for 10 years and thereafter to A for life provided he is then married. If at the end of 10 years A is married, he will acquire another interest in possession so no tax will be payable.

Where an interest in possession comes to an end and the life tenant then acquires an interest in possession in part only of the trust property tax will be payable on the part in which he does not acquire a new interest in possession.

Despite the above rules there is no tax on the termination of an interest in possession if the property then reverts to the settlor during the settlor's lifetime or to the settlor's spouse during the settlor's lifetime or within two years of his death.

Example
A settles property on B for life with a reversion to the settlor. No tax is payable when the property reverts to A on B's death.
  The reverter to settlor exception can be used to achieve a tax saving on the matrimonial home.

Example
Husband (H) dies and leaves the matrimonial home, valued at £250,000, to his daughter (D) and the rest of the estate to his wife (W). There is no inheritance tax to pay.
  D settles the house on her mother for life with reversion to herself. This is a potentially exempt transfer so there will be no tax to pay provided D survives seven years. There is no inheritance tax when the property reverts to D.
  It is free of capital gains tax too but will revert at its original value unless the settlement continues in which case it reverts at market value. Thus, to get the benefit of tax free uplift on the mother's death, D should settle the property on W for life, remainder to herself for life, remainder to her children with a power to determine her own life interest and appoint the property to herself.

The exemption for reversion to the settlor does not apply where the settlor has purchased the reversion.

Example
A settles property on B for life remainder to C. If A purchases C's remainder tax will be payable on B's death even though the property then reverts to A.

Since a person with an interest in possession is deemed to own the trust property absolutely, an advance of capital by the trustees to him does not give rise to tax since he is receiving property which is already treated for the purposes of inheritance tax as his own. An advance of capital to anyone else does give rise to tax since it brings the life tenant's interest in that property to an end.

Various exemptions and reliefs are available on the termination of an interest in possession including the following:

(a) The annual exemption of £3,000 (unless already used to exempt other transfers) is available where the termination occurs *inter vivos*.

(b) The spouse exemption applies unless the spouse has acquired the reversion for money or money's worth. (For example, settlement to A for life remainder to B—no tax on A's death if A is then married to B. Settlement to A for life remainder to X; B (A's spouse) buys X's reversion and then A dies—tax will be payable.)

(c) Business and agricultural property relief.

The exemptions for small gifts and normal expenditure out of income cannot be used.

5. REVERSIONS

7.011 A reversionary interest (that is a future interest) in settled property is usually excluded property and so no tax is payable on a transfer (*inter vivos* or on death) of such an interest. This rule is really just a consequence of the fact that the person with an interest in possession is deemed to own the trust property absolutely.

Example
Property is settled on A for life remainder to B. No tax is payable on B's remainder interest if B dies or gives away his interest during A's lifetime.

To prevent tax avoidance a reversionary interest is *not* excluded property (so that tax will be payable on the death of its owner or on an *inter vivos* transfer by him) in certain special cases.

D. Inheritance Tax—Settlements with no Interest in Possession

1. INTRODUCTION

7.012 There is no interest in possession in a settlement if no individual has "a present right to present enjoyment" of the trust property (*Pearson v I.R.C.* (1980) see para.7.003 above). The most common examples of such settlements are accumulation trusts and discretionary trusts. In the case of a settlement with an interest in possession, tax is payable on the death of the life tenant and on the termination of the life interest in other ways (see paras 7.009–7.011). In the case of accumulation and discretionary settlements this type of charge cannot arise so that special rules are required to prevent tax avoidance.

Where there is an interest in possession tax is chargeable once for each individual beneficiary's period of enjoyment of the property. The rules for settlements without an interest in possession are designed to achieve the equivalent of one full tax charge every generation thus establishing rough parity of treatment with other settlements and with circumstances where the property is not settled at all.

The settlement itself is treated as a taxable entity. It has its own cumulative total. It is always taxed at lifetime rates even if the initial creation was on death. The main feature is the "periodic charge" which is charged on the tenth anniversary of the creation of the settlement. It is charged on "relevant property" defined in s.58 as settled property (other than excluded property) in which there is no qualifying interest in possession. The regime does not apply to accumulation and maintenance trusts and other specially privileged trusts which are excepted from this charging regime and have their own system of taxation.

2. IHT ARISING ON CREATION OF A SETTLEMENT WITH NO INTEREST IN POSSESSION

If the transfer is *inter vivos*, it is an immediate chargeable transfer and tax **7.013** will be charged initially at half the death rates. Tax will be charged at the full death rates if the settlor dies within seven years of the transfer, although credit is given for any tax already paid. Tapering relief will be available if the settlor survives three years from the transfer. Grossing up will be required if the settlor pays the tax.

Example
Sam transfers £100,000 to a discretionary trust on January 1, 2004. His cumulative total immediately before the transfer was £177,000. He has no annual exemptions available. The trust bears the IHT (so no grossing up is required). The tax payable by the trust will be charged at 20 per cent on the excess over the nil rate band *i.e.* on £22,000.

$$\frac{20}{100} \times 22{,}000 = £4{,}400$$

If the transfer is on death, the property is taxed as part of the death estate before being transferred to the trustees of the settlement.

There is no reduction in the amount of tax if the settlor or his spouse is one of the discretionary beneficiaries since a discretionary beneficiary has no interest in the trust property for tax purposes. Furthermore, the fact that the settlor is a beneficiary will amount to a reservation of benefit thus leading to a possible charge on his death (see para.7.021 below).

It is necessary for the trustees to know the settlor's cumulative total at the time of the transfer as it will form part of the cumulative total of the settlement for all future transfers. It is, therefore, beneficial for the future taxation of the settlement if it is created at a time when the settlor has a low cumulative total.

The settlor should avoid making other settlements on the same day (other than charitable ones) as they will be classified as "related settlements". They will be added to the value of the settlement and will increase the tax paid by the settlement.

In *Rysaffe Trust Company (CI) v I.R.C.* (2002) a settlor signed five identical discretionary settlements on the same day. His solicitors dated them on different days. He sent a cheque for £50 to his accountants who credited £10 to each settlement. At a later date he transferred five parcels of shares in the same company to the five trusts. The Revenue argued that the initial creation of the settlements and the subsequent transfers were associated operations and, therefore, there was one settlement not five separate settlements. The taxpayer appealed. However, Page J. did not accept this. As a matter of general trust law there were five separate settlements not one. Although they were initially identical, they each contained powers of appointment and powers to appoint new trustees so that eventually they might be very different. There was no need to consider associated operations because the property was already "property comprised in a settlement" within the meaning of the charging section (s.63) without need to rely on the extended definition provided by s.268. Each holding of shares was a separate item of property held by the trustees by virtue of a disposition effected by a single operation not by virtue of a disposition effected by multiple operations.

3. IHT CHARGEABLE AFTER CREATION OF SETTLEMENT WITHOUT INTEREST IN POSSESSION

7.014   After creation, there are three possible occasions of charge to IHT:

(a) when property ceases to be "relevant property" between creation and the first 10 year anniversary;
(b) on each 10 year anniversary;
(c) when property ceases to be "relevant property" between 10 year anniversaries.

(a) Property ceasing to be relevant property before the first 10 year anniversary
A charge is imposed on the value of the property ceasing to be relevant property (s.65). Property may cease to be relevant property because the trustees are appointing capital to a beneficiary or because they are creating an interest in possession in some or all of the trust property. The charge is always based on lifetime rates. The actual rate of tax charged is 30 per cent of those rates as applied to a hypothetical chargeable transfer.
   Step one is, therefore, to calculate the hypothetical chargeable transfer. It is calculated by adding together the following:

—   property in the settlement immediately after commencement;
—   value of subsequent additions (at time added);
—   value of property in a related settlement (immediately after settlement commenced).

No account is taken of any subsequent changes in value.
   Step two is to calculate the tax at lifetime rates on the hypothetical chargeable transfer by joining the table of rates at the point reached by the settlor in the seven years before the creation of the settlement. Other chargeable transfers made on the same day are ignored (s.68(4)).
   Step three is to convert that tax into an average rate (equivalent to an estate rate). 30 per cent of that average rate is then used as the basis for calculating the charge to tax. This is referred to as the "settlement rate".

Step four is to calculate what proportion of the settlement rate will be applied to the transfer. One-fortieth of the settlement rate is charged for each complete successive quarter that has elapsed from creation of the settlement to the date of the transfer. This is referred to as the "effective rate". There is no charge if property ceases to be relevant property in the first quarter.

Example (continued)
Let us assume that the trustees of the trust created by Sam appoint £30,000 to one of the discretionary beneficiaries on November 30, 2005.   **7.015**

Step 1: Find value of hypothetical transfer
In our example the value of the hypothetical transfer is £100,000.

Step 2: Calculate tax at half rates on hypothetical transfer
In our example the settlor's cumulative total was £177,000 at the time the settlement was created leaving £78,000 of the nil rate band available. Tax will be charged at 0 per cent on the first £78,000 and 20 per cent on the last £22,000 *i.e.* £4,400.

Step 3: Convert the tax to an average rate and then take 30 per cent which will be the "settlement rate"

$$\frac{\text{Tax}}{\text{Value of Settlement}} \times 100 = \text{Average Rate}$$

$$\frac{£4,400}{£100,000} \times 100 = 4.4\%$$

Settlement rate is 30 per cent of 4.4 per cent, *i.e.* 1.32 per cent.

Step 4: Calculate the "effective" rate by reference to the number of quarters completed since the settlement was created
In our example there are seven completed quarters since the date the settlement was created so we take 7/40 of the settlement rate of 1.32 per cent and apply this to the fall in value of the trust property.

$$\frac{7}{40} \times \frac{1.32}{100} \times 30,000 = £69.30$$

If the tax comes from the trust fund the transfer will have to be grossed up.

(b) The first 10 year anniversary
Tax is charged on the value of the relevant property in the settlement immediately before the first ten year anniversary (s.64). Income only becomes relevant property where it has been accumulated (see SP8/86). Accumulation occurs when the trustees take an irrevocable decision to accumulate it although it can also occur after the expiry of a reasonable time.   **7.016**

Again step one is to calculate the value of a hypothetical chargeable transfer. It is calculated by adding together the following:

— current value of relevant property (this does not include income unless formally accumulated) in settlement immediately after

commencement;
— value of property in a related settlement (immediately after settlement commenced);
— value at the date the settlement commenced of any other property in the settlement which has not subsequently become relevant property.

Normally there will only be property in category one. The other two categories are anti-avoidance measures. Related settlements are included because transfers made on the same day are otherwise ignored and without this provision the settlor could save tax by setting up a number of small settlements instead of one large one. Non-relevant property is included to prevent the trustees switching value between relevant and non-relevant property.

Step two is to calculate the tax at lifetime rates on the hypothetical chargeable transfer by joining the table of rates at the point reached:

— by the settlor in the seven years before the creation of the settlement; plus
— any chargeable transfers made from the settlement in the first ten years.

Step three is to convert that tax into an average rate and to take 30 per cent of that average rate as the "settlement rate" to be applied to the relevant property in the settlement. As the highest rate of tax at lifetime rates is 20 per cent, the highest possible settlement rate is 30 per cent of that which is 6 per cent. It will be even lower if any of the trust property is eligible for business or agricultural property relief.

Example (continued)
Assume the assets remaining in the trust fund are worth £90,000 on January 1, 2014.

Step 1: Find value of hypothetical transfer
In our example the current value of relevant property is £90,000.

Step 2: Calculate tax at half rates on hypothetical transfer
In our example the settlor's cumulative total was £177,000 and £30,000 was appointed from the settlement so transfers to be taken into account are £207,000 leaving £48,000 of the nil rate band available. Tax will be at 0 per cent on the first £48,000 and 20 per cent on the last £42,000, *i.e.* £8,400.

Step 3: Convert the tax to an average rate and then take 30 per cent which will be the "settlement rate"

$$\frac{\text{Tax}}{\text{Value of Settlement}} \times 100 = \text{Average Rate}$$

$$\frac{£8,400}{£90,000} \times 100 = 9.333\%$$

Settlement Rate is 30 per cent of 9.333 per cent, *i.e.* 2.8 per cent.

Step 4: The settlement rate is applied to the property to be taxed to produce the tax payable

$$\frac{2.8}{100} \times £90,000 = £2,520$$

(c) Property ceasing to be relevant property between 10 year anniversaries
Tax is charged on the property ceasing to be relevant property. The rate of tax is a proportion of the effective rate charged at the first ten year anniversary. The proportion is one-fortieth for each complete successive quarter that has elapsed from the date of the first anniversary to the date of the transfer. There is no charge if property ceases to be relevant property in the first quarter.   **7.017**

Example (continued)
Assume the trustees appoint £20,000 to a discretionary beneficiary on November 15, 2015.

Step 1: Calculate the property ceasing to be relevant property
In our example the fall is £20,000.

Step 2: Calculate the effective rate by reference to the quarters completed since the previous anniversary
There are 11 completed quarters since the last 10 year anniversary so take 11/40 of the settlement rate (2.8 per cent) and apply this to the fall in value of the trust property.

$$\frac{11}{40} \times \frac{2.8}{100} \times £20,000 = £154$$

If the tax comes from the trust fund the transfer will have to be grossed up.

(d) Subsequent ten year anniversaries
The charge is calculated in the same way that it was calculated on the first ten year anniversary.   **7.018**

4. POINTS TO BE AWARE OF IN CONNECTION WITH THE TAXATION OF SETTLEMENTS WITHOUT AN INTEREST IN POSSESSION

Timing of appointments of capital
It will normally be preferable for trustees to appoint capital out of a trust immediately before an anniversary rather than immediately after one. This is because the charge to tax will then be calculated on the value of the trust property when the trust was created or on the previous anniversary rather than on its current value.   **7.019**

Example
Harry dies on May 30, 2003 with a nil cumulative total. He leaves a nil rate band legacy (£255,000) on discretionary trusts for his children and the residue to his wife.
   There is no inheritance tax on his death. By April 2013 the trust fund is worth £500,000. The trustees can appoint the whole of the fund to the children and there will be no inheritance tax liability.

If they wait until June to make the appointment, tax will be calculated on the new value of the fund so there will be a tax liability.

Additions of property to the settlement by the settlor

7.020 If the settlor adds property to the settlement by means of a chargeable transfer special rules apply (s.67(1)). The special rules do not apply where the transfer is exempt, for example because it is covered by the annual exemption.

Where the rules apply, the calculation of the periodic charge following the addition will be modified. When calculating the tax on the hypothetical chargeable transfer the settlor's cumulative total will be taken as the higher of the totals:

— immediately before creating the settlement plus transfers made by the settlement before the addition; and
— immediately before transferring the added property deducting from this latter total the transfer made on creation of the settlement and a transfer to any related settlement.

Whenever the modification would result in higher rates of tax, it will be preferable for the settlor to avoid adding property to the settlement and instead to create a new settlement.

Additional property added by persons other than the settlor will be treated as creating a separate settlement.

Reservation of benefit

7.021 Where a settlor creates a settlement without an interest in possession he may be a beneficiary of the settlement (*e.g.* he is one of the objects of a discretionary trust). In this case he has made a gift "subject to a reservation" and tax may, therefore, be payable *on his death* in respect of that property unless he has been excluded from benefit for seven years before he dies. See *I.R.C. v Eversden* (2002).

5. ANTI-AVOIDANCE PROVISIONS

7.022 A transfer to a discretionary trust is a chargeable transfer attracting inheritance tax at half the full rate. A transfer to a settlement with an interest in possession is a potentially exempt transfer and a transfer from such a settlement will be treated as a transfer by the person with an interest in possession, any tax payable being calculated by reference to his cumulative total and not to the original settlor's cumulative total.

Prima facie, it would seem possible for a person with a high cumulative total who wishes to transfer property to a discretionary trust to make use of a short-term interest in possession trust to save inheritance tax. The settlor would transfer the property to a trust in which a person with a low cumulative total would have an interest in possession for a short time. This would be a potentially exempt transfer. The property would then pass to a trust without an interest in possession. This would be a chargeable transfer, but the inheritance tax would be assessed by reference to the cumulative total of the person with the interest in possession.

To prevent the avoidance of tax by such means the Finance (No. 2) Act 1987 contains provisions designed to ensure that a transfer to a discretionary trust following a transfer to a trust with an interest in possession can be taxed by reference to the cumulative total of the original settlor where certain conditions are fulfilled.

6. ACCUMULATION AND MAINTENANCE SETTLEMENTS

Introduction

Where settled property is held in an accumulation and maintenance 7.023 settlement (as defined by s.71 of the Inheritance Tax Act 1984) special tax rules apply which are more favourable than the rules for settlements with or without an interest in possession. The object of the rules is to enable a settlor to give property without any tax penalty to young people with conditions attached which prevent them having access to income and/or capital at too young an age. The charges to tax on tenth anniversaries and on property leaving the settlement do not apply. The creation of an accumulation and maintenance settlement *inter vivos* is a potentially exempt transfer.

Definition

The accumulation and maintenance settlement rules apply to settled 7.024 property if four requirements (laid down in s.71 of the Inheritance Tax Act 1984) are satisfied:

(a) one or more persons will, on or before attaining a specified age not exceeding 25, become beneficially entitled to it or to an interest in possession in it; and
(b) no interest in possession subsists in it; and
(c) the income from it is to be accumulated so far as not applied for the maintenance, education or benefit of a beneficiary (*i.e.* one of the persons who will become entitled at 25 or a lower age); and
(d) *either*
    (i) not more than 25 years have elapsed since the beginning of the settlement (or later time when it satisfied the three requirements above); *or*
    (ii) all the beneficiaries had a common grandparent (or are the children, widows or widowers of the original beneficiaries who die before achieving the specified age).

We will consider each of the requirements in turn.

(a) *Entitlement at 25 or some lower specified age.* A settlement only satisfies this requirement if the beneficiaries *will* be entitled at 25 or some lower specified age. It is not sufficient that a beneficiary *may* be entitled at 25 or some lower specified age. Thus a settlement which gives "capital and income at 25 or on earlier marriage" satisfies the requirement since the beneficiary will get the property at 25 at the latest. A settlement which gives "capital and income on marriage or at 25 whichever is the later" does not satisfy the requirement.

It is impossible to have absolute certainty. Death can always prevent a beneficiary becoming entitled.

It is not necessary that the beneficiaries obtain a vested interest in *capital* at the specified age. It is sufficient that they acquire an interest in possession in the settlement, that is a right to income as it arises. Thus a settlement which requires income to be accumulated until 25 and then gives the income to the beneficiary is sufficient even if capital is never to vest in that beneficiary.

Section 31 of the Trustee Act 1925 gives the right to receive income to a beneficiary on reaching 18 where the vesting of capital is contingent on reaching a greater age or fulfilling some other contingency. Thus a settlement which gives capital to A at 30 (or any other age) satisfies this condition as long as s.31 has not been excluded since the right to income will then vest at 18.

Section 71 of the Inheritance Tax Act requires that an age of 25 or lower be "specified". It might be argued that where a beneficiary acquires a right to income at 18 under s.31 no age has been *specified*. However, the Revenue has stated that it regards the entitlement to income at 18 under s.31 as satisfying this requirement.

The requirement is that "one or more persons" will be entitled at a specified age. The "persons" can include unborn persons but s.71(7) of the Inheritance Tax Act 1984 provides that the condition is not satisfied "unless there is or has been a living beneficiary". Thus a settlement on "the children of A at 25" is not an accumulation and maintenance settlement if A is childless when the settlement is created (it will become one when A's first child is born). If the settlement were to the children of A and A had a child living at the time the settlement was made the settlement would remain an accumulation and maintenance settlement even if that child were to die since there would then "have been" a living beneficiary.

7.025   The possibility that trust funds may go to someone who does not qualify as a beneficiary of the accumulation and maintenance trust is usually fatal to accumulation and maintenance status. Thus, it is necessary to draft trusts carefully and to take particular care not to include powers of advancement and appointment which, if exercised, could result in entitlement being postponed beyond 25 or in property passing to non-qualifying beneficiaries. In some cases the mere existence of a power will compromise a trust's privileged status even if there is never any exercise of the power.

Thus, the mere *existence* of a power of appointment which will enable trustees to pay capital or income to non-qualifying beneficiaries will cause loss of accumulation and maintenance status.

Example

A trust is set up for the benefit of A's children contingent on them reaching 25 but there is power for the trustees to appoint capital or income to A's brother (who is now 26). The trust will not qualify for privileged status as there is no certainty that A's children will become entitled.

There would be no problem if the trustees had an overriding power to appoint capital or income amongst A's children as they saw fit while the children were under 25. The power does not infringe the s.71

requirement. It cannot be used to benefit anyone other than the class members and cannot postpone their entitlement.

To avoid the danger of trusts losing privileged status by oversight it is desirable to include a direction that no power shall be exercised in such a way as to prevent the trust qualifying as an accumulation and maintenance trust or to direct that appointments and advances shall not be made to any possible beneficiary who is 25 or older.

In *Lord Inglewood v I.R.C.* (1983) it was accepted that the mere *existence* in a trust of a common form power of advancement does not compromise the privileged status of a trust even though it could be used to postpone the vesting of property in a beneficiary beyond the age of 25. However, the *exercise* of such powers inappropriately may do so.

For the avoidance of doubt the Revenue confirmed ([1996] *Private Client Business* 76) that the payment by trustees of an accumulation and maintenance trust of trust funds direct to a school in payment of school fees will not compromise the privileged status of a trust.

(b) *No interest in possession.* Once there is an interest in possession in settled property it ceases to be subject to the rules for an accumulation and maintenance settlement. However, where there is more than one beneficiary each part of the settled property must be considered separately.

Example
A settlement is made for "such of the children of A as reach 25"; when the settlement is created A has been dead for some time and has two children, B aged 10 and C aged 16. The whole of the settled property will be subject to the rules for an accumulation and maintenance settlement for two years. When C reaches 18, he becomes entitled to half the income under s.31 of the Trustee Act 1925 and, therefore, obtains an interest in possesion in half the settled property. The other half of the property remains subject to the rules for accumulation and maintenance settlements. If C dies two years later there will be tax to pay on his half share (since he had an interest in possession); after his death the whole settled property will be subject to the accumulation and maintenance rules for a further four years until B obtains an interest in possession at 18.

(c) *Income to be accumulated so far as not applied for maintenance, etc.* The income must be either accumulated or used for the maintenance, **7.026** education or benefit *of the beneficiaries* (*i.e.* the persons who will be entitled at 25 or some lower age).

This requirement will not be satisfied if the trustees are given power to apply the income for other purposes (such as maintenance of persons other than the beneficiaries as defined).

The inclusion of a direction to accumulate for a period which would run beyond a beneficiary's 25th birthday would be fatal. For example a direction to accumulate for 21 years where a beneficiary is more than four years old.

(d) *Common grandparent or less than 25 years since settlement became an accumulation and maintenance settlement.* This requirement is satisfied where all the beneficiaries are children of the same person or grandchildren of the same person. The common grandparent need not be the settlor.

This requirement is also satisfied where the settlement provides for the replacement of beneficiaries who have a common grandparent but die before obtaining a vested right to capital or an interest in possession by their own children, widows or widowers.

Example
A settlement "to the children of A equally at 25 or if any of them shall die before that age such deceased child's share shall go to the children of such deceased child at 25" will be an accumulation and maintenance settlement.

Where the settlement is not on persons with a common grandparent it will only be an accumulation and maintenance settlement for 25 years. Since (as we shall see in para.7.028) adverse tax consequences will then apply, it is important in such a case to ensure that all property ceases to be subject to the rules for an accumulation and maintenance settlement within 25 years. If the settlement is on named persons this requirement cannot cause any additional problem (because they must achieve the specified age within 25 years to satisfy requirement (a) above).

Tax consequences
7.027   As stated above the lifetime creation of an accumulation and maintenance settlement is a potentially exempt transfer (see Chapter 4, para.4.002). Thus tax will only be payable where the settlement is created by will or as a result of the intestacy rules or where the settlor dies within seven years of creation. After the creation of the settlement there is no charge to tax on each tenth anniversary, nor on the death of a beneficiary before he acquires an interest in possession, nor on an advance of capital or income to a beneficiary, nor on a beneficiary becoming entitled to an interest in possession or an interest in capital. This usually means that there is no charge to tax other than on the creation of the settlement until after the property ceased to be settled (*i.e.* until the beneficiary gives the property away or dies after acquiring a vested interest in it).

However, tax will become payable at the end of 25 years if the settlement is still an accumulation and maintenance settlement and the beneficiaries did not have a common grandparent. Where tax does become payable the rate is dependent solely on the length of time the property has been in the settlement and is usually much higher than the rate for other settlements with or without an interest in possession.

The main advantages of an accumulation and maintenance settlement are that there is no initial charge if the settlement is created *inter vivos*, no periodic charges during the lifetime of the settlement and usually no charge when property leaves the settlement. In the case of other settlements without an interest in possession there is a charge on creation, on each tenth anniversary and when property leaves the settlement.

E. Inheritance Tax and Trustee Act 1925, s.31

Section 31 (see Chapter 11 for a full discussion) provides that where there is income available to an infant (whether he has a vested or a contingent interest) the trustees of the trust may at their sole discretion apply the whole or part of such income for or towards the infant's maintenance, education or benefit and to the extent that they do not they must accumulate the whole or part of such income. If, after reaching the age of 18, the beneficiary has not attained a vested interest in such income the trustees *shall* thereafter pay the income (together with any income produced by investments bought with accumulated income) to the beneficiary until the beneficiary either attains a vested interest or dies or until his interest fails. Section 31 is not part of the inheritance tax legislation. However, as seen above, the effect of the section on dispositions of property has considerable tax consequences. **7.028**

Where a gift is contingent (for example on the beneficiary reaching a certain age) the contingent beneficiary is entitled to income under s.31 if 18 or over. This means that such a beneficiary has an interest in possession for inheritance tax purposes. The death of such a beneficiary when an adult will, therefore, give rise to a charge to inheritance tax even though the contingency has not been satisfied.

Where a gift is contingent and there is a living beneficiary who is an infant the trustees have a discretion to use income for the maintenance, education and benefit of the beneficiary. There will, therefore, be a settlement without an interest in possession for inheritance tax purposes. The rules for accumulation and maintenance settlements will apply provided the infant will be entitled to capital or income at an age of 25 or less (he will be entitled to income at 18 unless the will has expressly excluded that right).

Where an infant is given a life interest the trustees have a discretion to use income for his maintenance, education and benefit. Any income not so used is accumulated, if the infant dies under 18 accumulated income is added to capital and devolves with capital. The infant does not, therefore, have an interest in possession until he reaches 18 and until that time the settlement will be an accumulation and maintenance settlement.

F. Settlements and Capital Gains Tax

1. Introduction

The basic structure of capital gains tax was explained in Chapter 5. In this section we will consider the possible liability to capital gains tax, in relation to disposals of trust assets or interests in a trust, of: **7.029**

(a) the settlor,
(b) the trustees,
(c) the beneficiaries.

The Capital Gains Tax legislation draws distinctions between settlements which are UK resident and those which are non-resident. In this book, we will only consider the rules applicable to the former.

2. DEFINITION OF SETTLEMENT FOR CAPITAL GAINS TAX PURPOSES

7.030 "Settled property" is defined, by Taxation of Chargeable Gains Act 1992, s.68, as any property held on trust other than property to which Capital Gains Tax Act, s.60, applies.

The property excluded from the definition of settled property by s.60 is assets held by a person:

(a) As nominee for another person; or
(b) As trustee for another person absolutely entitled as against the trustee. Such a bare trust often arises where property has been held on trust for a life tenant who has recently died and the trustees are holding the property while arranging to vest it in the remainderman. Another example of such a bare trust is where the trustees are preparing to transfer the assets to a beneficiary who has satisfied a contingency. The test for deciding whether a person is absolutely entitled as against the trustees is whether he has the exclusive right (subject only to paying the expenses of the trust) to direct how those assets shall be dealt with (s.60(2)). The beneficiary must, therefore, have the right to demand that the assets be handed over to him; or
(c) As a trustee for any person who would be so entitled but for being an infant or other person under disability. Thus, where land has been left to an infant, since an infant cannot hold a legal estate in land, trustees will have to hold the property until the child reaches 18. If he must satisfy a contingency (such as reaching 18) before he can become absolutely entitled to the property the exception does not apply (*Tomlinson v Glyn's Executor and Trustee Co.* (1970)).

Where the "trust" falls within one of the s.60(1) exceptions, the Taxation of Chargeable Gains Act applies as if the property were vested in the beneficiary and any acts of the nominee or trustee are treated as acts of the beneficiary. Thus, for example, when the trustees transfer assets to the remainderman after the death of the life tenant, no capital gains tax liability can arise.

Property held by two or more persons as joint tenants or tenants in common is not "settled property" provided they are together absolutely entitled to the property.

Trustees of settlements normally pay capital gains tax at a rate equivalent to the basic rate of income tax (in tax year 2003/04 this is

22 per cent). In the case of settlements under which income is to be accumulated or paid at the discretion of any person, the trustees pay capital gains tax at 34 per cent. This 34 per cent rate is payable on all trust gains whenever any part of the trust income for the year of assessment is liable to the additional rate of income tax. Where the settlor or spouse retain an interest in the settlement, gains are charged at the rates appropriate to the settlor (see below).

G. Capital Gains Tax Liability of the Settlor

1. CREATING THE SETTLEMENT INTER VIVOS

If the settlor transfers assets to trustees (whatever the terms of the settlement), this is a disposal. The gain or loss will be calculated in the normal way by deducting from the market value of the assets at the time of disposal, the deductions permitted by the Act, and any taper relief available (see para.5.006). The trustees will in turn acquire the assets at market value at the date of the disposal unless hold-over relief is claimed.   **7.031**

In certain cases hold-over relief may be claimed so that no immediate charge to capital gains tax arises (see para.5.014). Hold-over relief is available where the assets put into settlement are business assets. It is also available, regardless of the nature of the assets which are settled, where the creation of the settlement is a chargeable transfer for inheritance tax purposes but not where it is an exempt or potentially exempt transfer. This means that hold-over relief is available on the creation of a no interest in possession settlement. Where hold-over relief is available because there is a chargeable transfer, the settlor makes the election for relief, the trustees of the settlement are not required to agree.

Should the disposal give rise to a loss, that loss can only be set against gains made by the settlor on other transfers to trustees of the same settlement since settlors and their trustees are "connected persons" (Taxation of Chargeable Gains Act 1992, ss.18(3) and 286).

The potential liability to capital gains tax can arise even if the settlor has an interest as a beneficiary or is a trustee, or is the sole trustee, of the settlement (Taxation of Chargeable Gains Act, s.70).

Section 77 of the 1992 Act provides that where a settlor or his spouse has any interest in a settlement (for example, as a life tenant or as a beneficiary of a discretionary trust) gains of the settlement will be charged as gains of the settlor personally and not of the trustees. The settlor has a right to recover the tax paid from the trustees.

2. CREATING THE SETTLEMENT ON DEATH

If the settlement is created on death there will be no disposal and so no capital gains tax liability will arise. The deceased settlor's personal representatives will acquire the assets at their market value at death. This will also be the acquisition price of the trustees.   **7.032**

H. Capital Gains Tax—The Liability of the Trustees

1. CHANGES IN TRUSTEES

7.033   During the "life" of the settlement the persons holding office as trustees may change, whether by reason of death, retirement or removal. Whenever a new trustee is appointed the assets will have to be transferred to the newly constituted body of trustees. Section 69(1) of the Taxation of Chargeable Gains Act provides that settlement trustees are a continuing body of persons and disposals to the new trustees do not give rise to capital gains tax liability.

2. ACTUAL DISPOSALS

7.034   The trustees may wish to dispose of items of trust property and replace them with new items. They may wish to sell assets to raise cash, whether to meet expenses or to be able to make a cash advance to a beneficiary. Whatever the reason for the disposal, if the trustees make an actual disposal of trust property they may become liable to capital gains tax.

Whether a gain or loss arises will be determined in the usual way. The taper relief is available to trustees.

The trustees can set the exemptions and reliefs they are entitled to claim against any chargeable gains realised. The exemptions and reliefs to which they are entitled include:

(a) The annual exemption which is normally half the exempt amount available to an individual (so that trustees in tax year 2003/04 get £3,950). However, if the settlement is one of a number created by the same settlor the trustees of each settlement can claim one-tenth of the exempt amount available to an individual (so that such trustees in tax year 2003/04 will get £395) or, the annual exempt amount available to an individual (in tax year 2003/04 £7,900) divided by the number of trusts in the group, whichever is the greater.

(b) The principal private dwelling-house exemption given in the Taxation of Chargeable Gains Act 1992, ss.222, 223, provided the house disposed of has been the only or main residence of a person entitled to occupy it under the terms of the settlement (s.225). Therefore, provided the trustees have been given a power to permit the beneficiary to occupy the house the exemption will apply, whether the beneficiary is a life tenant or the beneficiary under a discretionary trust (*Sansom v Peay* (1976)).

(c) "Retirement" relief was available to trustees (under s.164(3) of the 1992 Act) until the end of tax year 2002/03 on the disposal of shares in a company or assets used in a business which form part of the settled property. However, this relief is only available:

(i) if there is a beneficiary with an interest in possession in the settlement who is at least 50 (or is retiring on the grounds of ill health) and

   (ii) *either* the shares are in a company which has been his family company for at least a year and of which he has been a working director for at least a year but he has now ceased to be a director

     or the assets have been used for at least a year by the beneficiary in his business.

(d) taper relief available in the normal way.

If a disposal gives rise to a loss the trustees may set that loss against any gains they have made in the year of disposal and may carry forward unabsorbed losses to set against gains made in future years.

3. DEEMED DISPOSALS

Persons becoming absolutely entitled as against the trustees

Where a person becomes absolutely entitled to trust property as against the trustees, the Taxation of Chargeable Gains Act, s.71(1), provides that "all assets forming part of the settled property to which he becomes so entitled shall be deemed to have been disposed of by the trustee, and immediately reacquired by him in his capacity as a trustee within section 60(1) ... , for a consideration equal to their market value". Any capital gains tax payable is assessed at this point and thereafter the trustee holds as a bare trustee.   **7.035**

Section 71(1) applies where:

(a) the trustees advance assets (other than cash) to a beneficiary (where he is a life tenant or a discretionary beneficiary); *or*

(b) a beneficiary satisfies a contingency and so becomes entitled to all or part of the trust property; *or*

(c) the settlement comes to an end as a result of the death of the life tenant and the remainderman becomes absolutely entitled to the property. (However, no tax is payable in this circumstance: see below, para.7.036.)

The deemed disposal and reacquisition takes place as soon as the beneficiary becomes absolutely entitled as against the trustees, even though the assets may not be transferred for some time afterwards. Thus, if a person is entitled to property provided he reached the age of 25, on his 25th birthday the trustees are deemed to dispose of the assets as settlement trustees and immediately to reacquire them as bare trustees for the beneficiary. Capital gains tax will be payable if a gain has arisen after taking account of exemptions, reliefs and allowances but there is no further liability when the assets are subsequently vested in the beneficiary.

Hold-over relief is available in certain circumstances when a beneficiary becomes absolutely entitled as against the trustees. If the settlement is an accumulation and maintenance settlement at the date the beneficiary becomes absolutely entitled, hold-over relief can be claimed by a joint election of trustees and beneficiary. The relief is also available on a joint election by trustees and beneficiary where there is a transfer by the trustees which is chargeable to inheritance tax; for example, an appointment of assets from a discretionary trust.

When a remainderman becomes absolutely entitled to the settled property following the death of the life tenant there is, again, a deemed disposal and reacquisition but no chargeable gain arises (s.73(1)(a)). This is in accordance with the general principle that death does not give rise to capital gains tax and so the remainderman has the benefit of a tax-free uplift in the base value of the settled property.

If the trustees have accrued losses from earlier transactions that they have been unable to set off against chargeable gains, s.71(2) provides that those losses are to be treated as if they accrued to the person becoming absolutely entitled, and not to the trustees.

In *Figg v Clark (I.O.T.)* there was a trust for the children of X who reached 21. In 1964 X had been paralysed from the chest down and was, therefore, incapable of fathering any more children. It was argued that the class closed at that point rather than on X's death. The court held that this was not so and that the class remained open until X's death. It would be unworkable to have to enquire into the exact date on which a person became incapable of fathering children. Consequently there is a presumption that persons remain capable of having a child until they die.

Death of the life tenant where the settlement continues

7.036 By s.72(1) of the Taxation of Chargeable Gains Act when a life interest in settled property (that continues to be settled after the death) comes to an end on the death of the life tenant, there is a deemed disposal and reacquisition at market value of the assets but no chargeable gain accrues on the disposal (subject to tax becoming payable on gains held-over when assets were transferred to the trustees).

Thus, if property is held on trust for persons in succession, for example "to A for life, remainder to B for life, remainder to C absolutely", on A's death there is a deemed disposal and reacquisition. However, no tax is payable on accrued gains unless gains were held-over when the trustees were originally given the assets. The trustees acquire the assets as trustees for B at the market value at the date of A's death. On B's death, the settlement comes to an end and C becomes absolutely entitled to the assets so that the provisions outlined in para.7.035 will apply.

I. Capital Gains Tax—The Liability of Beneficiaries

7.037 If a beneficiary is entitled to an interest in settled property, no chargeable gain arises on the disposal of the interest unless it was acquired by the beneficiary (or a predecessor in title) for consideration in money or money's worth, other than consideration consisting of another interest under the settlement (s.76(1)). Thus, if a life tenant sells his interest, no gain arises but the purchaser may face a tax liability on any subsequent disposal.

If the beneficiary is entitled under one of the types of trusts within s.60

of the Taxation of Chargeable Gains Act 1992 (*i.e.* broadly speaking where he is the beneficiary of a bare trust—see above, para.7.031), he is treated as if the assets were vested in him and so any disposals made by the trustees are taxed as if the beneficiary had disposed of the property. This means that the normal rules for calculating capital gains tax liability will apply and exemptions, reliefs and allowances the beneficiary is personally able to claim will be available; losses realised by the trustees can be used by the beneficiary (s.71(2)). Furthermore if the disposal by the trustees is to the beneficiary himself there is no capital gains tax liability.

J. Settlements and Income Tax—Introduction

In Chapter 6 we considered the general rules for the taxation of income and the particular rules that apply when a person dies. We saw that it is the personal representatives' responsibility to pay any outstanding income tax liability of the deceased and to pay tax on income that arises in the course of administering the estate. Once the administration period is complete the personal representatives' liability ceases. **7.038**

If the beneficiaries have absolute interests in the residue, the capital of the residue will be transferred to them (see para.6.021 for the income tax rules applying in these circumstances). However, if the will creates any type of trust which is to continue after the administration period the property will be vested in trustees and special tax rules will apply.

Will trusts are basically taxed in the same way as other trusts but since the settlor is dead when the trust becomes operative, the special anti-avoidance provisions relating to settlements contained in ss.660–694 of the Taxes Act 1988 (the "income deemed"provisions) cannot apply.

Trust income is taxed in two stages. The trustees are liable to tax on all the income of the trust (the rate depends on the type of trust). Beneficiaries who are entitled to income or who receive income from the trust are then assessed to tax. They may be charged further tax or have tax refunded to them, depending on their particular circumstances.

K. Income Tax—the Liability of the Trustees

The statutory income of trustees is calculated in the same way as for an individual by applying the rules of the various Schedules in the Taxes Act 1988. In calculating this figure, the trustees may deduct the expenses permitted by the appropriate Schedule. **7.039**

Thus, if the trustees are carrying on a trade, the income derived from the trade is assessed in accordance with the provisions of Sch.D, Case I of the 1970 Act and they can deduct allowable business expenses. However, they cannot deduct the expenses of managing the trust itself (*Aikin v MacDonald's Trustees* (1894)).

Having calculated the income of the trust the trustees are liable, provided the trust is not a discretionary or accumulation trust, to pay income tax at the basic rate on *all* of the rest of the income without the deduction of any personal reliefs (which are only available to "individuals" and for these purposes trustees are not "individuals"). Where the trustees receive dividends, the 10 per cent tax credit is treated as satisfying their liability to pay basic rate tax. Trustees are not liable to higher rate tax regardless of the amount of the income. If trustees make a payment which is income in the hands of the beneficiary, they will have to pay basic rate tax on it even though it is paid out of capital (Taxes Act 1988, s.349, and see para.7.044).

If income is paid directly to the beneficiary from its source, it is taxed in the hands of the beneficiary without the trustees paying tax (such a situation would arise where, for example, trustees ask a tenant of land owned by the trust to pay the rent to the beneficiary). If the trustees receive income net of tax, the tax credit will satisfy their liability to tax.

Section 686 of the Taxes Act 1988 requires the trustees of certain trusts (broadly discretionary or accumulation trusts) to pay a special trusts' rate of 34 per cent (Taxes Act, s.686(1A)) with the exception of the tax on dividends they receive. The rate is reduced to 25 per cent on dividend income. See para.7.041 below.

Thus, a trust which receives savings income will receive it net of 20 per cent tax; the trustees will then have to pay a further 14 per cent on the grossed up income.

The trusts' rate is paid on income which:

(a) is to be accumulated or which is payable at the discretion of the trustees or any other person;

(b) is not *before distribution* the income of any person other than the trustees not treated as income of the settlor;

   (The wording means that the trusts' rate does not apply where a beneficiary has a vested interest in income, *e.g.* a life tenant.

   Nor will it apply where income is deemed to be that of another person, *e.g.* the settlor. However, the income must be of that other person *before distribution*. Thus where income is treated as that of the settlor *if* it is paid to his infant unmarried child, the income is not income of the settlor before distribution and will attract the trusts' rate of tax);

(c) is not income of a charitable trust;

(d) exceeds the income applied in defraying the expenses of the trustees in that year which are properly chargeable to income (or would be so chargeable but for any express provisions of the trust).

The trusts' rate will, thus, be payable on income of a settlement which is treated as an accumulation and maintenance settlement for inheritance tax purposes (see above, para.7.013). It will also apply to most settlements which are treated as settlements without an interest in possession for inheritance tax purposes.

It should be noted that for the purposes of calculating liability to the trusts' rate the trustees deduct the trust expenses "properly" chargeable to income grossed up (at basic rate or lower rate) from the trust income.

The reason for this is that the trusts' rate is only chargeable on income which can be accumulated (and is not the income of any person other than the trustees). The income which can be accumulated is the trust income *after* the trust expenses have been paid. The expenses are grossed up at basic or lower rate to reflect the fact that they were paid from taxed income. Expenses "properly" chargeable to income are those so chargeable as a matter of general law not those made chargeable to income by the trust instrument (*Carver v Duncan* (1985)).

Example

A discretionary trust has £10,000 of income and £780 of expenses. Tax is **7.040** calculated as follows.

The trust expenses of £780 are grossed up at 22 per cent

$$780 \times \frac{100}{78} = 1,000$$

The 34 per cent trusts' rate is charged on the balance of the trust income.

$$9,000 \times \frac{34}{100} = 3,060$$

After payment of the expenses of £780 the basic rate tax of £220 attributable to them and the trusts' rate tax of £3,060 there is trust income of £5,940 remaining in the trustees' hands.

The trusts' rate is applied to "income". There is no provision requiring the rate to be applied to capital sums which are deemed to be income (*e.g.* to sums received on company buy backs).

When the trustees of such a trust make a payment to a beneficiary, they pay it net of the trusts' rate of tax. Therefore, the beneficiary will receive a tax credit of 34 per cent.

The application of these rules can be seen in the following example.

Example

The trustees carry on a trade and make a net profit of £20,000 after deduction of allowable expenses. They incur £780 expenses in the course of managing the trust.

(a) *If the trusts' rate is not payable.* The trustees pay basic rate tax (22 per cent) on the trust income of £20,000 (this amounts to £4,400). From their net income of £15,600 they will pay the expenses of £780 leaving £14,820 net income available for the beneficiaries.

Note:

The £780 of trust expenses have been paid from taxed income and have therefore "cost" £1,000. The beneficiary receives the amount of trust income left after payment of tax and expenses £14,820. The beneficiary must gross up this receipt at 22 per cent.

$$i.e. \text{ £14,820} \times \frac{100}{78} = \text{£19,000}$$

He will receive a certificate of deduction of tax and a tax credit for the basic rate tax on £19,000. He does not receive any tax credit for the tax paid by the trustees on the income used to pay the trust expenses and has no tax liability for that portion of trust income.

(b) *If the trusts' rate is payable.* The trustees' liability is calculated as follows:

	£	£
Trust Income		20,000
Less: Trust expenses grossed up		
$i.e. \text{ £780} \times \frac{100}{78} =$		(1,000)
Income liable to trusts' rate		19,000
Trusts' rate tax (£19,000 × 34%)		6,460

The income available to beneficiaries will be:—

	£	£
Trust Income		20,000
Less: Income tax (a) basic rate	(220)	
(b) trusts' rate	(6,460)	
		(6,680)
Income after tax		13,320
Less: expenses paid		(780)
Net available income		12,540

Note:
If the trustees pay to or apply any of the net available income for a beneficiary they must supply a certificate of deduction of income tax to that beneficiary. When calculating his statutory income the beneficiary will gross up any amounts received at 34 per cent. In the above example if the whole of the available income of £12,540 was applied to one beneficiary that beneficiary would include in his statutory income £12,540 grossed up to £19,000. He does not receive any tax credit for the tax paid by the trustees on the income used to pay the trust expenses and has no tax liability for that portion of trust income.

Dividends and the trusts' rate

7.041   From April 6, 1999, dividends are paid with a tax credit of 10 per cent. To make sure the tax liability on dividends of the same amount suffered by trusts attracting the trusts' rate did not increase as a result, the rate of tax on dividends received by such trusts was reduced to 25 per cent.

The reason for the reduction of the trusts' rate in these circumstances is best explained by a simple illustration. Prior to April 1999, if trustees received a dividend of £400, they needed to gross it up at the then applicable rate of 20 per cent—to £500. They would then pay 34 per cent on £500 (£170), leaving £330. After April 1999, if trustees receive the same dividend (of £400), it is grossed up at 10 per cent to £444 on which they pay 25 per cent (£111), leaving £333. The different rate of tax, therefore, ensures that the post-tax amount is much the same.

It is important to note that the 10 per cent tax credit on dividends is irrecoverable. That means the credits trustees receive on dividends cannot enter the "tax pool" (the total of tax they have paid on the trust income from whatever source which can be used to "frank" net income received by beneficiaries). This is because of the principle that the credits must remain irrecoverable even if they are passed through the trust to the beneficiaries.

While the trustees will be liable to tax of 25 per cent on the grossed up dividends, the net income they pay out will, in the beneficiaries hands, be treated as a new source of income (irrespective of that income's original source) carrying a 34 per cent tax credit. It will immediately be seen that there is potentially a mismatch between the amount of tax the trustees have paid on dividend income and the amount of tax credit the beneficiaries can claim on the trust income. Taxes Act 1988, s.687(2) provides that the trustees of the settlement are liable for the shortfall in tax.

How does this work? If trustees receive a dividend of £18,000, it will **7.042** carry with it an irrecoverable tax credit of £2,000. The dividend is, therefore, grossed up to £20,000 on which the trustees will be liable to pay 25 per cent (£5,000) but with the benefit of the £2,000 tax credit leaving £3,000 to pay. (However, only that amount of £3,000 enters the "tax pool".)

The trustees will then be left with net trust income of £15,000 in their hands. If they want to distribute all of that to the beneficiaries, the problem they face is that it will be grossed up at 34 per cent even though they have only paid 25 per cent on the gross amount. The problem is exacerbated by the fact that the 10 per cent tax credit on the dividend is not part of the "tax pool".

So what happens if they do distribute the £15,000? The beneficiaries will be deemed to receive it net of 34 per cent (so will have a tax credit of £7,727) which only the £3,000 in the "tax pool" can be used to meet. The result is that the trustees will have to pay a further £4,727 from capital (unless, as will often be the case, they have credits from other sources of income in the "tax pool").

Where there are no available tax credits in the tax pool and the trustees wish to avoid having to use capital to meet their s.687(2) liability, they should pay out only 66 per cent of the net dividend. On our figures they would pay £11,880 of the net dividend of £15,000 to the beneficiary who will receive it with a 34 per cent tax credit of £6,120. The trustees will retain £3,120 of the net dividend. The trustees are liable under s.687(2) to pay £6,120 to the Revenue. However, they have £3,000 available in the tax pool and they have the retained £3,120. There is, therefore, no need to use capital. The eventual effect of this is that they have used the £15,000 left after paying the trusts' rate of 25 per cent to pay the beneficiaries £11,880 and the Revenue £3,120.

This illustration shows that where the trustees choose to distribute and have no unused additional tax credits in the "tax pool", they will pay an effective rate of tax in excess of 34 per cent. This problem will be alleviated where the trustees have unused tax credits which will satisfy the additional tax liability. It can be avoided if the trustees accumulate the income rather than make distributions but this may result in a higher IHT liability when the capital of the trust is eventually paid out.

The question of when the trustees must pay the trusts' rate depends on whether or not a beneficiary has a right to trust income; this is discussed in the next paragraph.

L. Income Tax—the Liability of the Beneficiaries

The position differs depending on whether or not any beneficiary has a right to the trust income.

1. BENEFICIARIES WITH A RIGHT TO TRUST INCOME

7.043 A beneficiary who has a *right* to trust income is taxed on the income when it arises irrespective of whether or not it is paid over to him. Such a right arises when the beneficiary has a vested interest in the income of the trust. A direction to accumulate income will not destroy a vested interest in it provided the accumulated income *must* be paid to the beneficiary or to the estate of the beneficiary at some time.

Three examples of trusts where beneficiaries have vested interests in the income are where the beneficiary has:

(a) A life interest in a trust fund, for example "to A for life". (However, if A is under 18 and s.31 of the Trustee Act applies there will be no right to income and A will effectively have only an interest contingent on reaching 18.)

(b) A vested interest in accumulating income, for example "to A but the income to be accumulated for 10 years and then paid to A or A's estate". A has no right to receive the income immediately but it is certain that A or A's estate will receive it in 10 years' time.

(c) A right to income conferred by s.31 of the Trustee Act (for example, where a beneficiary has an interest in the capital of the fund contingent on reaching an age greater than 18 and has reached 18).

In these circumstances the trustees will have paid the basic rate tax on the trust income and the beneficiary will include in his "statutory income" for the appropriate tax year the income available to him, that is the gross trust income less the trustees' expenses grossed up at the appropriate rate depending on the sources of the trust's income (see the section on trust expenses in para.7.040). The grossed up income must be included even if no income is actually paid to (or applied for) the beneficiary. When the tax liability is calculated the beneficiary will claim a basic or lower rate tax credit. If his tax rate is less than the rate paid by the trustees he can reclaim tax. If he is a higher rate taxpayer he will have to pay the difference between his higher rate and the basic rate to the Revenue.

When calculating the tax liability the beneficiary is assessed on the income under the Schedule or Case of the Taxes Act 1988 appropriate to the source of the income (*Baker v Archer-Shee* (1927)). Most trust income will be derived from sources which would provide investment income in the hands of an individual. However, some trusts may derive their income from a trade carried on by the trustees. In such a case, the beneficiary would be assessed under Sch.D Case I although the income would be treated as *investment* income, not earned income, since it will not be income immediately derived by the beneficiary from the carrying on by him of the trade.

The following examples illustrate the way in which the tax liability of a beneficiary of a trust is calculated.

Example 1

The trustees of a trust for A for life, remainder to B receive £10,000 gross **7.044** income from the trust property and incur £780 expenses in managing the trust. A has a vested interest in the income of the trust fund and his only other source of income is a share of partnership profits of £30,000. He has no charges on income. The trustees pay to A £7,020 (that is the trust income of £10,000 less basic rate tax of £2,200 and the trust expenses of £780).

The tax liability of A is calculated as follows:

	£
Statutory income	
Profits (DI)	30,000
Net trust income grossed up	
at basic rate $\left(i.e. \text{ £7,020} \times \dfrac{100}{78}\right)$	9,000
Total income	39,000
Less: Personal relief	(4,615)
Taxable income	34,385

Tax liability is calculated as follows:

	£	£
£1,960 @ 10%	196	
£28,540 @ 22%	6,278	
£3,885 @ 40%	1,554	
		8,028
Less Tax Credit (£9,000 @ 22%)		(1,980)
To pay		6,028

Example 2

The facts are as in Example 1 except that the trustees receive a dividend of £9,000 (with a tax credit of £1,000) instead of the gross income of £10,000. The trustees pay A £8,220 (that is, the net dividend less the expenses of £780).

	£
Statutory income	
Profits (DI)	30,000.00
Trust income (dividend)grossed up at 10 per cent (£8,220 × 100/90)	9,133.33
Total income	39,133.33
Less: Personal relief	(4,615)
	34,518.33

Tax liability is calculated as follows:

	£	£
1,960 @ 10%	196	
28,540 @ 22%	6,278.80	
4,018.33 @ 32.5%	1,305.96	
		7,780.76

As a higher rate taxpayer, he is taxed at 32.5 per cent because this is the higher rate payable on grossed up dividend income. If he had been a basic rate taxpayer, he would have borne no further tax charge but if he was a non-taxpayer, he would not have been able to recover the dividend's tax credit (as that credit is irrecoverable).

Payments from capital

7.045   If a beneficiary with a vested interest in the trust income receives a payment that is income in his hands, he will pay income tax on it even if the trustees make the payment from capital (*Michelham's Trustees v I.R.C.* (1930)). This situation can arise where the trust fund bears an annuity. If the trust income is insufficient to meet the annuity, the trustees will have to make up the balance by using the capital of the trust. The annuity will be regarded as income in the hands of the beneficiary (*Brodie's Will Trustees v I.R.C.* (1933)).

The case of *Stevenson v Wishart* (1986) is interesting in that the Revenue failed in their contention that regular capital payments for nursing home fees should be treated as income. The position now appears to be that capital payments will not be treated as income payments unless

(a) as in *Brodie* they are designed to augment capital; or
(b) the trust instrument authorises the use of capital to maintain the beneficiary's standard of living; or
(c) the capital payment really amounts to an annuity.

2. BENEFICIARIES WITH NO RIGHT TO TRUST INCOME

7.046   A beneficiary will have no *right* to trust income if his entitlement to receive income depends on his satisfying a contingency or depends on the trustees exercising a discretion in his favour. The income is treated as the income of the trustees who will pay the basic or lower rate on savings income or the Sch.F dividend rate or trusts' rate of tax (the calculation was illustrated in para.7.039).

The most common examples of trusts falling within this category are discretionary trusts and trusts where the income is being accumulated for a person with no vested right to the income (such as accumulation and maintenance settlements as defined for inheritance tax purposes in Inheritance Tax Act 1984, s.71).

While the income is merely being accumulated, it is not taxed as part of the contingent beneficiary's income. However, if a payment of income is made to a beneficiary the amount paid must be treated as part of the beneficiary's income and he will have to gross it up at 34 per cent. A 34 per cent tax credit can be claimed and the beneficiary's excess liability or right to claim a rebate will then be calculated in the normal way.

This can best be illustrated by an example.

Example

The trustees hold property on trust for the children of A provided they reach the age of 25. The settlement satisfies the requirements of the Inheritance Tax Act 1984, s.71, with regard to the trustees' discretion as to maintenance, etc., and accumulation. The only child, X, is under 18 and the trustees decide to apply all the income of the trust to X (X has no other income). The trustees receive £20,000 gross income and incur £780 in trust expenses.

(a) The net income available for X's maintenance, education and benefit is £12,540 (the calculation was explained at para.7.039).
(b) X's tax liability:

Statutory income

	£
Trust income grossed up at 34%	
$£12,540 \times \dfrac{100}{66} =$	19,000.00
Less: Personal relief	(4,615)
Taxable income	14,385
Tax liability is:	
£1,960 @ 10%	196
£12,425 @ 22%	2,733.50
	2,929.50

From his total tax liability of £2,929.50 X can deduct his 34 per cent tax credit of £6,460. He has, therefore, a right to claim a rebate of £3,530.50, making his net receipts from the income of the trust £16,070.50.

Note:
Since the beneficiary can claim a 34 per cent tax credit on income applied for his benefit, the trustees should bear this in mind when deciding whether or not to apply income for the beneficiary.

Since the beneficiary only suffers income tax liability on income advanced to him, an accumulation trust may be advantageous from an income tax point of view for individuals suffering the higher rates of tax since the rate of tax on income accumulated is 34 per cent whereas the highest rate of tax on income received by an individual is 40 per cent. When the accumulations are later paid to a beneficiary they have become capital and so escape further income tax. However, inheritance tax may then be payable if it is not an accumulation and maintenance settlement as defined by the Inheritance Tax Act 1984, s.71 (see above, para.7.013), so that care should be taken with this method of saving tax. Furthermore this course would be most inadvisable if the beneficiaries would be paying less than 34 per cent tax since they can reclaim tax only in respect of income which has been advanced to them, not in respect of accumulated income. If the settlement gives trustees a discretion to pay income to beneficiaries or to accumulate it, the trustees could maximise tax-saving by exercising the discretion to the extent that the beneficiaries' income would not be liable to more than 34 per cent tax.

Demergers and Scrip issues

7.047   Demergers present serious problems for trustees. In a simple direct demerger the company declares a dividend from distributable profits and proceeds to satisfy it with an allocation of shares in the demerged company. It follows that the shares represent income so if they are paid to an interest in possession trust, the life tenant will be entitled to them.

From the point of view of the trust fund the consequences can be very serious. The capital value of the trust fund can be greatly reduced and the life tenant can receive a huge income benefit.

The trustees may not be happy with this result. They can sell shares before the demerger but this, being a disposal, may lead to an unwelcome capital gains tax liability.

What is the tax position?

7.048   The life tenant of an interest in possession trust is entitled to all income and is therefore entitled to the shares. The distribution is exempt from income tax provided the relevant conditions for an exempt distribution are complied with. (For capital gains tax purposes the Revenue now accepts that the shares being income belong to the life tenant so that there is no liability to tax—*Tax Bulletin*, October 1994.)

Where the trust is a discretionary one the receipt of the shares by the trustees is still an exempt distribution so there is no liability to income tax. (For CGT purposes the shares are treated as part of the trustees' original shareholding.)

If the trustees pay out shares to the beneficiaries there will be a charge to income tax at 34 per cent. (There will also be a charge to capital gains tax although hold over relief will be available.)

Demergers may also be done indirectly, *i.e.* the company declares a dividend and satisfies it with the issue of shares in a new company. This happened in the ICI/Zeneca demerger. In litigation arising from that demerger the court held that because it was an indirect demerger it was possible to regard the issued shares as capital of the trust fund. Therefore the new shares were held by the trustees as part of the capital.

Scrip Dividends

7.049   Companies are increasingly using this method. The "scrip" is offered as an alternative to a cash dividend; the value of the scrip will be substantially more than the value of the cash dividend; shareholders are able to turn their scrip into cash by effecting an immediate sale. Scrip dividends are popular with companies because it is not treated as a distribution and therefore ACT is not payable.

For individuals and trustees of discretionary trusts the tax position is as follows. The receipt must be grossed up at 20 per cent and is then subject to an additional tax charge (Taxes Act 1988, s.249) of 23 per cent of the market value of the scrip on the day of first listing. (For capital gains tax the new shares are pooled with the existing shares and the base cost is increased by the value of the scrip.)

Trustees of an interest in possession trust face the same problems as arise on demergers. Are the shares income and therefore the property of the life tenant or are they part of the trust capital? It is thought that there should be an apportionment. The scrip is added to capital but the trustees must then raise cash equal to the level of the cash dividend and pay that to the life tenant. (See *Law Society's Gazette*, July 1993, p.17.)

The tax treatment depends on how the shares are treated for trust law. See SP 4/94.

M. Income Tax, Capital Gains Tax and Trustee Act 1925, s.31

Income Tax

Section 31 of the Trustee Act is not a tax provision. However, since it can affect a beneficiary's right to income it can affect the income tax liability of trustees and beneficiaries.   **7.050**

Section 31 (see Chapter 11 for a full discussion) provides that where there is income available to an infant (whether he has a vested or a contingent interest) the trustees of the trust may at their sole discretion apply the whole or part of such income for or towards the infant's maintenance, education or benefit and, to the extent that they do not, they must accumulate the whole or part of such income.

If, after reaching the age of 18, the beneficiary has not attained a vested interest in such income the trustees *shall* thereafter pay the income (together with any income producd by investments bought with accumulated income) to the beneficiary until the beneficiary either attains a vested interest or dies or until his interest fails.

Once the infant reaches the age of 18 the trustees must decide what is to happen to income that has been accumulated (and therefore capitalised).

In all cases, except one, the accumulated income is added to capital and devolves with it. Thus, whoever takes the capital takes the accumulations.

The exceptional case is that of an infant with a life interest. If the infant reaches 18 any income which has been accumulated is paid to him. However, if the infant dies before reaching 18 the accumulated income is added to capital and devolves with it. An infant with a life interest, therefore, has no *right* to receive income until he reaches the age of 18 (since the trustees may decide to accumulate it) and cannot be certain of ever receiving the accumulations (since he may die before reaching 18).

Section 31 can, therefore, *give* certain beneficiaries a right to income where prima facie they had no such right under the terms of the trust. It can also *prevent* beneficiaries having a right to income which under the terms of the trust they would otherwise have enjoyed.

The effect, if any, of s.31 on income tax liability can be illustrated by examples.

(a) *T's will gives 20,000 shares to A for life (A is aged six).* If s.31 did not apply, A would have *a right* to receive the income from the shares and the trustees would pay the Schedule F rate (10 per cent) only on the dividends. A would include the grossed up income on his income tax return and might be liable to excess liability if his circumstances justified it.

However, if s.31 applies the trustees have a discretion whether to apply income for A's benefit and A, therefore, has no *right* to receive current income until he reaches 18. He has no right to receive accumulated income until he reaches 18. A is, therefore, treated as having an interest contingent on reaching 18. The trustees therefore pay the trusts' rate of tax (34 per cent). A will include income actually applied for his maintenance on his tax return. (Excess liability or a right to a rebate may arise depending on A's circumstances.) Once A reaches 18 he will obtain a right to current income. The trustees will then pay no further tax. The tax credit on the dividends will satisfy their basic rate tax liability.

(b) *T's will gives 20,000 shares to A if he reaches 25 (A is aged six).* If s.31 did not apply A would have no *right* to the income until reaching 25 and the trustees would pay lower rate tax *and* additional rate tax. Nothing would be included on A's tax return in respect of the trust income.

However, if s.31 applies A will have no right to the trust income *until* 18. The trustees will pay the trusts' rate. The trustees may choose to apply income for his benefit. Nothing will be included on A's tax return except to the extent that income is applied for his benefit. Amounts actually applied in this way will be included on A's tax return grossed up at 34 per cent. A may have to pay excess liability depending on his circumstances.

From 18 to 25 A will have a right to the income. The trustees will then pay no further tax. The tax credit on the dividends will satisfy their basic rate tax liability. A will include the grossed up amount in his tax return (grossed up at 10 per cent) and again may be liable to extra tax depending on his circumstances.

Note:
In the above examples the trustees would be paying basic (not lower) rate tax if the income were anything other than dividends.

Capital gains tax

7.051 Trustees pay capital gains tax on gains realised by them on trust assets at the rate of 22 per cent *except* in the case of accumulation or discretionary trusts when the rate is the trusts' rate (currently 34 per cent). A trust is an accumulation or discretionary trust where all or any part of the income arising to the trustees in a year of assessment is liable to the additional rate of income tax.

Thus, whenever s.31 alters the liability of trustees to pay the trusts' rate of income tax on any part of the trust income it also alters the rate at which capital gains tax is charged.

8. Grants

A. Types of Grant

A grant of representation is an order of the High Court. The High Court **8.001** has exclusive jurisdiction to make grants in England and Wales. Since October 1, 1971 the Family Division of the High Court has exercised the jurisdiction to make grants (s.1(4) of the Administration of Justice Act 1970). The Chancery Division and the county court have certain powers in probate cases but these do not include a power to make grants; these powers will be considered in Chapter 9.

There are three basic types of grant of representation:

(a) A grant of probate;
(b) A grant of letters of administration with will annexed; and
(c) A grant of letters of administration (commonly called a grant of simple administration).

A grant once made serves two main purposes. First, it establishes the authority of the personal representative. Secondly, it establishes either the validity of the deceased's will (in the case of probate or administration with will annexed) or that the deceased died without a valid will (in the case of simple administration).

Certain types of property do not devolve on the personal representatives when their owner dies. This applies to property which is the subject of a statutory nomination, property subject to a *donatio mortis causa*, certain payments from pension funds and insurance policies and, most importantly, property held by the deceased and another person (or persons) as joint tenants in equity. Such property is not included in the grant of representation. The ways in which it is dealt with on death is described in Chapter 21 (see paras 21.002–21.010).

B. Capacity to Take a Grant

Any person, including an alien, a minor, a corporation, a bankrupt, a **8.002** convicted criminal, or a mentally disordered person may be *appointed* an executor by a will. Similarly any such person may prima facie be entitled to a grant of letters of administration.

However, a minor cannot *take* a grant of representation and therefore the grant is made to an adult for the use and benefit of the minor. Such a grant will usually be limited to the period of incapacity so that the minor may take out a grant on attaining majority.

Similar rules apply to mentally disordered persons (that is persons who are incapable of managing their own affairs).

Where an alien resident outside the jurisdiction, a bankrupt or a criminal is entitled to a grant no special rules apply. However, in each case the court may exercise its discretion to pass over the person entitled and make a grant to some other person entitled (Supreme Court Act 1981, s.116).

After the coming into force of the Family Law Reform Act 1987 the fact that a person's parents were not married to each other at the time of his birth is irrelevant for the purposes of succession to property and is therefore irrelevant for the purpose of entitlement to a grant of representation (unless a contrary intention has been expressed in a will left by the deceased). Section 21 of the 1987 Act does provide, however, that a deceased person shall be presumed not to have been survived by any person whose parents were not married to each other at the time of that person's birth (or who is related through such a person). The presumption can be rebutted by evidence to the contrary. This provision is designed to facilitate the administration by making it unnecessary to carry out investigations.

C. Grant of Probate

1. THE EXECUTOR APPOINTED BY WILL

8.003   Normally the only person who may obtain a grant of probate is the executor appointed by the deceased in his will (or in a codicil validly supplementing or amending the will). An executor is a person appointed by the will to administer the deceased's property. The will may *appoint* any number of executors but not more than four persons may take out a grant in respect of the same part of the estate (power may be reserved to any others—see para.8.010).

Since most testators want to choose a person to administer the estate, a properly drafted will should expressly provide for the appointment of an executor; for example, by including a clause which says "I appoint X of [address] to be the executor of this will". The person named should be someone suitable to act as executor and who is willing to take a grant. The appointment may describe rather than name the executor; for example, "I appoint the Vicar of St James's Church in the parish of [...] to be the executor of this will" but such appointments are unwise since they may be ambiguous.

The appointment of an executor may be implied in cases where the will shows an intention that a particular person should perform the functions of an executor even though he is not expressly described as an executor. Such a person is described as "an executor according to the tenor of the will". For example, in *In the Goods of Baylis* (1865) the will directed that named persons should pay the debts of the estate and then hold the estate on trust for sale for the deceased's children. Lord Penzance held that since the "trustees" were to get in the whole estate, pay the debts and distribute the property the clear intention was that they should act as executors; therefore they were entitled to a grant. The appointment of a trustee without a direction that he is to pay the debts of the estate is not sufficient to make him executor according to the tenor (*In the Estate of McKenzie* (1909)).

A firm (for example, of solicitors) may be named as executors. However, since the office is a personal one this is treated as an appointment of all the individual partners in the firm. Great care should be taken with such appointments since in the absence of clear words to the contrary, the partners in the firm at the date on which the will is made (rather than the partners at the date of death) are the executors and they may be unavailable or unwilling to act at the time of the death. (The drafting problems connected with appointment of a firm will be considered in Chapter 22).

2. Appointment other than by will

A will may validly appoint someone to nominate an executor (in such a case the person appointed may nominate himself). Such a provision in a will would seldom be advantageous but, if included, a time limit should be imposed on the making of the appointment. **8.004**

One executor is always sufficient even where there is a minority or life interest. However, the court has a rarely exercised power to appoint an additional personal representative to act with a sole executor in the administration of the estate (Supreme Court Act 1981, s.114(4)). Such a person is not described as an executor but would seem to have the same powers as an executor.

Under the Administration of Estates Act 1925, s.22, trustees of settled land of which the deceased was tenant for life and which remains settled land after his death are deemed appointed executors in respect of the settled land alone. However, in accordance with r.29 of the Non-Contentious Probate Rules 1987, as amended, they will act as administrators not executors.

Under s.50(1)(a) of the Administration of Justice Act 1985 the court may appoint a person to be a personal representative in substitution for an existing personal representative. If the substitute is to act with an existing executor he is also an executor, in any other case he is an administrator.

3. Chain of representation (administration of estates act 1925, s.7)

Where the sole or last surviving executor dies before completing the administration of the estate a grant of letters of administration *de bonis non administratis* may be made to the person entitled under rule 20 of the Non-Contentious Probate Rules 1987 (see below, paras 8.033–8.036). Where one of a number of executors dies there is no need for a further grant; the remaining executor or executors having full power to complete the administration. **8.005**

However, where a sole or last surviving proving executor (other than an executor substituted under s.50(1)(a) of the Administration of Justice Act 1985) dies *having himself appointed an executor*, the latter, on taking a grant of probate in respect of the executor's estate, automatically becomes the executor of the original testator as well so that a grant of administration to the original estate is not needed (Administration of Estates Act 1925, s.7).

Example
A appoints B to be his executor and B appoints C. On A's death B will become his executor and may take a grant of probate. If B dies having taken a grant but without having completed the administration of A's estate and C takes a grant of probate of B's estate he will automatically become executor of A as well as B.

This is called the chain of representation. There may be more than two links in the chain. To continue the same example, if C appoints D to be his executor and C then dies without completing the administration of the estates and D takes out a grant of probate in respect of C's estate D will automatically become the executor of A and B as well as of C.

The chain of representation only applies where there is a grant of *probate* to the executor of a person who had himself taken out a grant of probate in respect of someone else's estate. Thus, the chain of representation is broken (and a grant of administration *de bonis non* is required) where:

(a) an executor dies intestate or without appointing an executor; or
(b) an executor dies having appointed an executor but that executor has predeceased; or
(c) an executor dies having appointed an executor but that executor fails to take out a grant in respect of the original executor's estate.

The chain of representation can be said to pass from *proving executor* to *proving executor*. There is, therefore, no chain of representation where no executor has been appointed. For example, A dies intestate, B takes out a grant of letters of administration and then B dies having appointed C to be his executor. C does not become the executor of A.

The appointment of an administrator will usually break the chain of representation. However, a temporary appointment does not do so.

Example
A appoints B to be his executor, B appoints C and dies. C is a minor when B dies. A grant of administration is made in respect of B's estate to D. D does not become A's executor. When, however, C reaches majority he may take out a grant of probate in respect of B's estate. If he does so he will then automatically become A's executor.

Similarly a person who becomes executor through the chain of representation may cease to be executor when someone else takes out a grant of probate in respect of the deceased's estate.

Example
A appoints B and C to be his executors: when A dies B is an adult and C a minor. A grant will be made to B alone but C is said to have "power reserved", *i.e.* he can take out a grant when he reaches majority. If B dies

without completing the administration of A's estate appointing D his executor while C is still a minor, D will become A's executor on taking out probate of B's estate. However, if on reaching 18 C takes out a grant in respect of A's estate, D will cease to be A's executor. This is because the chain of representation can only operate on the death of the *last proving* executor and C has now become a proving executor.

4. LIMITED, CONDITIONAL AND SUBSTITUTIONAL APPOINTMENTS

Most wills appoint one or more persons to act as executor for the whole of the deceased's estate and without limit as to time. However, an appointment may be limited, for example an appointment may: **8.006**

    (a) be limited in time (the appointment may, for example, appoint one person until another person reaches the age of majority);

    (b) be limited to certain property (for example, one executor may be appointed to deal with the deceased's general estate and another to deal with business property or literary effects).

Limited grants are dealt with in more detail in paras 8.023–8.032 below.

An appointment may also be conditional. For example, "I appoint A to be my executor provided he is a partner in the firm of A, B and Co at the date of my death."

A will may also validly provide for a substitutional appointment. For example "I appoint A to be my executor but if he is unable or unwilling to act then I appoint B." B may take out a grant once A has renounced probate or died.

5. EFFECT OF GRANT OF PROBATE

Conclusive proof of content and execution of will

A grant of probate in respect of a particular will is conclusive evidence as to the terms of the will of the deceased and that it was duly executed. If a will is found to be invalid (for example, because it is found not to have been properly executed or a later will is discovered) after a grant of probate, the probate must be revoked (see paras 8.038–8.040) if that will is to be made ineffective.   **8.007**

Confirmation of executors' authority

A grant of probate merely confirms the authority of the executor conferred by the will. The authority derives from the will. An executor may, therefore, deal with the estate of the deceased without first taking out a grant (see Chapter 11). However, a grant is in practice necessary to prove to other people that the executor has authority to deal with the property of the deceased and to pass a good title to any land in the estate.   **8.008**

6. EXECUTOR DE SON TORT

The term executor *de son tort* means literally executor as a result of his own wrong. The expression is unfortunate since the noun is wholly misleading and the adjectival phrase almost as much so. An executor *de*   **8.009** *son tort* is a person who deals with the estate of a deceased person by intermeddling with it as if he were an executor or administrator. Acts which have been held to amount to intermeddling include selling property, paying debts, collecting debts and carrying on the business of the deceased. However, acts of charity, humanity or necessity are not sufficient. Thus, arranging the deceased's funeral, ordering necessary goods for the deceased's dependents and protecting the deceased's property by moving it to a safe place have been held not to amount to intermeddling. In a recent case (*Pollard v Jackson* (1995)) it was held that a tenant, of part of the deceased's house, who kept the parts formerly occupied by the deceased clean and who burnt rubbish found there was not an executor *de son tort*. The steps he had taken could not be regarded as characteristic of executorship.

An executor *de son tort* has no authority to act in the estate of the deceased and can obtain no rights from his intermeddling. However, a person who is in fact the deceased's executor and who intermeddles loses the right to renounce probate and so can be cited to take a grant (see paras 10.052–10.055).

The effect of being an executor *de son tort* is that such a person becomes liable to the creditors and beneficiaries to the extent of the real and personal estate coming to his hands as if he were an executor (Administration of Estate Act 1925, s.28). He is also liable for inheritance tax to the extent of such property.

An executor *de son tort* can bring his liability to creditors and beneficiaries to an end by delivering the assets he has received (or their value) to the lawful executor or administrator before the creditors or beneficiaries bring an action against him.

7. POWER RESERVED TO PROVE AT A LATER DATE

8.010 A will may appoint several people to act as co-executors. It is unnecessary for them all to join in taking the grant if they do not wish to. Those who do not take the grant may renounce their rights but if they prefer not to renounce they may have power reserved to them to take the grant at a later date if it proves desirable. Where an application for probate is made and power is to be reserved to some executors to prove at a later date, notice of the application must be given to the non-proving executors. The oath for executors, filed when the application for the grant is made, must state that this notice has been given unless the court otherwise orders (Non-Contentious Probate Rules 1987, r.27(1)). Where the other executors are not named in the will and are partners in a firm of solicitors with the proving executors, the persons to whom power is reserved need not be given notice (r.27(1A)).

D. Grant of Letters of Administration with Will Annexed

1. CIRCUMSTANCES IN WHICH GRANT IS MADE

8.011 A grant of letters of administration with will annexed (also called a grant *cum testamento annexo*) is made when the deceased has a valid will and a grant of probate cannot be made to an executor. Such a situation arises where the will makes no appointment of an executor, where the executor predeceases, where the executor has validly renounced probate, where the executor is passed over by order of the court and where the executor has been cited but has not taken a grant of probate (see paras 10.052–10.055). A grant of administration with will annexed is also made in certain cases where an earlier grant of probate or administration with will annexed has been made but the personal representative appointed by the earlier grant has been unable to complete the administration of the estate (see paras 8.033–8.036).

2. PERSONS ENTITLED TO THE GRANT

Rule 20 of the Non-Contentious Probate Rules 1987 contains a list of the persons who are entitled to take out a grant of administration with the will annexed. The list follows the order of entitlement to property under the will. Persons who come earlier in the list will take a grant in preference to those who come later. If there is no executor able and willing to act, the following are entitled: **8.012**

(i) *Any residuary legatee or devisee holding in trust for any other person.* For example, residue is given to X and Y on trust for A and B. X and Y are the residuary legatees holding on trust and so have the first right to a grant. This is logical since the testator by appointing X and Y as trustees has shown that he is willing that they should deal with his property.

(ii) *Any other residuary legatee or devisee (including one for life), or where the residue is not wholly disposed of by the will, any person entitled to share in the undisposed of residue (including the Treasury Solicitor when claiming* bona vacantia *on behalf of the Crown).* For example, residue is given to A, B, C and D in equal shares; each will be entitled to take the grant. If D predeceased the testator and X was entitled to take the quarter of residue undisposed of, X would be equally entitled to the grant.

There are two provisos to this category:

(a) unless a district judge or registrar otherwise directs, a residuary legatee or devisee whose legacy or devise is vested in interest shall be preferred to one entitled on the happening of a contingency,

(b) where the residue is not in terms wholly disposed of, the district judge or registrar may, if he is satisfied that the testator has nevertheless disposed of the whole or substantially the whole of the known estate, allow a grant to be made to any legatee or devisee entitled to, or to share in, the estate so disposed of, without regard to the persons entitled to share in any residue not disposed of by the will.

For example the will says "I leave my home, Blackacre, all its contents and my bank account to my friend X". When the testator dies the property described in his will is substantially everything he owns. X can take a grant in preference to those family members who would be entitled to take residue under the intestacy rules.

(iii) *The personal representative of any residuary legatee or devisee (but not one for life, or one holding in trust for any other person), or of any person entitled to share in any residue not disposed of by the will.* For example, residue is given to A and B in equal shares; A predeceases the testator and X is entitled to take the half share of residue undisposed of. If X and B both die before taking a grant the personal representatives of either will be entitled to the grant.

(iv) *Any other legatee or devisee (including one for life or one holding in trust for any other person) or any creditor of the deceased.* For example, a house is left to A and £1,000 to B. Either is entitled to the grant unless a registrar otherwise directs. A legatee or devisee whose legacy or devise is vested in interest shall be preferred to one entitled on the happening of a contingency.

(v) *The personal representative of any other legatee or devisee (but not one for life or one holding in trust for any other person) or of any creditor of the deceased.* For example, if A and B in the previous example survive the testator but die before taking a grant the personal representatives of either will be entitled to the grant.

Rule 27(4) and (6) of the Non-Contentious Rules 1987 provides that where two or more persons are entitled in the same degree (*i.e.* come into the same paragraph above) a grant may be made to any of them without notice to the others (contrast the position with grants of probate, see paragraph 8.010) and that disputes between persons entitled in the same degree are to be decided by a district judge or registrar. (For the procedure see para.10.052.)

Living beneficiaries are to be preferred to the personal representative of deceased beneficiaries entitled in the same degree and adults to minors entitled in the same degree unless a district judge or registrar directs to the contrary (r.27(5)). If the whole estate of the deceased is assigned by the beneficiaries, the assignees have the same right to a grant as the assignors (r.24).

3. THE EFFECT OF A GRANT

Conclusive proof of content and execution of will

8.013   A grant of administration with will annexed is like a grant of probate in that it is conclusive evidence as to content and execution of the will.

Conferral of authority on administrator

8.014   A grant of probate merely confirms the authority of executors. However, a grant of letters of administration *confers* authority on the administrator and vests the deceased's property in him. Until the grant is made the property of a deceased who appoints no executor is technically vested in the Public Trustee (Law of Property (Miscellaneous Provisions) Act 1994, s.14). Once made the grant does not relate back to the date of death of the deceased except to the extent that relation back would (at the time of the grant) be beneficial to the estate (see para.11.005).

E. Grant of Simple Administration

1. CIRCUMSTANCES IN WHICH GRANT IS MADE

A grant of simple administration is made when there is no will capable of **8.015**
being admitted to probate (or of being annexed to letters of
administration).

Simple administration is appropriate in the vast majority of cases where
there is a total intestacy. However, if there is an admissible will which
does not deal with property (for example, a will merely appointing
executors) a grant of probate may be made. Similarly a will is admissible
to probate (or may be annexed to letters of administration) where it
purports to deal with property but all the gifts fail.

2. PERSONS ENTITLED TO TAKE A GRANT

Rule 22 of the Non-Contentious Probate Rules 1987 contains an order of **8.016**
the persons who are entitled to take out a grant of simple administration.
The order follows the order of entitlement to the estate on intestacy and
says that the persons entitled are, in the order listed and provided that
they have a beneficial interest in the estate:

(a) the surviving husband or wife of the deceased,
(b) children of the deceased (and the issue of a child who has
predeceased),
(c) the parents of the deceased,
(d) the brothers and sisters of the whole blood of the deceased (and
the issue of any brothers or sisters who have predeceased),
(e) brothers and sisters of the half blood of the deceased (and the
issue of any who have predeceased),
(f) grandparents,
(g) uncles and aunts of the whole blood (and the issue of any who
have predeceased),
(h) uncles and aunts of the half blood (and the issue of any who have
predeceased).

Since a beneficial interest is required the entitlement to a grant depends
in part on the size of the estate. For example, if the deceased died leaving
a spouse but no issue and with an estate of £80,000 (plus personal chattels)
the parents (if surviving) or brothers and sisters would not be entitled
under this provision since the estate would all go to the spouse. They
would, however, be entitled if the deceased's estate was £250,000.

Rule 22(2) provides that if no-one is entitled as being in any of the
above categories the Treasury Solicitor may take out a grant if he claims
bona vacantia on behalf of the crown.

Rule 22(3) provides that a grant may be made to a creditor of the
deceased or to a person who would be entitled to a beneficial interest in
the estate if there were an accretion to the estate provided that all those
entitled according to r.22(1) and (2) are cleared off. Thus, in the example
given above (a deceased with an estate of £80,000 and personal chattels
who is survived by spouse but no issue) the parents (if surviving) would
have a right to a grant if the spouse had been cleared off. If the

parents have predeceased then the brothers and sisters would have a right to a grant.

The personal representative of a person who survives the deceased but dies before taking a grant is entitled in the same degree as the person whom he represents (r.22(4)). However, unless a district judge or registrar otherwise directs, where a number of persons are entitled in the same degree, a person of full age is to be preferred to the guardian of a minor and a living person is to be preferred over the personal representative of a dead person (r.27(5)). Furthermore, blood relatives who are entitled to part of the estate are to be preferred to the personal representative of a spouse unless the spouse's estate is entitled to the *whole* of the estate as ascertained at the time of application for the grant.

Example
H dies survived by spouse and children. The spouse dies before obtaining a grant. The spouse's personal representative will be able to take a grant if the estate is not more than £125,000 plus personal chattels but if it is larger then the children will have priority.

3. EFFECT OF A GRANT

8.017   The effect of a grant of simple administration is the same as that of a grant of administration with will annexed except that it provides conclusive evidence of intestacy rather than as to the contents and terms of the will.

F. Renunciation

8.018   A person who is entitled to a grant of probate or administration may renounce his entitlement unless he has lost the right to renounce. Renunciation is made in writing to the registry. The most convenient way to deal with any renunciation is to submit it with the papers submitted by a person who does wish to take a grant.

An executor accepts office and thereby loses his right to renounce if he intermeddles in the estate (the principles are the same as those applying to a person constituting himself an executor *de son tort* so that the performance of acts of charity, humanity or necessity does not deprive the executor of his right to renounce). A potential administrator does not lose his right to renounce if he intermeddles. Both an executor and an administrator lose their rights to renounce if a grant is made in their favour.

A renunciation of probate by an executor does not operate as a renunciation of any right to administration which he may have unless that right is also renounced (Non-Contentious Probate Rules 1987, r.37(1)). However, a renunciation of administration in one capacity in effect operates to renounce *all* rights to a grant of administration.

Once a renunciation has been made it may only be retracted on the order of a district judge or registrar (r.37(3)). The Court will only allow the retraction of a renunciation if it can be shown to be for the benefit of the estate or of the persons interested in the estate (*Re Gill* (1873)).

G. Number of Personal Representatives

Section 114(1) of the Supreme Court Act 1981 provides that "probate or **8.019** administration shall not be granted ... to more than four persons in respect of the same part of the estate of a deceased person". This means that if more than four executors are appointed in respect of all or any part of the estate a grant can be made to only four of them. Power may be reserved to the others so that they can take a grant if a vacancy occurs (for example on the death of one of the four who has taken a grant). Similarly if more than four persons are equally entitled to a grant of administration (of either type) the grant cannot be made to more than four. If any dispute arises as to which of more than four persons are to take a grant it is resolved by a hearing before a district judge or registrar (Non-Contentious Probate Rules 1987, r.27(6)).

The minimum number of executors is always one, although the court has a discretion to appoint one or more additional personal representatives to act with the sole executor while there is a minority of a beneficiary or life interest subsisting in the estate (Supreme Court Act 1981, s.114(4)). An application for such an appointment may be made by any person interested in the estate or the guardian or receiver of any such person.

The minimum number of administrators is generally one, unless there is a minor beneficiary or a life interest in the estate where the appointment must normally be made to a trust corporation (with or without an individual) or to not less than two individuals (Supreme Court Act 1981, s.114(2)). However, the court has a discretion to appoint a sole administrator where there is a minority or life interest if it appears to the court "to be expedient in all the circumstances" (Supreme Court Act 1981, s.114(2)).

Where two administrators are necessary they may often be persons who have different entitlements to a grant.

Example
T dies intestate survived by a spouse and children and the estate is sufficiently large for the children to have an interest in it. The surviving spouse is entitled to a grant. A second administrator is required and so an adult child of the deceased may be co-administrator.

There is no requirement in cases of a minority or life interest that the numbers be maintained. Thus, if one of two administrators dies, the survivor can continue alone.

H. Special Rules as to Appointment of Personal Representatives

1. AFTER RENUNCIATION

It may appear from what has been said so far that the choice of executor **8.020** or administrator is automatic. However, this is far from being the case in all circumstances. The person with the best entitlement to a grant may renounce (see para.8.018 above) in which case the rules are applied as if that person had predeceased the testator. Thus:

    (a) if an executor renounces (unless there is another executor willing to act) a grant of administration with will annexed will be made to the person with the best entitlement to a grant under r.20;

    (b) if a person with the best entitlement under r.20 (or r.22 if there is an intestacy) renounces the person next in the list will have a right to a grant.

2. PASSING-OVER

8.021 The High Court has power under the Supreme Court Act 1981, s.116 to pass over the person entitled to a grant if "it appears ... to be necessary or expedient to appoint as administrator some person other than [the person entitled to take a grant]". When this power is exercised the court may appoint any person to be the administrator so that it does not necessarily appoint the person with the next best right to a grant or indeed a person with any right. Under s.115(1)(b) the Court also has power to grant administration to a trust corporation either solely or jointly with another person.

The power to pass over the person entitled to a grant is discretionary so that no exact rules can be laid down as to when the power will be exercised. However, two types of case may be recognised.

First, where the persons entitled request the appointment of their nominee. In *Teague and Ashdown v Wharton* (1871) Lord Penzance held that a mere request was insufficient to enable the court to pass over those entitled since "... persons entitled to grants ... are many of them persons who have no opportunity of knowing their own rights, and are not aware of the dangers that may beset them if they transfer these rights to other persons".

In *Re Potter* (1899) Gorell Barnes J. made a grant at the request of the persons who were entitled to a grant. It should be noted that in that case there were other special circumstances and that in his remarkably short judgment the judge seemed to place reliance on the fact that the appointment was made with the agreement of all the persons *interested* in the estate and not merely with the agreement of the persons entitled to a grant. It would seem, therefore, that the court will not pass over those entitled merely because they request that course.

Secondly, the Court may pass over a personal representative who is himself unsuitable for that office either in general or in the circumstances of the case. For example, in *In the Estate of Crippen* (1911) the deceased had been murdered by her husband; she had died intestate and normally he would have taken her property. He would also have been entitled to take a grant to her estate and, as he was dead, his personal representatives would have taken the grant. However, there is a rule of public policy that a person who slays another loses his entitlement to that person's property (see Chapter 16). The husband had, therefore, lost his beneficial entitlement to her estate and so his personal representative was passed over in favour of the wife's next-of-kin.

In *In the Estate of Hall* (1914) an executor who was in prison was passed over. In *Re Hall* (1950) the person entitled to administration was passed over on the ground that she could not be traced. In *In the Estate of Biggs* (1966) an executor had dealt with property in the estate without taking a grant (and was therefore debarred from renouncing probate—see para.8.009) but was now unwilling to continue acting despite the fact that he had been ordered to take a grant and that proceedings for contempt of court had been started against him. The court passed him over.

Finally, the case of *In the Goods of Edwards-Taylor* (1951) shows that the power to pass over is designed to control the appointment of personal representatives and cannot be used for a collateral purpose. In that case there was an application to pass over a beneficiary who was alleged to be mentally and physically immature. The application was made so that she would not be able to get possession of the deceased's estate immediately. The court refused to pass her over since the reason for the application was not concerned with the administration of the estate.

3. Administration of justice act 1985, section 50

Under s.50(1)(a) the court has power to remove an existing personal representative and appoint a substitute. Under s.50(1)(b) where there are two or more existing personal representatives it can terminate the appointment of one or more of those persons. The jurisdiction under s.50 is contentious business and accordingly is dealt with in the Chancery Division. **8.022**

I. Limited Grants

1. Introduction

Most grants are general in their effect. That is, they give the personal representative authority (or, in the case of probate, confirm his authority) to act for all purposes in the administration of the estate and extend to all the property in the estate without time limit. **8.023**

There are, however, three ways in which grants may be limited in their effect:

(a) they may be limited in time (for example, "until X reaches majority"); or
(b) they may be limited to part of the estate (for example, "limited to settled land"); or
(c) they may be limited as to a purpose, that is they may give the personal representative authority to deal with one particular aspect of the administration (for example, "limited to conducting or defending litigation").

2. GRANTS LIMITED AS TO TIME

Grants on behalf of minors

8.024 A minor cannot take a grant of probate or of administration. Where one of several executors appointed by a will is a minor the adult executors may take a general grant of probate immediately. Power is reserved to the minor who may take a grant of double probate when he reaches 18 (see paras 8.026–8.029 below). Where one of several potential administrators entitled in the same degree is a minor the grant will usually be made to the adults in preference to the guardians of the minor (Non-Contentious Probate Rules 1987, r.27(4)).

Where, however, the executors or the persons with the best entitlement to be administrators are all minors it is necessary to make a grant of letters of administration to some other person until the minors reach 18. This type of grant is commonly called a grant *durante aetate minore*; it may be a grant of administration with will annexed or a grant of simple administration. It confers on the administrator a general power to deal with the estate but is limited in time until the minor reaches 18. The grant will usually expire automatically on the minor reaching 18 although it is possible for some other time limit to be fixed (for example, the grant may be effective until the minor himself takes a grant). A grant *durante aetate minore* is made "for the use and benefit of the minor" and is therefore, made to the guardian of the minor (subject to the exceptions mentioned below) rather than to others entitled to the estate of the deceased.

The persons entitled to take a grant *durante aetate minore* under r.32 of the Non-Contentious Probate Rules 1987 (as amended by Non-Contentious Probate (Amendment) Rules 1991) are:

(a) a parent of the minor who has or is deemed to have parental responsibility under the Children Act 1989 or a guardian appointed under that act.

(b) an "appointed" guardian; that is someone appointed by a district judge or registrar under rule 32(2) either because there is no one eligible under the rule described above or because the registrar decides to pass over those persons;

(c) where there is a minority in the estate so that two administrators are required but there is only one person competent and willing to take a grant under the rules listed above that person may nominate a second administrator.

A Practice Direction of September 26, 1991 ([1991] 4 All E.R. 562) details the evidence of entitlement required for applications for grants on behalf of minors.

Mental incapacity

8.025 Where the executor or administrator is unable to act because of mental incapacity he *may* in some cases be passed over in favour of other applicants but normally a grant will be made to some other person for the use and benefit of the person suffering incapacity (r.35).

The grant is made in the following order of priority unless the district judge or registrar otherwise directs:

(a) to the person authorised by the Public Guardianship Office, Protection Division, to apply for a grant;

(b) where there is no person so authorised, to the lawful attorney of the incapable person acting under a registered enduring power of attorney;

(c) where there is no person authorised under paragraph (a) or (b) above the grant is to the person or persons entitled to the residuary estate of the deceased. In this case a medical certificate from a doctor who is responsible for the patient is required to prove incapacity.

Unless a district judge or registrar otherwise directs, no grant shall be made under this rule unless all persons entitled in the same degree as the incapable person have been cleared off.

3. GRANTS LIMITED AS TO PROPERTY

Where a grant is made limited to certain property up to four personal representatives may join in that grant and up to four in the grant made in respect of the rest of the estate.

8.026

Appointment of executors

A will may appoint different executors to deal with different parts of the estate. One example of this is an appointment of a literary executor to deal with literary effects and of a general executor to deal with the rest of the estate. The grant of probate taken by the literary executor will be limited to literary effects only. The grant taken by the general executor, if taken before the grant to the limited part of the estate, is described as a grant "save and except" the limited part; if taken after the grant of the limited part it is described as a grant *caeterorum*. There is no practical difference between these two types of grant.

8.027

The court's discretion

The court can make a grant limited to part of the estate in exercise of its discretion under s.116 of the Supreme Court Act 1981. However, the court will not make such a grant unless there are very exceptional circumstances and will usually pass over the person entitled to a grant altogether rather than make a limited grant.

8.028

Settled land

The legal title to settled land is vested in the tenant for life not in the trustees of the settlement. When the tenant for life dies and the settlement continues after his death, a grant limited to settled land is required in order that the settled land vests in the trustees of the settlement rather than the general personal representatives.

A grant of letters of administration is made to the trustees at the date of death or, where they fail to take a grant to the trustees of the date of grant or where no such trustees take a grant by the deceased's general personal representatives.

8.029

Where the property passes to a person absolutely entitled after death of the tenant for life the settlement comes to an end and the property devolves on the general personal representatives of the deceased tenant for life. There is, therefore, no need for special personal representatives in such a case (*Re Bridgett and Hayes Contract* (1928)). Similarly no special personal representatives are needed where a settlement is *created* by the will of the deceased. The general personal representatives will deal with administration of the property and will vest it in the tenant for life when administration is complete.

The above rules apply only to strict settlements under the Settled Land Act 1925. Where a person is entitled to a life interest under a trust of land (under the Trusts of Land Act, 1996) or a trust for sale, whether or not of land, the property is vested in the trustees and continues to be vested in them despite the death of the life tenant. The trust property does not, therefore, pass to any personal representative of the life tenant. Where a trust of land is created by will or intestacy, the general personal representatives will deal with the property and will vest it in the trustees.

4. GRANTS LIMITED AS TO PURPOSE

Grants ad colligenda bona

8.030   The purpose of a grant *ad colligenda bona* is to enable collection and preservation of the assets in the estate before a general grant is made so that any assets in danger may be preserved. Since the grant does not extend to distribution of the estate the will is not annexed to it. There are no particular rules as to who may apply for the grant; application is made to a district judge or registrar *ex parte* (Non-Contentious Probate Rules 1987, r.52(b)).

Although a grant *ad colligenda bona* is usually limited to collecting in the estate the court may grant power to sell or otherwise deal with the assets so as to preserve their value.

Grant ad litem

8.031   A grant *ad litem* is made to enable proceedings in court to be begun or continued on behalf of the estate of the deceased or against it. Any person interested in the litigation may apply *ex parte* to a district judge or registrar. Where someone wishes to bring a claim against an estate for family provision under the Inheritance (Provision for Family and Dependants) Act 1975 the Official Solicitor will usually be willing to take out a grant *ad litem*.

Grant pendente lite

8.032   Where there is a probate action in relation to an estate (for example, because the validity of an alleged will is in question), the court may appoint an administrator *pendente lite*, that is until the probate action is concluded. Any person who is a party to the probate action or interested in the estate may apply for the grant to be made but the grant will usually be made to an independent third party. The administrator will not usually be given authority to distribute any of the estate.

J. Incomplete Administration

In most cases the executor or administrator who first takes out a grant will **8.033**
complete the administration of the estate. Sometimes, however, the
original personal representative will die or otherwise cease to hold office
without completing the administration. In such a case, if there is no chain
of representation, a grant to some other person will be required. This will
either be a grant *de bonis non administratis* or a cessate grant depending
on the circumstances. Sometimes before the administration is completed
an executor is added by means of a grant of double probate. A grant of
double probate is made where one or some of a number of executors have
taken a grant with power reserved to others to take at a later stage and
one of those others now obtains a grant.

1. GRANT OF ADMINISTRATION DE BONIS NON

A grant *de bonis non administratis* is made to enable the administration of **8.034**
the estate to be completed following the death or incapacity of *all* the
previous personal representatives or the revocation of the previous grant.
(If one of the personal representatives becomes incapable the grant is
revoked and a further grant is made to the remaining personal
representatives; this is not, however, regarded as a grant *de bonis non*.)
Although the name "*de bonis non administratis*" means "concerning
unadministered goods" it is appropriate in cases where any type of
property, including realty, is unadministered.

There are three requirements which must be satisfied before such a
grant can be made:

(i) *The administration is incomplete.* Administration is complete once
the debts and legacies have been paid, accounts have been prepared and
any land or other assets remaining in the estate have been vested in the
beneficiaries by means of assents.

(ii) *There is no remaining personal representative.* A grant *de bonis non*
cannot be made following the death of one of a number of executors or
administrators since the remaining personal representatives have full
power to complete the administration. Similarly a grant *de bonis non*
cannot be made following the death of the last surviving executor if he has
appointed an executor who proves his will and so becomes an executor by
representation (see para.8.005 above).

(iii) *There has been a previous grant.* A grant *de bonis non* must always
follow a previous grant. An original grant is appropriate where an
executor has acted without a grant or someone has partly administered
the estate without any authority.

A grant *de bonis non* may be a grant of administration with will
annexed or a grant of simple administration. The order of priority for
taking the grant is governed by Non-Contentious Probate Rules 1987,
rules 20 and 22 which were explained above.

Usually the person (or persons) to whom the grant is made will be the
person who was entitled to a grant equally with the previous grantee or

who was next entitled after him. Where the previous personal representative was entitled to the whole of the estate the grant will usually be made to his personal representatives (the rule that living persons are to be preferred to the personal representatives of deceased persons only applies as between persons entitled in the same degree).

Where there is a minority or a life interest in the estate at the time when the application for the grant *de bonis non* is made two administrators will be required unless the court orders to the contrary or makes a grant to a trust corporation.

2. CESSATE GRANTS

8.035 A cessate grant is required where the original grant was limited in time and has ceased to be effective because the time has expired. The most common circumstances in which such a grant is required is where a grant of administration (with will or of simple administration) has been made to a guardian "for the use and benefit" of a minor who would be entitled to a grant but for his minority. When the minor reaches 18 the limited grant to his guardian automatically ceases to be effective and the minor is entitled to apply for a cessate grant. The cessate grant may be a grant of probate, administration with the will annexed or simple administration depending on the nature of the minor's entitlement.

A cessate grant is also appropriate in other circumstances where a grant is limited in time and the time expires. Thus if a will appoints an executor for life the executor's office ceases altogether with his death and so the chain of representation cannot provide the estate with an executor. A cessate grant is then made to any executor appointed in substitution for the deceased executor by the will (for example, the will may have appointed "A for life and thereafter B"). If no substitutional appointment has been made a cessate grant of administration with will is made to the person entitled under r.20. If a grant of simple administration is made for the use and benefit of a minor a cessate grant of simple administration is made to the minor when he reaches 18.

A cessate grant is theoretically different from a grant *de bonis non* since it is a general re-grant in respect of the whole estate rather than a limited grant in respect of the unadministered part. However, the practical effect of the two types of grant is the same.

3. DOUBLE PROBATE

8.036 A grant of double probate is made to an executor when he applies for a grant after a grant of *probate* has already been made to another executor. There are three types of case in which a grant of double probate is appropriate:

(i) Where one of a number of executors does not wish to take a grant immediately, does not wish to renounce and has not been cited to take or renounce probate, power will be reserved to him to take a grant later. He may then apply for double probate at any time.

(ii) Where one of a number of executors is a minor at the time of the original grant of probate to the others, power is reserved to him automatically and he can apply for double probate on reaching 18. If the original grant had been a grant of administration he would apply for a cessate grant not a grant of double probate. Thus where a will appoints several executors of whom some are adults and some minors a grant of probate will be made to the adults immediately and a grant of double probate to the minors on reaching majority. Where a will appoints a minor as the only executor a grant of administration with will annexed will be made to the guardians of the executor (or to the person entitled to residue if the minor executor was not so entitled) and a cessate grant of probate to the infant on reaching majority.

(iii) Where an executor is prevented from taking a grant by the rule which restricts a grant to four persons in respect of any part of an estate (Supreme Court Act 1981, s.114(1)) he may apply for a grant of double probate if a vacancy occurs (for example on the death of one of the four proving executors) since power is reserved to him in the original grant.

It should be noted that there is no possibility of double grants of *administration*. A potential administrator who does not prove in the original grant will only be able to take a grant later if a grant *de bonis non* or a cessate grant is needed or if a second administrator is needed because a life interest or minority arises.

When applying for a grant of double probate the oath must set out, in addition to the usual matters, particulars of the former grant. An office copy of the original grant should accompany the application.

K. Circumstances in which No Grant is Required

Since an executor's authority derives from the will rather than the grant of **8.037** probate certain steps may be taken without a grant. However, in nearly all circumstances a grant is eventually in fact required so that it can be produced to prove title to the assets of the estate.

There are a number of statutory provisions which enable certain assets to be dealt with without production of a grant but they are all concerned with relatively small amounts of property (see paras 12.008–12.010).

L. Revocation of Grants

1. JURISDICTION

In certain circumstances a grant may be revoked by the Chancery **8.038** Division (or county court) in contentious cases or by a district judge or registrar of the Family Division in non-contentious cases.

Where there is a dispute as to whether a grant should be revoked the case is contentious and every personal representative must be a party to the action. The original grant must be lodged with the court.

If there is no dispute as to the need for revocation the case is non-contentious. However, a grant cannot normally be revoked in non-contentious proceedings except on the application of the person to whom the grant was made.

2. GROUNDS FOR REVOCATION

8.039   A grant will be revoked if it is subsequently found that it ought not to have been made to the person to whom it was in fact made. This may arise in many ways: for example, where a fraudulent application is made by a person with no right to a grant; where a person thought to have predeceased is subsequently found to be alive and better entitled to a grant than the person to whom the original grant was made; where the grant was made despite the entry of a caveat; where a grant was made even though contentious probate proceedings were pending.

A grant will be revoked where a subsequent will is discovered (and in most cases where a subsequent codicil is discovered) or where it is found, after a grant, that the will was invalid or had been revoked before death.

A grant will be revoked where a personal representative becomes mentally or physically incapable, where he disappears or where he wishes to retire and the court agrees to this.

A grant will be revoked where the "deceased" is not in fact dead.

3. CONSEQUENCES OF REVOCATION

8.040   Section 27 of the Administration of Estates Act 1925 protects an original personal representative who makes or permits payments or dispositions in good faith. A person who makes a payment to a personal representative in good faith is also protected. Section 39 of the same Act provides that contracts for sale remain binding on and enforceable by the estate despite the revocation of the grant. Section 37 provides that a conveyance of any type of property remains valid despite revocation of the grant provided the conveyance is to a purchaser who gave valuable consideration in good faith (a conveyance is widely defined in this context and includes almost all dealings with property).

If property is transferred to the wrong beneficiary under a grant which is later revoked (for example, the property is distributed as on intestacy and then a will is found) the beneficiary is liable to return the asset or to refund its value. The true beneficiary is also entitled to trace the asset or its proceeds and to recover it from the person now in possession so long as it remains identifiable. However, there is no right to trace into the hands of a bona fide purchaser for value without notice.

9.   Probate Jurisdiction

A. Jurisdiction—Territorial Limits

Grants of representation are made by the English courts where property **9.001** of the deceased is situated in England and Wales and either an executor is appointed or such property is disposed of in England and Wales. A will which neither appoints an executor nor disposes of English property is not usually admitted to probate although the court has a discretion to issue a grant in such cases.

B. Nature of Probate Jurisdiction—Contentious and Non-Contentious Business

Probate jurisdiction is concerned with three things only. First, the **9.002** decision as to whether a document may be admitted to probate or annexed to a grant of administration as a testamentary document. Secondly, the decision as to who is entitled to a grant of representation in respect of the estate of a deceased person; thirdly, the decision to amend or revoke a grant.

Since 1970 probate business has been divided between the Family Division (which deals with non-contentious business), the Chancery Division (which deals with contentious business), and a county court which has a Chancery District Registry (which has concurrent jurisdiction to deal with contentious business where the value of the estate of the deceased does not exceed a limit laid down by rules of court, the present limit is £30,000).

Non-contentious business (which is also called common form business) is defined by Supreme Court Act 1981, s.128 as:

> "the business of obtaining probate and administration where there is no contention as to the right thereto, including—
>
> (a) the passing of probates and administrations through the High Court in contentious cases where the contest has been terminated, and
> (b) all business of a non-contentious nature in matters of testacy and intestacy not being proceedings in any action, and
> (c) the business of lodging caveats against the grant of probate or administration."

The vast majority of probate cases are non-contentious and are dealt with entirely by the Family Division. Non-contentious probate may involve a hearing before a district judge or registrar; for example a hearing may be required to decide between persons entitled to a grant in the same degree, or where the court is asked to pass over a person entitled to a grant in favour of some other person.

Where there is a dispute as to what document or documents should be admitted to probate, or as to who is entitled to take out a grant, or as to whether a grant should be revoked, contentious (or solemn form) proceedings may be necessary and will be brought in the Chancery Division or county court. In most cases non-contentious proceedings will begin first and the case will only become contentious when the dispute arises.

A grant of representation in common form does not prevent a probate claim for proof in solemn form from being brought later. Thus if, after the Family Division has granted probate, someone wishes to challenge the validity of the will he may issue a writ to start contentious proceedings.

Frequently where there is a dispute a caveat or citation will be entered but neither of these steps is, of itself, sufficient to start a contentious probate action.

After a probate claim is started, the case remains contentious until the dispute is finally decided by the Chancery Division or the county court. Once the dispute is disposed of, the case becomes non-contentious and so is returned to the Family Division which is responsible for the issue of the grant (the Family Division is the only court which actually makes grants).

C. Financial Limits

9.003   The jurisdiction of the High Court (Family and Chancery Division) is unlimited as to the amount of the estate. The county court has no jurisdiction in non-contentious cases and its jurisdiction in contentious cases is limited to cases where the estate is less than the county court limit at the time of death. (In valuing the estate for this purpose debts, funeral expenses and incumbrances are deducted as is property vested in the deceased as trustee and not beneficially.) The county court with jurisdiction is the one within whose area the deceased was resident at the date of death. Once proceedings have been commenced in the county court the principal registry should be informed so that no grant is made in common form in the estate. Proceedings in the county court are commenced by summons.

D. Probate Jurisdiction and Other Jurisdiction Concerning Wills

9.004   Probate jurisdiction is concerned only with what documents are admissible as testmentary documents and to whom grants should be made. Litigation concerning wills and administration of estates may, however, arise in at least three other ways:

    (a) there may be no dispute as to what should be admitted as a testamentary document but a dispute as to what it means (that is, a question of construction may arise);

(b) there may be a dispute as to how the estate should be administered by the personal representatives (so that an administration action becomes necessary); or

(c) there may be a claim against a personal representative who is alleged to have acted improperly (and so may be liable for the *devastavit* which he has committed).

Proceedings in each of these three types of case will usually be brought in the Chancery Division. When a question of construction is before the court, it is bound by the decision of the Family Division (or of the Chancery Division in earlier probate proceedings) as to the wording of the testamentary instrument. Questions of construction are not generally decided in probate proceedings except to the extent that it is necessary for the purpose of the probate action. Thus, it is appropriate for the court to decide, in probate proceedings, who the testator intended to appoint as executor and what parts of earlier wills or codicils have been revoked by a later testamentary document.

E. Solemn Form Procedure

We have already outlined the distinction between common form and solemn form probate. We intend to give no more than an outline of the solemn form procedure in the High Court (Chancery Division). (The procedure for obtaining a grant in common form cases is dealt with in Chapter 10.)   **9.005**

Probate claims are dealt with in Part 57 of the Civil Procedure Rules 1998 and the Practice Direction Supplemental to Part 57 which deals with rectification of wills and the removal of personal representatives as well as contentious probate. Part 57 (which was added to the Rules by the Civil Procedure (Amendment No 2) Rules 2001, SI 2001/1388) came into force on October 15, 2001.   **9.006**

The action is started by issuing a claim form under Civil Procedure Rules Part 7 in a Chancery District Registry or Chancery Chambers at the Royal Courts of Justice (or in the county court office if the case is in the County Court). A defendant served with the claim must file an acknowledgement of service within 28 days (or within 28 days of service of the particulars of claim if later). Any testamentary documents in the possession of the claimant must be lodged in the Court when the claim form is issued, any in the possession of the defendant must be lodged when he acknowledges service (CPR 57.5).

The claim form must contain a statement of the nature of the interest of the claimant in the estate and of the nature of each defendant's interest (CPR 57.7 (1), (2)). A party who disputes any such statement must say so in his statement of case. Similarly a party claiming that the testator did not know or approve of the contents of the will, lacked capacity or was subject to undue influence or fraud must say so and give particulars of the facts on which he relies (CPR 57.7 (3), (4)).

A default judgment cannot be obtained in a probate action. If service is not acknowledged the claimant can proceed with the action as if it had been acknowledged.

The normal rules about costs contained in CPR 44 apply to probate claims. Thus the court has a discretion as to who pays costs and the amount of costs. The costs are not automatically paid out of the estate. Generally the unsuccessful party will be ordered to pay the costs of the successful party. An executor who successfully proves a will is entitled to take his own costs out of the estate.

10.   Obtaining the Grant
(Non-Contentious Cases)

A. Probate Jurisdiction

Most non-contentious or common form probate business is dealt with in **10.001**
the Principal Registry of the Family Division in London or one of the
district registries (most of these district registries have sub-registries
attached to them). The judicial officers of the Principal Registry are called
district judges and those of the district registries are called registrars. In
cases of doubt or uncertainty a district judge or registrar may refer a
matter to a judge of the Family Division (Non-Contentious Probate Rules
1987, r.61). Registries do not have "catchment areas"; the choice of
registry is governed by convenience and personal preference.

It is not necessary for a personal representative to consult a solicitor.
The personal representative can make a personal application at the
Principal Registry or at a district registry or sub-registry or at certain local
probate offices served from the nearest registry. The procedure is simple
and will not be considered here. We are concerned only with the
procedure where a solicitor is acting for the personal representative.

B. The Papers Leading to a Grant

The solicitor must send or deliver the following: **10.002**

  (a) The Inland Revenue Account, if required, and cheque or money
      order for any inheritance tax due. If the grant is to be taken in
      England and Wales the completed account together with a
      remittance for tax and interest must normally be sent to Section
      K in Ferrers House, Nottingham (if the grant is to be applied for
      in Newcastle, payment should be made to the Edinburgh office)
      or taken by hand to Somerset House.

      The receipted account is returned to the solicitor who can then
      deliver it to the Principal or district registry with the other
      papers.

      Cheques should be made payable to "Inland Revenue" and
      crossed. (In certain circumstances the Inland Revenue may
      accept assets in satisfaction of the whole or any part of any
      liability to inheritance tax for example, works of art of "pre-
      eminent" standard under the Inheritance Tax Act 1984, s.230.)
  (b) The appropriate oath sworn or affirmed by the personal
      representatives before an independent solicitor.
  (c) Probate fees. A crossed cheque made payable to H.M. Pay-

master General should be used. If the estate is £5,000 or less there is no fee. If the estate exceeds £5,000 the fee is currently £50 (£130 for a personal application—that is where no solicitor is acting). The applicant may also obtain office copies of the grant for £1.

(d) The will (if there is one) and any codicils to it. A photographic copy of the will is normally annexed to the grant of representation by the registry. However, if the registrar considers that the will is unsuitable for photographic reproduction or if it contains inadmissible alterations or other irrelevant matter the registry will require the applicant's solicitor to supply a typewritten engrossment. In such circumstances, as an alternative to an engrossment the registrar has a discretion to allow a facsimile copy produced by photography in certain circumstances including:

(i) where a complete page is, or complete pages are, to be excluded;

(ii) where the original has been altered but neither re-executed nor republished and there is in existence a photocopy of the original executed document.

If the whole or part of the will has been written in pencil, a copy of the will in which the words which appear in pencil in the original are underlined in red ink must be lodged with the will.

If the original will has been lost or destroyed it may be possible to obtain an order admitting to proof the will as contained in a copy or reconstruction (Non-Contentious Probate Rules 1987, r.54(1)). If the original will is lodged in a foreign court a duly authenticated copy of the will may be admitted to proof without need for an order (Non-Contentious Probate Rules, r.54(2)). If the will incorporates standard clauses these need not be produced provided that the forms or clauses are contained in published documents and have previously been lodged with the senior district judge of the principal registry and accepted by him as sufficient lodgment for these purposes (Practice Direction issued by Senior District Judge Angel, April 10, 1995).

(e) Any affidavit evidence that may be required, for example an affidavit of due execution.

(f) Any renunciation by a person who would have been entitled to a grant in priority to the applicant (see para.8.018).

(Items (a), (b) and (e) are considered in more detail later in this chapter.)

Once the appropriate papers have been lodged at the registry all testamentary documents are photographed. Searches are made; one to ensure that no caveat has been entered against the estate and one to ensure that no grant of representation has already been issued. Searches are also made to ensure that no application for a grant has been made in a different registry and that no will has been deposited with the registry.

The papers are examined and if they are in order the grant of representation is prepared. A photographic copy of the will and codicils (if any) is attached to the grant. Grants are usually signed by a Probate Officer under the authority of the President of the Family Division; they are sealed with the seal of the Division. The grant is sent by post to the extracting solicitor together with any office copies which have been requested.

If there are defects in the papers the registry will contact the extracting solicitor so that the queries can be resolved.

C. Oaths

1. INTRODUCTION

Every application for a grant of representation must be supported by an oath. The oath is prepared by the solicitor acting for the personal representatives and it must be sworn (or affirmed) by the personal representatives before an independent solicitor.   **10.003**

The oath performs three functions:

    (a) It sets out the basis of the applicant's claim to be entitled to take the grant (for example, in the case of an executor it recites the fact that the applicant is the person named as executor in the will).

    (b) It requires the applicant to swear that he will duly collect in the assets of the deceased and duly administer the estate.

    (c) In the case of applications for grants of probate and letters of administration with the will annexed, the oath exhibits and identifies the will and any codicils to it.

The three most common oaths are the oaths leading to a first grant of probate, letters of administration with the will annexed or simple letters of administration. The three oaths are similar but differ in points of detail. Points common to all three oaths are considered first and then points relevant to specific types of oath.

2. FORM OF OATHS

The form which the oaths are to take is not laid down so that, provided the applicant swears to or affirms the facts which will lead to a grant in his or her case any words may be used. Precedents for the three common oath forms are included in the appendix.   **10.004**

3. POINTS COMMON TO ALL OATHS

Affirmation

An "oath" need not be sworn but can be affirmed. If a person wishes to affirm, the words "make oath and say" which appear twice in the body of the oath can be deleted and replaced by the words "do solemnly and sincerely affirm". The words "sworn by" in the jurat at the end of the form should then be deleted and replaced by the words "affirmed by".   **10.005**

Solicitor's name and address

The name and address of the extracting solicitor should appear in the top right hand corner of the oath. Correspondence concerning queries will   **10.006** then be sent to the solicitor and not to the personal representatives themselves. It is desirable to add the solicitor's reference immediately afterwards since the reference will then be included on the grant of representation when it is returned by the registry.

The deceased's name

10.007   The true and proper name of the deceased must always be given. The true and proper name of the deceased is normally the name in which the birth was registered or in the case of a married or divorced woman the surname of her husband (if she has adopted her husband's name). The true and proper name may have been changed by:

(a) deed poll; or
(b) habit and repute; however, a name is only regarded as changed by habit and repute if the former name has been completely abandoned over a period of time.

A testator may have been known by a name (or names) other than his true and proper name; such a name is not to be included on the oath unless it is necessary that the name appear on the grant of representation. It is necessary if the will was made in a name other than the testator's true and proper name or if property was owned in a name other than the true and proper name.

An explanation justifying the inclusion of the other name must either be given in a separate affidavit or, if it can be stated sufficiently concisely included in the oath. Examples of such concise explanations are:

1. "That the true and proper name of the deceased was Jane Brown but she made and duly executed the said will in the name of Jane LeBrun."

2. "That the true and proper name of the deceased was Jane Brown but certain property, to wit . . . is vested in her in the name of Jane LeBrun." In such a case at least one property held in the other name must be specified.

The deceased's address

10.008   The address given must have been the usual residential address including post code of the deceased at the time of death. In the case of an oath leading to a grant of probate or letters of administration with the will annexed if the latest testamentary document gives an address different from the last address of the testator that former address should be given but all other earlier addresses may be ignored.

The date of death of the deceased

10.009   This must be set out as it appears in the certificate of death. In cases where the precise date of death is uncertain the following wording is used:

> "who was known to be alive on . . . and whose dead body was found on . . ."

If a person is believed to be dead but his body has not been found (for example, because the deceased was aboard a ship which disappeared) the Family Division can make an order giving leave to swear that the person who is believed to be dead died "on or since" a certain date. The wording of such an order should be repeated in the oath.

Age of the deceased at death

If the precise age of the deceased is not known the best estimate possible   **10.010**
should be given.

Domicile of the deceased

If the deceased died domiciled in England or Wales this should be recited   **10.011**
as "England and Wales" (because England and Wales is one jurisdiction).
If there is any doubt as to domicile an affidavit setting out the fact should
be filed in support of the oath. The Administration of Estates Act 1971
provides that where a grant of representation is issued in England and
Wales, Scotland or Northern Ireland in respect of the estate of a person
who died domiciled in one of these countries, the grant will be recognised
in the other two countries provided it contains a statement of the
deceased's domicile. Thus, if a person dies domiciled in Scotland owning
assets in England and Wales, provided the Scots confirmation contains a
reference to the domicile of the deceased it will be recognised as the
equivalent of an English grant.

Settled land

Each oath must contain a paragraph relating to land settled before the   **10.012**
death of the deceased and continuing settled after his death. If there was
no such settled land comprised in the deceased's estate the paragraph is
left as printed.

If there was settled land the word "no" must be deleted. Normally such
settled land devolves not on the general personal representatives but on
the trustees of the settlement who take out a special grant of
representation limited to the settled land. Therefore normally in such a
case the general personal representatives must qualify the later
paragraph by inserting in the appropriate spaces the words "save and
except settled land". If however the settled land is to devolve on the
general personal representatives (for example, where they happen to be
the trustees of the settlement) the words "including settled land" must be
inserted. Since the Trusts of Land Act 1996 no new Settled Land Act
settlement can be created.

The personal representatives swear to collect and get in the real and
personal estate and to administer it

Each oath contains a paragraph which sets out the duties of a personal   **10.013**
representative (to collect, get in and administer the estate etc.). Nothing
need to be done to this paragraph unless the estate included settled land
in which case as stated in para.10.12 above the words "save and except" or
"including" settled land must be inserted.

Gross and net estate

Each oath contains a paragraph dealing with the gross and net value of the   **10.014**
estate *which passes under the grant.* The deponent(s) must swear to the
gross and net values. The paragraph contains two alternatives one of
which must be deleted.

    (a) "the gross estate passing under the grant not exceed £   and
        the net estate does not exceed £   , and this is not a case in

which an Inland Revenue Account is required" or
(b) "the gross estate passing under the grant amounts to £   and
the net estate amounts to £   "

The deponent is not concerned with the value of any part of the estate which does not pass under the grant. The following property does not pass under the grant: a life interest, joint property devolving by survivorship, property which is the subject of a *donatio mortis causa* or nomination. The test is whether the grant is necessary to establish a claimant's right to the property. The *gross* value of such property must be stated because the personal representatives swear that they will duly administer the estate, due administration of the estate includes the payment of debts; therefore, they must swear to gross figures not merely to net ones. The net value must be stated since probate fees are calculated on the basis of the value of the net estate passing under the grant.

If the gross estate passing under the grant does not exceed £220,000 and the other circumstances are such that no Inland Revenue Account need be delivered, that is, the deceased died on or after April 1, 1990 and the estate is an "excepted estate" (as defined in para.10.035 below) para.(a) should be completed and para.(b) deleted. If the recital that this is not a case where an Inland Revenue Account is required is omitted, the oath will be returned for the recital to be inserted and the oath resworn. Paragraph (a) must state that the net estate passing under the grant does not exceed the figure on which probate fees are payable.

Where an Inland Revenue account is required to be delivered para.(a) must be deleted and para.(b) completed with the precise values of the gross and net estate passing under the grant.

In para.(b) the figures for gross and net estate passing under the grant are the figures shown on page D18 of the Inland Revenue Account.

The jurat

10.015   The oath must be sworn by each deponent in the presence of an independent Commissioner for Oaths or solicitor. An independent solicitor is one who is not a member of the extracting solicitor's firm. The place and date of swearing must be given precisely; it is not sufficient to give the name of the town. If there is more than one deponent and each swears at a different time the name of each should be inserted in a separate jurat. Otherwise the name of the deponent(s) need not be inserted at all; it is sufficient for the jurat to refer to "the above named deponents." The wording of the jurat must be altered if there is to be an affirmation.

4. OATH FOR EXECUTORS

10.016   This oath is set out on page 401 of the Appendix.

"[I/we] ... /of ..."

10.017   The first paragraph of the oath for executors should commence with the words "I" or "we" as appropriate. The names, addresses and occupations or descriptions of each of the deponents should be inserted. The order of names should be the same as that given in the will and the order of names given on the oath will be repeated on the grant of representation. Sometimes the deponents wish to vary the order so that a trust corporation or professional person can be named first and in this case a letter of consent signed by the executors may be filed with the affidavit. However, if no such letter is filed the executors are presumed to have consented to the change.

The true and proper name of each of the executors must be given. Since one of the functions of the oath is to explain the basis of the claimant's right to take a grant by identifying him as the executor named in the will, it is necessary to give an explanation if the true and proper name differs from the name given in the will. The wording used will vary according to the circumstances:

(a) If the discrepancy is very small it is sufficient to say "in the will called" or if it is a mistake in the spelling "in the will written".

Example

"Jennifer Smith in the will called Jenny Smith"

(b) If a change of name was made by deed poll the date of the deed poll should be recited and the deed itself lodged for inspection.

Example

"Charles Coomb, formerly Charles Crumb who changed my name by deed poll dated the 5th day of December 1982."

(c) If the change of name was made on marriage the previous marital status should be given.

Example

"Jennifer Smith, married woman, formerly and in the will called Jennifer Brown, spinster."

(d) If the change of name was by habit and repute the fact that the former name has been completely abandoned must be recited.

Example

"That I was formerly known as David Button but assumed the name of David Betten on or about the 4th of December 1960 since when I have never used the name of David Button but have always been known as David Betten."

Relationship

It is quite common for a will to mention a relationship in the appointment of an executor for example, "I appoint my niece Frances Brown".

It is also quite common for testators to make a mistake in such relationships, for example referring to someone as a niece who is in fact a niece of the deceased's spouse. In such a case the oath must state that the deceased had no relative of that name and degree of relationship and recite such facts as will establish that the deponent was the person intended. If the will simply refers to "my wife" or "my husband" the oath must state that the deponent was the lawful spouse *at the time the will was signed.*

Address
The full, private and permanent address of the deponent must be given. A solicitor, or other person administering the estate in a professional capacity may give a professional address only. Other persons may give a business address in addition to a private address but only if it can be shown to be for the advantage of the estate.

Occupations or descriptions
The occupation of a male or female deponent must be given in precise language (if the person is retired the former occupation should be given qualified by the word retired).

If a woman has no occupation she may be described by reference to her marital status, *i.e.* as "spinster", "married woman", "widow" or in the case of a divorced woman as "single woman" or "single woman, formerly the wife of . . .". The marital status of female grantees does not appear on the grant of representation but if a woman so wishes the word "Mrs" or "Miss" can be included on the oath in which case they will also appear on the grant (Practice Note December 16, 1971—the Practice Note does not mention the possibility of including "Ms").

"Make oath and say that [I/we] believe the paper writing now produced to and marked by [me/us] to be the true and original last will and testament . . ."

10.018   This paragraph performs two functions:

    (a) it makes the oath binding on the deponents. (If the deponent wishes to affirm, the words "make oath and say" must be altered to "do solemnly and sincerely affirm" here, later in the oath (see para.10.019) and in the jurat); and

    (b) it identifies the documents which it is desired be admitted to probate. The deponent and person before whom the oath is being sworn must sign their names on each document. The signatures should be placed away from the text, if possible, since if the document is made unsuitable for photographic reproduction the Probate Registry will require an engrossment of the will.

If there are codicils to the will the words "with . . .codicils thereto" must be added to "the true and original last will and testament". If a codicil has been revoked by a later codicil, the earlier codicil must still be proved if it altered the terms of the original will or a previous codicil.

If the original will is unavailable the word "original" should be deleted. If the original is lodged in a foreign court an official copy (bearing the seal, if any, of the court) must be marked and the oath must refer to "the true last will and testament as contained in a true and official copy thereof". If the original will is lost or destroyed a court order must be obtained allowing probate to be obtained of a copy, draft or reconstruction. The oath must refer to "the true last will and testament as contained in a copy thereof" or " ... as contained in a completed draft thereof".

"And [I/we] further make oath and say that notice of this application has been given to the executor(s) to whom power is to be reserved"
Rule 27 of the Non-Contentious Probate Rules 1987 provides that notice **10.019** of an application for a grant of probate must be given to any executor to whom power is reserved. The oath for executors must therefore (in cases where power is reserved to an executor) include the paragraph set out above stating that such notice has been given. The district judge or registrar can dispense with the need to give notice if he is satisfied that to do so is impracticable or would result in unreasonable delay or expense. Application for such dispensation is made by letter. Where a partner (or partners) in a firm of solicitors applies for a grant it is not necessary to give notice to other partners to whom power is reserved unless they are named in the will.

When an executor wishes power to be reserved to him to prove at a later stage it is not necessary to include a statement to this effect in the oath; but the name of such an executor should be written in the margin.

"And [I/we] further make oath and say that [I/we] [am/are] ... the ... [executors/executrices] named in the said will."
If only some of the living executors named in the will wish to take probate **10.020** the number of such executors should be inserted for example, "we are two of the executors named in the said will."

If some of the executors are dead but all the living executors wish to take probate the living ones should be referred to as "the surviving executors". If only one executor was named in the will such a person is referred to as "the sole" executor.

If some of the proving executors are male and some are female, all should be referred to as "executors". If all are female, they should be referred to as "executrices".

If any executors have renounced probate this need not be referred to in the oath but the instrument of renunciation should be filed with the papers. It is not necessary for persons unwilling to take the grant to renounce. Instead power can be reserved to them to prove at a later date.

5. THE OATH FOR ADMINISTRATORS WITH WILL ANNEXED

The oath is set out on page 402 of the Appendix. **10.021**

Comparison with oath for executors
This oath is similar to that sworn by executors in that it refers to the will to **10.022** explain the basis of the deponent's claim to be entitled to administer the estate. It, therefore, has to identify the will in the same way that the oath for executors does. However, the oath must recite that the deponent is the person entitled in priority to take the grant and must explain that persons with prior rights (for example, persons appointed executors in the will)

have been cleared off. We will comment only on those parts of the oath which differ from the oath for executors.

["I/we] ... of ... "

10.023 The same details of name, address and occupations or descriptions that are given in the case of executors must be given for administrators; any discrepancy between will and oath must be explained. The order in which such names appear on the oath is determined by the extent of their interest in the estate.

"that ... minority ... life interests in [his/her] estate"

10.024 If a minority or life interest exists no matter how small it may be (but see para.10.027 for details of certain permitted deductions that may extinguish an apparent minority or life interest) the grant will usually have to be made to at least two individuals or to a trust corporation. Therefore, the oath must state whether or not there is a minority or life interest.

Clearing off persons with prior rights

10.025 The deponent must insert a paragraph explaining that any person with a prior right has been cleared off. Priority is governed by r.20 of the Non-Contentious Probate Rules 1987.

If the will did not appoint executors this must be recited. If the will did appoint executors the reason why they are not seeking a grant must be stated (for example, because an appointed executor died without taking a grant). Similarly the oath must state why any other person with a prior right is not seeking a grant. The reasons are likely to be:

(a) death, or
(b) renunciation, or
(c) failure to appear to citation.

The precise wording of such a recital will vary according to the circumstances, the following is a specimen:

> "That A, the sole surviving executor and trustee appointed in the will, predeceased the deceased [or survived the deceased but has since died without having proved the will] and that B, the residuary legatee and devisee for life named in the will, has renounced letters of administration with the will annexed and that C, the ultimate residuary legatee and devisee, has been duly cited to accept or refuse letters of administration with the will annexed. That in default of appearance of the said C to the said citation it was ordered by District Judge [...] of this Division on the ... day of ... 20..... that letters of administration with the will annexed be granted to [me/us]."

It is common practice for an applicant for a grant to file, with the other papers, the renunciation of any executor or any person having an interest prior to his own.

It is not necessary to clear off persons entitled in the *same* degree as the applicant. For example, if there are three specific legatees one of whom wishes to take a grant he must clear off persons with a *prior* right but not the other two specific legatees.

Recital of deponent's right to grant

After clearing off any person with a prior right the oath must state the exact capacity in which the applicant claims the grant. If the applicant is claiming as a person entitled under a partial intestacy the relationship (if any) must be given.   **10.026**

Examples

> "one of the residuary legatees and devisees named in the will."
> "one of the specific legatees and devisees named in the will."
> "a brother of the whole blood of the deceased and one of the persons entitled to share in the undisposed of estate of the said deceased."

If the person entitled to the grant is a minor and the applicants are taking a grant for his use and benefit the oath must recite this and must also show the applicants' authority to take such a grant. Suitable wording would be:

> "That A is the residuary legatee and devisee named in the said will and is a minor, the said A being the age of … and that there is no other person appointed or deemed to be appointed guardian of the said minor and that I, C, am the father and statutory guardian of the said minor and I, D, am the person nominated by an instrument in writing dated the … day of … 20….. under the hand of the said C, for the purpose of joining with him in taking a grant of letters of administration with will annexed of the estate of the said deceased."

Similarly if a grant is to be taken out for the use and benefit of a person who is mentally incapable of managing his own affairs the oath should state this and should show the basis of the applicant's right to take the grant; for example, that the applicant is the person authorised by the Court of Protection.

Permitted deductions

At the end of any oath immediately before the jurat it is always possible to insert additional necessary information. Sometimes it is desired to show details of "permitted deductions" from the value of the estate which may reduce the value of the estate below £125,000 or £200,000. This is done where the effect of such deductions will be to reduce the value of the estate to such an extent that no life interest or minority interest arise in respect of any undisposed of property so that it may be possible for the grant to issue to a sole administrator.   **10.027**

The permitted deductions are:

(a) the value of personal chattels,
(b) debts,
(c) inheritance tax payable from the estate without a right of recovery from any other person or property,
(d) fair and reasonable costs incurred and to be incurred,
(e) probate fees.

6. OATH FOR ADMINISTRATORS

10.028   The oath is set out on page 403 of the Appendix.

Comparison with oath for executors and oath for administrators with the will annexed
10.029   This oath is sworn where the deceased left no valid will. It follows that there is no will to identify and no need to refer to a will to establish the basis of the deponent's claim. Instead the oath must recite the relationship of the deponent to the deceased and show that all persons with a prior right have been cleared off. Only those parts of the oath which differ from the previous oaths will be commented on.

"[I/We] ... of ... "
10.030   The same details of names, addresses and occupations or description that are given in the case of executors must be given in the case of administrators although obviously in the case of an intestacy there can be no discrepancy between will and oath to require explanation. The order of names is governed by their priority to take a grant. A change can be made at the request of all applicants.

Clearing off persons with prior rights
10.031   Immediately after the words "died domiciled in ...intestate" the applicant must explain in what way persons with prior rights have been cleared off. Priority is governed by the Non-Contentious Probate Rules 1987, r.22. Clearing off is done either by stating that the deceased left no-one in the prior categories set out in r.22 or by stating that there were such people at the time of the intestate's death but they have since renounced their rights, failed to appear to a citation or died without taking a grant. A surviving spouse has first claim to a grant so if the intestate left no spouse the oath must first state that the deceased died intestate "a bachelor" or "a spinster" or "a widower" or "a widow" or "a single man" or "a single woman".

Any other persons entitled under r.22 are cleared off by stating that the deceased died *without* "issue", or "parent", or "brother or sister of the whole [or half] blood" or "their issue", or "grandparent", or "uncle and aunt of the whole [or half] blood" or "their issue".

If a person with a prior right has renounced, an example of the wording is as follows:

> "died intestate, a widow, without issue or parent (or any other person entitled in priority to share in her estate by virtue of any enactment) leaving B her brother of the whole blood and the only person entitled to her estate surviving her and that the said B has duly renounced letters of administration."

If a person with a prior right has survived the intestate but died before taking a grant, that person's personal representatives can apply for the grant and the wording is as follows:

"died intestate leaving W his lawful widow and the only person now entitled to his estate surviving him and that the said W has since died without having taken upon herself letters of administration of the said estate."

It is not necessary to clear off persons entitled in the same degree as the applicant. For example, if there are three children of the deceased one child does not need to clear off the other two.

"And further make oath and say that [I am/we are] ... of the deceased"
The applicant must here show the precise relationship to the deceased **10.032** and state whether he or she is "the only person entitled to the estate of the deceased" or "one of the persons entitled to share in the estate of the deceased" or "a person who may have a beneficial interest in the estate of the said deceased in the event of an accretion thereto."

A surviving spouse is described as "the lawful husband" or "the lawful widow." Since the Family Law Reform Act 1987 it is no longer necessary to describe a child as either "lawful" or "natural". An adopted child should be described as "lawful adopted". A child of a deceased uncle or aunt can be described as "a cousin german".

If the application is made by a grandchild, nephew or niece or cousin german the oath must recite that the parent through whom the claim is made died in the lifetime of the deceased.

It is not necessary to swear in the oath that those with an *equal* entitlement to a grant have been informed of this application (contrast the oath for executors where such a statement is required).

Permitted deductions
As with the oath for administrators with the will annexed details of **10.033** permitted deductions may be shown.

D. Inland Revenue Accounts and Payment of Tax

1. INTRODUCTION

A grant of representation will not, normally, be issued until the personal **10.034** representatives have lodged an Inland Revenue Account giving full details of the deceased's estate and until they have paid the amount, if any, of inheritance tax for which they are liable (Supreme Court Act 1981, s.109(1)). This account, where it is required, must generally be delivered within 12 months of the end of the month in which the death occurred or within three months after the applicant begins to act as personal representative if later. Certain estates are excepted from the requirement of delivering an account prior to the issue of the grant.

The purpose of the account is to enable the extracting solicitor acting on behalf of the personal representatives to list the deceased's assets and to calculate the inheritance tax liability, if any. The Inland Revenue will then check the extracting solicitor's "self-assessment" to tax to determine whether or not it is correct.

It should be emphasised that, unless the estate is an "excepted estate", the account must be delivered whether or not there is any tax to pay either on delivery of the account or at any time in the future. If tax is payable on delivery of the account, the personal representative's solicitor must send a cheque for the tax and form D18 (the "Probate Summary") to the Capital Taxes Office together with the account. The CTO retains the account and returns form D18 to the solicitor showing that tax has been paid. Form D18 is lodged with the Probate Registry when the application for the grant is made. If it is discovered at a later date that the Inland Revenue Account does not reflect the true circumstances of the deceased's estate a corrective account must be filed within six months of the discovery.

The advance of modern technology means that the Revenue will now accept computer generated facsimiles of Inland Revenue Accounts. The Revenue has issued a Statement of Practice (SP2/93) setting out the requirements for the acceptance of such forms. They must be "virtually indistinguishable" from the official forms and approval of the facsimile must have been obtained in advance from the Customer Service Manager.

2. "EXCEPTED ESTATES" WHERE NO INLAND REVENUE ACCOUNT NEED BE FILED

10.035 The obligation to file an Inland Revenue Account does not apply to "excepted estates". In the case of deaths after April 5, 2002 these are estates where:

(a) the value of the estate is attributable wholly to property passing under that person's will or intestacy or under a nomination of an asset taking effect on death or by survivorship in the case of a beneficial joint tenancy or under an interest in possession trust;

(b) any trust assets in which the deceased had an interest in possession were held in an interest in possession trust and do not exceed £100,000 in value;

(c) the total *gross* value of that property together with chargeable lifetime transfers referred to in para.(e) below did not exceed £220,000;

(d) of that property not more than £75,000 represented value attributable to property then situated outside the United Kingdom;

(e) that person died domiciled in the United Kingdom; and

(f) without having made any chargeable transfers (or potentially exempt transfers which have become chargeable as a result of the transferor's death within seven years) during his lifetime other than gifts of cash and/or quoted shares and securities not exceeding £100,000 in value.

Thus if the deceased died with a relatively small estate and a nil cumulative total, no account need be filed. For the purposes of determining the size of the estate, if the deceased was a joint tenant, only the value of his beneficial interest is taken into account when considering the £220,000 limit. If the estate later proves not to be an "excepted estate" because, for example, further property is discovered which increases the value of the estate, an Inland Revenue Account must be delivered within six months of the discovery.

An estate cannot be excepted if the deceased gave away property *inter vivos* subject to a reservation and at his death the reservation is still subsisting or if the reservation was released within seven years before the donor's death.

The Inland Revenue has power to require, by notice in writing within the "prescribed period", the delivery of an Inland Revenue account even where the estate is excepted. The "prescribed period" begins with the death and ends 35 days after the date of the first general grant of representation.

3. IHT FORM 200

Introduction

If the estate is not "excepted" from the need to do so the intending **10.036** personal representatives will have to complete and deliver the inland revenue account, form IHT 200. This form can be obtained at *www.inlandrevenue.gov.uk/cto/iht/htm* or by telephoning the Capital Taxes Office. Form 200 and its supplements together form a formidably long document. Form 200 itself consists of eight basic pages which summarise details of the assets of the estate. Details of the deceased and of the personal representatives are also included together with a calculation of the tax and a declaration as to the accuracy of the form. Depending on the circumstances of the estate up to 16 supplementary pages giving details of particular assets and exemptions are also required. A probate summary sets out details of the estate for probate purposes and, when approved by the CTO, is used to satisfy the Probate Registry that any tax payable before grant has in fact been paid. Finally there is a five page worksheet which is designed to help with the actual calculation of the tax. The eight pages of the form, the supplementary page for use where there is a will, the probate summary and the worksheet are reproduced in the Appendix at pages 416–429.

The rules as to calculation of inheritance tax and as to the liability to pay the tax were explained in Chapter 4. Form 200 is designed to allow self assessment of the tax liability taking into account:

(a) the amount of tax payable on the death estate taking into account any lifetime chargeable transfers and any exemptions and reliefs available on death;

(b) the amount of tax payable by the personal representatives on the one hand and trustees of any settlement in which the deceased had an interest on the other hand. (It will be recalled that personal representatives are responsible for the tax on joint property, property given away by a *donatio mortis causa* or nomination and foreign assets even though they do not vest in them and so are not part of the estate for probate purposes);

(c) the amount of tax payable on delivery of the account as opposed to tax payable by instalments.

The form also allows calculation of the value of the estate for probate purposes.

IHT 200 pages 1–2

10.037   The first page consists of details of the probate registry to be used, of the deceased and of the solicitor who is making the application for the personal representative (personal applications for probate or administration are permitted and are quite common but the procedure for dealing with inheritance tax is then quite different and is not dealt with further in this book). Page 2 enables the person completing the form to work out what supplementary pages are required to deal with particular types of assets and with any exemptions which are available. If any such pages are required, they should be completed first as they contain information which will be summarised in form IHT 200 itself.

IHT 200 pages 3–5

10.038   Page 3 is a list of the assets of the estate in the United Kingdom on which tax, if any, is payable by the personal representatives and may not be paid by instalments (and so is payable on delivery of the account). In the case of many items a supplementary page will already have been filled in to work out the total to be entered on page 3. Liabilities of the estate, funeral expenses and exemptions and reliefs on non-instalment option property are entered on page 4. The total non-instalment option property on page 3 less the deductions on page 4 thus provides a value of the chargeable assets in the United Kingdom on which tax is payable on delivery of the account by the personal representatives.

Page 5 is a list of the assets of the estate in the United Kingdom on which tax, if any, may be paid by instalments (and so is not payable on delivery of the account unless the personal representatives choose to do so). In many cases a supplementary page will already have been filled in to work out the totals to be entered on page 5. Liabilities and reliefs in respect of instalment option property are also entered on page 5.

Supplementary pages

Supplementary page D1 is reproduced in the appendix. This gives details of the will of the deceased if there is one.

The other supplementary pages (other than D18—see below) are not reproduced. It should be noted that some of these pages relate to property which is within the estate for tax purposes but not for probate purposes and on which the personal representatives are liable for tax (joint property—page D4, foreign property—page D15) and to settled property (page D5) which is not part of the estate for probate purposes and on which the personal representatives are not liable to tax.

Inheritance tax worksheet and pages 6–8

10.039   The worksheet is reproduced in the appendix at pages 424–427. Its purpose is to enable calculation of the amount of tax payable on death and to distinguish between what is payable on delivery of the account and what is payable by instalments and between what is payable by the personal representatives and what is payable by others.

The first page of the worksheet lists the assets which form part of the estate on which the personal representatives are liable to pay the tax. The second page lists other property which is taken into account to calculate the tax. This includes settled property on which the trustees are to pay the tax and the cumulative total of lifetime chargeable transfers (this information is needed to work out how much, if any, of the nil rate band is available on death). Care should be taken in completing the settled property boxes. Although it is not immediately apparent from the form, boxes WS4 and WS9 are only to be used where the personal representatives will pay the tax on the settled property (which they may choose to do in certain cases—usually because they happen also to be the trustees and so it is administratively convenient to deal with all the tax together), box WS11 will be completed where the trustees are to pay the tax. If the value of a trust fund is included in both places the calculation will overstate the value of the estate. The rest of the worksheet is used to calculate the amount of tax which is payable and how much of it is payable by instalments.

Once the worksheet is complete the information from it can be copied to pages 6 and 7 of form 200 itself. This will then show both the total amount of tax and the amount which is now due for payment.

Page 8 contains the declaration by the executor(s) or intending administrator(s) as the case may be that the form is correct and complete.

Probate summary D18

The probate summary serves two purposes. First, once the tax due on **10.040** delivery of the inland revenue account has been paid it is returned to the solicitor acting for the personal representatives. It is then sent with the other documentation leading to the grant to the Probate Registry to prove that the tax has been paid. Secondly, it enables the personal representatives to calculate the gross and net size of the estate for probate purposes. These figure can then be included in the oath as explained above.

Reduced form 200

In certain cases where it is clear that no tax is payable a "reduced" Inland **10.041** Revenue Account may be submitted. This consists of the eight pages of IHT 200 itself plus the probate summary (D18) without any supplementary pages. The current requirements for submitting a reduced account are:

(a) the deceased died domiciled in the United Kingdom;
(b) most or all the assets pass under the will or on intestacy to exempt beneficiaries (spouse, charity or national body) the gross value of any other assets not passing to an exempt beneficiary together with non-exempt gifts made within seven years before death does not exceed the IHT threshold at the date of death.

4. FURTHER FORMS

In addition to the forms already described, other forms may have to be **10.042** completed.

Corrective accounts and direct payaments

10.043 If the information originally provided by the personal representatives proves to be incorrect, whether as a result of a mistake or because they discover additional property or liabilities, a corrective account, Form D4, will have to be sent to Capital Taxes. If the alteration is trivial, they may dispense with the requirement.

It is possible for banks and building societies to pay funds direct to Capital Taxes. The personal representatives must complete Forms D20 and D21. See para.12.005.

Second or subsequent grants

10.044 If the applicant is applying for a grant of double probate or a cessate grant or a grant *de bonis non administratis*, Form A-5c is normally used.

Otherwise (for example, when a new grant is applied for after the previous grant has been revoked) IHT Form 200.

5. LATE PAYMENT, PENALTIES AND ESTIMATED ACCOUNTS

10.045 A failure to deliver an accurate account within the prescribed time limits may lead to the assessment of a penalty. The main provision relating to late delivery of an account is IHTA, s.245 which provides for a penalty of £100 plus £60 for each day that the account is late once the case has been referred to the Special Commissioners. The penalty does not apply if there is a reasonable excuse for the failure to comply with the time limit. The Revenue has issued guidance in leaflet IHT 13 as to what may be regarded as a reasonable excuse. The circumstances which will be so regard are quite limited. They do, for example, include life threatening illness, they do not include ignorance of the law, the difficulty of the case or pressure of time.

Penalties are also imposed (by s.247) in cases where the account proves inaccurate. In this case the amount of the penalty depends in part on whether there was any fraud or negligence involved and on the amount of the tax which could have been lost to the Revenue if the inaccuracy had not been discovered.

A particular problem arises in cases where a personal representative wishes to avoid delay in obtaining a grant but does not have complete information available. This is well illustrated by the case of *Robertson v I.R.C.* [2002] STC, 182. In that case the testatrix had left part of her property in Scotland to the Church of Scotland who were anxious for a quick sale. The executor submitted an account which dealt fully with most of the property. However, a cottage in Hertfordshire was yet to be valued. An estimated figure was included in the account which turned out to be far too low. A corrective account was submitted almost immediately and the correct amount of tax on the estate was paid within six months of the death (*i.e.* before the time when the tax would have become due if no account had been submitted). The Revenue were not therefore out of pocket as a result of the inaccurate estimate in the original account. nevertheless they imposed a penalty of £10,000 on the basis that the executor had not made "the fullest enquiries reasonably practicable" about the value of the property as required by IHTA, s.216(3A). The executor was successful on his appeal to the Special Commissioners on the basis that what he had done was in accordance with accepted practice, the fact that the original figure was an estimate was disclosed and there was no negligence involved. At a later hearing the executor was awarded his expenses of and relating to the hearing on the basis that the revenue had acted wholly unreasonably.

In the light of the Robertson case the Revenue has issued the following guidelines as to how they will deal with such cases in future (in their *IHT Newsletter*—Special Issue May 2002):

> "The Revenue is keen to provide assistance to personal representatives to enable them to fulfil their obligations without incurring penalties. In most circumstances we would expect the exact value of property to be given when form IHT 200 is submitted and not merely an estimate. However we accept that if there is a proven need to obtain a grant urgently personal representatives may find themselves in a position where they think that they need to submit an estimated account of the value of a particular item of property. In such circumstances they should ensure that they have made the fullest enquiries that are reasonably practicable before doing so, and the estimate should be as accurate as possible. The Personal Representative should, for example, contact the professional who is going to value the property formally to ensure that the estimate is a reasonable one."

E. Affidavit Evidence

1. AFFIDAVIT OF DUE EXECUTION

Before a will or codicil can be admitted to probate the district judge or registrar must be satisfied that it was duly executed.   **10.046**

If a will or codicil contains an attestation clause, which recites that the proper formalities were complied with, a presumption that the will was duly executed arises. Under the Non-Contentious Probate Rules 1987, r.12(1) if the will contains no attestation clause or the attestation clause is unsufficient or where it appears to the district judge or registrar that there is some doubt about the due execution of the will he must require an affidavit as to due execution before admitting the will to probate in common form. The affidavit should be from one of the attesting witnesses or, if no attesting witness is conveniently available, from any other person who was present at the time the will was executed. If no such affidavit evidence is obtainable, the district judge or registrar may (under r.12(2)) accept affidavit evidence from any person he may think fit to show that the signature on the will is in the deceased's handwriting or on any other matter which may raise a presumption in favour of due execution. The district judge or registrar may require notice of the application to be given to any person who may be prejudiced by the will. If the district judge or registrar after considering the evidence is satisfied that the will was not duly executed he must refuse probate and mark the will accordingly.

The maxim *omnia praesumuntur rite ac solemniter esse acta* may assist when actual evidence of due execution cannot be obtained. In certain circumstances it allows the inference to be drawn that the necessary formalities have been complied with.

> "The maxim expresses an inference which may reasonably be drawn when an intention to do some formal act is established; when the evidence is consistent with that intention having been carried into effect in a proper way; but where the actual observance of all due formalities can only be inferred as a matter of probability." *Per* Lord Lindley L.J. in *Harris v Knight* (1890).

The presumption can only be of use where the appearance of the document in question is consistent with the formalities having been complied with. The presumption applies very strongly where there is a formal attestation clause and less strongly where there is an informal clause or no clause at all. *In the Estate of Denning* (1958) is an example of the application of the presumption in the absence of an attestation clause. The dispositive part of a will, together with the testator's signature, was contained on one side of a piece of paper. On the reverse side two signatures were written in different handwriting, one below the other. Sachs J. applied the presumption and declared that the will was duly executed. He said:

> "that there is no other practical reason why the names should be on the back of the document unless it was for the purpose of attesting the will."

However, the presumption will not apply where the evidence suggests that the "will" was not executed in accordance with the formalities required by law even though the testator intended to execute a will. For example it will not validate a document where there is only one witness to the testator's signature.

2. AFFIDAVIT AS TO KNOWLEDGE AND APPROVAL

10.047 Under r.13 of the Non-Contentious Probate Rules 1987, before admitting to proof a will which appears to have been signed by a blind or illiterate testator or by another person by the testator's direction or which for any other reason gives rise to doubt as to the testator having had knowledge of the contents of the will at the time of its execution, the district judge or registrar must satisfy himself that the testator had such knowledge. Affidavit evidence may be required for this purpose under the Non-Contentious Probate Rules 1987, r.16.

A solicitor who is present when a will is signed by such persons ought to ensure that the attestation clause states that the will was read over to the testator and that the testator appeared to understand and approve the contents.

3. AFFIDAVITS OF ALTERATION, CONDITION AND DATE OF EXECUTION

10.048 The following matters are dealt with in Non-Contentious Probate Rules 1987, r.14.

Alteration
If a will appears to contain an unexpected alteration (other than the completion of a blank space) the district judge or registrar must require evidence to show whether the alteration was present at the time the will was executed (r.14(1)) and may require affidavit evidence for this purpose (r.16). In the absence of evidence to the contrary the alteration is presumed to have been made after execution. The district judge or registrar may, however, disregard an alteration which is of no practical importance (for example, an alteration to a legacy which has lapsed).

Incorporation
If a will contains a reference to another document in such terms as to suggest that it ought to be incorporated in the will the district judge or registrar may require the document to be produced and may call for such evidence in regard to the attaching or incorporation of the document as he may think fit (r.14(3)). Affidavit evidence may be required for this purpose (r.16).   **10.049**

Date of execution
If there is doubt as to the date on which a will was executed the district judge or registrar may require such evidence as he thinks necessary to establish the date (r.14(4)) and may require affidavit evidence for this purpose (r.16).   **10.050**

4. AFFIDAVIT OF ATTEMPTED REVOCATION

Any appearance of attempted revocation by burning, tearing or otherwise destroying must be accounted for to the district judge or registrar's satisfaction (r.15) and he may require affidavit evidence for this purpose (r.16). It is not desirable to attach anything to an original will since the existence of marks, pin holes, staple holes or clip impressions may suggest that there has been an attempted revocation in which case the district judge or registrar may call for affidavit evidence.   **10.051**

F. Caveats

A caveat is a notice entered at any probate registry by post or in person the effect of which is to prevent a grant of probate or administration being made without notice first being given to the person who enters the caveat, called the caveator (Non-Contentious Probate Rules 1987, r.44).   **10.052**

Once a caveat is entered it is effective for a period starting with the day after the day on which it is entered and ending six months after the day on which it was entered. A caveat may be renewed for an additional six months during the last month of the six month period and again in the last month of each successive six month period. The probate registry's own internal procedures ensure that no grant can be made in any registry while the caveat is effective. The caveat must contain the name and address of the deceased, the date and place of death and the name and address for service of the caveator.

Any person interested may issue a "warning" to the caveat under r.44(5). The index to caveats has been kept since August 1, 1988 at the Leeds District Probate Registry and not at the Principal Registry. As a consequence, warnings must be issued either personally, through the post or through the document exchange at Leeds District Probate Registry. The "person warning" must state the nature of his interest and the date of the will (if any) in the warning which must then be served on the caveator. The warning must also require the caveator to state the nature of his interest. A person whose application for a grant was blocked by a caveat may issue a warning since he is a "person interested".

Once the warning has been served on the caveator one of four things will happen depending on what right the caveator is alleging and what steps he chooses to take:

(a) *The caveator may withdraw his caveat* (r.44(11)). A caveator is free to withdraw his caveat at any time whether a warning has been issued or not. A caveator who withdraws after receiving a warning must give notice to the person warning. Once the caveat is withdrawn it becomes ineffective and the person warning is free to proceed with his application for a grant (unless, of course, there is another caveat in force).

(b) *The caveator may enter an appearance* (r.44(10)). An appearance should be entered within eight days of the service of the warning on the caveator. If it is not the person warning may thereafter take steps to "warn off" the caveator (see para.(d) below). An appearance can only be entered by the caveator if he has an interest contrary to that of the person warning. For example, entry of an appearance would be the appropriate step to take where the caveator claims to be an executor under a valid will and the person warning claims to be entitled to letters of administration on the grounds that the will is invalid. The appearance must be entered personally at the Leeds District Probate Registry.

Once an appearance has been entered, the caveat remains in force until a district judge (or, where the parties consent to the discontinuance of the caveat, a registrar) otherwise directs (r.44(13)). Often the entry of the appearance will be followed by the commencement of a probate action (although neither the warning nor the entry of the appearance itself amounts to the commencement of such an action). Where this happens the caveat is no longer necessary, since the fact that a probate action has been started has the effect of preventing a grant being made (r.45(3)).

(c) *The caveator may issue and serve a summons for directions* (r.44(6)). This step must be taken within eight days of service of the warning, otherwise the caveator risks being warned off. A summons for directions may only be issued by a caveator who has no interest contrary to that of the person warning. It is, therefore, the appropriate step to take where the caveator is entitled to a grant in the same degree as or a lower degree than the person warning but wishes to show cause why that person should not take a grant (for example because he is unsuitable and the caveator wishes the court to pass him over).

After a summons for directions has been issued there will be a hearing before a district judge (or in case of difficulty a High Court judge) at which he will decide to whom a grant should be made.

(d) *The caveator may do nothing.* In this case the person warning may file an affidavit after the time limit for entering an appearance (eight days) has expired (r.44(12)). The affidavit must show that the warning was served on the caveator. The caveat is then said to be "warned off" and is no longer effective so that the person warning is now free to proceed with his application.

G. Citations

Citations are documents issued by the principal or district registry which **10.053** call upon the party cited to show cause why a certain step should not be taken. They are used for a variety of purposes but all are designed to give a remedy where a person actually or possibly entitled to a grant is refusing to take steps to take the grant or to renounce so that others may do so. Although citations were formerly issued in contentious cases they are now only used in non-contentious cases.

There are three types of citation:

(a) A citation to take probate;
(b) A citation to accept or refuse a grant (of probate or letters of administration);
(c) A citation to propound a will.

1. CITATION TO TAKE PROBATE

An executor may normally renounce his right to take a grant. However, **10.054** once he has "intermeddled" (so as to constitute himself an executor *de son tort*) in the estate he is no longer free to renounce and so may be cited to take probate. The citation may be issued at the instance of any person interested in the estate but cannot be issued until at least six months after the testator's death nor at any time while proceedings as to the validity of the will are pending (Non-Contentious Probate Rules 1987 r.47(3)). An administrator does not, by intermeddling, lose his right to renounce and so he cannot be cited to *take* administration; (an administrator who intermeddles will, however, make himself liable up to the limit of assets coming into his hands as an executor *de son tort*).

2. CITATION TO ACCEPT OR REFUSE A GRANT

A citation to accept or refuse a grant may be issued at the instance of any **10.055** person who would be entitled to a grant if the person were to renounce (Non-Contentious Probate Rules 1987, r.47(1)). This type of citation is, therefore, used where a person with an inferior right to a grant wishes to force the person or persons better entitled to make up their minds whether to apply or not. Where there are several persons with a superior right they must all be cited before the person with the inferior right can take a grant. Where power has been reserved to a person to take a grant of probate, the proving executor may cite him to take or refuse probate (r.47(2)). In other cases it is not necessary or possible to cite a person with an equal right to take a grant since the court can issue a grant to any of the persons equally entitled.

A citation to accept or refuse a grant may be issued to a person with a right to either a grant of probate (unless he has lost the right to renounce) or letters of administration. A citation of this type may be made at any time after the death of the testator or intestate.

3. CITATION TO PROPOUND A WILL

10.056   The object of this type of citation is to force the persons interested in the alleged will to seek probate of it if they can. The application may be made by any person with a contrary interest (which in effect means a person who is entitled on intestacy or under an earlier will). The citation must be directed to all the persons interested under the alleged will and not only to the executors of it (Non-Contentious Probate Rules 1987, r.48(1)).

An executor of a will who doubts the validity of a later codicil is not entitled to cite the beneficiaries of the alleged codicil to propound it. His proper course is to bring a probate action in which he will seek to establish the validity of the will and the invalidity of the codicil.

4. PROCEDURE ON CITATION

A person (called a citor) who wishes to obtain a citation must first issue a caveat (Non-Contentious Probate Rules 1987, r.46(3)). The citor must then swear an affidavit confirming every averment in the citation (r.46(2)) and the district judge or registrar must settle the form of citation before it is issued (r.46(1)). Any will referred to in the citation must be lodged in a registry before the citation is issued unless it is not in the citor's possession and it is impractical to lodge it (r.46(5)). The citation will set out the steps which the court will take if the person cited does not show cause to the contrary.

A citation must normally be personally served on the person cited but other modes of service, including advertisement, may be ordered by the registrar (this will be done, for example, where the difficulty in obtaining the grant has been caused by the disappearance of the person entitled).

A person cited must enter an appearance within eight days of service (r.46(6)). If he does not the citor may apply for an order for a grant to himself if the citation was a citation to accept or refuse a grant (r.47(5)(a)). Where the person cited was cited to take probate he can be ordered to do so within a stated time if he fails to enter an appearance (r.47(5)(c)) although the court may exercise its discretion to pass him over (see, for example, *In the Estate of Biggs* (1966), para.8.021). If the person cited was cited to propound a will and has failed to enter an appearance the citor may apply for a grant in common form as if the will were invalid.

Where the person cited does enter an appearance he may show cause why the steps contemplated by the citation should not be taken.

Alternatively if he is now willing to take a grant he may apply *ex parte* to a registrar for an order for a grant (r.47(4)) to himself.

Where power to take a grant has been reserved to an executor a citation to accept or refuse a grant may be made at the instance of the proving executors (or the person who is executor by representation) against that person.

H. Standing Searches

An entry of a caveat has the effect of ensuring that notice of an application for a grant is given to the caveator. However, it is an abuse of the process of the court for a person to enter a caveat where there is no dispute as to an issue concerned with a probate matter (such as the validity of a will or a right to a grant of probate or administration). A person who merely wishes to know when a grant is made so that he can make a claim against the estate should not therefore enter a caveat. Such a person could, in most cases, enter a citation since a creditor is entitled to a grant of administration on clearing off the beneficiaries. However, it will usually be more appropriate for him to make a "standing search".   **10.057**

A standing search is made by lodging the appropriate form together with the prescribed fee at the principal or district registry or any sub-registry. An office copy of any grant made within 12 months before or six months after the search will then be given to the applicant. The period of search can be extended by further periods of six months on payment of a fee for each extension.

I. Guarantees

Before 1972 almost all administrators were required to enter into bonds for the due administration of the estate of the deceased. This requirement was repealed by the Administration of Estates Act 1971 and replaced by a much less stringent provision requiring a guarantee in certain limited circumstances and no guarantee or bond at all in most circumstances.   **10.058**

The present law is contained in s.120(1) of the Supreme Court Act 1981 which provides that:

> "... the High Court may ... require one or more sureties to guarantee that they will make good, within any limit imposed by the court on the total liability of the surety or sureties, any loss which any person interested in the administration of the estate of the deceased may suffer in consequence of a breach by the administrator of his duties as such."

The Non-Contentious Probate Rules 1987 (unlike the rules which they replace) do not require guarantees in any particular type of case.

11. Powers and Duties of Personal Representatives

A. Duties of Personal Representatives

1. DUTY TO COLLECT ASSETS

11.001 The first duty of a personal representative is "to collect and get in the deceased's real and personal estate" (Administration of Estates Act 1925, s.25 as amended by Administration of Estates Act 1971, s.9). Once the assets are collected the personal representative must administer the estate by paying debts and legacies and by disposing of the residue (these duties are dealt with in Chapters 15, 16 and 18). All duties of personal representatives must be performed with "due diligence". The personal representative must, therefore:

(a) take reasonable steps to collect money due to the deceased (by bringing proceedings if necessary);

(b) collect the assets as quickly as is practical. (Money which is due to the deceased and which is secured by mortgage or other charge need not be collected immediately unless the security is in danger.)

No absolute rule can be laid down as to what is a reasonable time for collection of assets nor as to what steps must be taken in order to collect assets. In each case the personal representative will only be liable for loss resulting from his failure to act if he has acted unreasonably.

2. PROOF OF TITLE TO ASSETS

11.002 The personal and real property of the deceased devolves on the personal representatives at death, in the case of an executor or on the making of the grant, in the case of an administrator. This only applies to interests in property which continue notwithstanding the death so that a life interest does not devolve on the personal representatives nor does an interest in joint property (which passes to the remaining joint tenant(s) by right of survivorship). The legal title to property held by the deceased as a trustee devolves on the personal representative if the deceased was a sole trustee but on the remaining trustees if there are any at the time of death. If the deceased owned an interest as a tenant in common in equity, it will devolve on the personal representatives, unless it was a life interest in which case it will cease to exist on death.

An interest held as beneficial joint tenant will not devolve on the personal representatives but will pass by right of survivorship to the surviving joint tenant(s). Property subject to a nomination or *donatio mortis causa* will not devolve on the personal representatives, it can be claimed by the nominee or donee immediately after death.

Insurance policies on the deceased's life written in trust for third parties or taken out under the Married Women's Property Act 1882 are not assets of the estate. Such policies are payable to the trustees on proof of death; a grant of representation is not required. The personal representatives will not be concerned in the collection of the proceeds of such policies (unless there is no trustee named in which case the proceeds will be paid to them—even so the proceeds will still not be assets of the estate). A lump sum payable under a discretionary pension scheme is not an asset of the estate and the personal representatives are not concerned in its collection. The trustees of the pension scheme will pay direct to the person(s) they have selected.

In order to collect the assets which devolve on them personal representatives will have to prove their entitlement to the people who are in possession of the assets at the time of death. This can be done by production of the original grant of probate or administration or of an office copy of the grant. Office copies can be obtained from the registry on payment of a small fee. Personal representatives should apply for sufficient office copies to enable them to deal with the estate of the deceased promptly—the more items of property included in the estate the greater the number of copies which should be obtained. It is not, however, necessary to have a copy for each item of property. A person in possession of estate assets must hand over the assets on production of the original or office copy grant which he must then return to the personal representatives.

3. ENFORCEMENT OF PERSONAL REPRESENTATIVES' DUTIES

A personal representative who accepts office (by taking a grant or by acting as executor) is liable for loss resulting from any breach of duty which he commits. A breach of duty by a personal representative may consist of misappropriating the property of the deceased for his own benefit, maladministration (such as distributing to the wrong people even though in good faith) or negligence (such as an unreasonable delay in dealing with the collection or distribution of the estate). Any breach of duty by a personal representative is called a *devastavit*. **11.003**

An action may be brought against the personal representative by a beneficiary or creditor who is not paid in full as a result of a *devastavit* by a personal representative. A personal representative can protect himself against certain types of breach of duty in a number of ways (see Chapter 14). In particular a personal representative cannot be held liable to an adult who has consented to the way in which he has performed his duties with full knowledge of the circumstances.

Where several personal representatives are appointed each is liable for his own breach of duty but not for breaches by his co-executor or co-administrator. However, a personal representative who permits a breach of trust by another personal representative will be liable since he has then failed to perform his own duty of safeguarding the estate. He may also be liable in negligence (see 4. Duty of Care below) if he fails to attend to his duties and thus allows a breach by another personal representative to go unnoticed.

4. DUTY OF CARE

11.004 The Trustee Act 2000 provides for a single duty of care which applies to trustees. Section 1 provides:

> 1. (1) Wherever the duty under this subsection applies to a trustee, he must exercise such care and skill as is reasonable in the circumstances, having regard in particular—
>
> (a) to any special knowledge skill or experience that he has or holds himself out as having, and
>
> (b) if he acts as trustee in the course of a business or profession to any special knowledge or experience that it is reasonable to expect of a person acting in the course of that kind of business or profession.

Under s.35 the duties set out in the act apply to personal representatives as well as to trustees.

Schedule 1 provides that the duty applies to personal representatives and trustees when:

1. exercising any power of investment whether conferred by the act (as to which see section 12 below) or otherwise (for example under the terms of the will)
2. exercising a power to acquire land
3. entering into arrangements appointing agents, nominees or custodians (see section 10 below) or reviewing such agents' arrangements
4. exercising the power to insure (see section 6 below)

The statutory definition of the duty of care and when it applies is so similar to the common law position that it is unlikely to have any significant impact. Schedule 1 para.7 allows exclusion or restriction of the duty (in the case of personal representatives, the exclusion or restriction must be in the will). The inclusion of this provision in the Act was controversial and the possibility of an amendment is being considered by the Law Commission.

B. Powers of Personal Representatives before Grant

11.005 The authority of an administrator derives from *the grant*. The powers of an administrator before the grant is made are, therefore, very limited.

An administrator may not bring any action before grant and if he purports to do so a later grant does not cure the defect in the original proceedings (*Ingall v Moran* (1944)). A new action must be brought once the grant has been made. In order to protect an estate from wrongful injury in the period between death and the obtaining of the grant the authority of an administrator will relate back for the limited purpose of giving validity to acts done before letters of administration were obtained. However, such relation back occurs only in those cases where the acts done are for the benefit of the estate. The test of whether or not an act is for the benefit of the estate is entirely objective. Thus in *Mills v Anderson* (1984) an "administrator" agreed before the grant to accept on behalf of the estate a sum in full and final settlement of a claim for damages. It later became apparent that the settlement was too low. It was held that there could be no question of the administrator's authority relating back to validate the agreement as it would not be to the benefit of the estate.

An administrator has no power to vest property in any person before obtaining a grant.

In the period between death and grant of administration the property of the deceased vests in the Public Trustee (Law of Property (Miscellaneous Provisions) Act 1994, s.15).

The power of an executor derives from *the will* of the deceased and not from the grant which merely confirms his authority. An executor can therefore, in principle, exercise all his powers without obtaining a grant. An executor can sue or be sued before obtaining a grant. If he brings an action (for example, against a creditor) the action is valid even though no grant has been issued. However, before judgment is entered in his favour a grant must be obtained since the court will, at that stage, require proof of his authority to act as executor if the action depends on his title to act in that capacity.

An executor is also entitled to deal with the collection and distribution of the estate without first obtaining a grant. In practice, collection of assets without a grant may prove impossible since the persons in possession may refuse to hand them over without proof of the executor's title. Similarly, as far as distribution is concerned, a purchaser will require proof of title before paying for assets. A beneficiary in whose favour an assent or conveyance of a legal estate in land is made is entitled to have a notice of the assent or conveyance endorsed on the original grant of representation; thus, the grant will have to be obtained before the assent is made.

Certain assets can be dealt with without the production of a grant (see paras 12.008–12.010).

C. Implied Administrative Powers

1. INTRODUCTION

Trustees are given many powers by the Administration of Estates Act 1925, the Trustee Act 1925 and the Trustee Act 2000. The powers of "trustees" under these acts are also given to personal representatives. The Trustee Act 2000 came into force on February 1, 2001; it extends the powers of trustees and personal representatives and removes many of the restrictions contained in earlier legislation as well as imposing a statutory duty of care on trustees and personal representatives (see 4. above). The act applies to wills made before as well as after the commencement date.

It is always possible for a testator to exclude an implied power by

11.006

stating in the will that it is not available to the personal representatives or trustees.

2. POWERS OF PERSONAL REPRESENTATIVES TO SELL, MORTGAGE AND LEASE

11.007 Section 39 of the Administration of Estates Act 1925 (as amended by the Trusts of Land and Appointment of Trustees Act 1996) gives the personal representatives very extensive powers. Section 39(1)(i) preserves the common law powers of personal representatives to sell and mortgage personal property included in the estate. In relation to realty they are given (by section 39(1)(ii)) all the functions of a trustee of land under the Trusts of Land and Appointment of Trustees Act 1996. This provision effectively gives them the same powers as an absolute owner.

A receipt given by a personal representative for money, securities or other personal property is a sufficient discharge to the person paying or transferring (Trustee Act 1925, s.14) unless that person acts in bad faith (for example, by purchasing property at a fraudulent undervalue) in which case the transaction is vitiated and a beneficiary or creditor of the estate may have the transaction set aside. If trustees sell land, it is necessary for a receipt to be given by at least two trustees or a trust corporation. However, a sole personal representative may give a good receipt for capital money (Law of Property Act 1925, s.27(2)).

The personal representatives obviously have very wide powers to sell assets and raise money. These powers are necessary since cash is required for a number of purposes in connection with the administration; for example, the payment of funeral, testamentary and administration expenses, inheritance tax, debts and pecuniary legacies. Deciding *which* assets to sell is a complex decision and the personal representatives have to consider a number of matters; for example, which assets have been specifically given to beneficiaries, which assets occur first in the statutory order for property available for payment of debts (see Chapter 15), which assets will fetch the best price and which assets will attract the least liability to tax for the estate and for the beneficiaries. These matters are discussed more fully in Chapter 12.

3. POWER TO APPROPRIATE

11.008 Section 41 of the Administration of Estates Act 1925 gives the personal representatives power to appropriate any part of the estate in or towards satisfaction of any legacy or interest or share in the estate of the deceased, provided that such an appropriation does not prejudice any specific beneficiary.

Example
T leaves X a pecuniary legacy of £1,000 and the residue of the estate to Y. The residue includes a clock valued at £750. The personal representatives may let X take the clock in partial satisfaction of the legacy.

An appropriation can only be made by the personal representatives if the appropriate consents are obtained. There are two situations to consider.

(a) *If the beneficiary is absolutely and beneficially entitled to the legacy* the consent required is that of the beneficiary or, if the beneficiary is an infant or mentally incapable of managing his own affairs, the consent must be that of the beneficiary's parent or guardian or receiver.

(b) *If the legacy is settled* the consent must be that of the trustees (provided they are not also the personal representatives) or of the person for the time being entitled to the income provided such a person is of full age and capacity. If the personal representatives are the only trustees and there is no person of full age or capacity for the time being entitled to the income no consents are required. However, in this case the appropriation must be of an investment authorised by law or by the will. This limitation as to the type of property appropriated does not exist in other cases.

The asset is valued at the date of the appropriation, not at the date of death (*Re Collins* (1975)); if the asset is rising in value, therefore, a pecuniary legatee will be anxious that the appropriation be made as quickly as possible. The personal representatives will have to ascertain and fix the value of assets for this purpose as they see fit but must strive to be fair to all beneficiaries. A duly qualified valuer should be employed where necessary. Thus, in *Re Bythway* (1911) it was held that an executrix was not entitled to appropriate to herself shares in an unquoted company at her own valuation.

If the asset is worth more than the legacy to which the beneficiary is entitled it would appear that the power granted by s.41 cannot be exercised since in such a case the asset cannot be said to be appropriated "*in or towards satisfaction*" of the legacy (*Re Phelps* (1980)). The personal representatives can, however, exercise their power of sale under s.39 of the Administration of Estates Act 1925 to sell the asset to a beneficiary in consideration of a part payment of cash and the satisfaction of the legacy.

Because s.41 requires consent, the Inland Revenue regard appropriation as a "conveyance or transfer on sale" so that any instrument giving effect to the appropriation attracted *ad valorem* stamp duty (*Jopling v I.R.C.* (1940)). For that reason it was common for wills to provide that the personal representatives need not obtain the consent of a legatee to an appropriation. The Stamp Duty (Exempt Instruments) Regulations 1987 exempt from duty all instruments giving effect to an appropriation in or towards satisfaction of a general legacy executed on or after May 1, 1987. Such instruments must be certified as falling within the appropriate category of the Schedule to the Regulations. (See para.22.040.)

Where a personal representative sells an asset to a beneficiary partly in consideration or satisfaction of a legacy and partly in consideration of an additional cash payment it would appear that *ad valorem* stamp duty may have to be charged on any instrument effecting the transaction. This is because it cannot be said in such a case there has been an appropriation *in or towards* satisfaction of a legacy. Such a transaction may be regarded as a sale for other tax purposes—for example, capital gains tax (*Passant v Jackson*).

The Intestates' Estates Act 1952 provides that the surviving spouse of a person who dies intestate has a *right* to require the personal representatives to appropriate any dwelling house comprised in the residuary estate in which the spouse was resident at the time of the intestate's death in or towards satisfaction of the spouse's entitlement (see Chapter 3). Since the spouse can compel the personal representatives to make the appropriation there is no contractual element and *ad valorem* stamp duty has never been payable. (Sch.2, para.5(2) of the Act gives the spouse the right to *require* appropriation even where the house is worth more than the spouse's entitlement, provided equality money is paid).

4. POWER TO APPOINT TRUSTEES OF A MINOR'S PROPERTY

11.009   When a personal representative vests property in a beneficiary absolutely entitled (or person otherwise entitled to assets, for example, a trustee) the personal representative obtains a discharge from liability by means of a receipt signed by the person entitled. In the absence of an express direction to the contrary in the will a minor cannot give a good receipt for money or securities nor can his parents, guardian or adult spouse give one on his behalf (a married minor can give a good receipt for income). Personal representatives who, without authority, pay a child's legacy to a parent, guardian or adult spouse are in danger of personal liability to account to the minor when the minor attains majority. To overcome this difficulty the Administration of Estates Act, s.42 gives personal representatives power, where a minor is absolutely entitled to property, to appoint a trust corporation or two or more individuals, not exceeding four (whether or not including one or more of the personal representatives) to be trustees of the property for the minor. The personal representatives may transfer property to the trustees and a receipt signed by those trustees will be a good discharge to the personal representatives. However, the power is not available where the minor merely has a contingent interest. In the absence of express authority the personal representatives will either have to continue holding the property until the minor reaches majority or use one of the alternatives set out in Chapter 18 (appropriation, payment into court).

5. POWER TO POSTPONE DISTRIBUTION

11.010   Section 44 of the Administration of Estates Act 1925 provides that the personal representatives are not bound to distribute the estate of the deceased before the expiration of one year from death. This does not affect their duty to pay debts with due diligence and simply means that a beneficiary cannot insist on earlier payment of a legacy, even if a testator directed payment within a short period after the death. In a case where such a direction for payment is included in the will a pecuniary or general legatee is merely entitled to interest from the date fixed for payment.

(There are cases where there is a right to interest from the date of death—see Chapter 16.) The personal representatives cannot necessarily be compelled to pay a legacy even after the 12 month period has expired although they may thereafter be required to explain the delay and all pecuniary and general legatees (other than contingent ones) will thereafter be entitled to interest at 6 per cent per annum.

6. POWER TO INSURE

The statutory power of insurance is contained in s.19 of the Trustee Act **11.011** 1925 as substituted by s.34 of the Trustee Act 2000. The substituted section gives a much wider power to personal representatives than did the original s.19. Personal representatives now have power to insure any property in the estate against risks of loss or damage due to any event and power to pay the premiums out of the estate. The duty of care under s.1 of the Trustee Act 2000 applies to the "exercise of the power to insure". Some commentators suggest that this may make personal representatives liable for loss resulting from failure to insure where the failure is negligent. However, on a literal interpretation a failure to insure cannot be regarded as the exercise of the power.

7. POWER TO RUN A BUSINESS

A deceased person may have run a business either as a sole trader, a **11.012** partner or through the medium of a limited company. The personal representatives of such a person must consider their position in relation to the business and determine what powers and duties, if any, they have.

Sole traders

Where the will is silent the personal representatives have implied power **11.013** to continue the business *for the purpose of realisation only*, that is to enable it to be sold as a going concern. Such a period will not usually exceed one year (*Re Crowther* (1895)). It is preferable to give them express power to continue the business so long as they see fit (thus avoiding the possibility of a forced sale in a poor market).

Unless the will makes express provision the personal representatives will only have authority to use those assets used in the business at the date of the deceased's death. It may be desirable to give them power to use other assets of the estate if they see fit.

When the personal representatives have authority to carry on a business they are personally liable for any debts they incur. However, they are entitled to an indemnity from the estate. If the business is being carried on for the purpose of *realisation only* the right of indemnity may be exercised in priority to all creditors of the deceased and beneficiaries. If the business is being carried on under authority given by the will the right of indemnity may be exercised in priority to beneficiaries but not in priority to creditors of the deceased. The reason for this is that the beneficiaries are bound by the terms of the will but the creditors of the deceased are not (unless a creditor has expressly assented to the carrying on of the business). In this case the indemnity extends only to assets which the will authorised them to use.

Partnerships and limited companies

11.014 Where a partner or shareholder in a limited company dies the personal representatives of the deceased normally have no power to intervene in the management of the business. Death dissolves a partnership unless, as is usually the case, the partnership agreement provides otherwise.

A company is a legal person which continues to exist despite the death of shareholders or directors. In the case of a "one man" company there may, however, be difficulties in directing its activities once the major shareholder/director dies.

In either case the personal representatives will be mainly concerned with ascertaining the beneficial entitlement to the deceased's interest in the business and, if appropriate, arranging a sale of the interest. It is important that personal representatives should be aware that a partnership agreement frequently contains provisions relating to death of partners. For example, many agreements provide for automatic accruer of a deceased's share of goodwill and/or for the exercise by surviving partners of an option to purchase the deceased's share in the capital assets. Similarly the Articles of Association of a company or an agreement between the shareholders may give other shareholders pre-emption rights or options to purchase a deceased shareholder's shares. Personal representatives should discover whether or not such rights exist and should not look only at the deceased's will.

8. POWER TO MAINTAIN MINORS

11.015 Section 31 of the Trustee Act gives trustees (and personal representatives) a power to apply available income for the maintenance, education or benefit of minor beneficiaries.

What happens to income—the general rule

11.016 Where a testator directs that property is to be held on trust for beneficiaries (for example "to A if A becomes a solicitor"), the question arises of what happens to any income produced by the property after death. If the testator has left express directions, they must be carried out. If not, there are general rules (see Chapter 16). We can summarise these rules by saying that most testamentary gifts carry with them the right to intermediate income. This means that income produced by the property is added to capital and devolves with it, so that whoever becomes entitled to the capital also becomes entitled to the intermediate income. Certain gifts do not carry with them the right to intermediate income; the most common example of such a gift is a contingent pecuniary legacy (apart from certain exceptional contingent pecuniary legacies dealt with in Chapter 16). A contingent pecuniary legatee is entitled to nothing but the capital (unless there is a delay in payment after the contingency has been fulfilled in which case the legatee becomes entitled to interest). In such a case if the legacy fund is invested any interest produced is paid to the residuary beneficiary or, if there is none, to the person entitled on intestacy.

The effect of s.31 of the Trustee Act

Section 31 of the Trustee Act provides that where property is held for a   **11.017**
minor beneficiary and the gift carries with it the right to intermediate
income the trustees have a discretion as to what they do with that income,
whether the minor's interest is vested or contingent. The trustees are
entitled under s.31 to choose to apply the income for the maintenance,
education and benefit of the minor but to the extent that they do not, they
must accumulate it. In exercising this discretion they are directed to
consider the age and requirements of the minor, the circumstances of the
case generally and in particular what other income, if any, is applicable for
the same purposes. If they have notice that more than one trust fund is
available for those purposes the trustees must so far as is practicable,
unless the entire income of the funds is applied or the court otherwise
directs, apply only a proportionate part of each trust fund. Accumulated
income may be applied during the minority of the beneficiary as if it were
income of the current year.

Example

T makes two settlements. T gives his shareholding in X Co. to trustees to
hold for A if A reaches 25 and his shareholding in Y Co. to trustees to hold
for B for life, remainder to C. At T's death both A and B are minors. A has
a contingent interest, B has a vested interest. The trustees may choose to
apply the income from the respective shares for the benefit of A and B but
in so far as they do not apply it, they must accumulate it.

Section 31(1) provides that if the minor reaches 18 and still has an
interest which is contingent the discretion of the trustees ceases and from
that date they *must* pay the income to the beneficiary until the
contingency is fulfilled or the gift fails. In the above example, therefore, as
soon as A reaches 18 the trustees must pay current income to A until A
reaches 25 or dies without fulfilling the contingency. B will be entitled to
current income at 18 and until his death.

Once the minor reaches 18 (or marries earlier) the trustees must
consider what is to happen to income which has been accumulated.
Section 31(2) provides that with one exception (dealt with below) such
accumulations are to be added to capital and will devolve with it. Thus, if a
gift is contingent on reaching 21 the beneficiary will be entitled to both
capital and accumulations if he reaches 21 but if he does not they will both
pass to the person entitled in default.

The exceptional case where accumulations do not devolve with capital
is that of a minor with a life interest. Section 31(2) provides that *if* such a
minor reaches 18 he is entitled to any income that has been accumulated.
If he fails to reach 18 (or marry earlier), the accumulations will devolve
with the capital. The effect is that a minor with a life interest has no right
to receive income until he reaches 18 (or marries earlier); he can neither
insist on receiving income as it arises nor can he be certain of receiving the
accumulations.

Example

T gives his shareholding in Y Co to trustees to hold for A for life
remainder to B. A is aged 6 at the time the settlement comes into effect.

Until A reaches 18 the trustees must accumulate the income to the extent that they do not choose to apply it for the benefit of A. If A dies before reaching 18 the accumulated income (together with the shares in Y Co) will pass to B. If A reaches 18 the trustees must pay the accumulated income to A.

Express clause varying s.31

11.018 A professionally drawn will may extend the statutory power of maintenance to give the trustees an unfettered discretion (so that, for example, they need not consider other sources of income available to the minor).

Where a gift is contingent on reaching an age greater than 18 (for example, 25) the person drafting the will should consider removing the right to receive income at 18. One reason for removing the right is that its existence gives the beneficiary an interest in possession at 18 for inheritance tax purposes. If such a beneficiary dies aged between 18 and 25 the value of the trust property will be included in his estate when calculating inheritance tax payable even though the beneficiary had no right to capital (see Chapter 7). Another reason for considering the removal of the right to income at 18 is that if the right remains and the settlement is converted into an interest in possession settlement at 18, holdover relief for capital gains tax will not be available when the beneficiary becomes absolutely entitled to capital at 25. If the settlement were to continue as an accumulation and maintenance settlement until 25, holdover relief would be available. However, draftsmen should also be aware of the capital gains tax *disadvantage* of removing the right to income; any gains realised by the trustees will be liable to capital gains tax at the additional rate, instead of at the basic rate. (See Chapter 7.)

9. POWER TO ADVANCE CAPITAL

11.019 Section 32 of the Trustee Act provides that trustees (and personal representatives) have an absolute discretion to apply capital for the advancement or benefit of any person who has either a vested or contingent interest in capital. Property may be advanced under this section to new trustees to be held upon new trusts containing powers and discretions not contemplated by the original instrument (although the perpetuity period will run from the time that the original settlement was created).

If a beneficiary with a contingent interest dies after receiving an advance and without fulfilling the contingency the trustees have no right to recover property from the estate of the deceased beneficiary. The section does not apply to land or capital money under a Settled Land Act settlement (it does, however, apply to the proceeds of sale of land held upon trust for sale).

There are three limitations on the statutory power:

    (a) The trustees may only advance up to one-half of the benefici-ary's vested or presumptive share. (For example, if a settlor gives a trust fund of £30,000 to be divided amongst X, Y and Z provided they reach 25, each has a presumptive share of £10,000.

The trustees may advance up to half of £10,000 to each or any of them.) If an advance is made to a person who dies without fulfilling the contingency, the trustees have no right to recover the advance from that person's estate.

(b) Any advance made must be brought into account when the beneficiary becomes absolutely entitled.

(c) Any person with a prior interest (*e.g.* the right to receive income from the trust property) must consent to the advance.

It is common for a will to include an express clause removing the three limitations and to leave the trustees to exercise an unfettered discretion.

10. POWER TO DELEGATE—TRUSTEE ACT 2000

The power of personal representatives to delegate is now contained in Part IV (ss.11–27) of the Trustee Act 2000. Under s.11 personal representatives may delegate any or all of their "delegable functions" to an agent. The delegable functions are defined as any functions except: decisions as to how or whether assets should be distributed, decisions as to whether fees or payments due should be made out of income or capital of the trust fund, exercise of powers under other enactments or under the will (which must be dealt with under those enactments or in accordance with the terms of the will), the appointment of nominees and custodians (ss.16 and 17, see below). The power to delegate is further restricted in the case of charitable trusts.

11.020

More than one agent may be appointed (s.12(2)) but if two or more agents are to exercise the same function they must do so jointly. A personal representative may be appointed as agent but a beneficiary may not be (s.12(1) and (3)). The terms on which the agent is appointed are set by the personal representatives and may include provision for remuneration (s.14(1)). Sub-delegation by the agent, any restriction on the agent's liability and any permission for the agent to act where a conflict of interest might arise are only permitted if "reasonably necessary" (s.14(2) and (3)).

Section 15 imposes special restrictions on the appointment of agents in the case of asset management. Asset management is defined as the investment of assets, and the acquisition and disposal of property (s.15(5)). In these cases the agreement authorising the exercise of the functions must be in writing or evidenced in writing (s.15(1)). The personal representatives must supply the agent with a policy statement giving guidance as to how the asset management functions should be exercised (s.15(2)(a)) and the agreement must require the agent to comply with the policy statement or any replacement of it (s.15(2)(b)).

Section 16 contains provisions which allow personal representatives to appoint nominees to hold property. This power enables personal representative, for example, to vest shares in a nominee to facilitate management of the investments. Section 17 enables personal representatives to appoint "custodians" to undertake the safe custody of assets, documents or records. A nominee or custodian must be carrying on business as such for these appointments to be made (unless it is a body corporate controlled by the personal representatives).

Section 22 requires personal representatives to keep under review the appointments of agents nominees or custodians and the terms under which they act. Provided that the personal representatives comply with the duty of care in appointing and reviewing agents, nominees and custodians they are not liable for any acts or defaults of the agents nominees or custodians. They would, of course, be liable for their own act in making the appointment or in deciding the terms of appointment if they were negligent in doing so.

In drafting a will the implication of these rules and the restrictions contained in the statutory provisions should be considered. In some cases it may be appropriate to provide for the delegation of all powers of personal representatives not just the "delegable functions" as defined by the Act. It may also be appropriate to dispense with the need for a policy statement, to allow sub-delegation by the agent, restriction on the agent's liability and permission for the agent to act where a conflict of interest might arise whether or not "reasonably necessary". In particular it may be appropriate to allow delegation to a beneficiary.

11. INDEMNITY

11.021   Section 31 of the Trustee Act 2000 provides that personal representatives are entitled to reimbursement from the estate for expenses properly incurred. Similarly, under s.32, they are entitled to reimburse agents nominees and custodians.

12. POWERS OF INVESTMENT

11.022   Part II (ss.3–7) of the Trustee Act 2000 simplifies and liberalises the law relating to investment by personal representatives. Section 3(1) provides that a personal representative "may make any kind of investment that he could make if he were absolutely entitled to the assets" of the estate. This is called the "the general power of investment". It does not include a power to invest in land (but s.8 does contain such a power—see below and loans secured on land are permitted under s.3). In exercising the general power of investment or any other power of investment (such as one provided in the will) personal representatives must, under s.4, have regard to "standard investment criteria". These criteria are the suitability to the estate of the kind of investment chosen and the need for diversification of investments in so far as is appropriate to the circumstances of the estate.

Under s.5 personal representatives must take advice in making and reviewing investments. The advice must be "the advice of a person who is reasonably believed by the [personal representative] to be qualified to give it by his ability in and practical experience of financial and other matters relating to the proposed investment" (s.5(4)). However, under s.5(3) advice need not be taken if the personal representatives "reasonably conclude that in all the circumstances it is unnecessary or inappropriate to do so".

These provisions apply to wills made before as well as after the commencement of the Act on February 1, 2001. The power to invest may be restricted in the will.

The overall effect of these provisions is to free personal representatives from the restrictions formerly imposed on them by the Trustee Investment Act 1961. However, the potential liability for negligence is increased where more speculative investments are chosen. It is arguable that a failure to consider making investments could also be a failure to have regard to the "standard investment criteria" and so also give rise to a claim for negligence. However, it is also arguable that a failure to consider making investments is not an exercise of a power at all and so outside the scope of Part II altogether.

13. POWER TO PURCHASE LAND

Section 8 of the Trustee Act 2000 gives personal representatives the **11.023** power to buy land in the United Kingdom (freehold or leasehold) as an investment, for occupation by a beneficiary or for any other reason. The power can be restricted by the will. The general duty of care applies to the exercise of the power.

D. Administrative Powers Granted by Will

As indicated in the previous section it is common to extend many of the **11.024** statutory powers of trustees and personal representatives. It is also common to confer on them certain additional powers such as the power to make loans to beneficiaries or to advance capital to a surviving spouse to whom a life interest has been given. These matters are dealt with more fully in Chapter 22.

E. Rights of Beneficiaries During the Administration

As we have seen it is the function of the personal representatives to **11.025** administer the deceased's estate by collecting the assets, paying off the debts and liabilities and distributing the estate to the beneficiaries under the will or the intestacy rules. The beneficiaries may wish to know what rights they have against the personal representatives during the administration period.

1. THE RIGHT TO COMPEL DUE ADMINISTRATION

Beneficiaries have no equitable interest in assets
The assets of the deceased vest in the personal representatives and those **11.026** assets come to the personal representatives "in full ownership without distinction between legal and equitable interests" (*Commissioner of Stamp Duties (Queensland) v Livingston* (1965)). In view of this, until the administration of the estate is complete, the beneficiary, whether under a will or intestacy, can have neither a legal nor an equitable interest in the

deceased's assets (*Dr Barnardo's Homes National Incorporated Association v Commissioners for Special Purposes of the Income Tax Acts* (1921)). A personal representative cannot be regarded as holding the assets of the estate on trust for the beneficiaries since, until the administration has been completed, it is impossible to say which assets will be available to the beneficiaries and which will have to be used to pay debts and administration expenses. A trust can only exist where there are "specific subjects identifiable as the trust fund" (*Commissioner of Stamp Duties (Queensland) v Livingston*, above). The effect of this is that the beneficiaries cannot claim the assets until the administration has been completed because until then the beneficiaries cannot be certain of entitlement to any assets. They cannot object simply because the personal representatives sell, or intend to sell, an asset given to them in the will. They can only object if the asset should not be sold because, for example, there is no need to sell the asset in the circumstances.

The beneficiaries' chose in action

11.027 Although the beneficiaries have no legal or equitable interest in the deceased's assets, they do have a chose in action; that is a right to ensure that the deceased's estate is properly administered.

The chose in action can be transmitted to another person, as is illustrated by the case of *Re Leigh's Will Trusts* (1970). In this case the testatrix left "all shares which I hold and any other interest ... which I may have" in a named company. She did not hold any shares in that company but at the date of her death she was the sole beneficiary of her husband's estate which included shares in that company. It was held that the gift took effect as a gift of her chose in action in her husband's estate.

The position of specific legatees

11.028 While the general rule is that beneficiaries acquire merely a chose in action, in *I.R.C. v Hawley* (1928) it was suggested that a specific legatee takes an equitable interest in the property given under the terms of the will from the date of death, even though the property may be used to discharge the debts and liabilities of the estate by the personal representatives in whom the legal estate will vest.

However, this decision is inconsistent with the personal representatives receiving both the legal and equitable interests, as suggested in *Commissioner of Stamp Duties (Queensland) v Livingston* above. In *Re Hayes' Will Trusts* (1971) Ungoed-Thomas J. said "no legatee, devisee or next of kin has any beneficial interest in the assets being administered". In view of this conflict it seems likely that even a specific legatee will have only a chose in action to ensure due administration.

2. GENERAL ADMINISTRATION ACTIONS

11.029 Where difficulties arise while the estate being administered, whether because of a problem which the personal representatives have encountered or a dispute arising over the conduct of the administration (for example, where the beneficiaries allege that the personal representatives have committed a *devastavit*) an application can be made to the court to have the difficulty resolved. These proceedings which are intended to ensure that the administration is conducted properly are called "administration proceedings". There are two types of administration proceedings:

(a) actions for general administration of the whole or part of the estate by the court. If the court makes such an order the personal representatives cannot exercise their powers to sell or distribute the assets without the consent of the court. The order stops time running under the Limitation Act for creditors' claims; or
(b) actions for specific relief, such as the determination of one specific problem.

Administration proceedings are not necessarily the result of any wrong-doing. The court's held may be sought by the personal representatives themselves if they are anxious about a particular point; this is particularly likely in the case of an action for specific relief and this is, therefore, dealt within Chapter 14 which is concerned with protection of personal representatives. Alternatively, the beneficiaries may seek the help of the court; this is more likely in the case of a general administration action and, therefore, the rest of this section deals with such actions.

Jurisdiction
The Chancery Division of the High Court has jurisdiction in these matters **11.030** but the following also have jurisdiction:

(a) the county court if the estate does not exceed in amount or value the county court limit (at present £30,000), and
(b) the bankruptcy court if the estate is insolvent.

The parties
The action can be commenced by any personal representative, any **11.031** beneficiary under the will or intestacy or any creditor. All the personal representatives must be made parties to any action; those who consent are made plaintiffs and those who do not are made defendants CPR, 63.

The order for administration
If the whole estate is to be administered under the court's direction the **11.032** court can order that an account be taken of:

(a) property that forms part of the residue of the estate which has come into the possession, either of the personal representatives or of some other person by the order or for the use of the personal representatives;
(b) the deceased's debts and funeral and testamentary expenses. If the deceased died more than six years before the date of the order the court can order that an enquiry be made as to whether any such liability of the deceased remains outstanding;
(c) legacies and annuities;
(d) any parts of the deceased's estate that have not yet been collected or distributed after enquiries have been made and any charges attaching to such property have been ascertained.

If an instance of wilful default is established against the personal representative the account may be ordered on the footing of wilful default, that is that the personal representative accounts for property which would have come into his possession but for his wilful default.

Once accounts and enquiries have been taken and made, the court will order distribution to the beneficiaries.

As an alternative to making a general order the court can order that:

(a) specific accounts and inquiries be taken and made to deal with particular problems that have arisen; or

(b) the personal representative should produce particular accounts within a stated period of time.

Costs

11.033   The personal representatives are entitled to have their costs paid from the assets of the estate, unless they have acted unreasonably or unless the result of such an order would be to diminish the estate to such an extent that claimants to it would be unfairly prejudiced (*Evans v Evans*). The costs of other parties are in the court's discretion.

Appointing a judicial trustee

11.034   Where the personal representatives cannot administer the estate and are unwilling to incur the expense of an administration action they (or a beneficiary) can apply for a judicial trustee to be appointed. He will be appointed to act either alone or with others and can be appointed to replace the existing personal representatives. Since he is an officer of the court, once appointed, he does not need the court's consent to exercise his powers.

Substitution or removal of personal representative

11.035   The High Court has a discretionary power under s.50 of the Administration of Justice Act 1985 on an application made by a beneficiary of an estate (or by or on behalf of a personal representative):

(a) to appoint a substitute to act in place of an existing personal representative; or

(b) where there are two or more existing personal representatives to terminate the appointment of one or more, but not all, of these persons.

F. Other Remedies of Beneficiaries

1. PERSONAL ACTION AGAINST PERSONAL REPRESENTATIVES

11.036   When a personal representative accepts office he accepts the duties of the office. A failure to carry out those duties properly is a *devastavit* for which the personal representative will be personally liable to the disappointed beneficiaries (or next of kin). The court may, however, grant relief either wholly or partly from personal liability to a personal representative for a breach of trust where it appears that a personal representative acted honestly and reasonably and ought fairly to be excused (Trustee Act 1925, s.61).

2. THE RIGHT TO TRACE

A beneficiary (or next-of-kin or creditor) has the right to trace and recover *property* of the estate (or property representing property of the estate) from the personal representative or from any recipient of it other than a bona fide purchaser for value (or person deriving title from such a purchaser). The right to trace is lost where the property of the estate has been dissipated or where tracing would produce an inequitable result.   **11.037**

Example
X, a personal representative, takes £1,000 belonging to an estate he is administering and spends it on a car which he gives to Y. The beneficiaries can recover the car from Y. If Y sells the car for £900 to Z, a bona fide purchaser for value, the beneficiaries have no right to trace the car into the hands of Z. They can, however, recover the £900 from Y. If Y dissipates the £900 by spending it on a holiday the right to trace is lost.

In some cases a beneficiary may prefer to rely on tracing rather than on bringing a personal action against the personal representatives (for example, where he is anxious to recover a particular asset rather than its value). In some cases the personal remedy may be valueless (for example, where the personal representative is bankrupt) so that tracing may be the only effective remedy.
    A full discussion of the law on tracing is beyond the scope of this book and the reader is referred to any standard equity textbook.

3. A PERSONAL ACTION AGAINST RECIPIENTS OF ASSETS OF THE ESTATE

Where all the other remedies of a beneficiary, next-of-kin or creditor have been exhausted a personal action may be brought against a person who has wrongly received assets of the estate. This was established by the judgment of the House of Lords in *Ministry of Health v Simpson* (1951). In this case, personal representatives had paid large sums of money to various charities in the mistaken belief that they were entitled to do so under the terms of the will. The next-of-kin of the deceased had established that the personal representatives were not so entitled and had exhausted their personal remedies against the personal representatives. They had been able to trace some of the payments into the hands of the charities and to recover them. However, some of the charities had dissipated the money with the result that the right to trace was lost. It was held that the next-of-kin were able to bring an action against the recipients personally to recover an amount equal to that which had been wrongly paid to them.   **11.038**

12. Practical Considerations During Administration

A. Introduction

12.001 In previous chapters we have studied the legal rules that are relevant to the administration of an estate. When applying the legal rules the circumstances of the estate and of the beneficiaries must be borne in mind. In this chapter we will consider some of the problems which can arise.

B. Raising Money to Pay Debts and Inheritance Tax

1. INTRODUCTION

12.002 Before the personal representatives can obtain a grant of representation they will need to pay any inheritance tax that is due. However the problem which faces them is that in order to get access to money in the deceased's bank or building society or to raise money by selling assets they will normally need the grant. They will therefore need to find a way of raising money to pay the tax which does not require a grant of representation.

2. BORROW MONEY FROM A BANK

12.003 One of the most common methods of raising money is to borrow it from a bank. The bank may be the deceased's bank or the personal representatives may prefer to approach their own bank.

Banks normally insist on an undertaking being given by the personal representatives to the effect that they will account to the bank from the first realised assets of the estate. If the personal representatives have appointed solicitors to act for them, the bank may require a further undertaking to be given by the solicitors. In this case the solicitor should obtain the personal representatives' irrevocable authority to give an undertaking.

The disadvantage of borrowing from a bank is that the loan will carry interest. Therefore, irrespective of any undertaking that has been given, the loan should be outstanding for as short a time as possible. It is advisable to arrange the loan immediately before the application for the grant is to be made and, once the grant has been obtained, to use it to realise sufficient assets to repay the debt quickly.

The Income and Corporation Taxes Act 1988, s.364(1) provides that the personal representatives may for the purposes of calculating income tax liability deduct interest paid as a charge on their income to the extent that it is paid on a loan to meet an inheritance tax liability on the delivery of the Inland Revenue Account, in respect of personal property to which the deceased was beneficially entitled immediately before his death and which vests in the personal representatives (or would do so if the property were situated in the United Kingdom). Even if the loan satisfies this requirement, the interest is only deductible to the extent that it is paid in respect of a period ending within one year from the making of the loan. Furthermore, the personal representatives must open a separate loan account, and not merely allow the deceased's bank account to become overdrawn.

The liability to pay interest may make this method unattractive to personal representatives and to beneficiaries.

3. BANKS RELEASING FUNDS OF THE DECEASED

An interesting article in *The Law Society's Gazette*, September 14, 1994 **12.004** revealed differences in the attitudes of the major banks to releasing funds of the deceased held by the bank. It is clearly always worth contacting the deceased's bank to find out whether they will release funds for this purpose.

4. DIRECT PAYMENT SCHEME

With effect from March 31, 2003 the Revenue agreed a scheme with the **12.005** British Banker's Association and the Building Societies Association whereby personal representatives can draw on money held in the deceased's accounts to pay inheritance tax due on delivery of IHT 200.

The scheme is voluntary so personal representatives should check whether the particular bank or building society is part of the scheme. The procedure is set out in the Guidance Notes to Form D20.

Personal representatives must obtain a Capital Taxes reference number for the deceased using Form D21 at least two weeks before sending the IHT 200. They must complete and sign a separate Form D20 for each bank or building society from which they wish to transfer money. They send the completed D20 to the relevant institution which will then transfer the sum requested to Capital Taxes. Once Capital Taxes receives notice of the payment it will link the payment to Form IHT 200 and return Form D18 to the personal representatives. The whole process will take longer than paying by cheque. However, this should be offset by the saving in time and cost of arranging a loan.

5. NATIONAL SAVINGS PRODUCTS AND BRITISH GOVERNMENT STOCK— PROCEEDS PAID DIRECT TO THE REVENUE

IHT 11 sets out the procedure whereby such products can be used to fund **12.006** inheritance tax.

Where an estate includes National Savings investments or British Government stock on the Bank of England register (for example War Loan, Treasury Stock and Exchequer Stock), it is possible to arrange for the payment of IHT from such products direct to the Revenue without the need to encash them. However, the Revenue itself warns that this process may take up to four weeks. The procedure should, therefore, not be used in cases where a grant is needed urgently.

The first step is to write to the appropriate National Savings Department or, in the case of Government Stock, to the Bank of England to obtain a letter giving:

- the value of the deceased's letter at the date of death; and
- the National Savings Bank or Bank of England Reference Department

The solicitor should send those letters to the Pre-Grant Section of Capital Taxes together with a letter detailing the investments to be used, a completed Inland Revenue Account and a form D-18.

If the amount transferred is sufficient to cover the tax due, the Revenue will receipt Form D-18 and return it so that the solicitor can apply for a grant. If any additional tax is due after the transfer of funds, the Revenue will give information as to the amount of the shortfall.

6. Borrow from a beneficiary

12.007   Beneficiaries may object to the personal representatives borrowing money from banks to meet the inheritance tax liability since the interest paid will reduce the income from the estate available to them. In many cases, the beneficiaries have to accept the payment as unavoidable but it may be possible to borrow money from a beneficiary interest-free.

Since the loan will facilitate the administration, beneficiaries will often be amenable to such a suggestion, provided they have the money available. This may come from their own resources or from the proceeds of an insurance policy taken out by the deceased and payable direct to the beneficiary. Such a policy may be a Married Women's Property Act 1882, s.11 policy or one written in trust for a particular person. In such cases the insurance company will simply require proof of death, in the form of a death certificate and will not require production of a grant.

If the deceased contributed to a superannuation scheme and a lump sum is paid by the trustees to a beneficiary on the death, the beneficiary may be willing to use such a sum to make an interest-free loan.

Where easily realisable property (such as money in a building society account) was held jointly with the deceased, the survivor may be willing to lend to the personal representatives out of such property.

The beneficiary will be reimbursed from the assets of the estate once the grant has been obtained.

7. Sale of assets

12.008   An executor's authority derives from the will, whereas an administrator's authority derives from the grant. An executor, therefore, has power to sell assets before a grant of representation is made whereas an administrator has no such power. However, an executor may find that it is, in fact, difficult to sell some types of assets since a prospective purchaser may insist on seeing the grant in order to confirm that the person claiming to be the executor is, in fact, the person entitled to the grant. Moreover, while the executors may be able to sell items of moveable personal property such as clothes, paintings and furniture such items may not raise sufficient funds. Land cannot be sold without the grant because the purchaser will want to examine the original grant and endorse a memorandum of the sale on the original grant.

8. ASSETS HANDED DIRECT TO INLAND REVENUE

Generally, inheritance tax is required to be paid by cheque. However the Revenue has a discretion to accept assets in total, or partial, satisfaction of the tax liability on an estate (Inheritance Tax Act 1984, s.230).   **12.009**

To be acceptable, land must have some kind of amenity value and the public must be able to enjoy reasonable access. Other items which the Secretary of State is satisfied are pre-eminent for their national, scientific, historic or artistic interest are also acceptable.

9. SUMS PAYABLE WITHOUT A GRANT

Small payments
Various provisions permit small sums to be paid or transferred on death without the need to produce a grant of representation. In all cases this power is discretionary, not obligatory and orders made under the Administration of Estates (Small Payments) Act 1965 place an upper limit on these payments of £5,000. If the sum due to the deceased is in excess of £5,000 the grant is needed for the *whole amount*, not just the excess over £5,000.   **12.010**

Subject to the £5,000 limit the payment can be made to the person appearing to be entitled to the grant or to be beneficially entitled to the sums in respect of *inter alia*:

(a) Money held in the National Savings Bank, Trustee Savings Bank, Savings Certificates or Premium Bonds. It should, however, be noted that despite these rules the Director of Savings will, in practice, require sight of a grant if the deceased held more than £5,000 *in total* in the National Savings Bank, Savings Certificates and Premium Bonds. In certain circumstances, the Director of Savings must obtain a statement from the Inland Revenue to the effect that either no inheritance tax is payable or that it has been paid, before he will make the payment without the production of the grant;

(b) Moneys payable on the death of a member of a trade union, an industrial or provident society or a friendly society;

(c) Arrears of salary, wages or superannuation on benefits due to employees of government departments;

(d) Police and firemens' pensions, Army and Air Force pensions.

Schedule 7, para. 1 of the Building Societies Act 1986 contains corresponding provisions in respect of moneys invested in a building society.

These small payments may be a useful source of funds to pay inheritance tax for personal representatives and may be preferable to seeking loans from beneficiaries.

C. Sale of Assets—Which to Sell?

1. INTRODUCTION

12.011 When the personal representatives have to sell assets whether to raise money to pay inheritance tax or in the course of administering the estate after the grant has been obtained, they must bear in mind a number of considerations:

    (a) the terms of the will,
    (b) the wishes of the beneficiaries,
    (c) the tax consequences of selling individual items.

2. THE TERMS OF THE WILL AND THE WISHES OF THE BENEFICIARIES

12.012 When deciding which assets to sell first, the personal representatives must have due regard to the statutory order for payment of debts (see Chapter 16). Should the personal representatives use the wrong items to satisfy the debts then "marshalling" may be necessary so that the appropriate beneficiary bears the burden of the debt. Therefore, if the will gives specific items of property to beneficiaries these items should not be considered for sale until the other assets in the estate have been exhausted.

When the personal representatives are choosing which assets to sell, the wishes and needs of the beneficiaries should be considered. For example, if the residuary beneficiary wants a valuable antique which has not been specifically dealt with in the will, his wishes should be respected if at all possible.

3. FUTURE DESTINATION OF PROPERTY

12.013 If the terms of the will or the intestacy rules create a trust, the personal representatives should ensure that any property retained is suitable in view of the nature of the trust. The personal representatives should consider the needs of the beneficiaries when deciding whether to retain high income as opposed to high capital growth investments.

4. THE SALE OF SHARES

12.014 The sale of shares in a quoted company should cause few problems but if the shares are in an unquoted company it may be less easy to find a market for the shares. In this circumstance, the personal representatives could seek a buyer among the other members of the company. The company itself may be willing to buy the shares under the provisions of s.162 of the Companies Act 1985. When a payment is made by the company in these circumstances to the deceased member's personal representatives any profit made on the sale will attract income tax liability unless the requirements of ss.219–229 of the Income and Corporation Taxes Act 1988 are satisfied. (The details of these rules are beyond the scope of this book.)

Clearly, where unquoted shares are concerned, the personal representatives must take professional advice as to the price they should obtain for the shares. They should also be aware of the fact that the company's Articles of Association may contain pre-emption rights.

5. TAX CONSIDERATIONS—INHERITANCE TAX

The sale of assets does not normally affect the amount of inheritance tax payable. However, Inheritance Tax Act 1984, ss.178–198 contains provisions giving relief where certain assets are sold for less than their market value at the date of death.

12.015

Relief for sales of shares at a loss

If "qualifying investments" are sold by the "appropriate person" within 12 months of the death at less than their market value at the date of death, the sale price can be substituted for the market value at the date of death. Depending on the size of the death estate and the deceased's cumulative total, this may lead to a repayment of tax.

12.016

"Qualifying investments" are shares and securities which are quoted at the date of death, on a recognised stock exchange or the unlisted securities market and units in authorised unit trusts (Inheritance Tax Act 1984, s.178(1) and Finance Act 1987, s.272). The relief also applies to any such investments held in a settlement of which the deceased was a life tenant.

The "appropriate person" is defined in s.178(1) as "the person liable for tax attributable to the value of those investments or, if there is more than one such person, and one of them is in fact paying the tax, that person". In view of the wording of the definition, it is important that the sale be made by the person who has paid the tax (usually the personal representatives or trustees) if the relief is to be available. For example, if the personal representatives had paid the inheritance tax on quoted shares, they must be the ones to sell those shares. The relief would not be available if the shares were vested in a specific legatee even if the legatee sold the shares at a loss within 12 months.

The loss is calculated by deducting the sale price from the market value of the shares at death. However, the Revenue have the power to substitute the best consideration which could reasonably have been obtained (s.179(1)(b)). Expenses incurred as a result of the sale, such as stockbrokers commission and stamp duty, cannot be used to increase the loss.

Example

On X's death he had made chargeable transfers up to the limit of his nil rate band and had a death estate of £300,000 including shares in a public quoted company worth £3,000. Inheritance tax was paid on the estate. If X's personal representatives sell the holding for £2,500 within 12 months of the death, they can claim relief and so receive a rebate equal to the tax paid on the £500 reduction in value.

If a number of sales of qualifying investments are made within the 12 month period the sale proceeds of all transactions must be aggregated to discover the overall gain or loss. If, overall, a loss has arisen the claim for the relief may be made. If, overall, a gain has been made the Revenue cannot demand extra inheritance tax but no loss relief can be claimed on the particular shares sold at a loss.

Example
The figures for X's estate are the same as for the previous example save that X held shares in three separate public companies, each holding being worth £1,000 at his death. If X's personal representatives sell the three holdings for £500, £750 and £1,250 respectively within 12 months of the death, they must aggregate the three sale prices to calculate the overall loss of £500. It is *not* possible to take account only of the first two sales.

The relief is available whenever a sale is made by the appropriate person within the specified period but, if the sale proceeds are reinvested by the appropriate person in other qualifying investments within two months of the last such sale, the loss relief available will be reduced or extinguished (s.180(1)). This is because the purpose of the reliefs is to give assistance where shares are sold to raise money to pay inheritance tax or other debts. If the sale is to improve the estate's portfolio of investments, the relief will not be available to the personal representatives.

If the sale is to be eligible for the relief, it must occur within 12 months of the death. The operative date is the sale date unless there was a contract to sell in which case, the contract date determines whether the sale qualifies for relief.

A problem existed for personal representatives who found themselves at the end of the 12 month period from death holding shares where the quotation had been suspended. Clearly the personal representatives could not sell the shares and, therefore, no relief was available. However, the Finance Act 1993, s.199 inserted a new s.186B into the Inheritance Tax Act providing that the shares can be treated as sold immediately before the end of the 12 month period for their value at the time.

If qualifying investments held by the appropriate person are cancelled within the period of 12 months from death without being replaced by other shares or securities, they are to be treated as sold by the appropriate person for nominal consideration of £1 (IHTA, s.186A).

The inter-relation of inheritance tax loss relief on shares and capital gains tax

12.017 When sales which can potentially give rise to claims within para.12.014 take place, the personal representatives will realise an allowable loss for capital gains tax purposes. If the election for the inheritance tax relief is claimed, however, the sale price becomes the personal representatives' acquisition value for capital gains tax (Inheritance Tax Act 1984, s.187 and Taxation of Chargeable Gains Act 1992, s.274). The personal representatives will then be treated for capital gains tax purposes as selling for the same amount as the acquisition value and will not be able to claim a capital gains tax loss.

Inheritance tax is chargeable at 40 per cent on the value of the portion of an *estate* exceeding the nil rate band (after cumulation). Since capital gains tax is payable by personal representatives at 34 per cent of the chargeable *gain*, it will always be preferable to claim inheritance tax loss relief unless the amount of the capital gains tax loss is more than the amount by which the nil rate band is exceeded and there are (or are likely to be) future gains against which the loss can be set in excess of any exemption or relief the personal representatives can claim.

Relief for sales of land at a loss

If the deceased was entitled to an interest in land at the time of death and that interest is sold for less than the market value at death, the personal representatives can claim to have the sale price substituted for the market value at death, provided the sale takes place within four years of death, the operative date being the date of the contract for sale (ss.190–198 of the Inheritance Tax Act 1984). This can lead to a rebate in the way illustrated in para.12.016. **12.018**

As with sales of quoted shares the sale must be by "the appropriate person" which has the same meaning as in para.12.016 above. Furthermore section 196 prevents the claim being made where the sale is to one of the beneficiaries (or to certain persons closely connected to a beneficiary). Section 191 provides that small decreases in value are ignored. Thus, the relief is not available if the reduction in the value of the interest is less than either £1,000 or 5 per cent of its value on death, whichever is the lesser.

The Revenue are given the power to substitute the best consideration that could reasonably have been obtained on the sale if this is higher than the sale price, thereby preventing the personal representatives artificially creating or increasing the loss.

Sections 192 to 195 require certain adjustments to be made which may reduce the amount of loss relief that can be claimed. For example, when the sale proceeds are reinvested in any other interest in land within four months of the last qualifying sale, the relief may be reduced or extinguished.

Where several interests in land are sold within three years of death, if one is revalued in order to claim loss relief, all the interests sold must be revalued. If any interest has increased in value, there may be more inheritance tax to pay as a result. Care must, therefore, be taken when deciding whether to make the claim in these circumstances since if the personal representatives make an overall *gain*, additional inheritance tax *can* be levied. (This is an important distinction as compared with the position on shares.)

In the case of sales in the fourth year after death sales for more than value at date of death are ignored. Exchange of contract is not a "sale". See *Jones (Ball's Administrators) v IRC* (1997).

The inter-relation of inheritance tax loss relief and capital gains tax

12.019 Unlike the provisions which deal with loss relief on the sale of shares, the provisions which deal with loss relief on the sales of interests in land contain no section which states expressly that the capital gains tax acquisition value is to be reduced in the event of a claim for inheritance tax loss relief. However, s.274 of the Taxation of Chargeable Gains Act 1992 provides that where a value has been "ascertained" for inheritance tax purposes, that figure will become the acquisition value for capital gains tax purposes. In cases where land is sold for more than death value but no inheritance tax is payable (e.g. because the property passes to an exempt beneficiary), it would be beneficial to elect to substitute the sale price for capital gains tax purposes. This is not possible, see *Stonor v IRC* (2001).

6. TAX CONSIDERATIONS—CAPITAL GAINS TAX

12.020 Personal representatives will, prima facie, be liable to pay capital gains tax at 34 per cent on gains made on sales of assets. However, as personal representatives are chargeable only on gains arising since death and as relief may be available to exempt gains, in many cases, no capital gains tax will be payable.

If the personal representatives vest assets in the beneficiaries, the beneficiaries will acquire the assets at their market value at the date of death. When the beneficiaries dispose of the assets they will be chargeable at their own rates on any gains realised by them and entitled to the benefit of any allowable losses realised by them. The personal representatives will not have any capital gains tax liability on such disposals.

If the personal representatives wish to sell assets, they should, when deciding which assets to sell, consider the possibility of a capital gains tax liability arising. They should consider the following factors:

(a) *Will a chargeable gain arise?* The assets may have risen in value since the date of death. However, the personal representatives will be able to claim an annual exemption in the tax year of death and the two following tax years. The amount of this exemption is the same as that available to individuals. Where possible sales of assets which have risen in value during the administration should be spread over two or more tax years so that more than one annual exemption may be claimed.

(b) *Will a loss arise?* A loss must be set off against any gains which the personal representatives realise in the same tax year. To the extent that the loss cannot be set off against gains of the same tax year, it is carried forward and set off against gains made by the personal representatives in future tax years. If the personal representatives are unlikely to make future gains they may wish to consider vesting the loss-making asset in a beneficiary, thus allowing the beneficiary to sell the asset. The beneficiary can then set the loss off against any gain that he may make in the future. If the assets sold are shares or land, the inheritance tax loss relief discussed above should be considered.

(c) *Is it better to sell an appreciating asset or a depreciating one?* Selling an asset that is increasing in value may avoid the payment of tax but equally will deprive the estate of a valuable asset. Selling a depreciating one will give rise to a loss which may lead to a tax saving but the personal representatives must not delay too long before selling since the value of the estate may be unnecessarily reduced. However, it would be foolish to sell if there is any possibility of the asset recovering its value in the near future.

(d) *What are the wishes of the beneficiaries?* When choosing which assets to sell and which to retain, the personal representatives should consult with the beneficiaries to obtain their views. Most beneficiaries will want to ensure that the value of their entitlement is maintained so will advocate selling depreciating assets and retaining appreciating ones. However, a beneficiary with a substantial capital gains tax liability from other disposals might agree to receive a depreciating asset so that he can sell it, thus realising a loss that can be set against his gains. Similarly a beneficiary with unrelieved losses can have an appreciating asset vested in him. The asset can be sold by the beneficiary, the gain being reduced by his allowable losses.

Where assets are held for a charity, it is likely that the charity will want the asset to be appropriated to it and sold on its behalf as bare trustee. This can result in a saving of capital gains tax as compared to the position where the assets are sold by the personal representatives and the proceeds transferred to the charity. It is important to comply with the necessary formalities. There should be a written appropriation and a record of the instruction to sell. Most major charities are familiar with the necessary steps and many have helpful leaflets. The Institute of Legacy Managers website (*www.ilmnet.org.uk*) has a precedent available. It is well worth talking to charities early in the administration and keeping them informed of developments.

(e) *Higher rate beneficiaries.* A beneficiary may want an asset which has been left to him to be sold. A beneficiary who is a higher rate taxpayer will prefer the *personal representatives* to sell assets which show capital gains and then to pay the proceeds to himself rather than vesting the asset in the beneficiary. This is because personal representatives pay capital gains tax at 34 per cent. Therefore, unless such a beneficiary has an unused annual exemption tax will be saved if the personal representatives sell and make the *proceeds* available to the beneficiary.

D. General Duties

In addition to the detailed points set out above, the personal representatives must bear in mind more general considerations when administering the estate. The personal representatives must ascertain the deceased's debts and liabilities, obtain the grant, pay debts and distribute the assets to the beneficiaries. **12.021**

While administering the estate they must ensure that the value of assets are maintained.

This obligation will be discharged in a number of ways. The personal representatives must ensure that when any asset is damaged or falls into disrepair it is repaired. This can be expensive and so they should take out insurance cover. If the deceased had taken out property insurance the personal representatives should as soon as possible after the death notify the insurance company and either have their interest noted on the policy or a fresh policy issued.

For estates which include shares, personal representatives must constantly review their portfolio, taking expert advice as appropriate, and ensuring as far as possible that the portfolio maintains its value. Therefore the personal representatives must consider selling shares that are dropping in value with a view to replacing them with a better investment. Equally the personal representatives should avoid speculative investments even though they might realise substantial profits. Any investments other than stocks and shares of the deceased should also be looked at criticially.

Finally the personal representatives should ensure that they complete their task quickly and efficiently by anticipating difficulties before they arise (so far as possible) and not delaying the performance of their duties.

13. Duties of Solicitors

A. The Extent of the Solicitor's Duty

The solicitor's duty is to prepare a will which carries out the client's **13.001** testamentary intentions and to take any other steps which are necessary to give effect to those wishes. A failure by the solicitor to draft a will so as to comply with the client's wishes is an especially serious matter since the mistake which has been made is not likely to become apparent until the client is dead or may never be discovered at all. It is too late to correct certain types of mistake once the client is dead. The will (or part of it) may be refused probate on the grounds that the client did not have knowledge and approval of the contents but this will not necessarily ensure that the testator's true wishes are put into effect. Section 20 of the Administration of Justice Act 1982 allows rectification of a will to correct clerical errors or failure to understand the client's instructions but as we saw in Chapter 2 this does not enable every type of mistake to be corrected. Even if rectification is possible the mistake will cause considerable delay and expense.

A beneficiary who suffers loss as a result of the failure of the solicitor to carry out his duty is all too likely to sue the solicitor who acted for the testator. In *White v Jones* (1995) the House of Lords held that the solicitor's assumption of responsibility towards his client should be held in law to extend to the intended beneficiary in circumstances where the beneficiary would otherwise have no remedy. The result of this decision has been a proliferation of cases alleging breach of duty on the part of solicitors in relation to the drafting and execution of wills.

B. Duties Relating to the Preparation of the Will

The solicitor must clarify the terms of the retainer

Any ambiguity will be resolved in favour of the client. In *Gray v Buss* **13.002** *Murton* (1999) a trainee solicitor believed that he was being asked to give an opinion as to whether or not a will had been validly executed (which it had). The clients believed that he was advising them on whether the will was effective (which it was not). The firm was held liable to the clients on the basis that it was for the solicitor to establish the extent of the retainer. In *Hurlingham Estates Ltd v Wilde & Partners* (1997) Lightman J. said that in the absence of a retainer limiting liability it was necessary to consider whether the solicitor "should reasonably have appreciated" that the client "needed his advice and guidance" on the tax aspects of the transaction. Any limitation on the retainer would have to be in writing to enable the client to consider it and give informed consent.

The solicitor must prepare the will with reasonable speed

13.003   In *White v Jones* itself solicitors received a letter on July 17 instructing them to prepare a new will but had not prepared the will for execution by the time the testator died on September 14. The firm had to compensate the disappointed beneficiaries.

In *X v Woollcombe Yonge* (2001) a solicitor prepared a will for a terminally ill client within a week but the client died before it was ready. Neuberger J. suggested that seven days would be a sufficiently short period "in most cases" where the client was "elderly or likely to die". In this case the testatrix, although terminally ill, was not expected to die within the next couple of weeks. She was planning to move to a hospice and raised no objection when told that the solicitor would bring the will some time in the following week. The amount of time taken was not unreasonable. However, "where there is a plain and substantial risk of the client's imminent death, anything other than a handwritten rough codicil prepared on the spot for signature may be negligent".

It is beneficial to agree a time-frame with the client for preparation of the will. This is good practice in itself but, beyond that, may be of assistance if the client dies before the will is ready for execution. The duty owed by the solicitor is to the client and is to produce a legally effective will which carries out the client's intentions. If the solicitor has carried out the terms of the agreement, it will be much more difficult (though not impossible) for the beneficiaries to allege breach of duty.

Take instructions from the client in person wherever possible

13.004   It is possible to take instructions in writing or via the internet but there may be problems as a result. Principle 24.01, *Guide to Professional Conduct* says:

> "Can I draft a will on the basis of the testator's written instructions alone?
>
> Yes, but you must consider carefully whether this is safe, bearing in mind the inherent dangers, e.g. lack of sufficient information, the difficulties in fully advising the client and ensuring capacity, and the possibility of fraud and undue influence."

Ideally solicitors should not accept instructions from an intermediary. The court was extremely critical of the solicitor in *Richards v Allen* (2001) who accepted instructions from his sister-in-law without ever seeing the testatrix.

Be careful of conflicts of interest. It is common to see married couples together but many solicitors are not happy doing this and there may be tensions particularly in the case of second marriages. In *Hines v Willans* (2002) a solicitor was held liable for breach of duty arising from a conflict of interest. He had an appointment to see a wife on the following Monday, but made a will for her husband disinheriting her and (at his own suggestion) prepared a notice of severance of the couple's joint tenancy.

Be alert to the possibility of undue influence. If a client expresses a wish to save inheritance tax by making lifetime gifts is he/she under pressure from one or more of the children? Does the client understand what he is doing and what could happen in the future? Make sure everything is confirmed in writing and try to see the client in the absence of family members who may be exerting pressure.

Try to establish that the client has testamentary capacity
Where a solicitor fails to check a testator's capacity and prepares a will **13.005** which later turns out to be invalid, there may be a claim from the estate that it has been reduced by the costs of the dispute. See *Worby v Rosser* (1999) and *Corbett v Bond Pearce* (2001).

It is, therefore, important for practitioners to carry out their duties with regard to capacity.

The so-called "Golden Rule" was developed by Templeman J. (as he then was) in *Kenward v Adams* (1975) and *Re Simpson (Deceased)* (1977). It was referred to with approval in *Buckenham v Dickinson* (1997) and by Rimer J. in *Re Morris (Deceased), Special Trustees for Great Ormond Street Hospital for Children v Rushin and others* (2001).

Templeman J. said:

> "In the case of an aged testator or a testator who has suffered a serious illness, there is one golden rule which should always be observed, however straightforward matters may appear, and however difficult or tactless it may be to suggest that precautions be taken: the making of a will by such a testator ought to be witnessed or approved by a medical practitioner who satisfies himself of the capacity and understanding of the testator, and records and preserves his examination and findings.
>
> There are other precautions which should be taken. If the testator has made an earlier will this should be considered by the legal and medical advisers of the testator and, if appropriate, discussed with the testator.
>
> The instructions of the testator should be taken in the absence of anyone who may stand to benefit, or who may have influence over the testator.
>
> These are not counsels of perfection. If proper precautions are not taken injustice may result or be imagined, and great expense and misery may be unnecessarily caused."

It is often difficult to get medical evidence particularly in urgent cases. Always prepare a full attendance note detailing the steps you took to establish testamentary capacity.

Clients with borderline testamentary capacity are often vulnerable to undue influence. Try to see the client alone. In *Killick v Pountney* (2000) an important factor in the court's decision that there had been undue influence was the fact that the beneficiary had been present for some of the time at the interview.

The House of Lords in *Barclays Bank v Ettridge and other appeals* (2001) reviewed the law on undue influence in the context of charging one spouse's interest in the matrimonial home as security for the debts of the other. One practical recommendation made was that the interview with the client must be in the absence of the person benefiting from the transaction. There must be a clear explanation of the nature and consequences of the act. It is then for adult persons of competent mind to decide whether they will do an act. The solicitor does not need to approve of the client's decision. Independent and competent advice does not mean independent and competent approval.

In exceptional cases where it is glaringly obvious that the spouse is being grievously wronged, Lord Nichols said that the solicitor should decline to act further. Many practitioners are concerned that the effect of not acting is merely that the client will be coached better and taken elsewhere and by the person exerting the influence. However, in *Powell v Powell* (1900) Farwell J. said that a solicitor "ought not to go on, if he disapproves, simply because he thinks that someone else will do the work if he does not".

Be clear what property the testator owns and in what capacity

13.006   Clients do not always remember how they own property. In *Chittock v Stevens* (2000) a house was believed to be in joint names but eight months after the death of the husband (partially intestate) it was discovered that it had been in his sole name. It is desirable to either check the basis of ownership or record that the will has been prepared on the basis of the information provided by the client. Resolve any ambiguities or uncertainties with the client.

Joint property is particularly problematic. In *Carr-Glynn v Frearsons* (1998) the testatrix (aged 81) consulted a solicitor to make a will leaving her interest in a property "Homelands" to her niece. She owned the property with her nephew and was uncertain as to whether she owned it as beneficial joint tenant or tenant in common.

Her solicitor prepared a will and advised her that the gift of "Homelands" could not take affect if she held it as a beneficial joint tenant. The solicitor asked if the testatrix wanted her to obtain and check the deeds. The testatrix said that she would do it herself. She did not do so and when she died it was discovered that she had owned the property as beneficial joint tenant.

The Court of Appeal found that the solicitor was in breach of her duty which extended beyond the mere preparation of the will to steps necessary to give effect to the client's testamentary intentions. Many people consider the decision rather harsh but according to the Court of Appeal the solicitor's breach lay in not explaining to the client that she could have served a notice of severance without having to obtain the deeds. Had the solicitor given this explanation, there would presumably have been no liability even if the client declined to serve the notice.

A beneficial joint tenancy also caused a problem in *Re Woolnough* (2002). The firm of solicitors overlooked the fact that serving a notice of severance is just one way of severing a joint tenancy (see para.21.008) and did not realise that severance had occurred before death.

There may also be cases where property held in joint names is actually held on a resulting trust for the party who provided the funds. See *Aroso v Coutts* (2002), *Goodman v Carlton* (2002). Explore the nature of ownership while the client is alive and it is possible to clarify and record it. In a case where property is in the name of one party but another may have an interest (*e.g.* where one party has moved in with another and has made substantial contributions to the costs of the property) it may be desirable to suggest changes in the legal ownership so that the position is clear.

Does anyone else have an interest in property "owned" by the client as a result of proprietary estoppel?
See *Gillett v Holt* (1998) in which the Court of Appeal confirmed that a **13.007** promise to leave property by will can give rise to a claim in proprietary estoppel. The necessary elements are a promise relied on by the promisor resulting in detriment to the promisee so that it would be unconscionable for equity not to provide a remedy. The promisee will not necessarily receive everything he feels he is entitled to. The Court of Appeal has gone out of its way to emphasise that any award must be proportionate to the detriment suffered, the claims of creditors and of other beneficiaries of the estate. See *Campbell v Griffin and West Sussex County Council* (2001), *Jennings v Rice* (2002).

Does the client have a general power of appointment?
If so, it is important to clarify the client's wishes for the trust property. The **13.008** trust property will pass as part of a general residuary gift where the power has not been expressly exercised. However, it is preferable to exercise the power expressly to avoid later allegations that the client was not aware of the effect of the residuary gift. See *Gibbons v Nelsons (A Firm) & Others* (2000).

The solicitor's role in taking instructions should not be entirely passive
The solicitor should ensure that the client is not under some **13.009** misapprehension as to the effect of his instructions which if corrected might lead to different instructions. It is not possible to give an exhaustive list of all the points which should be drawn to a client's attention but the following are among the most important:

(a) Jointly held property will pass to the surviving joint tenant even if the will says otherwise.
(b) If dependants and certain relatives are not provided for family provision claims may be made.
(c) Gifts of specific items will be adeemed if the items are sold or changed in substance unless specific provision is made.
(d) Unless contrary provision is made most types of gift will lapse (and fall into residue or pass on intestacy) if the donee predeceases. A gift will, however, take effect if the beneficiary survives for a very short time or is deemed to survive under s.184 of the Law of Property Act 1925. This may not correspond with the client's wishes so that a survivorship clause should be considered.
(e) Unless contrary provision is made in the will, a person taking a property charged with a debt takes it subject to that debt (Administration of Estates Act 1925, s35). Check the testator's wishes in relation to a specific gift of an asset which is (or may be at the time of death) charged with a debt.
  Be particularly careful where there is life assurance linked to the debt. Make sure that there is no ambiguity as to where the proceeds of the policy are going. Normally the testator will want the person who is responsible for the debt to take the benefit of the policy so as to have funds available. This may require careful

drafting.

(f) Payments from pension funds and insurance policies may be payable to beneficiaries independently of the terms of the will. In the case of pension schemes where lump sums are payable at the discretion of the trustees of the scheme, it is usually possible for an employee to leave a statement of his wishes for the destination of the sum payable. Such a statement is not binding on the trustees but will be considered by them. A client who has the benefit of such a scheme should be advised to make a statement.

C. Duties Relating to the Execution of the Will

The solicitor must offer to oversee the execution of the will

13.010 As we saw in para.2.010 the case of *Esterhuizen v Allied Dunbar* (1998) suggests that a solicitor must make the following offer:

- the solicitor will attend the client at home and oversee execution; or
- the client can come to the solicitor's office and have execution overseen; or
- if the client prefers he can execute the will at home.

If the client executes the will at home the solicitor should send a letter explaining exactly how to execute the will.

The solicitor must offer to check the will after the execution

13.011 In *Ross v Caunters* (1980) the solicitor sent the testator a letter with the will saying that attestation was required by "two independent witnesses". When the will was returned to the solicitor, one of the witnesses had the same surname as one of the beneficiaries. The solicitors did not query this. The witness was married to the beneficiary who, therefore, lost her entitlement. Megarry, V.C. found that the solicitor had been negligent because he had failed:

- to warn the testator that a spouse of a beneficiary should not witness;
- to check whether the will was properly attested;
- to observe that the attesting witness was the spouse of a beneficiary;
- to draw this to the attention of the testator.

In *Gray and Others v Richards Butler (A Firm)* (2000) the judge accepted that a solicitor owes a duty to a testator, at execution *and also when the will is returned after execution.*

If retained to arrange execution, do so within a reasonable time

13.012 In *Hooper v Fynmores (A Firm)* (2002) a solicitor prepared a will for an elderly client, in early September 1997, increasing the claimant's share in residue by £40,000. The solicitor who prepared the will wrote to the client asking if he would like him to bring out for signature.

On September 8 the client was admitted to hospital. On September 10 the claimant left a message with the firm of solicitors explaining that the client had gone into hospital. On September 16 an old friend of the client telephoned the solicitor to say that he was having tests and would be in touch when he was home from hospital. The solicitor considered that he had been "stood down".

The client later arranged that the solicitor would visit him on October 13. However, the solicitor himself went into hospital and cancelled the appointment. He did not arrange a new appointment and did not discuss the possibility of sending a substitute. The client died on October 21 without executing the will. The Court of Appeal found that the solicitor had been negligent.

Initially the solicitor was entitled to rely on the client's instructions relayed through a close and reliable friend postponing action. However, the position changed when the further appointment was made. A solicitor has a duty to satisfy himself that a delay in executing a will resulting from the cancellation of an appointment will not be disadvantageous to the client. If necessary, the solicitor should appoint a substitute. An appointment with an elderly client in hospital should not to be cancelled unless the client is agreeable to it.

Sometimes clients are unwilling to execute a will. A solicitor is not required to ensure that a client executes a will. There may be circumstances where continuing to press a client could amount to undue influence. It will normally be appropriate to write to clients reminding them that the will has not been executed and asking if they want any alteration to be made.

Do not allow a client to execute will conditionally
See *Corbett v Newey* (1996) where solicitors allowed the testatrix to sign **13.013** the will but not date it. Her intention was that it should not come into operation until certain lifetime gifts had been completed. The will was not valid because it had not been executed unconditionally. The solicitors had to compensate the disappointed beneficiaries.

D. Duties Relating to Records

Full attendance notes are a solicitor's protection against false allegations. **13.014** In addition, the discipline of preparing them may also help to avoid a mistake. Courts place a great deal of weight on good contemporaneous notes but are unimpressed by those prepared after the event and particularly those prepared from memory in the knowledge of future litigation (see *Killick v Pountney* (2000)). It is sensible to take instructions for a will in the same form so that important questions are not omitted. Many people find using a checklist helpful.

It is particularly important to clarify in correspondence any limitations imposed on the extent of the service (see para.13.015 below) or on the extent of the solicitor's knowledge of the client's assets (see para.13.006 above).

A solicitor who is present at the execution of a will by a testator who is frail (whether mentally or physically) should always make a full and careful attendance note. (See para.13.014 above.)

After execution the solicitor should "make up" a copy of the will (*i.e.* write in particulars of the date, signature and witnesses) or take a photocopy for his file. Made-up copies and photocopies are admissible as proof of the terms of the will if the will is lost (see para.2.31). It is especially important to keep a copy if the will itself is to be kept by the client or deposited elsewhere such as at a bank. The solicitor's filing system must be so arranged that the original will (if kept by the solicitor) and copy can be found many years after execution. Nothing should be attached to an original will since the presence of pin holes or clip impressions may lead to an allegation of attempted revocation in which case affidavit evidence will be required. (See para.10.051.)

E. Duties Relating to General Advice

13.015 A solicitor who has agreed to prepare a will for a client is under an obligation to take any steps necessary to put the client's testamentary wishes into effect. The solicitor should, therefore, explain any problems, disadvantages and necessary steps. It is possible to limit the terms of the retainer (for example by offering to draft a will but not to offer detailed advice on tax planning without a separate charge) but as we have already seen the obligation is on the solicitor to clarify the terms of the retainer (*Gray v Buss Murton* (1999)).

The solicitor must have written evidence of the retainer to have any hope of success (see *Hurlingham Estates Ltd v Wilde & Partners* (1997)). Writing is required, not merely as evidence of what has been agreed, but so that the client can consider (and discuss with others) the position and its implications independently of the solicitor. Furthermore, even if the client consents, the solicitor will not be able to rely on the consent unless it is informed. In particular the client must understand whether the limitation is one which is reasonable and whether it is necessary for the client to seek advice elsewhere.

A solicitor cannot gain protection from liability by claiming to rely on counsel's opinion. In *Estill v Cowling, Swift & Kitchin* (2000). An estate suffered unnecessary inheritance tax because an inappropriate discretionary trust was established in the testatrix's lifetime.

Arden J. said that a solicitor does not abdicate his professional responsibility when he seeks the advice of counsel: "He must apply his mind to the advice received. But the more specialist the nature of the advice, the more reasonable is it likely to be for a solicitor to accept and act on it."

If the solicitor has accepted a general retainer to put the client's testamentary wishes into effect, it may also be appropriate to advise on other methods of disposal such as lifetime gifts and on the possible advantages of taking out insurance policies expressed to be for the benefit of third parties. If the solicitor thinks it necessary he may also advise the client to obtain expert investment advice. If the solicitor himself gives investment advice he must be authorised under the Financial Services and Markets Act 2000.

It is also very important to warn clients that a will should never be regarded as permanent. Changed circumstances should lead to a review of the will (particularly changes in family circumstances such as marriage, separation, divorce and the birth of children and changes in financial circumstances such as inheritance of property or retirement). A solicitor who is acting for a client in relation to other matters (such as a divorce) should always suggest the making of a new will if he suspects it may be desirable. When advising a married client who intends to make a will it is desirable to suggest that the spouse also considers making a will so that the dispositions of the spouses can be considered together.

Although it is a breach of the rules of professional conduct for a solicitor to tout for business there can be no objection to a solicitor informing his existing clients of changes in the law which make it desirable for them to make new wills. However, this may lead to suggestions that the solicitor owes a continuing contractual duty to the clients. See *Hines v Willans* (1997).

A solicitor is not under an obligation to keep a client informed of changes in the law unless the firm has accepted a continuing retainer.

F. Solicitor as Beneficiary

Where a person is a beneficiary of a will which he has himself prepared **13.016** positive evidence will be required of the testator's knowledge and approval of the contents of the will (*Wintle v Nye* (1959)). Where the will is simple and short and the testator has had an opportunity to read it, the court may not require any additional evidence (see *Fuller v Strum* (2000)). The Law Society has directed that a solicitor receiving a benefit from a client must *insist* that the client goes to another solicitor for independent advice and for the drafting of the will. It is not sufficient that the client is merely *advised* to take such advice (see para.2.033).

Neither of these rules prevents a solicitor from preparing a will which appoints the solicitor or his partner as an executor even though the will contains a charging clause.

G. Duties of Solicitor Acting for Personal Representatives

Personal representatives will frequently retain a solicitor to act for them **13.017** in the administration of an estate. The personal representatives are then the solicitor's clients. The beneficiaries or family of the deceased are not. If there is any dispute arising out of the administration the solicitor must be careful not to allow an actual or potential conflict of interest to arise by advising the beneficiaries or family of the deceased while he continues to act for the personal representatives.

It is particularly important that the solicitor reminds the personal representatives that they owe their duty to the estate and not to particular beneficiaries. They should remain neutral if there is a dispute between beneficiaries. Where personal representatives incur costs by acting to further the interests of one set of beneficiaries at the expense of another, they will be penalised by the court. See *Tod v Barton and Royal Society of Chemistry* (2002) and *Breadner v Granville-Grossman* (2001).

The duties of a solicitor in acting for personal representatives include giving advice and taking action in the administration on the clients' behalf. Immediately after the death the solicitor will be called upon to obtain any will of the deceased, advise on its validity and take steps to obtain a grant including the preparation of the appropriate oath and the Inland Revenue Account (if required). In some cases it will also be necessary to obtain affidavits in support of the application (such as affidavits of due execution).

Once the grant has been obtained the solicitor's duty is to advise the personal representatives on their duties. In particular the solicitor will be required to advise on the collection and realisation of the estate, the payment of debts and the distribution of the estate to the beneficiaries.

In *Cancer Research Campaign and Others v Ernest Brown & Co (A Firm) and Others* (1997) Harman J. reviewed the authorities to decide whether or not executors had an obligation to inform legatees of a gift made to them in advance of distribution. He concluded that they had not on the basis that a legatee has no specific right in any asset in the estate. They have merely a chose in action to compel the proper administration of the estate. The estate may have such heavy debts that there is nothing left for legatees. Solicitors acting for executors could not be under any more extensive liability and so they had no obligation either. This was unfortunate for the legatees in question who would have varied their entitlement to achieve a tax saving had they been informed within the two year time period.

However, there is no doubt that it is good practice to inform beneficiaries of their interest in an estate. Even the authorities relied upon by Harman J. suggest this.

Missing beneficiaries cause problems for personal beneficiaries. Solicitors must explain that the duty of the personal representatives is to distribute the estate to those entitled and advise on the possible ways of dealing the situation (see Chapter 14).

Once the administration is complete the solicitor will prepare (or will supervise the preparation of) the estate accounts prior to the distribution of residue. Solicitors have frequently been criticised for failure to prepare such accounts promptly.

14. Protection of Personal Representatives

A. Introduction

Personal representatives are personally liable for any loss arising from a **14.001** failure to carry out their duties. If they have incurred personal liability they may be able to obtain relief in one of three ways.

(a) *The will may contain a relieving provision.* Many wills include a clause limiting the liability of personal representatives to liability for wilful fraud or wrongdoing and giving protection from liability for mistakes made in good faith. In *Armitage v Nurse* (1997) Millett L.J. held that a clause purporting to exclude liability for everything except actual fraud was not repugnant or contrary to public policy. There is a core of obligations that beneficiaries must be able to enforce against trustees in order to give effect to the trust, but these obligations do not include the duties of skill, care, prudence and diligence. However, there is an increasing feeling that such clauses are not normally appropriate for professional trustees who are paid and can insure against the risk of liability. The Law Commission is currently consulting with a view to preventing professional trustees excluding liability.

(b) *The court may grant relief under Trustee Act 1925, s.61.* The court has a discretion to grant relief where a trustee "has acted honestly and reasonably and ought fairly to be excused".

For example, this discretion was exercised in *Re Kay* (1897) where a personal representative paid a legacy which appeared small in comparison to the estate at a time when he was unaware of liabilities which exceeded the total value of the estate.

(c) *The beneficiaries may grant a release.* The personal representatives can obtain a release from personal liability from all the beneficiaries affected by the breach. Such a release is only effective where the beneficiaries induced the personal representatives to perform the wrongful act (*Trafford v Boehm* (1746)) or if the beneficiaries are *sui juris* and fully aware of the breach.

(d) *Limitation.* Where personal representatives have incurred personal liability, they may be able to plead the defence of limitation. Creditors cannot bring an action against personal representatives for non-payment of debts after a period of six years has elapsed from date of distribution of the estate (Limitation Act 1980, s.2). Beneficiaries cannot bring an action against the personal representatives to recover land or personalty after the expiration of 12 years from the date on which the right of action accrued (Limitation Act 1980, ss.23 and 15(1)). No limitation period applies where a personal representative is fraudulent or where the personal representative is in possession of trust property or the proceeds thereof. The limitation period will not start to run against a beneficiary who is under a disability or where there has been fraud, concealment or mistake (Limitation Act 1980, ss.28, 38 and 32).

Personal representatives will obviously be anxious to avoid incurring personal liability. It is possible for them to prevent personal liability ever arising by complying with certain statutory provisions which offer protection. Where a solicitor acts on behalf of personal representatives, the solicitor should endeavour to ensure that they obtain protection. These methods of obtaining protection are considered below.

B. Statutory Advertisements (Trustee Act 1925, s.27)

14.002 Personal representatives who have distributed the assets of the deceased are personally liable to any beneficiaries or creditors for any unpaid debts and liabilities even though they were unaware of them at the time for distribution (*Knatchbull v Fearnhead* (1837)). However they can protect themselves from such liability by advertising for claimants under Trustee Act 1925, s.27.

1. THE ADVERTISEMENTS

14.003 Under s.27, the personal representatives may give notice of their intention to distribute the assets of the estate, requiring any person interested to send in particulars of his claim (whether as a creditor or as a beneficiary *Re Aldhous* (1955)) to the personal representatives within a stated time, not being less than two months from the date of the notice. This notice must be brought to the attention of the general public by:

(a) placing an advertisement in the *London Gazette*; and
(b) placing an advertisement in a newspaper circulating in the district in which land to be distributed (if any) is situated; and
(c) giving "such other like notices, including notices elsewhere than in England and Wales, as would, in any special case, have been directed by a court of competent jurisdiction in an action for administration". (In an action for administration the court would order the advertisement to be placed in such local or national newspapers as might be appropriate having regard to the circumstances of the case. In cases of doubt, personal representatives should apply to the court for directions as to where to place the advertisements since failure to comply with all the requirements denies them the protection of the section).

2. SEARCHES

14.004 Section 27(2) provides that personal representatives are not freed "from any obligation to make searches or obtain official certificates of search similar to those which an intending purchaser would be advised to make or obtain". Although this subsection does not list the searches that have to be made the prudent personal representative will make the same searches as a purchaser of land would make in the Land Registry or Land Charges Register, as appropriate, and the local land charges register, as well as searching in bankruptcy against the deceased and any beneficiary receiving assets.

3. DISTRIBUTING THE ESTATE

Once the time limit on the notices has expired the personal representatives can distribute the estate having regard only to the claims of which they have notice. If a claim is made after distribution by someone of whom they had no notice, the personal representatives are not personally liable. In these circumstances the disappointed claimant must recover the assets from the persons who received them from the personal representatives. So as to avoid delay in the distribution of the estate, these searches and advertisements should be made as early in the administration as possible. The section does not relieve personal representatives from liability if they have actual knowledge of a claim. For example, if they know of a debt they are under an obligation to pay it even though the creditor does not respond to the advertisement. **14.005**

A problem with s.27 is that having decided what are the appropriate newspapers, it may prove difficult actually to place the advertisement. For example in *Re Gess* (1942), the deceased was Polish and died in England in 1939. Due to the war, no advertisements could be placed in Polish newspapers. Section 27 was of no assistance to the personal representatives who had to seek a different form of protection (they obtained a *Benjamin Order*—see para.14.010 below).

4. CONTINGENT LIABILITIES

Although s.27 gives protection against claims of which the personal representatives have no notice, it gives no protection where personal representatives have distributed the estate with knowledge of a future or contingent liability. **14.006**

If the personal representatives know that a debt will fall due at some time in the future, they will simply set aside a fund to meet that future liability when the time comes. Contingent liabilities are less easy to deal with. For example the deceased may have guaranteed a debt from a third party; the personal representatives cannot know whether or not the estate will be called upon to honour the guarantee. Similarly, there may be a threat of legal proceedings against the estate; while the personal representatives may suspect that the plaintiff will not take the matter further they cannot be certain of this. The personal representatives must decide what to do in such a case and there are four courses of action open to them.

First, they can set aside assets from the estate sufficient to meet the contingent liability should it actually arise. This course of action will be unpopular with the beneficiaries since they will only receive the assets once the personal representatives decide the contingent liability can no longer arise (for example when the loan guaranteed by the deceased is paid off or the plaintiff in the proposed action abandons his claim). It does, however, give the personal representatives total protection provided they have set aside sufficient assets.

Secondly, they can distribute all the assets to the beneficiaries but obtain the beneficiaries' agreement to indemnify the personal representatives if the liability ever crystallises. This will be more popular with the beneficiaries but the personal representatives should be wary since an indemnity is only as financially sound as the beneficiary who gives it. Thus, if the personal representatives distribute assets to a beneficiary who spends the money received on a holiday an indemnity from him will be worthless if he has no other assets. Furthermore, it may not be possible to obtain an indemnity; for example, where a beneficiary is a minor, mentally incapacitated or simply refuses to give one. Even where an indemnity has been obtained from a beneficiary who is financially sound, the inheritance may have been invested in assets which are not easily realisable, for example, a house. In this case calling in the indemnity could cause severe financial hardship, since the beneficiary would have to sell his house to meet his obligation.

14.007   Thirdly, the personal representatives could insure against the liability arising. If cover can be obtained (and it depends very much on the risk involved) the only expense will be the premium on the policy; the assets will pass to the beneficiaries free of any liability as far as they are concerned. Provided the premium is not too high, the beneficiaries are likely to find this the most attractive solution.

Finally, as a last resort the personal representatives can apply to the court for directions. This is obviously an expensive option and personal representatives may wonder if the cost can be justified. However, they should apply where the potential liability is large and insurance cover is not available. In the case of *Re Yorke (Deceased), Stone v Chatway* (1997) Lindsay J. gave guidance on this subject in the context of possible liability in the estates of deceased Lloyd's names. As only a court order can give complete protection it cannot be wrong for executors of Lloyd's Names to insist upon the protection of a court order. For a fuller discussion see below.

The Inheritance Tax Act 1984 created several problems for personal representatives. Where a person dies within seven years of making a potentially exempt transfer such a transfer becomes chargeable. The *inter vivos* transferee is primarily liable for the tax but the personal representatives of the transferor become liable if the tax remains unpaid for 12 months. There is no obligation to report potentially exempt transfers *inter vivos* and such transfers may remain undiscovered until after the personal representatives have distributed the assets. Moreover, the discovery of hitherto unknown *inter vivos* transfers will increase the cumulative total of the transferor at the date of death; this may result in the withdrawal of the nil rate band from all or part of the death estate with a consequent increase in the amount of inheritance tax due.

Personal representatives who are solicitors acting in the course of their practice may be protected by their insurance.

Non-solicitor personal representatives and solicitors who are not acting in the course of their practice have no such protection.

The problem is much less pressing since the Revenue issued the following statement published in *The Law Society's Gazette*, March 13, 1991:

> "It may be helpful if I say that the capital taxes offices will not usually pursue for inheritance tax personal representatives who:
>
> - after making the fullest enquiries that are reasonably practicable in the circumstances to discover lifetime transfers, and so
> - having done all in their power to make full disclosure of them to the board of Inland Revenue
>
> have obtained a certificate of discharge and distributed the estate before a chargeable lifetime transfer comes to light.
>
> This statement of the board's position is made without prejudice to the application in an appropriate case of s.199(2) of the Inheritance Tax Act 1984.
>
> I am writing in similar terms to the Law Society of Scotland.
>
> DY Pitts
> Director Capital and Valuation Division, Inland Revenue."

It is clearly important that personal representatives do make adequate enquiries as the above statement only applies where the personal representatives have made "the fullest enquiries that are reasonably practicable in the circumstances".

5. Deceased lloyd's names

14.008 The well publicised problems at Lloyd's meant that many Names were faced with unquantifiable losses. To solve the problems Equitas was created. Names waived their claims against Lloyd's and in return received debt and litigation credits and reinsurance of outstanding open years into Equitas. All business for 1992 and prior years of account was reinsured to close with Equitas upon payment of the appropriate premium.

If the resources of Equitas prove inadequate and it fails, there is a possibility that claims could be made against the Names (or their estates). This presents a problem for personal representatives who face the possibility of personal liability if they distribute the estate without providing for this contingent liability.

The Society of Trust and Estates Practitioners brought the test case (*Re Yorke (Deceased), Stone v Chataway* (1997) referred to in para.14.007, hoping that the judgment would remove the need for individual applications to be made for all estates in a similar position. The judgment did not achieve this. It approved the use of Equitas but said that personal representatives would face different levels of risk depending on the circumstances of the case and that they could only obtain full indemnity by applying to court for directions. It was accepted that in appropriate cases, judged to be low risk, personal representatives could take indemnities or rely on insurance.

There is a streamlined form of application available which will be heard by a Master rather than a judge. This is dealt with in Practice Statement, *Chancery Division: Estates of Deceased Lloyd's Names* (2001) which replaced the 1998 Practice Direction.

The procedure applies to cases where the only, or only substantial, reason for delaying distribution of the estate is the possibility of personal liability to Lloyd's creditors and:

(a) all liabilities of the estate in respect of syndicates of which the Name was a member for the years of account 1992 and earlier have been reinsured into the Equitas Group; and

(b) all liabilities of the estate in respect of syndicates of which the Name was a member for the years of account 1993 and later are in respect of syndicates which have closed by reinsurance in the usual way;
— are protected by an Estate Protection Plan issued by Centrewrite Ltd; or
— are protected by EXEAT insurance cover provided by Centrewrite Ltd.

The Practice Direction contains a specimen witness statement to support the claim form and a specimen draft order although both are likely to need adapting to suit the circumstances of the case.

6. BANKRUPT BENEFICIARIES

14.009 There is a risk of personal liability for a personal representative who pays a legacy direct to a bankrupt beneficiary rather than the trustee in bankruptcy. Bankrupts must tell their trustees in bankruptcy about acquisition of property. Personal representatives can, therefore, safely hand over money to a bankrupt beneficiary on proof that the bankrupt has complied with his or her duties under the Insolvency Act 1986, in particular ss.307 and 312, to inform the trustee in bankruptcy of everything affecting the bankrupt's property.

However, personal representatives should be alert to potential problems if a bankrupt beneficiary suggests that the money should be paid over in a way which is at all unusual. If concerned, they should consider seeking the assistance of the court or as a last resort, paying money into court under the Trustee Act 1925, s.63).

It is not usually necessary to enquire about the financial status of beneficiaries, but it is a different matter if personal representatives have notice that there may be a query about a particular beneficiary. A bankruptcy search in Form K16 under the Land Charges Act could be made (against any name a beneficiary might use) or the personal representatives could contact the Insolvency Service.

C. Benjamin Orders and Alternatives

The personal representatives will not be protected by s.27 if they are **14.010**
aware of the rights of a claimant but simply cannot find him. In these
circumstances the personal representatives can apply to the court for a
Benjamin Order permitting them to distribute the estate on the basis of a
particular assumption.

For example, in the case from which the order took its name (*Re
Benjamin* (1902)), the deceased by his will left a beneficiary a residuary
gift. The beneficiary disappeared some nine months before the testator
died and despite advertisements the beneficiary did not claim his share of
the estate. In the circumstances the court permitted the assets to be
distributed as if the beneficiary had predeceased the testator. The order
may allow the estate to be distributed on some other footing. Thus in an
unreported case the estate was distributed on the basis that a child who
predeceased the testatrix left no child surviving the testatrix.

In *Re Gess, Gess v Royal Exchange Assurance* (1942), the
administrators of a Polish national, who died domiciled in England, were
unable to advertise for Polish claimants against the estate because of the
outbreak of war. They knew of some debts and applied for permission to
distribute the estate. The court held that they could distribute the estate,
after setting aside a fund to meet the known Polish liabilities, without
making further inquiries or advertisements on the basis that all the debts
and liabilities of the estate had been ascertained.

Naturally there must be some factual basis for the assumption set out in
the order so that full inquiries must be made by the personal
representatives before the court will grant the order. The court will
obviously require evidence. An order may be made without the court
inquiring further into the circumstances if it is satisfied that the statutory
advertisements have proved unsuccessful in tracing the missing person.
The making of the order is not conditional on the personal
representatives having complied with the requirements of s.27 as to
advertisement and searches; the court will decide what, if any,
advertisements ought to be made.

If the assumption on which the order was made proves to be wrong,
because the supposedly dead beneficiary is shown to be alive, he can claim
his share of the assets from the other beneficiaries. However, the personal
representatives are relieved of personal liability in these circumstances.
Once an order is obtained, the personal representatives need take no
further steps to protect themselves.

The drawback to applying for a Benjamin Order is that it is an
expensive procedure. In *Evans v Westcombe* (1999) the court approved
the purchase of an insurance policy to cover the possibility of a missing
beneficiary returning as an alternative to seeking a Benjamin Order. It
said that personal representatives, particularly of small estates, should
not be discouraged from seeking practical solutions to difficult
administration problems without the expense of resort to the court. The
court also said that it did not wish to restrict the use of insurance to cases
where the personal representative was not beneficially entitled.

Unfortunately the case also demonstrates the weakness of insurance. It may be difficult to quantify the amount to be insured. In *Evans* the missing beneficiary was entitled to half of the residue. The personal representative, therefore, obtained a policy for just over half the value of the estate. She was not advised to consider the possibility of interest. When the missing beneficiary returned, he demanded interest from the date of distribution of the estate. The court agreed that he was entitled to interest but there were no funds available to pay him. On the facts, the court was willing to relieve the personal representative from liability under the Trustee Act 1925, s.61. She had sought legal advice and shown herself willing to follow it and had been unaware of the possibility of interest.

It would have been preferable for the personal representative in *Evans* to have employed genealogists to trace the missing beneficiary and to have charged the cost to the estate. There have been huge improvements in the techniques used by genealogists and it is unusual for them to be unable to trace a missing beneficiary. In any event most insurance companies will now require evidence from genealogists before they will consider insurance. It is normally better practice to use a firm which charges an hourly rate rather than one which takes a contingency fee (typically 30 per cent) from the entitlement of the beneficiary.

D. Illegitimate and Adopted Beneficiaries

14.011   The Family Law Reform Act 1987 abolished the concept of illegitimacy. This means that a person may take on the intestacy of a relative even though he, the relative or some person through whom they are related was born of parents who were not married to each other at any time. Similarly, references to relationships in wills made after April 4, 1988 are, unless a contrary intention appears, construed as including persons whose parents never married or who are related through such persons. The statutory protection previously given to personal representatives who distribute an estate in ignorance of such potential beneficiaries has been withdrawn. However, with respect to intestacy only, a person whose father and mother were not married to each other at the time of his birth is presumed not to have been survived by his father or by any person related to him only through his father unless the contrary is shown.

These rules leave personal representatives in a difficult position. Inquiries should be made of relatives or others to discover any beneficiaries who may exist, and naturally these inquiries should be conducted with the maximum delicacy and tact. Presumably, if personal representatives advertise under the Trustee Act 1925, s.27 and wait the appropriate period they will obtain the protection of that section. However, they may wish to consider the possibility of insuring against liability and of taking indemnities from the known beneficiaries.

A personal representative is protected if he distributes an estate in ignorance of an adoption of which he does not have notice. Disappointed beneficiaries can claim their share of the estate from the other beneficiaries but not from the personal representatives. The personal representatives, therefore, need take no special steps to protect themselves.

E. The Personal Representatives' Liability in Respect of the Deceased's Leaseholds

1. GENERAL

On death, a leasehold interest held by the deceased devolves on his personal representatives by operation of law, whether or not they enter into possession of the premises. The nature of their liability for rent or breach of covenants depends on whether their liability is: **14.012**

(a) representative, that is deriving from their office; or
(b) personal, that is arising when they enter into possession of the premises as assignees of the deceased's interest.

2. REPRESENTATIVE LIABILITY

The personal representatives are liable as the deceased's personal representatives for rent due, and any breach committed prior to the death as well as for rent due and breaches committed from death to the expiry, or assignment of the lease (unless the deceased was the original lessee in which case the personal representatives are liable until the expiry of the lease irrespective of any assignment).   **14.013**

In their representative capacity the personal representatives are liable to discharge any liability on a lease to the extent of the assets of the deceased which they have received. If the deceased was an assignee of the lease, the personal representatives can end their liability by surrendering or assigning the lease. If the deceased was the original lessee, assignment will not end their liability. The Trustee Act 1925, s.26, however, protects the personal representatives from further liability once they have assigned (this protection cannot be excluded by the terms of the will). Section 26 as amended provides that the personal representatives will not be liable for a future claim if they do three things.

(a) satisfy all existing liabilities under the lease which may have accrued and been claimed up to the date of the conveyance to a purchaser or beneficiary; and
(b) where necessary, set apart a fund to meet any future claims that may be made in respect of any fixed and ascertained sum which the lessee agreed to lay out on the demised premises, although the period for so doing may not have arrived; and
(c) assign the lease to a purchaser, legatee, devisee, or other person entitled to call for a conveyance.

Thereafter the personal representatives may distribute the deceased's residuary real and personal estate to or amongst the persons entitled thereto without setting aside a fund to meet any future liability under the lease and the personal representatives will not be personally liable in respect of any subsequent claim under the lease.

The lessor can follow the assets of the estate into the hands of the beneficiaries and claim payment from the assets or their proceeds (s.26(2)).

3. PERSONAL LIABILITY

14.014 Personal liability arises when the personal representatives enter into possession, whether physically or constructively (for example, by receiving rent from a sub-tenant). The personal representatives are then personally liable for the rent and for any breaches of covenant arising while the lease is vested in them as assignees of the deceased's interest. As the personal representatives are not the original lessees, liability ceases once the personal representatives assign their interest.

Oddly, there are different limits on the extent of the personal representatives' personal liability. For rent, the liability is limited to the amount actually received (or that which with reasonable diligence might have been received) during their period as assignees (*Rendall v Andreae* (1892)). For breaches of other covenants the personal representatives are liable without limit.

The personal representatives have no protection under s.26 against *personal* liability; they should either obtain an indemnity from the beneficiaries or create an indemnity fund from the estate. This fund will be distributed to the beneficiaries once the personal representatives cease to be personally liable, for example, as a result of assigning the lease of termination. Such a fund may be unpopular with the beneficiaries who are likely to prefer an immediate distribution of property. It is, therefore, modern practice to insure against this liability, thus reducing the drain on the estate's assets.

F. Liability for Acts of Agents

14.015 The Trustee Act 2000, s.11 gives trustees and personal representatives wide powers to appoint agents (and nominees and custodians under s.16 and s.17). The appointment can be on such terms as they see fit subject to the limitations contained in s.14(3) and s.20(3). They will have to comply with the requirements of s.15 if they wish to delegate their asset management functions.

Section 23 provides that they will not be liable for any act or default of the agents, nominees or custodians unless they failed to comply with the statutory duty of care:

(a) when making the appointment, or
(b) when reviewing the appointment as required by s.22.

G. The Six Month Time Limit

The Inheritance (Provision for Family and Dependants) Act 1975 (see   **14.016**
Chapter 20) gives personal representatives protection provided they wait
until the expiry of six months from the grant of representation before
distributing the estate, if the court then permits an out-of-time application
to be made. Similarly, if the personal representatives wait for the same
period before distributing the estate, they suffer no personal liability if the
court then makes an order permitting an out-of-time application to have
the deceased's will rectified under s.20 of the Administration of Justice
Act 1982. However in neither case are the successful applicants denied
the right to recover assets from the beneficiaries who received them from
the personal representatives.

Personal representatives are wise to wait six months from the grant
distributing the estate.

H. Administration Proceedings for Specific Relief

As we have seen if the personal representatives distribute the estate to the   **14.017**
wrong person or become liable for some expense that was not properly
incurred for the benefit of the estate, they are (unless specifically
protected) personally liable to make good any loss.

In cases of doubt, prudent personal representatives will apply to the
court (Chancery Division or county court where the net estate does not
exceed in amount or value the county court limit, at present £30,000).

Applications are made under CPR, Pt 64.2. It is possible to apply for a
general "administration order". This means that the whole
administration is carried out under the direction of the court. This is an
expensive and time-consuming process and the court will only make such
an order if it considers that the issues between the parties cannot properly
be resolved in any other way.

It is much more common to ask the court to determine a specific
question. Practice Direction 64 gives the following examples of claims
which may be made:

(1) *a claim for the determination of any of the following questions*—
    (a) any question as to who is included in any class of persons
        having:
           (i)   a claim against the estate of a deceased person;
           (ii) a beneficial interest in the estate of such a person;
               or
           (iii) beneficial interest in any property subject to a
               trust;
    (b) any question as to the rights or interests of any person
        claiming:
           (i)   to be a creditor of the estate of a deceased person;
           (ii) to be entitled under a will or on the intestacy of a
               deceased person; or
           (iii) to be beneficially entitled under a trust;
(2) *a claim for any of the following remedies*—

    (a) an order requiring a trustee—
        (i) to provide and, if necessary, verify accounts;
        (ii) to pay into court money which he holds in that capacity; or
        (iii) to do or not to do any particular act;
    (b) an order approving any sale, purchase, compromise or other transaction by a trustee; or
    (c) an order directing any act to be done which the court could order to be done if the estate or trust in question were being administered or executed under the direction of the court.

Actions are brought in the Chancery Division by issuing a Part 8 claim form. All the personal representatives must be made parties and any persons with an interest in or claim against the estate can be made a party if it is appropriate having regard to the nature of the order sought. The trustees will be expected to have canvassed with all the adult beneficiaries the proposed or possible courses of action before applying for directions and to set out the details of the consultation undertaken in their witness statements.

The costs incurred by *all* the parties involved in the action for specific relief are usually paid from the estate provided it can be shown that there was a problem which justified the application being made.

The trustees or the party concerned may apply to the court at any stage of proceedings for an order that the costs of any party (including the costs of the trustees) shall be paid out of the fund (a "prospective costs order").

I. Administration of Justice Act 1985, s.48

14.018 Where there is doubt as to the construction of a will, s.48 allows the High Court, without hearing any argument, to authorise the personal representatives to act in reliance on a written opinion of a barrister of at least 10 years' standing. The Court will not make such an order if there is any dispute as to the construction since it would then be inappropriate to make an order without hearing argument. This provision allows a speedy resolution of difficulties of administration. The order will protect the personal representatives from any action for breach of duty.

15.   The Payment of Debts

Personal representatives have a duty to pay the debts of the deceased and **15.001** must do so with due diligence (*Re Tankard* (1942)). Different rules as to the payment of debts apply depending on whether an estate is solvent or insolvent.

A. The Solvent Estate

An estate is solvent when the assets are sufficient to pay funeral, **15.002** testamentary and administration expenses and debts and other liabilities in full. Provided these can be paid, it is irrelevant that legacies cannot be paid in full. The beneficiaries of the estate will be concerned to know which assets of the estate will be used in payment of the debts and which will be available for distribution.

Section 34(3) of the Administration of Estates Act 1925 provides that assets shall be taken in the order set out in Part II of the First Schedule to the Act. However, special rules apply where property of the deceased was charged during the deceased's lifetime with payment of a debt. This situation will be considered first.

1. DEBTS CHARGED ON PROPERTY

Where a debt has been charged on property of the deceased *during the* **15.003** *lifetime of the deceased* (for example, a mortgage debt charged on the deceased's house) Administration of Estates Act 1925, s.35 provides that such property will be primarily liable for payment of that debt. Thus, a beneficiary who accepts the property must accept it subject to the mortgage. The deceased may exclude s.35 by showing a contrary intention in the will, a deed or other document. A charge is usually expressly created by the deceased but may also arise by operation of law; for example an Inland Revenue charge for unpaid tax or a charge imposed by the court on land belonging to a judgment debtor.

The case of *Re Birmingham* (1959) illustrates the difference between a simple debt and a debt charged on property. T agreed to buy Blackacre from V for £3,500; contracts were exchanged and T paid a deposit of £350. T died before completion. In her will T left Blackacre to her daughter, D, and the residue to R. T's solicitors completed the purchase of Blackacre. The court held that D took Blackacre subject to an unpaid vendor's lien for the balance of the purchase price. However, the solicitor's costs were to be paid from the general estate since at the time of T's death they were not charged on Blackacre.

Several properties charged with one debt

15.004   If several properties are charged as security for one debt, each property bears a proportionate part of the debt (s.35(1)) and thus, if each property is given to a different beneficiary, each beneficiary will take his property subject to a charge for a proportionate part of the debt. This is so even if some of the properties are specifically given by the will while some merely pass as part of the residue. In *Re Neeld* (1962) the Court of Appeal said that in such a case the testator is not to be presumed to have thrown the whole debt on to the properties comprised in the residue.

Separate debts

15.005   Where separate properties are charged with separate debts and the debt charged on one property exceeds the value of that property the amount of the deficit will be made up from the deceased's general estate and not from the other charged properties. This will be so even if all the charged properties are given to one beneficiary (*Re Holt, Holt v Holt* (1916)). The only exception is where the testator makes it clear that a gift of several different properties is *one* gift the whole of which is to be treated as charged with several different debts. In that case the deficit will be made up from the other charged properties (*Re Kensington* (1902)).

The rights of creditors

15.006   Section 35 is only concerned with competition amongst beneficiaries as to the property to be used to pay debts. It does not affect the rights of creditors. A secured creditor may be paid by the personal representatives from the general estate instead of from the charged property; if this happens the doctrine of marshalling will apply as between the beneficiaries so that ultimately the debt falls on the charged property (see below, para.15.023).

Options to purchase

15.007   A testator may give an option to purchase a property in the will. The option may be at an undervalue but even so the person exercising it will be treated as taking the property as a purchaser not as a beneficiary. A purchaser is entitled to have any debt charged on the property paid off from the general estate (*Re Fison's Will Trusts* (1950)) so that he will take the property free from any debt charged on the property.

2. CONTRARY INTENTION

Methods of showing contrary intention

15.008   Section 35 may be varied if the testator shows a contrary intention. Contrary intention is not shown by a simple direction in the will (or any other document) that debts be paid from *residue*; such a direction is to be construed as relating only to debts other than those charged on particular items (s.35(2)(a) and (b)). An additional indication of intention is required. Thus a gift of specific property *free from the debt* charged on it will suffice; as will an express direction that a mortgage or other charge be paid from residue. Less obviously, if a testator directs that debts be paid from a special fund (*other than residue*) the direction will be construed as extending to all debts including those charged on specific items of property.

For example, if a testator has a mortgage debt charged on Blackacre and in his will directs that "my debts be paid from the proceeds of sale of my shares in X company and the residue of my estate be held for A", all the testator's debts including the mortgage debt will be paid from the proceeds of sale. If the special fund is insufficient to pay off all debts, any unsatisfied balance of a charged debt will remain charged on the property and will not be paid from the general estate (*Re Fegan* (1928)).

Taking instructions

A solicitor drafting a will for a client should always inquire whether there are any debts charged on property. If there are, the solicitor should ask whether or not the client wishes such debts to be paid from the general residue and draft the will accordingly.   **15.009**

Mortgage protection policies

The most common example of a debt charged on property during the deceased's lifetime is a mortgage. A client who wishes to make a will should be asked about his mortgage arrangements so that he can consider from what source the mortgage debt is to be paid. It is, however, becoming increasingly common for mortgagors to take out a mortgage protection policy. This is a life assurance policy which, on the mortgagor's death, pays either a fixed amount (equal to the original loan) or an amount sufficient to pay off the amount of the loan outstanding at the date of death (*i.e.* a reducing amount). If the proceeds are to be paid to the estate of the mortgagor they will increase the size of the estate for inheritance tax purposes. The policy may, however, be written in trust for a named beneficiary or assigned to the lender, in which case the proceeds will be paid to that person and will not increase the size of the deceased's estate for inheritance tax purposes.   **15.010**

If two people are buying property jointly they normally each take out such a policy. The terms of the policy may state that the proceeds are to be paid to the surviving joint tenant to the exclusion of the estate of the deceased; if no such statement is included the parties may write each policy in trust for the other. A solicitor, drafting a will, should inquire whether such a policy exists and, if one does, should make sure that the client takes it into account when deciding what directions to leave as to the payment of the mortgage debt.

If the client has bought a house in his or her sole name and has a mortgage protection policy which has not been assigned to the lender, the solicitor should point out the desirability of considering leaving the proceeds of the policy to the person who is taking the property subject to the mortgage, so that there will be funds available to that beneficiary for the discharge of the mortgage debt.

3. THE STATUTORY ORDER FOR UNSECURED DEBTS

The deceased may make express provision for the payment of debts. In the absence of such provision the statutory order of application of assets   **15.011** applies and is set out in Part II of the First Schedule to the Administration of Estates Act. It is as follows:

(1) Property of the deceased undisposed of by will, subject to the retention thereout of a fund sufficient to meet any pecuniary legacies.

(2) Property of the deceased not specifically devised or bequeathed but included (either by a specific or general description) in a residuary gift, subject to the retention thereout of a fund sufficient to meet any pecuniary legacies, so far as not already provided for.

(3) Property of the deceased given for the payment of debts.

(4) Property of the deceased charged with the payment of debts.

(5) The fund, if any, retained to meet pecuniary legacies.

(6) Property specifically devised or bequeathed, rateably according to value.

(7) Property appointed by will under a general power (including the statutory power to dispose of entailed interests) rateably according to value.

Undisposed of property

15.012 Such property may arise where a will does not deal with all the assets of the deceased (*i.e.* where there is no residuary gift); it may also arise where a residuary gift fails wholly (*i.e.* where the residuary beneficiary predeceases the testator) or partly (*i.e.* where residue is given to two or more beneficiaries in *equal shares or equally* and one or more of the beneficiaries predeceases the testator, the share of the predeceased beneficiary lapses and passes to the testator's next-of-kin). Before debts are paid from the undisposed of property a fund is set on one side for payment of any pecuniary legacies.

Residue

15.013 Any general gift of property, that is one which is not comprised in a specific bequest or devise, will be a residuary gift. Thus in *Re Wilson* (1967) T made some specific and pecuniary legacies and then gave "all my real estate and the residue of my personal estate". Pennycuick J. held that T's devise of realty fell within para.(2) despite the fact that there was no prior specific devise.

Before any debts are paid from residue, a fund is set on one side for payment of pecuniary legacies to the extent that sufficient property was not set aside from any undisposed of property.

Property specifically given for or charged with payment of debts

15.014 Property is specifically *given* for payment of debts where a testator *directs in the will* that it be used for this purpose and leaves no directions as to what is to happen to any balance left over after the debts are paid, for example, "my debts are to be paid from the proceeds of my premium bonds".

Property is *charged* with payment of debts when a testator *directs in the will* that it be used for this purpose and directs that any balance left over after the debts are paid be given to a particular beneficiary; for example "my debts are to be paid from the proceeds of sale of my shares in A Co and any balance is to go to X" or "I give X the proceeds of sale of my shares in A Co subject to payment of debts". This is quite different from the "charge" referred to in s.35 which deals with debts charged *during the deceased's lifetime* on particular assets. In the case of s.34 the assets were unincumbered during the deceased's lifetime and the charge is imposed by the will.

The retained pecuniary legacy fund
A fund will have been set on one side from the undisposed of property **15.015** and/or residue to meet pecuniary legacies; if necessary that fund (or part of it) is taken to pay debts. Pecuniary legacies abate proportionally unless the deceased directed that certain legacies be paid in priority to the others.

"Pecuniary legacy" is defined widely in s.55(1)(ix) of the Administration of Estates Act to include an annuity, a general legacy and a demonstrative legacy in so far as not discharged out of designated property (for definitions see paras 16.004 and 16.005).

Property specifically devised or bequeathed rateably according to value
The order makes no distinction between devises and bequests; both are **15.016** equally available.

(a) *Value* means value to the testator. Thus a mortgage charged on the property would be deducted when calculating the value of the property but a legacy charged on the property by the testator in the will would not (*Re John* (1933)).

Example
T owns Blackacre value £10,000 but subject to a mortgage of £4,000. T owns Whiteacre value £10,000. T's will gives Blackacre to B and Whiteacre to W but charges Whiteacre with payment to L of a legacy of £6,000. There are debts to pay of £2,000 (apart from the mortgage) and no other assets. Blackacre had a value to the testator of £6,000 (£10,000 – £4,000). Whiteacre had a value to the testator of £10,000.
Therefore:

$$\text{Blackacre bears } \frac{6,000}{16,000} \times 2,000 = \text{£750 of the debts}$$

$$\text{Whiteacre bears } \frac{10,000}{16,000} \times 2,000 = \text{£1,250 of the debts}$$

In addition Blackacre is charged with payment of the mortgage (unless the will directed otherwise) and Whiteacre with payment of the legacy.

(b) *Option to purchase.* T's will may give a person an option to purchase property at a stated price. This price may well be at an undervalue in which case the will gives the "purchaser" a benefit. The personal representatives may wonder whether such property is available for payment of debts as if it were a specific gift.

In *Re Eve* (1956) Roxburgh J. directed that when personal representatives were calculating what property to use for payment of debts they should not regard property subject to an option to purchase as equivalent to a specific gift of that property. They should first calculate whether once the purchase price for the property was paid there would be sufficient assets to meet all the debts of the testator. If there would, the purchaser is free to exercise the option and will purchase the property subject to the option. If there would not, the option cannot be exercised and the personal representatives must take the property and use it for payment of debts. Roxburgh J. concluded that "the property subject to an option is the last to be available for the payment of debts. For, indeed, in so far as the property subject to the option is required for the payment of debts, the option over the property cannot be exercised at all and the benefit of it is totally destroyed by the operation of law".

Property appointed under a general power of appointment

15.017 Where the testator has a general power of appointment (that is, a power to appoint property to anyone he pleases) and exercises the power *expressly* in the will, such property is taken last for payment of debts.

Section 27 of the Wills Act 1837 provides that where a testator has a general power of appointment which is not exercised expressly in the will it is deemed (subject to a contrary intention in the will) to have been exercised by any general gift contained in the will. Thus, for example, if X has a general power of appointment over Blackacre but makes no mention of the power or of Blackacre in the will a general gift of "all the rest of my property" or "all my realty" would be sufficient to dispose of Blackacre. However, if (as a result of s.27) property is included in a general gift it will be treated as available for payment of debts as part of residue not as property subject to a general power.

Property outside the statutory order

15.018 Property subject to a *donatio mortis causa* or to a statutory nomination is available for payment of debts but is not mentioned in the statutory order. It would, therefore, be taken after all the other assets were exhausted. According to *Re Eve*, if a testator gives a person an option to puchase property at an undervalue the property subject to the option is taken to pay debts when it is necessary to do so because all other assets are exhausted, and not otherwise. It is, however, impossible to say in what order assets subject to an option to purchase, *donatio mortis causa* or nomination would be taken as between themselves.

4. VARIATION OF THE STATUTORY ORDER

15.019 A testator has a right to vary the statutory order. There are two ways in which this is commonly done.

A gift of residue "subject to" or "after" payment of debts

15.020 If residue is given to several beneficiaries in equal shares and one of those beneficiaries predeceases the testator that share of residue lapses and becomes undisposed of property. Undisposed of property is normally taken first for payment of debts and any balance will then be available to the testator's next-of-kin. If, however, the testator directs that residue be taken *after* payment of debts (or gives the residue *subject* to payment of debts) that is construed as an express direction that debts be paid from the whole residue before it is divided into shares. Thus, the living beneficiaries and the testator's next-of-kin will bear a proportionate part of the debt and will, therefore, receive a proportionate share in the balance.

Example

(a) *No contrary intention.* T gives certain specific bequests and leaves the residue to A and B in equal shares. B predeceases T. The estate, after setting aside the specific bequests but before paying debts and other liabilities, amounts to £20,000. Debts amount to £8,000. B's lapsed share amounts to £10,000. The debts will be paid from that lapsed share leaving a balance of £2,000 available to T's next-of-kin. A will take £10,000.

(b) *Contrary intention.* The same situation but T leaves the residue *after payment of debts* to A and B in equal shares. The debts must be paid from the £20,000 before it is divided into shares. £12,000 will be left after payment of debts and A and T's next-of-kin will divide this equally. A will, therefore, take £6,000 and T's next-of-kin will take £6,000.

Property "given for" or "charged with" payment of debts—intention to exonerate residue
If a testator merely gives property for or charges property with payment **15.021** of debts this will not in itself be sufficient to vary the statutory order. Such property will merely fall within paras (3) or (4) of the statutory order (*i.e.* property specifically given or charged with payment of debts) and will, prima facie, be taken after property within paras (1) and (2) of the statutory order (*i.e.* undisposed of property and residue) is exhausted. However, if the will shows an intention to exonerate the property which would otherwise be taken first, this will vary the statutory order. It has been held that where a will contains a gift of residue to a beneficiary together with a direction that debts be paid from a specified fund this shows an intention to exonerate the residue and the statutory order will be varied.

In *Re James* (1947), for example, the testator charged certain specific property with payment of debts and gave the residue to his wife. Roxburgh J. held that the will showed a clear intention to exonerate the residue and therefore the debts would be paid from the charged property.

Conversely in *Re Gordon* (1940) a testatrix directed that her debts be paid from a sum of £50 and any balance therefrom be paid to a named charity. There no gift of residue. It was held that the statutory order was not varied as there was no indication of an intention to exonerate other property; therefore, the debts were to be paid from the undisposed of property and the £50 was to be paid in full to the charity.

Presumably any form of words could be used in a will to show an intention to exonerate other property. Thus in *Re Gordon* had T expressly declared that debts were to be paid from the £50 "in exoneration of any undisposed of property" the result would have been different.

Desirability of making express provision for payment of debts

15.022 When drafting a will it is desirable to discuss with the testator the possibility of making express provision for the payment of debts since this will allow a testator to consider the question of debts and to make his own decision as to the property to be used.

5. THE DOCTRINE OF MARSHALLING

15.023 If a personal representative takes assets falling within one of the later paragraphs in the statutory order to pay debts before assets falling within the earlier paragraphs are exhausted, the creditors will be entirely unconcerned. Creditors merely want payment; the source of the payment is irrelevant to them. A beneficiary, on the other hand, will be very concerned if property which that beneficiary hopes to take is wrongly used to pay debts. Marshalling is a way of adjusting the assets so as to compensate a disappointed beneficiary where a payment has been made from the wrong assets.

Example

X is administering the estate of T. T's will left shares in ABC Ltd (value £2,000) to S and the residue of the estate to R (the residue consists of land worth £20,000). There is a debt of £2,000 to pay. The debt *should* be paid from residue. If X uses the shares to pay the creditor, S will be disappointed. However, S can be compensated from property falling within any of the earlier paragraphs. S is therefore entitled to £2,000 from the residuary assets.

B. Insolvent Estates

1. INTRODUCTION

15.024 An estate is insolvent if the assets are insufficient to pay all the funeral, testamentary and administration expenses, debts and liabilities. The beneficiaries of the deceased's will or the deceased's next-of-kin under the intestacy rules will receive nothing and the creditors of the estate will not all be paid in full.

There are three methods of administering an insolvent estate:

1.   The most economic and straightforward method is for the deceased's personal representatives to do so under a normal grant of representation. Creditors are entitled to take a grant. If a creditor wants to administer and those entitled in priority will neither renounce nor get on with the job, the creditor can use the citation process to try and clear them off or apply to the registrar to pass them over under the Supreme Court Act 1982, s.116. There is no need for the person appointed to be a qualified insolvency practitioner (Administration of Insolvent Estates of Deceased Persons Order SI 1986/1999 art.4(3)).

2. It is possible for the court to take over the administration by making an administration order under CPR, Pt 64. This means that the personal representatives act under the direction of the court. The courts are not anxious to undertake such a role and professional advisers rarely consider this route.

3. The other alternative is for the estate to be administered by a trustee in bankruptcy following an insolvency administration order made by the bankruptcy court. Creditors or personal representatives can petition and in either case the order vests the estate in the Official Receiver. Subsequently a trustee in bankruptcy will be appointed. The creditors will normally appoint the trustee in bankruptcy and creditors' committee.

The Administration of Insolvent Estates of Deceased Persons Order 1986 provides that, whether the estate is administered by a trustee in bankruptcy or by the deceased's personal representatives the same rules apply to:

- the respective rights of creditors;
- provable debts;
- the valuation of future and contingent liabilities; and
- the priority of debts.

In general, therefore, it does not matter whether the estate is administered by a trustee in bankruptcy or by the deceased's personal representatives.

However, there are certain situations where a trustee in bankruptcy has advantages.

1. Challenging lifetime transactions for the benefit of the estate
A trustee can challenge transactions: **15.025**

- under the Insolvency Act 1986, s.339 if made at an undervalue within "the relevant time" (two years ending with death or five years if the deceased was insolvent at the time or became so as a result of the transaction Insolvency Act 1986, s.341 as modified by the Administration of Insolvent Estates of Deceased Persons Order);
- under the Insolvency Act 1986, s.423 if made at an undervalue for the purpose of putting assets beyond the reach of creditors;
- under the Insolvency Act 1986, ss.340–342 which have preferred some creditors at the expense of others.

PRs cannot make such an application.

2. Disclaiming onerous property
A trustee can disclaim onerous property even if he/she has gone into   **15.026**
possession, attempted to sell it or in some other way exercised rights of ownership (Insolvency Act 1986, s.315). Onerous property is defined in s.315 as any:

- unprofitable contract; and
- property in the deceased's estate which is unsaleable or not readily saleable, or is such that it may give rise to a liability to pay money or perform any other onerous act.

For example, therefore, any lease which contains covenants on the part of the tenant can be disclaimed.

3. Dealing with the deceased's dwelling house

15.027   Other people may have an interest in assets of the deceased (typically a spouse in the matrimonial home). Personal representatives and trustees in bankruptcy can apply to the court for an order for sale. Where the application is first made by the trustee in bankruptcy more than 12 months after the deceased's property vested in him, the court will assume, unless there are exceptional circumstances, that the interests of the creditors outweigh all other considerations (Insolvency Act 1986, s.335A(3)). Where the application is made by personal representatives, there is no such assumption so they may have more difficulty.

Note that when the insolvency provisions of the Enterprise Act 2000 come into effect, there will be a limit of three years on the period during which the trustee in bankruptcy can deal with a bankrupt's interest in a dwelling house which is the sole or principal dwelling house of the bankrupt, the bankrupt's spouse or a former spouse.

It is possible for personal representatives to apply for the appointment of a trustee in bankruptcy if it becomes apparent that there are reasons justifying it at any stage of the administration.

It is important to consider the position as to payment of professional charges where an estate is insolvent. The rules for ordinary personal representatives have changed as a result of the Trustee Act 2000, s.35(3)(b). A solicitor's charges whether made under an express charging clause or under the statutory power contained in s.28 are no longer regarded as a legacy but as "administration expenses". As such they have priority over the preferential debts listed in the Insolvency Act 1986.

A trustee in bankruptcy can charge for his or her services and again the charges will be administration expenses and have priority over preferential debts.

A solicitor appointed as executor should bear in mind that, although administration expenses have priority, the estate may be too small to cover them. Therefore, if there is a chance that an estate will be insolvent, it is important to assess the risk before committing a substantial amount of time to the estate. Solicitor–executors, and indeed, other executors, may want to renounce. It is important not to intermeddle in an estate which may be insolvent.

Where personal representatives are administering an estate which is (or may turn out to be) insolvent it is important that they observe the correct order for payment of creditors. This is:

(a) funeral, testamentary and administration expenses, and then
(b) the bankruptcy order.

This order cannot be varied by the testator. If the personal representatives do not follow the statutory order they will incur personal liability for "superior" debts which have been left unpaid. Therefore, if there is any possibility that an estate may be insolvent the personal representatives should observe the statutory order when paying debts.

2. ASSETS AND LIABILITIES

When a living person is declared bankrupt there are special rules of bankruptcy which swell the bankrupt's assets. These rules also apply to an insolvent estate by virtue of the Administration of Insolvent Estates of Deceased Persons Order 1986 (SI 1986/1999). The same Order provides that where a bankruptcy petition is presented and then the debtor dies, the bankruptcy proceedings may continue despite the death of the debtor.

15.028

All debts and liabilities, present or future, certain and contingent, liquidated or unliquidated are provable against an insolvent estate. If the value of a liability is uncertain (because it is contingent or for any other reason) its value must be estimated (Insolvency Act 1986). A debt which is statute-barred is not provable where the estate is insolvent.

3. AVAILABILITY OF JOINT PROPERTY

A Court of Appeal decision (*Re Palmer (Deceased) (A Debtor)*(1994)) held that jointly held property passed to the co-owner on death as usual and was not available to the administrator of the estate.

15.029

The effect of this decision has been reversed by a new s.412A inserted into the Insolvency Act 1986 by the Insolvency Act 2000, s.12. The trustee of a deceased insolvent can now apply to the court to recover the value of the deceased's former interest in joint property from the survivor for the benefit of the estate. The trustee can only make the application where the petition for the insolvency order is presented after April 2, 2001 and within five years from the date of death. When deciding whether or not to make the order the court must have regard to all the circumstances of the case including the interests of the creditors and the surviving joint tenant. Unless the circumstances are exceptional, the court must assume that the interests of the creditors outweigh all other considerations.

4. SECURED CREDITORS

A creditor may have security for a debt; for example a bank may have given a loan to the deceased and taken a charge over the deceased's house or other assets as security. Such a creditor has a choice.

15.030

(a) He may rely on his security and not prove for his debt at all. This is a safe course provided the security is sufficient to cover the debt.

(b) He may realise the security and if the security is inadequate prove for any balance as an unsecured creditor.

(c) He may value the security and prove for any balance as an unsecured creditor. Care must be taken in such a valuation. If the creditor puts too low a value on the security the personal representatives can insist on redeeming it at that value leaving him to prove as an unsecured creditor for the balance. If he puts too high a value on it and proves as an unsecured creditor for the balance, he will prove for an insufficient amount.

(d) He may surrender his security and prove for the whole debt as an unsecured creditor.

In so far as the secured creditor obtains payment by realising the security, he has priority over all unsecured creditors of the estate and receives payment in priority to the funeral, testamentary and administration expenses.

5. FUNERAL, TESTAMENTARY AND ADMINISTRATION EXPENSES

15.031   These are paid in priority to all unsecured debts and liabilities of the deceased and are paid in priority to preferred creditors. Where an estate is insolvent "reasonable" funeral expenses are likely to be on a lower scale than would be the case with a solvent estate. Personal representatives' charges now rank as administration expenses (Trustee Act 2000, s.35).

6. OTHER DEBTS AND LIABILITIES

15.032   The Administration of Insolvent Estates of Deceased Persons Order 1986 provides that the bankruptcy order is to apply to the payment of all other debts and liabilities.

The bankruptcy order
15.033   The bankruptcy order is as follows:

> (a) Preferred debts.
> (b) Ordinary debts.
> (c) Deferred debts.

Within each category the debts rank equally and if the assets are insufficient to meet the debts of one category in full all debts in that category abate proportionally.

Creditors can claim for debts which are contingent, future or the value of which can only be estimated (Insolvency Act 1986, s.382(3)).

Where a trustee in bankruptcy is administering the estate, the trustee must estimate the value of any debt which is uncertain. This is subject to the court's overall supervision. Once estimated by the trustee or by the court, this is the amount which is treated as due (Insolvency Act 1986, s.322(4)).

Where personal representatives are administering the estate, they must estimate the value of the debt. If the other creditors do not accept the valuation, the personal representatives should apply to the court for directions under CPR, Pt 64.

15.034   *Preferred debts include*:

> (a) Wages or salary or accrued holiday remuneration owed by the deceased to an employee in respect of the whole or any part of the period of four months before death, such amount not to exceed the limit prescribed by the Secretary of State (currently £800).
> (b) Sums due from the deceased in the 12 month period before death in respect of Class 1 or Class 2 contributions under the Social Security Act 1975 (or the Social Security (Northern Ireland) Act 1975).
> (c) Sums due from the deceased under Schedule 3 to the Social

Security Pensions Act 1975 in respect of contributions to occupational pension schemes and State scheme premiums.

(d) Sums due from the deceased to the Inland Revenue on account of deductions of P.A.Y.E. income tax which the deceased was liable to make from wages or salary paid during the period of 12 months before death (less repayments due to the deceased from the Inland Revenue).

(e) Value added tax referable to the six month period before death and which became due during that period.

If a landlord carries out a distraint on the deceased's goods within three months of death the preferred creditors have a first claim on the goods (or the proceeds of sale). This is to prevent a landlord making use of the special remedy of distraint to obtain payment from the assets of the estate before the preferential creditors. However the landlord is entitled to replace in the order of priority any creditor who is paid as a result of such a claim (Insolvency Act 1986). So to this extent a landlord will get priority over other ordinary creditors.

If the landlord recovers an amount in excess of six months' rent accrued due before death any excess must be held for the estate.

When the insolvency provisions of the Enterprise Act 2000 come into effect, Crown preference will be abolished. The following categories will lose their preferential status:

- sums due to Inland Revenue;
- sums due to Customs and Excise; and
- social security contributions.

Ordinary debts
These are all other debts which are not deferred. **15.035**

Interest
Any surplus remaining after the payment of preferred and ordinary debts **15.036** shall be used to pay interest on preferential and ordinary debts from death till payment (ordinary debts ranking equally with preferential debts for this purpose). The rate of interest payable is whichever is the greater of:

(a) the rate specified in s.17 of the Judgments Act 1838 at death; and
(b) the rate otherwise applicable to that debt.

Deferred debts
Deferred debts are debts owed in respect of credit provided by a person **15.037** who (whether or not the deceased's spouse at the time the credit was provided) was the deceased's spouse at the date of death. Such debts are payable after the payment of preferred and ordinary debts and the interest thereon.

7. LIABILITY FOR UNPAID DEBTS

Personal liability of personal representatives
If a personal representative pays an inferior debt knowing of the **15.038** existence of a superior debt, the payment is taken as an admission by him

that he has sufficient assets to pay all debts of which he has notice which rank in priority to the inferior debt. He will, therefore, be personally liable to pay all such debts.

However, he is not personally liable if, without undue haste, he pays an inferior debt without notice of a superior one. (This is unlike the position of a personal representative who pays a *beneficiary* without notice of the existence of a debt of the deceased).

Limited protection

15.039   A personal representative is under a duty to pay all debts in the same category *pari passu* (*i.e.* proportionately) and has no right to prefer one creditor above others in the same class.

However, under s.10(2) of the Administration of Estates Act 1925 there is limited protection for a personal representative who pays a debt in full at a time when he has no reason to believe the estate is insolvent. A personal representative who makes a payment in such circumstances to a creditor (including himself, unless he took a grant of representation in the capacity of creditor) in not liable to account to other creditors of the *same* class as the creditor who has been paid, if it subsequently appears that the estate is insolvent.

The section does not protect a personal representative against creditors in a *superior* category nor does it protect a personal representative who had any reason to believe that the estate was insolvent.

8. The problem of bankrupt beneficiaries

15.040   A personal representative who pays a legacy direct to a beneficiary who is bankrupt rather than to the trustee in bankruptcy runs the risk of personal liability (see further *Law Society's Gazette*, February 24, 1993).

Where there is no reason to suspect bankruptcy it is unlikely that the personal representatives would be held liable. However, where there are any grounds for suspicion they should make a bankruptcy search in Form K16 at the Land Charges Registry. Where a beneficiary is known to be bankrupt, the personal representatives should pay to the trustee in bankruptcy on production of a notice under the Insolvency Act 1986, s.307 (unless the trustee in bankruptcy indicates otherwise).

16.   Legacies and Devises

A. Legacies and Devises

A legacy is a gift in a will of personalty; a devise is a gift in a will of realty. **16.001**

B. Classification of Legacies

Legacies may be classified as specific, general, demonstrative, pecuniary **16.002**
or residuary. The classification is important because different types of
legacy have different characteristics.

1. Specific legacies

A specific legacy is a gift of a particular item of property owned by the **16.003**
deceased at the time of death and distinguished from all other property
owned by the deceased of a similar type.

> Examples of specific legacies are:
>
> "I give the gold ring I bought in Manchester to X."
> "I give my shares in ABC Ltd to Y."

Specific legacies suffer from the disadvantage that they may fail as a result
of the doctrine of ademption. Ademption means that a specific legacy fails
if the subject-matter has ceased to form part of the deceased's estate at
death. This may be because the property has been sold or has completely
changed its substance. The disappointed beneficiary will receive no
compensation from the rest of the estate. Only specific legacies suffer
ademption; therefore when construing a will the court tends to construe a
legacy as general rather than specific where possible (*Re Rose* (1949)).
(For a fuller discussion of ademption, see paras 16.014–16.019.)

As we saw in Chapter 15 specific legacies (and devises) are available for
payment of debts, but only after such items as undisposed of property,
residue and any retained pecuniary legacy fund have been exhausted.

2. General legacies

A general legacy is a gift in a will of an item of property which is not **16.004**
distinguished from property of a similar type. If the deceased does not
own property at the date of death corresponding to the description in the
will, the personal representatives must purchase suitable property using
funds from the estate. In determining from which part of the estate such
funds are to be provided a general legacy is treated as a pecuniary legacy
so that the same rules which apply to the incidence of pecuniary

legacies—see paras 16.040–16.046—apply to the incidence of general legacies.

An example of a general legacy is:

"I give 100 shares in ABC Ltd to Y."

This is a gift of *any* 100 shares in ABC Ltd. The mere fact that at the time of making the will the testator owned exactly 100 shares in the company is not sufficient to turn the legacy into a specific legacy (*Re Willcocks* (1921)). If a legacy is to be construed as specific there must be a clear indication in the will itself that the testator is referring to particular property owned at the time of the will. A general legacy is not liable to ademption but will be taken for payment of debts before specific legacies. (See para.16.008.)

3. DEMONSTRATIVE LEGACIES

16.005 A demonstrative legacy is "in its nature a general legacy but there is a particular fund pointed out to satisfy it" (*per* Lord Thurlow, *Ashburner v MacGuire* (1786)).

Examples of a demonstrative legacy are:

"I give £100 to X to be paid from my current bank account."
"I give £100 to Y to be paid out of my National Savings Certificates."

A demonstrative legacy combines the attributes of general and specific legacies. It is treated as a specific legacy to the extent that the particular fund is in existence at the date of death and is therefore taken for payment of debts after general legacies. If, however, the particular fund is not in existence at the date of death the legacy is not adeemed (as a specific legacy would be). Instead it is treated as a general legacy and paid from any other property available in the estate.

4. PECUNIARY LEGACIES

Description

16.006 A pecuniary legacy is a gift in a will of money. Most commonly a pecuniary legacy is general (for example, "I give £100 to X") but it may be specific (for example, "I give the £100 I keep in a box under the bed to Y") or demonstrative (for example, "I give £100 to Y to be paid from my current bank account)".

Annuities

16.007 An annuity is a pecuniary legacy payable by instalments.

The Administration of Estates Act 1925, s.55(1)(x)

16.008 *Special definition.* Section 55(1)(x) defines a "pecuniary legacy" for the purposes of the Act. The expression

"includes an annuity, a general legacy, a demonstrative legacy so far as it is not discharged out of the designated property, and any other general direction by a testator for the payment of money, including all death duties free from which any devise, bequest or payment is made to take effect."

Thus, a gift of "the £100 I keep in a box under my bed" being a specific legacy is not treated as a pecuniary legacy for the purposes of the Administration of Estates Act; the £100 would, therefore, rank with the other specific legacies for payment of debts.

Availability for payment of debts. In the order of availability of property for payment of debts set out in the Administration of Estates Act, the fund set on one side for payment of pecuniary legacies is taken fifth, whereas specific legacies (and devises) are taken sixth after the retained fund has been exhausted. If only part of the retained fund is required for payment of debts the various pecuniary legacies will abate proportionally (unless the testator indicated that one legacy was to be paid in priority to the others in which case the indication is binding on the personal representatives).

5. RESIDUARY LEGACIES

A residuary gift in a will passes the property of the deceased not otherwise disposed of. It may be a gift of the entire net estate if no other dispositions have been made or it may be a gift of what is left after payment of specific and general gifts. It may be limited to personalty not otherwise disposed of but more usually it will not be so limited and will pass all property whether realty or personality. **16.009**

C. Devises

A devise is a gift of realty and can be either specific or residuary. If specific it is subject to the rules on ademption. **16.010**

D. Failure of Legacies and Devises

1. INTRODUCTION

A gift made in a valid will can fail for a number of reasons. Some of the more important are listed below: **16.011**

- (a) disclaimer;
- (b) ademption;
- (c) the beneficiary predeceases the testator;
- (d) divorce;
- (e) uncertainty;
- (f) the beneficiary witnesses the will;
- (g) the gift is contrary to public policy or for an illegal or immoral purpose;

    (h) the gift is conditional and the condition is not fulfilled;

    (i) the doctrine of satisfaction;

    (j) the gift is induced by force, fear, fraud or undue influence (this has already been considered in Chapter 2);

    (k) the gift infringes the rules against perpetuity or accumulations (a consideration of these rules and their consequences is beyond the scope of this book).

2. EFFECT OF FAILURE

16.012   Any legacy or specific devise which fails will fall into residue unless the testator has included a substitutional gift. If a residuary gift fails, the property is undisposed of and passes under the intestacy rules to the testator's next-of-kin.

3. DISCLAIMER

16.013   No one can force another to accept a benefit under the will. Beneficiaries are free to disclaim any property given by will. However, it is not normally possible to pick and choose—unless the will provides to the contrary, the whole of a gift must be disclaimed or the whole must be accepted; if, however, two entirely separate gifts are made one may be accepted and the other disclaimed. Once a person has accepted any benefit from a gifted property (for example, income from or interest on it) it is too late to disclaim. (It may, however, be possible to vary the terms of the deceased's disposition by a variation agreement.) A fuller discussion of the practical considerations involved in disclaimers and variations will be found in Chapter 19 below.

    A voluntary disclaimer made during the lifetime of a testator is ineffective (see *Smith v Smith* (2001)). This is because, until the death, a beneficiary has no interest to accept or disclaim; he has a mere expectation of an interest.

4. ADEMPTION

Introduction

16.014   As we saw in para.16.003 and in para.16.010, a specific legacy or devise will fail if the subject-matter does not form part of the testator's estate at death. Ademption may occur as a result of sale or destruction of the asset or a change in substance. A disappointed beneficiary has no rights to receive the proceeds of sale where property has been sold nor any rights to the proceeds of any insurance policy where property has been destroyed. There are a number of aspects of the doctrine of ademption which warrant fuller consideration.

A change in substance

16.015   A change in substance will cause ademption to take place but a mere change in form will not. It is sometimes difficult to decide whether a change is one of substance or of form. In *Re Clifford* (1912), T gave 23 "of the shares belonging to me" in a named company. After the date of the will the company changed its name and subdivided each share into 4. Swinfen Eady J. held that the legacy was not adeemed since the subject-matter remained exactly the same although changed in name and form. The beneficiary, therefore, took 92 of the new shares. In *Re Slater* (1907), a testator made a gift of shares in Lambeth Waterworks Company. After the date of the will the company was taken over and amalgamated with other waterworks companies into the Metropolitan Water Board which issued stock to replace shares held in the old companies. The Court of Appeal held that the legacy was adeemed since the new stock was in an entirely different organisation.

In *Re Dorman, Smith v National Childrens Home and Others* (1994) the deceased left the sums contained in a named deposit account to the trustees of a settlement in which she had enjoyed a life interest. These sums represented income of the trust fund which she had received but not spent. After the date of the will these accounts were closed on her behalf and the sums transferred to an account bearing a higher rate of interest (this was done under an enduring power of attorney—see below). The court held that because the accounts were so similar and were funded in the same way there was no change of substance and no ademption.

Effect of republication

If a legacy has been adeemed and the testator afterwards makes a codicil **16.016** which republishes the will, it normally has no effect on the ademption. For example, if T left Blackacre to B, sold Blackacre, then made a codicil republishing the will B would still have no rights to the traceable proceeds of sale even if they were identifiable.

However, as a result of the republication the will may be construed in such a way that a gift which would otherwise have been adeemed will be saved. For example, T gives "the house in which I now reside to X." Such a gift is a specific devise and if T sells the house after the date of the will it will be adeemed; if T buys another house X is not entitled to the replacement. However, if T makes a codicil to the will after the purchase of the replacement house, the will is republished as at the date of the codicil and, since the wording used in the gift is wide enough to cover *any* house in which T is residing at the appropriate time, X will be entitled to the replacement house.

A codicil republishing a will can only have the effect of passing a replacement asset if the wording used in the original will is sufficiently wide. If, for example, T gave "the 3 stone diamond ring I bought in London in 1971 to X" and the ring was stolen the gift would be adeemed; if the ring was insured T might use the insurance money to buy an identical three stone ring but even if T made a codicil republishing the will the wording would be too specific to cover the replacement and X would get nothing.

The effect of the doctrine of conversion

When a vendor enters into a binding contract to sell realty the equitable **16.017** doctrine of conversion applies so that the vendor is treated from the date of the contract as having an interest in the proceeds of sale rather than in the realty. If T makes a will leaving freehold property, Blackacre, to B and then enters into a binding contract to sell Blackacre, the devise is adeemed from the date of the contract. If T dies between contract and completion B is entitled to any rent or other income Blackacre may produce until completion but B is not entitled to the proceeds of sale, which will fall into residue.

The anomalous rule in *Lawes v Bennett* (1785) can in certain circumstances convert property retrospectively; this may lead to ademption. If T makes a will leaving Blackacre to B and residue to R, later grants an option to purchase Blackacre to O and dies before the option has been exercised, Blackacre passes to B. However, if O subsequently decides to exercise the option this effects a retrospective conversion so that Blackacre is deemed to have been converted into proceeds of sale from the date of T's death. The sale proceeds are therefore paid to R and not to B—B is not, however, required to repay any rents or income received since the date of death.

The rule in *Lawes v Bennett* was extended to a gift of shares subject to an option to purchase in *Re Carrington* (1932). The result was that, when the option to purchase the shares was exercised, the shares were deemed to have been sold as at the date of the testator's death. The gift of shares was treated as adeemed and the proceeds of sale fell into residue.

If the will is made or republished after the date of the grant of the option the testator is deemed to have intended to pass to the beneficiary the property *or* the proceeds of sale so that no ademption will take place even if the option is exercised. The beneficiary will be entitled to the proceeds of sale (*Drant v Vause* (1842)).

Property to be ascertained at date of death

16.018   A testator may make a gift of assets to be ascertained at the date of death, for example a gift of "all the shares in ABC Co. which I own at my death". Such a gift is not subject to the doctrine of ademption as such, although it will fail if the testator owns no assets corresponding to the description at the date of death.

Problems when drafting a will

16.019   The effect of the doctrine of ademption should always be explained to a client who wishes to make a bequest or devise of a specific item.

It is possible to include words of substitution so that a testator might give "my shares in ABC Co. or any shares representing that investment at the time of my death." However, such a gift may well create problems for the personal representatives in identifying such shares, particularly if the death occurs some time after the will is made. It may, therefore, be preferable simply to point out to the client the importance of reviewing the will periodically so that it can be changed if an asset specifically given is sold, destroyed or substantially changed.

Alternatively, it may be possible to word the gift so that the precise property is to be ascertained at the date of death (as suggested in para.16.018 above) or to give a pecuniary legacy in substitution for a legacy failing by reason of ademption.

Mental incapacity of donor

When a person becomes mentally incapable of managing his own affairs a receiver under the Mental Health Act 1983 will have to be appointed unless the person has granted an enduring power of attorney. There is obviously a danger that the receiver or donee may, if unaware of the terms of the Will, deal with the assets of the estate in such a way as to risk ademption. The Mental Health Act 1983 contains provision to ensure that ademption does not occur. Section 101 provides that (in so far as circumstances allow) testamentary beneficiaries shall take the same interest in substituted property as they would have taken in the original property. This makes it unnecessary for the receiver to apply to the Court of Protection for a new will to be made. However, there is no corresponding provision for dealings by the donee of a registered enduring power of attorney. The result is that the donee must either check the terms of any will and try to avoid action which will result in ademption or if (as is likely) this is impossible, apply to the Court of Protection for a statutory will. The dangers of such ademption were illustrated in *Re Dorman, Smith National Childrens Home and Others* (1994), although on the particular facts of the case the court was able to find that ademption had not taken place.

5. BENEFICIARY PREDECEASES TESTATOR

Introduction

In order to take a gift under a will a beneficiary must survive the testator. **16.020** If the beneficiary predeceases the testator a legacy will lapse and fall into residue or if it is a residuary gift will pass under the intestacy rules. A beneficiary need only survive for a very short period—a minute or a second will suffice.

If a gift is to joint tenants or is a class gift, it will not lapse unless all the joint tenants or members of the class predecease the testator; if one joint tenant or class member survives the testator, that one person takes the whole gift. If a gift is to tenants in common, the share of any tenant who predeceases the testator will lapse.

A testator cannot exclude the doctrine of lapse by declaring that it is not to apply. A testator can, however, include a substitutional gift providing that if the beneficiary predeceases, the property is to pass to another person.

A solicitor should always point out to a client the possibility that a beneficiary may predecease so that the client can consider including a substitutional clause. It is also common to include a survivorship clause in a will. A survivorship clause states that a beneficiary is only to take a benefit under the will if the beneficiary survives the testator for a stated period (usually 28 days). The effect is to prevent a beneficiary who only survives the testator by a very short period from benefiting under the will. The importance of such a clause is obvious when it is remembered that a beneficiary may be *deemed* to survive under the Law of Property Act 1925, s.184 (see para.16.021 below). Without a survivorship clause, the testator's property would pass under the terms of the beneficiary's will or to the beneficiary's next of kin under the intestacy rules. Such a devolution of property might be contrary to the testator's wishes.

Substitutional and survivorship clauses, as well as giving the testator control over the ultimate destination of his property, may have the effect of saving inheritance tax overall. For a fuller discussion of this topic see Chapter 22.

Where the order of deaths is uncertain

16.021 *The statutory presumption.* It can sometimes happen that there is no evidence as to the order in which people have died, for example where two people die in a car accident. In such a case, s.184 of the Law of Property Act 1925 provides that for the purposes of succession to property the deaths are presumed to have occurred in order of seniority so that the elder is presumed to die first. The section applies equally on intestacy (with one exception which will be considered later).

Example

```
     Mother          Mother
       |               |
     Harold    =    Winifred

       30              29
```

Harold and Winifred both die in a car accident; the order of their deaths is uncertain. They have each made wills leaving all their property to the other. They have no children. Each has a mother who survives.

Harold, being the elder, is presumed to die first. His property therefore passes under the terms of his will to Winifred who is presumed to have survived him. His property forms part of her estate. The gift in Winifred's will to Harold lapses and her estate (which now includes Harold's property) passes to her mother under the intestacy rules. It is unlikely that Harold would have wished his property to pass to Winifred's mother in preference to his own; had he included a survivorship clause in his will his property would not have passed to Winifred and so would not have gone to her mother.

Exceptions to the doctrine of lapse

16.022 There are three situations where, despite the fact that a beneficiary has predeceased a testator, a gift will not fail.

  (a) Gifts in discharge of a moral obligation.
  (b) Section 32 of the Wills Act 1837.
  (c) Section 33 of the Wills Act 1837.

Both (a) and (b) are of comparatively minor importance and can be dealt with briefly; (c), however, warrants a more detailed examination.

Gifts in discharge of a moral obligation

16.023 If a testator makes a gift to beneficiary in order to discharge a moral obligation and the beneficiary predeceases the testator the gift will not lapse but will form part of the beneficiary's estate. Examples of gifts which have been held to be in discharge of a moral obligation are a direction to pay a statute-barred debt (*Williamson v Naylor* (1838)) and a mother's direction that the creditors of her deceased son be paid (*Re Leach's Will Trusts* (1948)).

The precise limits of the rule are uncertain and it may be that it applies only to directions to pay debts and not to ordinary gifts (*Stevens v King* (1904)).

Section 32 of the Wills Act 1837

Section 32 provides that a gift of entailed property will not lapse if at the death of the testator there are any issue living who are capable of taking under the entail. The testator can exclude the section by showing a contrary intention in the will.

16.024

Section 33 of the Wills Act 1837

The section. Section 33(1) (as substituted by the Administration of Justice Act 1982) applies where a testator dies after December 31, 1982. (The rules contained in the original s.33 which applied before 1983 are not dealt with in this book.) The substituted s.33 provides that where:

16.025

- (a) a will contains a devise or bequest to a child or remoter descendant of the testator; *and*
- (b) the intended beneficiary dies before the testator, leaving issue; *and*
- (c) issue of the intended beneficiary are living at the testator's death.

then, unless a contrary intention appears by the will, the devise or bequest shall take effect as a devise or bequest *to the issue* living at the testator's death.

Section 33(3) provides that such issue take "according to their stock, in equal shares if more than one, any gift or share which their parent would have taken."

Thomas leaves Catherine a legacy of £20,000 in his will but Catherine predeceases Thomas. Normally the gift to Catherine would fail; however, as a result of s.33 the gift does not fail but passes equally to Giles and Gertrude who take £10,000 each.

Section 33 goes on to provide that no issue shall take whose parent is living at the testator's death and so capable of taking.

Example

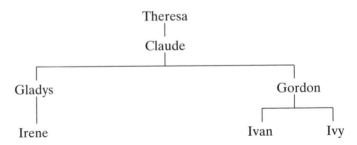

Theresa leaves Claude a legacy of £20,000. Claude and Gordon predecease Theresa. The gift does not lapse but passes to Theresa's issue. Gladys receives one-half (her issue are entitled to nothing as she is still alive); Gordon has predeceased Theresa and therefore his share of £10,000 is divided equally between his issue, Ivan and Ivy, who take £5,000 each.

The section does not make it clear whether, where a gift is contingent, substituted beneficiaries must satisfy the same contingency as primary beneficiaries. Etherton J. in *Ling v Ling* (2002) said that they must.

Class gifts. Section 33(2) provides that where:

(a) a will contains a devise or bequest to a class of persons consisting of children or remoter descendants of the testator; and
(b) a member of the class dies before the testator, leaving issue; and
(c) issue of that member are living at the testator's death.

then, unless a contrary intention appears in the will, the devise or bequest shall take effect as if the class included the issue of its deceased member living at the testator's death. Under s.33(3) the issue take *per stirpes* according to their stocks, in equal shares if more than one, the share which their parent would have taken and no issue whose parent is living at the time of the testator's death shall take.

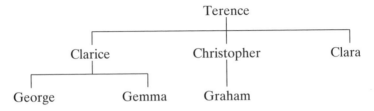

Terence leaves £30,000 to be divided "amongst all my children". Clarice predeceases Terence. Her one-third share (£10,000) will be divided *per stirpes* amongst such of her issue as survive Terence. Section 33(3) will apply so that no issue shall take whose parent is living at the testator's death. Therefore Graham will take nothing.

Contrary intention. Both s.33(1) and s.33(2) are expressed to be **16.026** subject to contrary intention. There is, however, some uncertainty as to precisely what constitutes "contrary intention" for this purpose. The original s.33 of Wills Act 1837 stated that it was not to apply when an interest was determinable at or before death. Thus, that section did not save a life interest to a child of the testator who predeceased, nor a gift to a child of the testator as a joint tenant or as a member of a class who predeceased leaving surviving joint tenants or class members; nor did it apply to a gift contingent on an event which had not occurred when the child predeceased. The substituted s.33 does not contain such exclusions and it is not clear whether or not a testator making gifts on such terms thereby demonstrates a contrary intention. If a testator does not wish the issue of a deceased child (or remoter descendant) to take a benefit the safest course is to include a provision stating what is to happen in the event of such predecease. (See the discussion of the new s.33 and will drafting below.)

In *Ling v Ling* (2002) the court had to consider whether or not a will expressed contrary intention. The gift was to children "*living at my death*". The court held that those words achieved nothing. They merely stated expressly what would otherwise be implicit, that a class is normally composed of those members, if any, in existence at the death of the testator. To amount to contrary intention there would have to be words making it clear that issue were not to be substituted.

Children whose parents were not married and children en ventre sa mere. Section 33(4) provides that for the purposes of s.33 the illegitimacy of any person is to be disregarded. Thus, a child whose parents were not married can take in the same way as a child whose parents were married. The subsection also provides that a child *en ventre sa mere* is living for the purposes of the section.

The effect of the substituted s.33 on will drafting. As explained above if a testator does *not* want s.33 to apply it is desirable for the avoidance of doubt to state in the will what is to happen where a child predeceases. However, even in those cases where a gift to a testator's deceased child (or remoter descendant) *is* to pass to the child's issue, it is desirable to include an express provision to this effect rather than to rely on the section for the following reasons:

(a) If the substitution is set out in the will, a solicitor can be certain that the effect of the statutory provision is brought to the attention of the client; this gives the client the opportunity to request an alternative if the statutory provision does not correspond with his wishes.

(b) If the gift to the testator's child (or remoter descendant) is contingent it is desirable to provide expressly for the possibility that the child might survive the testator but die without fulfilling the contingency leaving issue.

(c) If the gift to the testator's child (or remoter descendant) is contingent it is desirable to state expressly whether or not a substituted beneficiary is to take subject to the same contingency.

In cases where a gift is made to anyone other than a child (or remoter descendant) of the testator (for example "to the children of my brother") an express substitutional gift to issue *must* be included if the testator wants the gift to pass to issue in substitution for a beneficiary who predeceases. Section 33 applies only to gifts to the testator's children (or remoter descendants).

6. DIVORCE

Wills Act 1837, s.18A as amended by the Law Reform (Succession) Act 1995

16.027   As we saw in Chapter 2, in cases where a marriage is dissolved or annulled the former spouse is to be treated as having died on the date of dissolution or annulment. Thus, any gifts made by will to a spouse and appointments of spouse as executor will fail.

The effect of the s.18A amendment on will drafting

16.028   The fact that the former spouse is to be treated as *dying* on the date of dissolution or annulment means that the will drafting problems revealed by *Re Sinclair* are no longer relevant.

A substitutional gift expressed to take effect "if my spouse predeceases or does not survive me for [a specified period]" will now take effect if the primary gift to the spouse fails as a result of s.18A.

It is no longer *necessary* to include the words "or fails for any other reason". However, it is still *desirable* to include such words in case of failure from some other unforeseen reason—for example, forfeiture. See *Re Jones (Deceased)* (1997).

In any event it is always desirable to suggest that clients who are contemplating divorce should review their wills and that they should do so as early as possible since the mere fact of separation (or even a decree of Judicial Separation) will not revoke testamentary dispositions.

7. UNCERTAINTY

Introduction

16.029   If it is impossible to identify either the subject-matter or the objects of a gift, it will fail for uncertainty.

Uncertainty of subject-matter

16.030   Gifts of "some of my best table linen" (*Peck v Halsey* (1726)) or of "a handsome gratuity" (*Jubber v Jubber* (1839)) have been held to be void for uncertainty. (In some cases such gifts may now be saved by the Administration of Justice Act 1982, s.21).

A gift may prima facie be of an uncertain amount and yet be capable of assessment in which case it will not fail. For example, a clause giving a beneficiary a power to select such items as he wishes is valid; so also is a direction that a beneficiary enjoy "a reasonable income" from the testator's properties (*Re Golay* (1965)) since the court can, if necessary, determine what is a reasonable income.

Uncertainty of objects

If the beneficiaries are not clearly identified the gift will fail. Thus, a gift to   **16.031**
"the son of A" where A had several sons fails for uncertainty (*Dowset v Sweet* (1753)). It is, therefore, important when drafting a will to take care to check the names of individuals and institutions intended to benefit. The only case where a gift will not fail for uncertainty of objects is where a testator wishes to make a charitable gift and does not sufficiently identify the charity which is to benefit. The gift will not fail so long as it is clear that the gift is for exclusively charitable purposes. The court will direct a scheme to give effect to the gift.

8. THE BENEFICIARY WITNESSES THE WILL

The general rule

Section 15 of the Wills Act provides that a gift made to a beneficiary fails   **16.032**
if:

   (a) the beneficiary witnesses the will; or
   (b) the spouse of the beneficiary witnesses the will.

The validity of the will itself is not affected. The rule exists to ensure that wills are reliably witnessed by independent persons.

Beneficial gifts only

Section 15 applies only to beneficial gifts. Thus, if a gift is made "to X as   **16.033**
trustee to hold for Y" and X or X's spouse witnesses the will the gift does not fail. The gift would fail if Y or Y's spouse witnessed the will.

Subsequent events irrelevant

It is the time of execution which is important. Subsequent events are   **16.034**
irrelevant. Thus, if a witness marries a beneficiary *after* the date of execution of the will the gift remains effective (*Thorpe v Bestwick* (1881)). Similarly, if a gift is to the holder of an office or to a person fulfilling a description the gift will remain effective even though a witness later takes up the office or comes to fulfil the description (*Re Ray's Will Trusts, Public Trustee v Barry* (1936)).

Gift made or confirmed by independently witnessed will or codicil

A gift will not fail if there is a codicil or will which can be said to confirm   **16.035**
the will and which is not witnessed by the beneficiary (or the beneficiary's spouse). It is not necessary to find any express reference to the gift in the independently witnessed will or codicil. In *Re Trotter* (1899) T made a gift by will to B, a witness; there were two later codicils to the will; B did not witness the first but did witness the second. The court held that, as there was one independently witnessed codicil, the gift to B did not fail.

Secret trusts

16.036 If T creates a secret (or half secret) trust in favour of X and X or X's spouse witnesses the will, X does not lose his entitlement. This is because X takes under the trust and not under the will (*Re Young* (1951)).

Superfluous attesting witnesses

16.037 In the case of a testator dying after May 29, 1968, the Wills Act 1968 provides that the attestation of a will by any beneficiaries or their spouses is to be disregarded if without them the will is duly executed.

Thus, if a will is witnessed by three people, one of whom is a beneficiary (or spouse of a beneficiary) that person may take a gift in the will; however, if two of the three witnesses (or their spouses) are beneficiaries their signatures cannot be disregarded and neither can take.

If a person (other than the testator) has signed a will, it is presumed that the signature is as a witness. The presumption can be rebutted—for example, by evidence that the signature was to indicate approval of the testator's disposition. If a beneficiary (or spouse of a beneficiary) is able to show that a signature was in such a capacity, there is no question of loss of entitlement.

A charging clause used to be regarded as a pecuniary legacy. However, the Trustee Act 2000, s.28 provides that a charging clause is no longer a legacy for the purposes of the Wills Act 1837, s.15 or for the purposes of abatement of legacies.

This means a solicitor can witness a will containing a charging clause even though the solicitor (or the firm in which the solicitor is a partner) is appointed executor. The right to charge will not be forfeited.

Because a charging clause was regarded as a legacy, it used to be necessary to provide that a solicitor's charges be paid "*in priority to other pecuniary legacies*". This was to prevent them abating with the other pecuniary legacies where the estate was too small to pay all pecuniary legacies in full. As the Trustee Act 2000, s.28 provides that such clauses are no longer legacies, there is no question of abatement and such clauses are unnecessary.

9. THE GIFT IS FOR AN ILLEGAL OR IMMORAL PURPOSE OR CONTRARY TO PUBLIC POLICY

16.038 Such a gift cannot take effect. The principles to be applied in deciding whether a gift is illegal, immoral or contrary to public policy are the same as in the law of trusts. The law relating to public policy is not fixed but changes with the passage of time. In *Gray v Barr* a broad principle of public policy was expressed as being "that no man should be allowed to profit at another person's expense from his own conscious and deliberate crime". Thus, if one person, B, is found guilty of murder of another, T, B cannot take any benefit under the will of T or under the intestacy rules if T dies intestate. Any person claiming from B's estate (for example, B's issue) are also excluded. If B is found guilty of the manslaughter of T it was said in *Re H (Deceased)* that the rule of public policy will apply to prevent B taking any benefit if the person has been found guilty of deliberate, intentional and unlawful violence but not otherwise. The rule of public policy will not apply if the killing was carried out while B was insane within the McNaghten rules.

In *Jones v Roberts* (1995) the rule was applied where a person had been convicted of manslaughter of his parents on the grounds of diminished responsibility. He was criminally responsible for his actions and had used deliberate, intentional and unlawful violence.

This rule of public policy has been modified by the Forfeiture Act 1982. The Act does not apply where a person has been convicted of murder but applies in any other case where one person has unlawfully killed another (for example, manslaughter) and is precluded by reasons of public policy from taking an interest in property. An offender may apply to the court within three months of the date of conviction (s.2) for an order modifying the forfeiture rule in respect of any beneficial interest which the offender would have acquired from the deceased (but for the forfeiture rule) *inter alia*:

(a) under the deceased's will or on intestacy;
(b) on a nomination by the deceased;
(c) as a *donatio mortis causa* (s.2(4)(a)).

An application may also be made where property had been held on trust for any person and as a result of the deceased's death but for the forfeiture rule the offender *would have* acquired an interest in the trust property (s.2(4)(b)).

Section 4(5) of the Act *appears* to provide that where there is more than one interest in property to which the forfeiture rule applies the Court may exclude the rule in respect of any *but not all* and where there is one such interest the Court may exclude the rule in respect of *part only* of that interest. However, in one of the first applications to come before the Court (*Re K* (1985)) Vinelott J. stated that the Act was a private members bill and is not couched in technical language but is intended to be understood by persons other than lawyers specialising in property and trust matters. He said that in his view s.4(5) was intended to enlarge the power of the court by making it abundantly clear that the court is not bound to relieve against the forfeiture rule entirely or not at all but that the court is free if it chooses to modify the effect of the rule to a limited extent. His first instance judgment was approved by the Court of Appeal.

16.039 The court must not make an order unless satisfied that the justice of the case requires the forfeiture rule to be modified having regard to the conduct of the offender and of the deceased and to such other circumstances as appear to the court to be material (s.2(2)).

No application may be made after the expiry of the three month period (s.2(3)).

A personal representative, who is administering an estate where the deceased was unlawfully killed by another person who would but for the forfeiture rule have received any of the interests in the property set out above, should wait for the expiry of the three months from conviction before distributing such property to others.

Section 3 of the Act provides that the forfeiture rule is not to be taken to preclude any person from making an application under the Inheritance (Provision for Family and Dependants) Act 1975. Such an application can be made if the requirements of *that* Act are complied with. Thus, an applicant must be able to show that the disposition of the deceased's estate effected by the will or by the intestacy rules did not make reasonable financial provision for the applicant (*Re Royse* (1984)).

Re Jones (Deceased) (1997) and *Re DWS* (2000) make it clear that a person whose interest has been forfeited is not to be treated as having predeceased. Hence, a substitutional gift expressed to take effect only if the beneficiary predeceases will not come into effect. If there is an intestacy, the statutory trusts will not apply to allow substitution of issue as issue cannot take if their parent is "living".

In *Dunbar v Plant* (1998) the Court of Appeal allowed relief from forfeiture to the survivor of a suicide pact in relation to the proceeds of an insurance policy taken out by the survivor's fiance (he had died as a result of the pact). The court held that the survivor had committed the criminal offence of aiding and abetting her fiance's suicide and, therefore, the forfeiture rule applied. However, the Forfeiture Act 1982, s.1(2) allows courts flexibility in applying the rule in cases where public policy demands a more sympathetic approach. Accordingly, she was granted full relief from forfeiture.

10. FAILURE OF A CONDITION

16.040   If a legacy is conditional on an event or circumstance which at the date of death is impossible or not present, the legacy will fail. However, the court may be able to construe the will in such a way that the legacy is found not to be conditional on the event or circumstance.

In *Watson v National Children's Home* (1995) a testator left half of his estate to one charity and the other half to a second charity conditional on the latter caring for his domestic pets. If the second charity did not agree to do so the residue would pass entirely to the first charity.

At the time of his death the deceased had no pets. The first charity argued that the gift to the second charity failed because the second charity could not fulfil the condition. The court held that the condition was impossible to fulfil and should be regarded as spent. As such the second charity took the gift absolutely. The clause had to be construed as requiring the charity to care for any of the deceased's pets but if there were none the gift should still pass. If the gift was not construed in this way, it would be deemed ambiguous and extrinsic evidence would be admitted under s.21 of the Administration of Justice Act 1982. The deceased had clearly stated that only if the charity refused to look after his pets should the gift fail.

It may be that a condition attaching to a legacy is void. In *Nathan v Leonard and National Association For Mental Health* (2002) the deceased directed that, if any one of the beneficiaries contested the will, the entire estate was to go to a married couple who were taking two thirds of the residue and who she was anxious to provide for adequately. One of the other residuary beneficiaries made a claim under the Inheritance (Provision for Family and Dependants) Act for further provision be made for him from the estate. The married couple contended that this brought the forfeiture clause into effect.

There were three issues:

(a) Was the forfeiture clause void either for repugnancy or because it was contrary to public policy?

(b) If it was valid, had it been breached?

(c) If breached, was the gift over to the married couple effective?

The court held that the clause imposing forfeiture was not repugnant. A condition is only repugnant if it is inconsistent with ownership. There is nothing inconsistent about a gift subject to divesting. Inconsistency only arises if the gift purports to limit the incidents of ownership, such as the ability to sell.

Equally, although the condition might well have a strong deterrent effect on a beneficiary who was contemplating making a claim under the Act, that did not in itself make the condition contrary to public policy.

Making an Inheritance Act claim would amount to contesting the will for this purpose and would breach the clause.

However, it was clear that some words had been mistakenly omitted from the final sentence of the codicil. Since it was impossible for the court to say what the omitted words were, the condition failed for uncertainty. The legacies were, therefore, free from the condition.

11. THE DOCTRINE OF SATISFACTION

The equitable presumption of satisfaction is based on the assumption that **16.041** a parent would wish to treat his children fairly and would not wish to make provision for one of his children twice over at the expense of his other children. In appropriate circumstances equity will presume that the second gift satisfies the first. It is merely a presumption and can be rebutted by evidence of the testator's intention.

The presumption of satisfaction has various aspects. We are here concerned with the ademption of a legacy as a result of a subsequent portion. The topic may sound rather outdated but there have been a number of recent cases confirming that the presumption is still active.

A *"portion is ... very broadly speaking, a gift intended to set up a child in life or to make substantial provision for him or her ..."* per Lindsay J. in *Re Cameron (Deceased)* (1999).

It is only lifetime gifts which are classified as "portions" that cause problems in this context. A mere gift is not a portion. There must be an idea of making a permanent provision for the child.

In *Taylor v Taylor* (1875) it was held that paying for the son's entry into Middle Temple, buying him an army commission (after he had given up the idea of law) and buying him a mining business (after he had given up the idea of the army) were all portions. However, other lesser payments including paying his gambling debts were not.

In *Re Cameron* (1999) it was held that it was irrelevant whether the gift was made by the father or the mother (or someone else *in loco parentis*). The gift in *Re Cameron* was actually made *on behalf of* the mother under an enduring power of appointment. Moreover, it was made to not to the legatee but to the child of the legatee to cover school fees.

In *Race v Race* (2002) Behrens J. concluded that the rule against double **16.042** portions can now apply to gifts of land (previously there was some suggestion that it applied only to personalty).

In *Casimir v Alexander* (2002) Hart J. held that the age of the child was irrelevant. The child in question was an old-age pensioner. The gift was a house and thus not a means of assisting her to earn her own livelihood. The gift was capable of being a portion as the key element is the permanent nature of the provision rather than the age or status in life of the donee. However, on the facts, there was sufficient evidence to rebut the presumption. The deceased regarded his daughter as having "earned" the gift through her long years of caring for him and his wife. Moreover, it was a condition of the gift purchase that she would continue caring for her father in the new house. This meant that there was a motive for the lifetime gift which differentiated it from the testamentary gift.

When deciding whether or not a legacy has failed, it is the donor's intention at the time of the later gift that is important not the intention at the time of the will. Evenso, if it is apparent at the time a will is made that a testator is intending to make a subsequent gift to one child, it will be sensible for the testator to make a written statement as to his present intention and place it with the will.

E. Incidence of Pecuniary Legacies

1. INTRODUCTION

16.043 Throughout this section the term "pecuniary legacy" is used in the Administration of Estates Act sense to cover a general legacy, an annuity or a demonstrative legacy so far as it is not discharged from the designated property.

If a will gives a pecuniary legacy to a beneficiary, the personal representatives will need to know from which part of the estate they are entitled to take assets to pay the legacy. We saw in Chapter 15 that personal representatives have exactly the same problem when deciding which assets are to be used for payment of debts and that there are statutory rules which govern availability of assets for payment of debts. The position with regard to pecuniary legacies is, however, much less certain. This area of the law has been described as "tortuous" and "notoriously obscure" (*per* Salt, Q.C., Ch., in *Re Taylor's Estate* (1969)). It is most desirable that anyone drafting a will should avoid any problems of statutory interpretation by stating expressly what property is to be taken for payment of pecuniary legacies.

However, in the opinion of the writers this tortuous area has been simplified by the Law Reform (Succession) Act 1995.

2. NO UNDISPOSED OF PROPERTY

16.044 The pre-1926 rules still apply which means that pecuniary legacies are payable from residue. Under the rule in *Greville v Brown*, where a testator gives residue (both real and personal) in one mass to a beneficiary the realty is available to pay pecuniary legacies *but only* in so far as the personalty is exhausted. The precise wording of the gift is irrelevant so long as the testator makes it clear that there is one single gift consisting of both realty and personality. An example of such wording is "I give all my residue, both real and personal, to X."

Under the rule in *Roberts v Walker* where a testator directs that pecuniary legacies be paid from a mixed fund of realty and personality, the legacies are payable *proportionately* from both realty and personality. An example of such wording would be "I give my residue, real and personal, on trust for sale to my trustees to use the proceeds to pay my legacies and hold any balance for X".

The question of the extent to which realty is available will only rarely be of any importance.

For example, if residuary realty is given to one person, R, and residuary personality to another person, P, R will obviously want to insist that legacies be paid exclusively from personality (P will be equally anxious that realty be made available).

3. UNDISPOSED OF PROPERTY

The Trusts of Land and Appointment of Trustees Act 1996 amends the Administration of Estates Act 1925 to read as follows:

16.045

> "(1) On the death of a person intestate as to any real or personal estate, that estate shall be held in trust by his personal representatives with the power to sell it.
> (2) The personal representatives shall pay out of—
>   (a) the ready money of the deceased (so far as not disposed by his will, if any); and
>   (b) any net money arising from disposing of any other part of his estate (after payment of costs),
> all such funeral, testamentary and administration expenses, debts and other liabilities ... and out of the residue of the said money the personal representative shall set aside a fund sufficient to provide for any pecuniary legacies bequeathed by the will (if any) of the deceased."

The effect of the amended s.33(2) is, therefore, to make undisposed of property primarily liable for payment of pecuniary legacies. Ready money will be used first but thereafter it is irrelevant whether the undisposed of property is realty or personality.

Example
T's will leave a pecuniary legacy of £6,000 to L and the residue to A and B in equal shares. A predeceases T and the gift to him lapses. The estate amounts to £20,000. There are no debts. Since s.33(2) expressly directs that pecuniary legacies be paid from money arising from disposing of *any* part of the estate as to which the deceased was intestate, the pecuniary legacy will be paid from the lapsed share of residue irrespective of whether it is realty or personality. Therefore B gets £10,000 and A's lapsed share of £10,000 is used to pay L's legacy of £6,000. The balance of £4,000 left after payment of the pecuniary legacy will pass under the intestacy rules to T's next of kin.

4. ARE THERE ANY CIRCUMSTANCES IN WHICH S.33(2) DOES NOT APPLY?

16.046　Before the amending of s.33 by the Trusts of Land and Appointment of Trustees Act 1996 it was clear that the direction to pay pecuniary legacies contained in s.33(2) related only to the proceeds of the *statutory* trust for sale imposed by s.33(1). The statutory trust for sale could not apply if a will imposed an *express* trust for sale because there cannot be two trusts for sale, one statutory and one express, applying to the same property (*Re McKee* (1931)). The express trust took precedence over that imposed by s.33(1). If s.33(1) did not apply then neither did s.33(2) which deals with the proceeds of sale arising under the statutory trust.

Example
A testator died before January 1, 1996 leaving a pecuniary legacy of £6,000 to L and directing that the residue was to be held *on trust for sale* for A and B in equal shares. A predeceased T and the gift to him lapsed. The estate amounted to £20,000. Since the testator had imposed an express trust for sale on the residue there was no room for a statutory trust for sale to apply to the residue. Thus, s.33(1) did not apply to the undisposed of property and therefore s.33(2) (which dealt only with the proceeds of sale arising from the statutory trust) could not apply. The question then arose of what property was to be used to provide for the payment of the legacy to L. Unfortunately the answer was by no means certain.

There were several conflicting cases—*Re Midgley* (1955), *Re Beaumont's Will Trusts* (1950), and *Re Taylor's Estate* (1969). The better view was that when s.33(2) did not apply, the payment of legacies was still governed by the pre-1926 rules. The result was that legacies were not payable primarily from undisposed of property.

The position may now have been simplified by the Trusts of Land and Appointment of Trustees Act 1996.

It seems to the writers that in the amended s.33 the link between the two subsections is broken. Pecuniary legacies are to be paid from cash in the estate at death or produced by the sale of *any* part of the estate and, therefore, it is irrelevant whether the undisposed of property is held on a statutory or an express trust.

If this interpretation of the new section is correct it removes an area of unnecessary complexity and uncertainty from the administration of estates. Where the will makes no special provision for the payment of pecuniary legacies, they will always be paid from cash either contained in the estate at death or resulting from the disposal of any part of the estate as to which the deceased was intestate.

5. WILL DRAFTING

16.047　Despite the probable simplification of the law it is clearly desirable when drafting wills to state expressly what property is to be used for payment of pecuniary legacies. For example, a testator may leave residue "subject to payment of legacies". It is common for trusts for sale to direct that legacies be paid from residue before division into shares; this is certainly a solution to the problem of uncertainty but it does not necessarily reflect the wishes of testators. Many testators might prefer a direction that, where residue is left on trust, in the event of any share of residue lapsing, pecuniary legacies should be paid from the lapsed share of residue, thus reducing the amount passing under the intestacy rules.

F. Income from and Interest on Legacies and Devises

1. INTRODUCTION

A personal representative cannot be compelled to pay legacies and distribute the estates before the expiry of one year from the death (Administration of Estates Act 1925, s.44). Even in a very simple administration there will inevitably be delay between the death and the distribution. Beneficiaries will want to know what rights they have to income or interest in that period.   **16.048**

This section is concerned with the rights of a beneficiary:

(a) to receive *income* which has been produced by assets in the period between the death of the testator and the vesting of the assets in the beneficiary; and

(b) to receive *interest* paid from the estate on the value of a pecuniary (or general) legacy in the period between the death of the testator and the payment of the legacy to the beneficiary.

2. INCOME

Some assets by their very nature are incapable of producing income (for example, a painting, a ring, a piece of furniture) in which case the question of a beneficiary's right to income is irrelevant. Other assets do, however, produce income (for example, a house which is rented to a tenant, company shares, government stock). We are concerned with the rights of beneficiaries to receive this income. It is necessary to distinguish the following types of gift: **16.049**

(a) immediate specific gifts;

(b) contingent and deferred specific gifts;

(c) immediate residuary gifts;

(d) contingent and deferred residuary gifts.

Immediate specific gifts

A specific legacy or devise which is to take effect immediately carries with it the right to any income accruing to the property in the period between the death of the testator and vesting. The beneficiary is not, however, entitled to receive the income *as it arises*; instead, the beneficiary must wait until the personal representatives vest the property in the beneficiary by means of an assent. The assent operates retrospectively to give the beneficiary the right to receive the income which has accrued since the date of death.   **16.050**

An assent can be oral in the case of all assets other than land, for which a written assent is required. An assent indicates that the asset is not required for payment of debts and is available to the beneficiary. (See

Chapter 18.) A specific beneficiary must bear all liabilities relating to the asset after the assent and thus must bear any costs of transporting, insuring or transferring the asset unless there is a direction to the contrary in the will. It is common for a clause to be included in a professionally drawn will directing that such expenses be paid from residue.

Contingent and deferred specific gifts

16.051 An example of a contingent specific gift is "to X if X becomes a solicitor" and an example of a deferred specific gift is "to X after the death of A". Prior to 1925 neither type of gift carried with it the right to receive income. However, s.175 of the Law of Property Act 1925 provides that such gifts do carry with them the right to income (unless the testator has indicated otherwise). Such income will, therefore, be added to the capital and will devolve with it. Income can, however, only be accumulated and added to capital for so long as the statutory rule against accumulations permits (Law of Property Act 1925, ss.164–166 as amended by the Perpetuities and Accumulations Act 1964, s.13). Thereafter the income will either fall into residue or pass under the intestacy rules.

Immediate residuary gifts

16.052 An immediate residuary gift whether of realty or personalty carries with it the right to income accruing after the testator's death.

Contingent and deferred residuary gifts

16.053 Contingent residuary bequests have always carried the right to income, contingent residuary devises carry the right to such income as a result of the Law of Property Act, s.175. In the absence of contrary direction such income will be added to capital (subject to the rule against accumulations) and will devolve with it.

Section 175 does not mention *deferred* (or deferred, contingent) bequests which are, therefore, subject to the pre-1926 rules and do not carry the right to income. In the absence of a direction to the contrary income will pass to the person entitled to undisposed of property.

There is some uncertainty as to whether a *deferred* residuary *devise* carries the right to income. The better view appears to be that it does with the result that income will be added to capital (subject to the rule against accumulations).

The effect is that probably all residuary gifts carry the right to income apart from deferred (or deferred, contingent) residuary bequests. Examples of such gifts would be "my personalty to X after the death of A" or "my personalty to X after the death of A if X becomes a solicitor".

Apportioning income

16.054 It is necessary to consider how the income accruing after death is to be ascertained and we will, therefore, look at the effect of the Apportionment Act 1870.

In the absence of any direction to the contrary in the will s.2 of the Apportionment Act 1870 provides that: "All rents, annuities, dividends and other periodical payments in the nature of income ... shall, like interest on money lent, be considered as accruing from day to day and shall be apportionable in respect of time accordingly". Interest is required at common law to be apportioned on a daily basis.

An asset which has been specifically devised or bequeathed may produce income which is paid to the personal representatives after the death of the deceased but which covers a period partly before and partly after the death. The personal representatives will have to decide whether the whole of the income passes to the specific beneficiary or whether it must be apportioned; if it is apportioned that part of the income attributable to the period before death will fall into residue and only that part which is attributable to the period after death will pass to the specific beneficiary.

Example

T leaves shares in ABC Ltd to X and residue to R. A dividend of £365 is declared for a period, 100 days of which precede the death and 265 days of which follow the death. The dividend must be apportioned between X and R. R will get the pre-death income attributable to the 100 day period and X will get the post-death income attributable to the 265 day period.

$$R \text{ will get } \frac{100}{365} \times £365 = £100$$

$$X \text{ will get } \frac{265}{365} \times £365 = £265$$

If the dividend is declared for a period which wholly precedes the death but is not actually paid until after the date of death it will not pass to the specific beneficiary; it will be treated as belonging to the deceased and will, therefore, form part of the residue. If a payment is made *before* death for a period falling partly before and partly after (or even wholly after) the death no apportionment is required and the specific beneficiary is not entitled to claim any portion of the advance payment from the estate. (Apportionments will also be dealt with in Chapter 18.)

Apportionments may involve personal representatives in complicated calculations and they are often regarded as more trouble than they are worth. The result is that most professionally drawn wills exclude the need to apportion so that if rents, dividends or other income are paid after death such income will pass entirely to a specific beneficiary even if it did partly relate to a period preceding the death.

Whether the need to apportion has been excluded or whether it applies is of no relevance when it comes to determining the liability of beneficiaries to income tax. Such liability is determined by reference to the income tax rules explained in Chapter 6. Similarly the exclusion of the need to apportion has no relevance to the valuation of the estate for inheritance tax purpose. Such valuation is determined by reference to the inheritance tax rules explained in para.4.019. The exclusion is only effective for distribution purposes and does not affect the Revenue.

3. INTEREST

Introduction

16.055 Interest is paid to a pecuniary legatee (or general legatee or demonstrative legatee if the designated fund has been exhausted) from the time at which the legacy is payable. The interest is to compensate the legatee where payment of the legacy is delayed. The interest is paid from residue and is treated as an administration expense. The testator may make express provision for the payment of interest and order that more or less interest be paid.

Rate of interest

16.056 Where disputes arise as to the administration of an estate, the court has power to order personal representatives to account under CPR 64 (which replaces RSC, Order 85 in its entirety) and can also order the payment of interest. Under RSC Ord 44 r.10 interest ordered by the court was normally at six per cent per annum. Under the CPR, PD40, para.15 interest is *"at such rate as the court shall direct"*.

This change in the rules on the rate of interest makes life a little difficult for personal representatives administering estates out of court. In the past it was thought that the rate of interest paid by personal representatives should follow the rate ordered by the court unless there were special circumstances. There is now no fixed rate and, therefore, nothing for personal representatives to follow. This makes it more important for testators to consider including provision for payment of interest in the will. Where there is no such provision, personal representatives may wish to agree a rate of interest with pecuniary legatees and residuary beneficiaries.

Time for payment

16.057 In the absence of any direction to the contrary from the testator, the general rule is that a legacy is payable one year from the testator's death (this period is sometimes referred to as the executor's year). It may well be impossible to pay a legacy at the end of the year because of problems with the administration. If the legacy is not paid by the end of that period the legatee becomes entitled to interest from that date.

A testator may specify that a legacy is to be paid at a particular date; for example "£2,000 to X to be paid immediately after my death" in which case interest will be payable from the date specified. Similarly, if a testator directs that a legacy is contingent on the happening of an event or is deferred until a future date interest will be payable not from the end of the executor's year but from the date of the specified event or the future date. However, if a testator directs that a contingent or deferred legacy be severed from the rest of the estate and set aside for the benefit of the legatee it will carry interest from the end of the executor's year.

Four special cases when interest is paid from death

16.058 There are four exceptional cases when a pecuniary legacy (or general legacy or demonstrative legacy if the designated fund has been exhausted) carries interest from the date of death.

(a) *Satisfaction of a debt.* A legacy to a creditor which is to satisfy a debt carries interest from the date of the death unless the will fixes a later date for payment.

(b) *Legacy charged on realty.* For historical reasons a vested legacy charged on realty carries interest from the date of death, unless the testator fixed a later date for payment.

(c) *Legacy to a testator's minor child.* If a testator gives a legacy to his minor child or to a minor to whom he is *in loco parentis* the legacy carries interest from the date of death. The rule is an old one designed to provide maintenance for the child; if, therefore, any other fund is designated for its maintenance, the legacy will not carry interest.

Moreover, the rule only applies where the legacy is given to the child directly; interest is not payable from death if the legacy is given to trustees to hold for the child (*Re Pollock* (1943)).

Interest is payable from death if the legacy is contingent on the child reaching full age or marrying earlier but it is probably not so payable if the contingency has no reference to the child's minority (for example reaching an age greater than majority).

(d) *Legacy to a minor with intention to provide maintenance.* If a testator gives a legacy to any minor (not necessarily the testator's own child or a person to whom the testator is *in loco parentis*) and shows an intention to provide for the minor's maintenance it carries interest from death unless the will designates some other fund for maintenance. Unlike the previous rule interest will be carried from death by a legacy contingent on reaching an age greater than majority.

Will drafting
A person who is drafting a will may prefer to make express provision for the payment of interest rather than leaving personal representatives and beneficiaries to rely on these rather technical rules.   **16.059**

Options to purchase
A will may give someone the right to purchase an asset of the estate. If the will is silent, the asset is valued at market value at the date of death. See *Re Bliss* (2001). An open market valuation differs from a probate valuation in that it takes into account matters such as a right of occupation granted by will which a probate valuation would ignore. *Re Bliss* also decided that the valuation should not take into account events subsequent to death unless the will directed otherwise. In *Re Bliss* the option to purchase was subject to the right of the deceased's husband to occupy part of the property. A few months after the death and before the option had been exercised, he moved out and indicated that he would not return. The valuation was still to be carried out subject to his right to occupy.

Re Bowles (2003) held that time for the exercise of an option will not be of the essence where the will contains no prescribed consequences for failure to act in time. The testator's will gave a beneficiary the right to buy part of a farm at the amount agreed between the executors and the Capital Taxes Office. He had to be informed of this right within six months of the testator's death and then had three months to decide whether he wanted to exercise the option. Almost three years after the death agreement had still not been reached with the Capital Taxes Office. The court held that the time limits were directory in nature and that the beneficiary was entitled to wait until the price was ascertainable. From then he would have a reasonable time to exercise the option. To have found that the time limits were mandatory might have defeated the testator's intention.

17.   Construction of Wills

Entire books have been written on the principles governing the **17.001**
construction of wills. One chapter can do no more than give a very brief
introduction to some of the more important principles involved.

Questions of construction are dealt with by the Chancery Division.

A. The Object of the Court is to Ascertain the Testator's Expressed Intention

1. The basic rule

The object of the court is to ascertain the testator's intention *as expressed* **17.002**
in the will. In other words the court is simply concerned to determine the
meaning of the words written; it will not speculate or conjecture as to what
the testator's "real" intention may have been. Thus, in *Re Rowland* (1963)
a testator made a will leaving all his property to his wife but in the event of
her death "preceding or coinciding" with his own everything was to go to
his brother. The testator and his wife were declared dead after a boat on
which they were sailing disappeared. The wife was the younger and was,
therefore, presumed to have survived her husband. The court declared
that the substitutional gift to the brother could not take effect as there was
no evidence that the wife's death had preceded or coincided with her
husband's; she might have survived him. The husband might well have
"really" intended his brother to take in such circumstances but the court
was not at liberty to speculate. "The will must be in writing and that
writing only must be considered." (*Per* Harman L.J.) Similarly in *Re Jones*
(1998) the will gave the testatrix's whole estate to her son with a gift to two
nephews if the son predeceased. The son killed the testatrix and so the gift
to him was forfeited (see para.16.038). The Court of Appeal held that as
the son had not predeceased, the nephews could not take. The Court
could not speculate as to what the testatrix would have wanted in these
circumstances.

Where the wording of a gift is too vague to be given a specific meaning
the court cannot rewrite the gift which, therefore, fails for uncertainty
(see paras 16.029–16.031).

2. Ordinary words given their ordinary meaning

If the words used in the will are clear and unambiguous, it is not possible **17.003**
for the court to attribute to them meanings they do not normally bear in
order to produce a result which is thought to be more in accordance with
the testator's intentions. If, however, such an interpretation gives rise to

some obvious absurdity or is manifestly inconsistent with the will read as a whole, the sense of such words may be modified or extended so far as is necessary to avoid the consequences but no further. The mere fact that a disposition seems rather strange is not sufficient to justify departing from the ordinary meaning of words.

Some words have several meanings in which case the court must try and determine in what sense the testator used the word. "Money" is a good example of such a word since it can mean merely notes or coins, can include money "in the bank" or can be used loosely to cover assets in general. The House of Lords in *Perrin v Morgan* (1943) took the view that the word was capable of having a very wide meaning indeed and that courts should carefully consider the context before attributing a narrow meaning to the word (particularly if the result of such an interpretation would be to leave a large part of the estate undisposed).

3. TECHNICAL WORDS MUST BE GIVEN THEIR TECHNICAL MEANING

17.004   If a testator uses a technical word or expression, for example "my realty" or "my personalty", such an expression must be given its technical meaning unless the will shows a *very* clear intention to use it in a different sense. Thus, in *Re Cook* (1948) a testatrix in a home-made will left "all my personal estate" to X, there were no other gifts in the will and the greater part of her estate consisted of realty. Harman J. held that the expression "personal estate" was a technical one and must be given its technical meaning despite the fact that doing so meant that the bulk of the testatrix's property passed on intestacy.

In *D'Abo v Paget (No. 1)* (2001) a will left property to A for life then on trust absolutely "for the child or other issue of [A] who if the devolution of the said property . . . had been subject to limitations in strict settlement [to A] and his issue would have taken on the death of [A]". The court held that the use of the words "child or issue" showed that a gift to one person was intended and so the elder daughter alone would take even though strict settlements normally divide the estate between daughters as tenants in common.

4. THE DICTIONARY PRINCIPLE

17.005   A testator is free to show that words used in the will are used in an unusual way. This may be done expressly, by including a definition clause; for example, a testator may say that wherever he refers to "my monkey" he means "my son". It is more likely, however, that the will as a whole may suggest that an unusual meaning is attached to one word. Thus, in *Re Lowe* (1890) a testator made a gift "to all my children, apart from X". (X was illegitimate.) At that time the word "children" did not include illegitimate children unless the testator indicated that he wanted it to do so. It was held that the specific exclusion of X indicated that the testator regarded the word "children" as including illegitimate ones, so that all the testator's illegitimate children, apart from X, could take.

5. RECTIFICATION OF A WILL

Section 20 of the Administration of Justice Act 1982 provides that "if a **17.006** court is satisfied that a will is so expressed that it fails to carry out the testator's intentions, in consequence:

(a) of a clerical error; or
(b) of a failure to understand his instructions,

it may order that the will shall be rectified so as to carry out his intentions".

A fuller discussion of this provision is contained in para.2.031.

B. Extrinsic Evidence

1. THE GENERAL RULE

The general rule is that the court construes the words written in the will **17.007** and will not admit extrinsic evidence of the testator's intention. However there are certain circumstances where extrinsic evidence is admissible. The first three are long established; the others were introduced by the Administration of Justice Act 1982.

2. WHERE THE WORDS USED ARE NOT APT TO FIT THE SURROUNDING CIRCUMSTANCES

This is sometimes referred to as "the armchair principle". "You may place **17.008** yourself, so to speak, in [the testator's] armchair, and consider the circumstances by which he was surrounded when he made his will to assist you in arriving at his intention," *per* James L.J., *Boyes v Cook* (1880). An illustration of this rule is *Thorn v Dickens* (1906) where the testator left "all to mother" but did not have a mother living at the time he made his will; extrinsic evidence of the testator's circumstances was admitted to show that he was in the habit of calling his wife "mother" with the result that she was able to take. Similarly, in *Re Fish* (1893) the testator left property to "my niece, Eliza Waterhouse" but did not have a niece of that name; extrinsic evidence was admitted to show that his wife had a great-niece of that name and it was found that the testator had used the word "niece" in a wide sense so that the great-niece was able to take the gift. In both these cases there was no-one who fitted the description used in the will. If there had been (for example, if in *Thorn v Dickens* the testator's mother had been alive at the time the will was made) no extrinsic evidence could have been admitted and the apparent beneficiary would have taken. Declarations made by the testator as to his intention are not admissible; only evidence *of the surrounding circumstances* is admissible.

3. WHERE THERE IS A LATENT AMBIGUITY

A latent ambiguity is one which does not become apparent until an **17.009** attempt is made to give effect to the dispositions in the will. Thus, if a testator makes a gift of "my motor car" and it turns out that at the time of the will, he owned six cars or, if a testator makes a gift to "my nephew, John Jones" and it turns out that he had several so named, extrinsic evidence *including evidence of declarations made by the testator* as to his intention will be admitted to show which car was intended to be the subject-matter of the gift or which nephew was intended to benefit. If there is no evidence available the whole gift will fail for uncertainty.

An example of a latent ambiguity in *Re Jackson* (1933). The testator made a gift "to my nephew, Arthur Murphy"; he had one illegitimate nephew and two legitimate nephews of that name. At that time illegitimate relationships were ignored unless the will showed a contrary intention. Therefore, had there been only one legitimate nephew that nephew would have fitted the description and would have taken the gift (even if there had been evidence that the testator's *intention* was that that person should not take). However, as there were two such nephews there was a latent ambiguity and extrinsic evidence, including evidence of the testator's intention, was admitted. This evidence showed that, in fact, the testator had intended to refer to the illegitimate nephew and he, therefore, took the gift.

4. To rebut a presumption of equity

17.010 In certain circumstances equity raises presumptions; for example, that a legacy from a father (or person *in loco parentis*) to his child will be adeemed if the father (or person *in loco parentis*) after the date of the will gives the child an *inter vivos* portion. These presumptions may be rebutted by extrinsic evidence (including evidence of declarations made by the testator as to his intention).

5. The administration of justice act 1982

17.011 In the case of deaths occurring after December 31, 1982, s.21 provides that extrinsic evidence *including evidence of declarations as to the testator's intention* may be admitted to assist in the interpretation of a will in so far as:

(a) any part of it is meaningless,
(b) the language used in any part of it is ambiguous on the face of it,
(c) evidence other than evidence of the testator's intention shows that the language used in any part of it is ambiguous in the light of the surrounding circumstances.

An example of subsection (b) is a gift of "my money" or "my effects".

Paragraph (c) appears to have extended the existing rules on extrinsic evidence in two ways. First, evidence of surrounding circumstances (though not direct evidence of the testator's intention) can now be admitted to *raise the possibility* that an ambiguity exists, whereas, prior to the 1982 Act, evidence could only be admitted where the words did not fit the surrounding circumstances. Thus, where a testator makes a gift to "my niece, Ann" it would now be possible to admit evidence to show that, although the testator had only one niece called Ann, there was a niece of his spouse also called Ann. Secondly, it is now possible to admit direct evidence of the testator's intention in cases other than latent ambiguity.

In a helpful judgment (*Re Williams, Deceased* (1985)), Nicholls J. stated the principles to be applied when considering the admissibility of extrinsic evidence. He reminded practitioners that the section is merely *an aid* to construction. Thus, evidence may be admitted to show which of several possible meanings a testator was applying to a particular word or phrase (for example "my money", "my effects"). The meaning may be one which without the evidence would not have been at all apparent but so long as the word or phrase is *capable* of bearing that meaning in its context this does not matter. However, it may be that the extrinsic evidence reveals a meaning attached by the testator to a word or phrase which no matter how liberal the approach of the court, the word or phrase cannot bear. The court will not allow extrinsic evidence to vary or contradict the language used in the will since this would amount to rewriting the will for the testator and this can only be done, if at all, under the rectification provisions.

C. The Will Speaks from Death

1. Section 24 of the wills act 1837

Section 24 provides that as regards property every will shall be construed **17.012** "to speak and take effect as if it had been executed immediately before the death of the testator, unless a contrary intention shall appear by the will". Thus, a gift of "the contents of my house" will pass the contents owned at the date of death, not merely those owned at the date of the will.

2. Contrary intention

A will may expressly state that the testator is giving an asset owned at the **17.013** date of the will. In the absence of an express statement, certain words and expressions are commonly found to show contrary intention.

"My"

If the testator couples the word "my" with a gift of a specific item (for **17.014** example, "my piano") it is possible that the court will construe the gift as a gift of the particular piano owned at the date of the will. Therefore, if the piano is sold or destroyed after the date of the will the gift is adeemed and cannot pass a piano purchased later and owned at the date of the death. However, if the word "my" is coupled with a description of property capable of increase or decrease (for example "all my shares") there is no contrary intention and the gift will pass any shares owned at the time of death.

"Now" or "at present"

The use of such words will be taken as showing a contrary intention (that **17.015** is, as referring to the date the will is made) if they are an essential part of the description. Thus, in *Re Edwards* (1890) the testator made a gift of "my house and premises where I now reside". After the date of the will he let a part of the property. The court held that the word "now" indicated a contrary intention so that the whole of the property occupied at the time the will was made (including the part subsequently let) passed to the beneficiary, not merely the part occupied at the date of the death.

If, however, the words are regarded as mere additional or superfluous description which has simply become inaccurate by the date of the will the court is unlikely to find that they show a contrary intention. In *Re Willis* (1911) a testator gave "all my freehold house and premises situated at X and known as Y and in which I now reside". After the date of the will he acquired two further plots of land which he enjoyed with the original house. The court held that there was no contrary intention so that the gift was to be construed at the date of death; thus the additional plots were included.

3. SECTION 24 HAS NO APPLICATION TO PEOPLE

17.016 Section 24 only applies to property; as regards people a will is construed at the date it is made (unless there is a contrary intention).

A gift made "to the eldest son of A" is construed as a gift to the person fulfilling that description at the date the will is made. If that person predeceases the testator the gift fails and does not pass to the eldest *surviving* son.

It is important to remember that where a will is republished it is construed as if made at the date of the republication.

If a testator makes a gift to a beneficiary who fulfils a particular description (for example "the wife of X") and to the testator's knowledge no-one fulfils that description at the date of the will the court will construe the gift as one made to the first person to fulfil the description. Once a person has fulfilled the description the gift is construed as a gift to that person even if the description later becomes inaccurate; thus, if in the previous example X and his wife were divorced after the date of the will she would still be entitled to the gift on Y's death, even if X had remarried.

D. Property Subject to a General Power of Appointment

1. GENERAL AND SPECIAL POWERS OF APPOINTMENT

17.017 Instead of making an outright gift of property to a named beneficiary, a testator may give one person a power to appoint property to others. The power may be entirely unlimited, so that the appointer can appoint to anyone, in which case it is referred to as a "general" power, or the power may be limited, so that the appointer can appoint only amongst certain specific people (for example the children of X), in which case it is referred to as a "special" power of appointment.

A person with a general power of appointment is free to deal with the property exactly as he pleases and is therefore for many purposes treated as the owner of the property subject to the general power of appointment. For example, if a person exercises such a power by will, the property subject to the power is available for payment of the deceased's debts. (See Chapter 15.)

2. METHOD OF EXERCISING A GENERAL POWER OF APPOINTMENT

A testator may make an express appointment by will but this is not **17.018** essential. Section 27 of the Wills Act provides that, where a testator has a general power of appointment exercisable by will, it can be exercised by any general devise or bequest without the necessity for an express reference to the power. A general devise or bequest is one where the subject-matter is described in a general manner, for example "all my leasehold land", "all my land in Hampshire" or "all my shares". If property subject to a general power is to pass under the terms of such a gift, it must correspond to the general description.

Section 27 is subject to contrary intention. However, the court will not readily find such an intention. Thus in *Re Jarrett* (1919) the fact that the testator had made an express appointment in the will which failed was found not to show a contrary intention and the subject-matter of the power passed as part of the residue.

The section does not apply if the terms of a general power of appointment require an express reference to the power or the property. Special powers of appointment are not covered by the section and therefore need to be expressly exercised (unless the terms of the power provide otherwise).

E. Special Rules Relating to Children

1. ADOPTED CHILDREN

The Adoption Act 1976 applies to any adoption order made by a court in **17.019** the United Kingdom, the Isle of Man or the Channel Islands and to certain foreign adoptions. It provides that when construing the will of a testator who dies after December 31, 1975:

(a) an adopted child is to be treated as the legitimate child of the married couple who adopt it or, if the adoption is by one person, as the legitimate child of that one person (but not as a child of any actual marriage of that person); and

(b) an adopted child is to be treated as if it were not the child of any person other than the adopting parent(s).

It is immaterial whether the adoption order is made before or after the testator's death. For example, if T gives property "to A for life, remainder to the children of A" any child adopted by A, whether before or after T's death, will be entitled to share in the gift, unless there is any contrary intention shown.

Where a disposition by will depends on the date of birth of a child or children the disposition is to be construed, in the absence of contrary intention, as if:

(a) the adopted child had been born on the date of the adoption; and

(b) two or more children adopted on the same date had been born on that date in the order of their actual births.

Example

T makes one gift "to the children of A living at my death" and one gift "to the children of A born after my death". T dies in 2006 and after T's death A adopts a child who was born in 2004. This child is treated as born on the date of the adoption and is therefore not a child living at T's death and cannot take under the first gift. However, it is a child born after T's death and can take under the second gift.

It is expressly provided that these rules do not affect any reference to the *age* of a child. Thus, if T gives property "to the first child of A to reach age 25" and A has a natural child born in 1978 and an adopted child adopted in 1980 at age 12, it is the adopted child who will reach age 25 first and be entitled to the gift. A gift to "the eldest child of A" would probably not be construed as containing a reference to an age so that the general rule would be applied; thus, the adopted child would be treated as born on the date of the adoption and therefore as being younger than the natural child.

2. Children whose parents were not married

17.020 In any will or codicil made after April 4, 1988 references to relationships are construed without regard to "whether or not the father and mother of either [person], or the father and mother of any person through whom the relationship is deduced, have or had been married to each other at any time" (Family Law Reform Act 1987, s.1(1)). Thus a gift "to my children" includes both legitimate and illegitimate children. A gift "to my grandchildren" includes all the testator's children's children regardless of whether the testator was married at any time and regardless of whether his children were married at any time. The will may show a contrary intention should the testator so wish.

In the case of wills and codicils made after December 31, 1969 and before April 4, 1988, the Family Law Reform Act 1969, s.15 applies. This makes provision the effect of which is similar, in most respects, to the 1987 Act.

F. Class Gifts

1. The class closing rules

Necessity for such rules

17.021 A class gift is a gift of property to be divided amongst persons fulfilling a general description (for example "the children of A", "the children of A who reach 18"). The size of any individual's share will depend upon the number of persons who fulfil the description. This makes distributing the property difficult since until A dies it is always possible that the number of persons fulfilling the description will increase. Personal representatives would, therefore, have to wait till A's death before giving any child a share in the property.

To avoid this inconvenient result, certain rules of construction known as "the class closing rules" have been developed; the effect of the rules is to close a class at an artificially early date in order to allow earlier distribution. Beneficiaries who are born after the class has closed lose their entitlement; the unfairness that this may cause is thought to be outweighed by the convenience of allowing early distribution. However, if a testator does not want the class to close early the rules can always be expressly excluded (subject to the rules against perpetuity). Clear words should be used to exclude the rules. An example of sufficiently clear wording is "to the children of A *whenever born*".

The precise details of the rules vary according to the type of gift (immediate, deferred or contingent) but the principle is that the class closes as soon as there is one beneficiary entitled to immediate distribution.

Throughout this section the word "living" includes a child *en ventre sa mere*.

Immediate class gifts

An example of such a gift is "to the children of A". If there is any child of A living at the date of the testator's death the class closes and the personal representatives distribute to the class members then in existence (*Viner v Francis* (1789)). No child born after the class has closed can take any interest. If there are no children living at that date, there is no class closing rule applicable and the class will remain open until A dies.   **17.022**

Deferred class gift

An example of such a gift is "to X for life remainder to the children of A". In this case the property cannot be distributed while X is alive and the class, therefore, remains open until X dies. It will include any children living at the testator's death and any children born thereafter and before the death of X. If any such child dies before the property is actually distributed, his share will be paid to his estate. No child born after the class has closed can take any interest. If there were no children living at the testator's death and none born before X's death, there is no class closing rule applicable and the class will remain open until the death of A.   **17.023**

Contingent class gift

An example of such a gift is "to the children of A who reach 18". If any child has reached 18 when the testator dies, the class closes at that date and will include any child living at that date who reaches the age of 18. If a child dies without fulfilling the contingency his "share" is divided amongst the other members of the class who fulfil the contingency. If no child has reached 18 at the date of the testator's death, the class remains open until a child reaches 18 and will include any child living at that date who reaches 18. Again if any child dies without fulfilling the contingency his "share" is divided amongst any others who do fulfil the contingency. No child born after the class has closed can take any interest.   **17.024**

Deferred and contingent class gifts

17.025 An example of such a gift would be "to X for life, remainder to the children of A who reach 18". In this case the property cannot be distributed whilst X is alive and the class, therefore, remains open until X's death. It will close at X's death if any child living at the testator's death has reached 18 and will include any children living at the testator's death or born since who reach 18. If any child, living at the testator's death, reaches 18 but dies before distribution the class closes on X's death and the share of the deceased child is paid to his estate. If no member of the class has reached 18 at the time of X's death the class remains open until the first child reaches 18. No child born after the class has closed can take any interest.

2. ACCELERATION OF THE DATE FOR CLOSING A CLASS

17.026 If there is a postponed class gift (for example "to X for life, remainder to the children of Y") it may happen that the prior interest fails, perhaps because the life tenant predeceases the testator or because the gift to the life tenant is void. In such a case the gift to the class is accelerated so that it is treated as an immediate class gift. The class will, therefore, close at the testator's death (if there are any members then living) and any later born children will be excluded (*Re Johnson* (1893)).

A life tenant may wish to disclaim or surrender the life tenancy and the question then arises of whether one person can by voluntarily dealing with his own interest affect the membership of the class. In *Re Davies* (1957) Vaisey J. held that where a life tenant disclaimed, the gift to the class would be accelerated and would close immediately thereby excluding any later born members. However, the decision has been criticised as not reflecting the probable wishes of a testator; Goff J. refused to follow it in *Re Harker's Will Trusts* (1969) and held that where a life tenant surrendered her life interest the class would remain open until her death.

3. GIFTS OF A SPECIFIED AMOUNT TO PERSONS FULFILLING A DESCRIPTION

17.027 If a testator gives "£1,000 to each of the children of A", it is not a class gift since the amount each child is to receive does not vary according to the number of persons fulfilling the description. However, problems arise in distributing such a gift and these problems are similar to the problems which arise in connection with class gifts. The number of persons fulfilling the description may increase at any time before A's death and so the personal representatives cannot know how much money they should retain to cover the possibility of future children being born. In order that the personal representatives should be able to complete the distribution without difficulty, there is a rule of construction which provides, in the absence of a contrary intention, that only persons who are alive at the testator's death can take; if there is no-one alive at that date fulfilling the description, the entire gift fails. This is a drastic rule but it enables the personal representatives to distribute the estate without having to worry about retaining assets to cover a possible future liability.

4. CLASS GIFTS TO CHILDREN OF THE TESTATOR WHO PREDECEASE

Normally a person who predeceases the testator can take no benefit **17.028** under a class gift. Section 33 of the Wills Act 1837 as substituted by Administration of Justice Act 1982, s.19 provides that, in the absence of contrary intention, where a class gift is made to children or remoter issue *of the testator* and a member of the class predeceases the testator leaving issue who survive the testator, the issue take *per stirpes* the share which their parent would have taken (see para.16.025).

G. Deciding Whether a Gift is Absolute or Limited

1. SECTION 22 OF THE ADMINISTRATION OF JUSTICE ACT 1982

Testators who draft wills without professional advice sometimes give **17.029** property to X and then direct that on X's death what remains should pass to Y. This is because non-lawyers often think that it is possible to give the rights of an absolute owner to persons in succession. The effect of such an attempt depends on the precise words used in the will but may be construed in any of the following ways:

(a) an absolute gift to X, the gift over to Y failing, either as a trust which is void for uncertainty, or because it is repugnant to X's absolute interest;
(b) a life interest to X, with remainder to Y absolutely;
(c) a life interest to X, with remainder to Y absolutely but subject to X's power to dispose of the capital *inter vivos*.

Section 22 of the Administration of Justice Act 1982 introduces a presumption where a testator gives property to his *spouse* in terms which would in themselves give an absolute interest but by the same instrument purports to give *his issue* an interest in the same property, the gift to the spouse is presumed to be absolute despite the purported gift to issue. The presumption applies in the case of deaths occurring after December 31, 1982.

This section solves the problem of unintended life interests in the case of gifts to spouses and issue but problems still remain where such a gift is made to persons other than spouses.

2. THE RULE IN LASSENCE V TIERNEY

This rule attempts to reconcile inconsistent provisions in a will. "If you **17.030** find an absolute gift to a legatee in the first instance and trusts are engrafted or imposed on the absolute interest *which fail* either from lapse or invalidity or any other reason, then the absolute gift takes effect so far as the trusts have failed, to the exclusion of the residuary legatee or next of kin, as the case may be." (*Hancock v Watson* (1902).) The rule imputes to T an intention that the absolute gift be modified only so far as is necessary to give effect to the trusts.

Example

T gives property to A absolutely and later in the will directs that the property given to A absolutely is to pass, after A's death, to the children of B. If B dies without children, A (or A's estate) will be entitled to the capital.

The difficulty in such cases is deciding whether or not there was an absolute initial gift. It is comparatively simple to find such a gift where the testator makes the absolute gift in the will and engrafts the trust in a later codicil or where, as in the previous example, there is an absolute gift followed by a later clause engrafting the trust but difficult questions of construction will arise where a series of gifts is made in one continuous sentence.

18. Completing the Administration

Once the personal representatives have paid all the debts and liabilities of **18.001**
the estate they must vest the available assets in the beneficiaries who are
entitled to them and must prepare an account to show the amount of
residue available to the residuary beneficiaries.

A. Assents

1. POSITION OF BENEFICIARIES BEFORE ASSENT

As we saw in paras 11.024–11.027 a beneficiary (with the possible **18.002**
exception of a specific beneficiary) under a will or a person entitled under
the intestacy rules has no legal or equitable proprietary interest in any
asset comprised in the estate. He has merely a chose in action in the estate
(*i.e.* the right to have the deceased's estate properly administered) and he
only obtains rights to assets when the personal representatives indicate by
means of an assent that these assets are not required for the purposes of
the administration.

2. ASSENTS IN RESPECT OF PURE PERSONALTY

Where there is a will
An executor (and probably an administrator with the will annexed) **18.003**
passes title to pure personalty by means of an assent. An assent is an
indication from the personal representative that a particular asset is not
required for the purposes of the administration. It is not required to be in
particular form; it can be oral (for example where a personal
representative tells a beneficiary that his legacy is ready for collection) or
implied from conduct (for example where a personal representative
allows a beneficiary to take possession of an asset). The beneficiary
actually derives title from the will not from the assent; the effect of the
assent is merely to activate the gift in the will.

If particular formalities are required to transfer the legal title to an
asset, the assent cannot itself pass the legal title. In such a case once the
assent has been made the personal representative holds the asset as
trustee for the beneficiary until the appropriate formal requirements have
been complied with. Most choses in action require special formalities;
money in a Post Office Savings Bank, Trustee Savings Bank or National
Savings Certificates require withdrawal or transfer forms; company
shares require a share transfer. Although the personal representatives
may have themselves registered as members of a company, s.183 of the
Companies Act 1985 provides that unless the articles of the company

state otherwise a personal representative may transfer stocks and shares without being first registered. There are no formalities required by law to transfer money from a bank account; a letter of instruction should be sent to the bank manager together with an office copy of the grant of representation.

In the case of a specific legacy (but not a residuary or general legacy) the assent is retrospective to the date of death so that the legatee becomes entitled to income produced by the subject-matter of the gift since the testator's death. Thus, in *I.R.C. v Hawley* (1928) the personal representatives did not make an assent of company shares in favour of a specific legatee for nearly three years after the testator's death. It was held that, because an assent to a specific legacy is retrospective, once the assent had been made the Inland Revenue were entitled to assess the beneficiary to income tax on dividends which had been declared in the intervening years. Similarly, after assent a specific legatee is responsible for the costs of transferring the property. This includes costs of packing, delivering and insuring bulky or delicate chattels and the costs of obtaining a share transfer for company shares.

In *Re Clough-Taylor, Coutts & Co v Banks and Others* (2003) an asset specifically bequeathed had been taken by a third party who alleged that the deceased had given it to him during her lifetime. The court held that the executor has no duty to take anything other than normal or routine steps to collect in assets and deliver them to specific legatees. The specific legatee would have to bear the cost of any litigation to recover the asset. The court said it would be helpful—though not strictly necessary—for the executor to assign to the legatee any cause of action it had in relation to the chattel.

Many testators would prefer such costs to be paid from residue and it is, therefore, common for an express direction to this effect to be included in a will.

Where there is an intestacy

18.004   At common law an administrator had no power to assent in the case of an intestacy (Williams, *Law Relating to Assents*, p. 96). Section 36(1) of the Administration of Estate Act 1925 gives administrators as well as executors the power to make title to land (freehold or leasehold) by means of a written assent but it does not mention other property. Administrators must therefore pass title to other property by the method appropriate to the nature of the subject-matter. Chattels, money and bearer securities pass by delivery, shares, stock and debentures by transfer and most other choses in action by assignment.

3. ASSENTS IN RESPECT OF LAND

Administration of Estates Act 1925, s.36

18.005   In general a document which is to convey or create a legal estate in land must be a *deed* (Law of Property Act 1925, s.52(1)). However, as an exception to this rule, s.36(1) of the Administration of Estates Act gives personal representatives (both executors and administrators) power to *assent* to the vesting of any estate or interest in land (whether freehold or leasehold) in any person entitled (whether beneficially, as trustee or as personal representative of a deceased beneficiary who is entitled to property) *whether by devise, bequest, devolution, appropriation or otherwise*. An assent is a form of conveyance and becomes an essential link in the title of the assentee.

"*Devolution*" covers a person taking under the intestacy rules. The meaning of "*or otherwise*" presents some problems. The other words in the section all refer to transactions which a personal representative would be called upon to effect in the course of the administration of the estate. Probably therefore the words "or otherwise" should be construed *ejusdem generis* and should not be taken to cover any transaction which is not part of the administration; thus, if a personal representative is selling property or is asked by a beneficiary to transfer the property to a purchaser from the beneficiary the personal representative should not risk using an assent but should use a conveyance. There is in any event little advantage to using an assent in such a case for while it may be a rather shorter document, *ad valorem* stamp duty is payable on a sale whether an assent is used or whether a conveyance to the purchaser is used.

Form of assent

Section 36(4) of the Administration of Estates Act provides that "an assent shall be in writing, signed by the personal representative and shall name the person in whose favour it is given and shall operate to vest in that person the legal title to which it relates; and an assent which is not in writing or not in favour of a named person shall not be effectual to pass the legal estate". **18.006**

It is clear that an assent of land by a personal representative in favour of another person must comply with the requirements of s.36(4) if it is to pass the legal estate. According to Pennycuick J. in *Re King's Will Trusts* (1964) the same requirements must be complied with where a personal representative wishes to vest land in himself (whether beneficially or as trustee or as personal representative of another deceased). The reasoning of Pennycuick J. has been criticised by various writers (see R. R. A. Walker (1964) 80 L.Q.R. 328) but even if the criticisms are justified the provision of a signed, written assent by a personal representative in his own favour is hardly an onerous task and has the merit of avoiding any possible doubt or uncertainty.

It is important to remember that a personal representative is always free to convey land by means of a deed and will often choose to do so (for example, where indemnity covenants are required from the beneficiary).

The effect of an assent

Section 36(2) of the Administration of Estates Act provides that an assent relates back to the date of death of the deceased unless a contrary intention appears. This is unlike the position in respect of assents of personalty where only an assent to a specific legacy relates back. Thus, a specific or residuary devisee would appear to be entitled to any rents or profits produced by land from the date of death of the deceased. **18.007**

Protection of purchasers and beneficiaries

18.008   A person in whose favour an assent or conveyance is made may require that notice of the assent is endorsed on the grant of representation at the cost of the estate under s.36(5).

A purchaser will insist that a conveyance from personal representatives contains a statement that the personal representatives have not previously given or made any conveyance or assent in respect of the legal estate. If this statement is incorrect it cannot prejudice the title of any previous *purchaser*; but if there was a previous assent in favour of a *beneficiary* the purchaser will take the legal title in preference to that beneficiary if, and only if, there was no notice of the previous assent endorsed on the grant of representation *and* the purchaser accepted the conveyance on the faith of the statement in the conveyance (s.36(6)).

There is no point in such a statement being included in an assent in favour of a beneficiary since s.36(6)) only protects *purchasers*.

A purchaser has no right to examine a will to ascertain that land was assented to the person actually entitled. However, s.36(7) protects such a person by providing that in favour of a purchaser, unless notice of a previous assent or conveyance has been endorsed on the grant of representation, an assent or conveyance made by a personal representative is "sufficient evidence that the person in whose favour [it] is given is the person entitled to have the legal estate conveyed to him". The section only says that an assent is "sufficient" evidence not "conclusive" evidence; thus, if facts have come to the purchaser's knowledge before completion which indicate that the assent was in fact made in favour of the wrong person, the purchaser cannot rely on the assent (*Re Duce and Boots Cash Chemists (Southern) Ltd's Contract* (1937)).

Protection of personal representatives

18.009   A personal representative will not want to distribute assets until satisfied that all liabilities have been dealt with. Section 36(10) provides that personal representatives may, as a condition of giving an assent or making a conveyance, require security for the discharge of any duties, debts or liabilities to which the property is subject (for example, a mortgage debt or charge for inheritance tax). If reasonable arrangements have been made for discharging such liabilities, however, the personal representative cannot refuse to make the assent to a beneficiary entitled to the property.

If the personal representative is uncertain whether or not land will be required for the payment of liabilities he may under s.43 of the Administration of Estates Act allow a beneficiary to take possession of the land prior to the making of a formal assent. The personal representative can subsequently retake possession of the property and dispose of it if it becomes necessary in the course of the administration.

If the deceased owned land which was subject to covenants for breach of which the personal representatives will remain liable (for example where the deceased was an original lessee or where there have been indemnity covenants) the personal representatives will wish to protect themselves by obtaining an indemnity covenant from the beneficiary.

They will therefore have to use a deed when transferring the property to the beneficiary instead of merely an assent.

B. Personal Representative or Trustee

1. PERSONAL REPRESENTATIVE FOR LIFE

A personal representative retains office for life and is not discharged from **18.010** office even when all the debts and liabilities have been paid and all the assets distributed. If there are any subsequent accretions to the estate (for example if a debt which had been regarded as irrecoverable is paid to the estate or if someone dies leaving a legacy to the deceased which is saved from lapse by one of the exceptions to the doctrine of lapse) the personal representative must distribute such accretions and conversely if legal proceedings are brought or claims made against the estate the personal representatives must deal with them on behalf of the estate.

2. COMPARISON WITH TRUSTEES

A personal representative may be a trustee of property left by will or **18.011** passing under the intestacy rules. This may be because:

- (a) the testator expressly appointed the personal representative as trustee; or
- (b) the testator left property on trust but did not expressly appoint trustees; or
- (c) a trust arises under the intestacy rules (although there is some doubt as to whether administrators become trustees in such a case).

Even where a personal representative is not also a trustee there are certain similarities between personal representatives and trustees:

- (a) Personal representatives, like trustees, are in a fiduciary position. They must act with the utmost good faith and must not profit from their position.
- (b) The provisions of the Trustee Act 1925 apply equally to personal representatives where the context admits.

However, there are also important differences:

- (a) The function of a personal representative is to wind up the estate and distribute the assets, whereas the function of a trustee is to hold assets for the beneficiaries.
- (b) Executors (and probably administrators) have joint and several authority to deal with *personalty* (they must act jointly if they are to convey *land* although one personal representative can enter into a contract for sale binding on any other personal representatives *Fountain Forestry Ltd v Edwards* (1975)). Trustees must always act jointly.
- (c) A sole personal representative may give a good receipt for money for the sale of land whereas at least two trustees (or a

trust corporation) are required.

(d) The period of limitation is 12 years against a personal representative but only six years against a trustee.

(e) If a sole personal representative dies without having completed the administration there will either be transmission of office under the chain of executorship or a grant *de bonis non administratis* must be taken out by the person entitled under the Non-Contentious Probate Rules 1987. If, however, a sole or last surviving trustee dies the trust property devolves on the trustee's personal representatives.

(f) A trustee has power to appoint additional or substitutional trustees. A personal representative has normally no power to appoint additional or substitutional personal representatives (although a person entitled to administration may nominate another administrator in certain cases where two administrators are needed because of a minority or life interest).

(g) Personal representatives owe their duty to the estate as a whole, trustees to the individual beneficiaries (*Re Hayes Will Trusts* (1971)).

(h) When personal representatives transfer assets to a "legatee" there is no gain or loss for capital gains tax purposes. The legatee takes over the acquisition value of the personal representatives (together with any expenses of transfer). When a beneficiary of a trust becomes absolutely entitled as against the trustee there is a deemed disposal and may be a charge to capital gains tax. Where the will directs that the personal representatives are to hold on trust, the beneficiary may become absolutely entitled before the personal representatives have assented the assets to themselves as trustees. In such a case the beneficiary takes as legatee and not as trust beneficiary.

In view of such differences it is obviously important where a personal representative is also a trustee to ascertain at what point the personal representative ceases to hold assets as personal representative and starts to hold them as trustee.

3. Transition from Personal Representative to Trustee

Intestacy

18.012   Under the Administration of Estates Act 1925 undisposed of property may have to be held on trust either for a spouse for life or on the statutory trusts until a beneficiary achieves a vested interest. There is some doubt as to whether administrators on intestacy ever become trustees in the true sense or whether they continue to hold property as administrators. The better view would seem to be that they do not become trustees. However, Romer J. in the case of *Re Yerburgh* (1928) stated that administrators become trustees as soon as all liabilities have been discharged and the amount of residue to be held on trust has been ascertained. Romer J. went on to state that the administrators ought to mark the moment when residue was ascertained by making an assent to the property vesting in themselves as trustees. It is unclear whether the judge meant that the assent was essential in order to vest the property in the administrators in their capacity as trustees or whether he meant that the assent was merely desirable in practice in order to indicate that the change in capacity had occurred, the change occurring automatically once the residue was ascertained.

Where the will does not appoint the personal representative as trustee
In the case of a specific legacy, once personal representatives have indicated by means of an assent that an asset is not required for payment of debts the asset is held on trust for the specific beneficiary (*Re Grosvenor* (1916)).   **18.013**

In the case of residue the position is rather unclear. In *Harvell v Foster* (1954) the Court of Appeal stated that the personal representatives remain liable in their capacity as such for the residue of the estate until it is vested in the beneficiary entitled. If the vesting is delayed (as it may be for example where the beneficiary is a minor and cannot give a good receipt) liability as a personal representative will continue and the personal representatives will not become trustees.

It is difficult to see why, if *Re Yerburgh* is correct, there should be a conversion to trustees in the case of intestacy but not in a case where there is a will.

Where the will appoints the personal representative as trustee
If personal representatives are directed to hold residue on trust there is some authority for saying that as soon as liabilities are discharged and the residue ascertained the personal representatives automatically start to hold the property in their capacity as trustees (*Re Cockburn's Will Trusts* (1957)). However, the position is far from clear and there are dicta in *Attenborough v Solomon* (1913) which suggest that the change does not take place automatically but only when the personal representatives assent the property to themselves in their capacity as trustees.   **18.014**

An assent is certainly desirable since it will avoid any doubt as to whether or not a change in capacity has occurred.

C. Receipts and Discharges

1. INTRODUCTION

A beneficiary discharges a personal representative from liability by means of a receipt signed by the beneficiary. A residuary beneficiary normally signs the estate accounts.   **18.015**

2. PECUNIARY LEGACIES

It used to be common for solicitors to ask pecuniary legatees, who wished to receive their legacies in the form of a cheque sent through the post, to sign a receipt in advance. The Law Society's Land Law and Succession Committee considered this practice and on October 14, 1992 stated in the *Gazette* that it considered that: **18.016**

"... it is no longer reasonable or necessary for legatees and beneficiaries to be asked to sign receipts in advance of payment being made and that such a practice is bound to generate additional correspondence and thus to add unnecessarily to the cost of the administration of the estate."

Precedents for simple forms of receipt for the payment of pecuniary, specific and residuary legacies are available. However, solicitors may find it more convenient to ask the legatee or beneficiary to acknowledge receipt by signing and returning a duplicate copy of the letter accompanying the cheque. In any case, s.3 of the Cheques Act 1957 provides that:

"An unindorsed cheque which appears to have been paid by the banker on whom it is drawn is evidence of receipt by the payee of the sum payable by the cheque."

So far as residuary beneficiaries are concerned, the solicitor will normally send them copies of the estate accounts (already approved by the personal representatives). The Law Society's Committee recommends sending a cheque at the same time:

"... with a request that the beneficiaries acknowledge payment by signing a receipt either endorsed on the accounts or supplied separately and with the receipt to include, if needed, a discharge to the personal representatives."

Obviously, there may be cases where there has been ill feeling during the administration and the solicitor anticipates that the residuary beneficiary may be difficult. In such a case, the Committee recommends that:

"... residuary beneficiaries should be sent in advance copies of the approved accounts and be asked to sign a form of receipt and discharge to the personal representatives on the basis that they will be sent a cheque immediately upon the solicitors receiving the form back signed."

The following form of receipt is a Plain English redraft by Richard Oerton of the form originally produced by the Land Law and Succession Committee. It appeared in "Clarity".

"THE LATE ....

The estate accounts show the final sum due to me as £ ....

I approve the accounts and will accept that sum in full satisfaction of all my claims against the estate.

Please pay it by a crossed cheque in my favour and send it to me by post."

Although it is common to include a discharge to the personal representative in the form of a receipt, it could only be effective if the beneficiaries had been given full and accurate details of all dealings with the estate assets and liabilities.

3. Minors cannot give a good receipt for money

Unless the will provides otherwise, a minor cannot give a good receipt for **18.017**
money (*Re Somech* (1957)). A married minor can give a good receipt for
income but not for capital (Law of Property Act 1925, s.21). The parent or
guardian of a minor used not to be able to give a good receipt on behalf of
the minor without express provision in the will. However, the Children
Act 1989 has changed this. Section 5 provides that all parents with
parental responsibility have the same rights, powers and duties as
guardians appointed under the Children Act. These rights are set out in
s.3 and include "the right to receive or recover in his own name *for the
benefit of the child*, property of whatever description and wherever
situated, which the child is entitled to receive or recover".

There may be circumstances where the testator may not be happy to
allow the parent or guardian to receive the legacy. It does not appear that
the personal representatives would be entitled to withhold the legacy so
the best course would be to leave the legacy to trustees to hold for the
benefit of the minor.

Under the Administration of Estates Act 1925, s.42 personal
representatives have power where a minor is absolutely entitled to a
legacy to appoint a trust corporation or at least two individuals (and not
more than four) to hold the property on trust until the minor reaches 18.
The trustees can give the personal representatives a good receipt.
However, s.42 does not apply where the infant's interest is contingent (for
example on reaching 18). It does not appear that personal representatives
could make such an appointment if the parent or guardian of the minor
demanded the legacy.

D. The Equitable Rules of Apportionment

These rules exist to try to achieve fairness between tenants for life and **18.018**
remaindermen. If residuary personalty is left to persons in succession
there is an obligation under the rule in *Howe v Lord Dartmouth* (1802) to
sell wasting, hazardous, and unauthorised assets. Pending sale the tenant
for life is not entitled to the income from such assets since otherwise he
might obtain a benefit from the personal representatives' delay. Instead
he is entitled to interest at four per cent per annum on the value of the
assets. Any surplus income is treated as capital and invested in authorised
investments. This rule exists to protect remaindermen.

The rule in *Re Earl of Chesterfield's Trusts* (1883) exists to protect the
life tenant. There is an obligation to sell reversionary interests and other
non-income producing assets. There will inevitably be some delay before
such a sale can be effected and no income is earned during the period.
Therefore the proceeds of sale of such assets are not treated as exclusively
capital but are apportioned between capital and income under the rule in
the *Re Earl of Chesterfield's Trusts*.

Although these rules were originally developed to achieve fairness
between the life tenant and the remainderman they lead to extremely
complicated calculations and most professionally drawn wills exclude
them as a matter of course. Where, as is usually now the case, trustees

have wide powers of investment which include power to acquire wasting and non-income producing assets, such assets will be authorised investments and the Rules in *Howe v Lord Dartmouth* and *Re Earl of Chesterfield's Trusts* will have no application. There will, therefore, be no need to exclude them.

There is another type of equitable apportionment known as the *Rule in Allhusen v Whittell* (1867). This rule probably still applies. It is, therefore, advisable to exclude it in wills which create successive interests. This rule provides that where residue is left to persons in succession debts and other outgoings (such as legacies) are to be treated as paid partly from capital and partly from income accruing to that portion of capital during the period between the testator's death and the payment of the outgoings. The principle is that the life tenant is entitled to income from the net residue after payment of debts and other liabilities but not to income from those assets which are needed for the payment of debts and which, therefore, do not form part of the net residue.

Example
A leave will residue to L for life, remainder to R. The personal representatives wish to pay legacies of £11,000 one year after T's death. The estate has produced income at the rate of 10 per cent per annum. The legacies will be treated as paid with £10,000 of capital and £1,000 of income. Thus the net residuary estate will be reduced by £10,000 and the income of the estate will be reduced by £1,000.

Like the other equitable apportionments the rule exists to achieve fairness between life tenant and remainderman. It is, however, usually excluded in professionally drawn wills. If it is not excluded it will affect the capital and income accounts presented to the residuary beneficiaries. The Inland Revenue will ignore any apportionments effected under this rule and will assess the liability of the estate to income tax on all the trust income before apportionments.

E. The Legal Rules of Apportionment

18.019 As explained in para.16.053, income is treated as accruing on a daily basis under the common law rules of apportionment of interest and the Apportionment Act 1870. Thus, income received after death must be apportioned if it relates to a period part of which falls before and part of which falls after death.

Most professionally drawn wills exclude the need for such apportionments. If the will creates a trust in favour of a life tenant the need for apportionments should be expressly excluded on the life tenant's death as well as on the testator's death.

Even if the will does exclude the need for apportionments, the exclusion is only effective for *distribution* purposes. Apportionments will still have to be made to calculate the value of the estate at death for *inheritance tax purposes* (see para.4.019). Moreover, when calculating the liability of the estate to *income tax* no apportionments are made no matter what the will says; any income which is payable after death is treated as income of the estate and not of the deceased even though part or all of the income may be attributable to a period falling before death (however, as we saw in Chapter 6 there is an income tax relief available where income has been apportioned and charged to inheritance tax). The position is rather different on the death of a life tenant of a trust. For income tax purposes the Inland Revenue will follow the terms of the trust instrument. If that does not exclude the need for apportionment of income on the death of a life tenant the income tax liability will be apportioned between the life tenant's estate and the person next entitled but if it does exclude the need for apportionment, tax on all income payable after death will be treated as the liability of the person next entitled.

F. Accounts

1. THE PURPOSE OF ACCOUNTS

The personal representatives will prepare a variety of accounts for different purposes. At an early stage of the administration they must complete an Inland Revenue Account (unless the estate is an "excepted estate" in which case no Account is required). They will also keep records of any income of the estate so that any income tax liability of the estate can be calculated.   **18.020**

In addition, before the personal representatives can complete the administration they must produce estate accounts for the residuary beneficiaries. The purpose of such accounts is to list all the assets of the estate, all the debts, liabilities and expenses that have been paid, all the legacies that have been paid and then to show the balance which is available for distribution to the residuary beneficiaries. The personal representatives will also show how the entitlement of each residuary beneficiary is to be paid. Thus, if the personal representatives propose to pay part of the entitlement in cash and to transfer assets *in specie* to make up the balance this must be explained. The residuary beneficiaries signify their approval of the accounts by signing them and acknowledging receipt of any amount due. This discharges the personal representatives from liability (see para.18.021).

2. THE FORM OF THE ACCOUNTS

There are no rules as to the form of estate accounts. However, they *must* be clear and easy to understand since their purpose is to convey information to the residuary beneficiaries. An account may be prepared vertically showing assets less liabilities or as a double sided account showing receipts on one side and payments on the other.   **18.021**

An account normally commences with a narrative which sets out such matters as the date of death of the deceased, the date of the grant of representation, a summary of the dispositions made in the will (or of the effect of the intestacy rules), the value of the gross and net estate and any other information relevant to the administration (for example, whether any interim payments have already been made to the residuary beneficiaries, whether it is proposed to transfer assets *in specie* to the residuary beneficiaries). The purpose of such a narrative is to make the account more intelligible to the beneficiaries. In order to cut down the amount included on the account details of investments may be relegated to separate schedules.

It is usual, except in the case of very small estates, to divide the account into a capital account and an income account. Such a division is essential if a life interest has been created in the residue since one person will be entitled to capital and another to income.

If separate capital and income accounts are prepared it will be necessary, unless the need to apportion has been excluded, to make apportionments of any income received after death which is attributable partly to the period before and partly to the period after death. The former will be shown on the capital account as part of the residuary cash. The latter will be shown on the income account; if the income-producing asset was specifically bequeathed the income will pass to the specific beneficiary, if it was not it will pass as part of the residuary income.

18.022   If residuary personalty has been left to one person for life, remainder to another, equitable apportionments of certain types of income and of the proceeds of sale of certain types of asset may have to be made for *distribution* purposes. These were discussed in para.18.018 above. If such apportionments of income and capital are made they will obviously affect the entries made in the Estate Accounts. However, it is usual for professionally drawn wills to exclude the need for equitable apportionments.

A simple estate account is set out below.

MRS AMY TESTOR DECEASED

Mrs Amy Testor of the Restwell Nursing Home, Bognor Regis, died on January 4, 2003 at the age of 96.

Probate of her will was granted by the Principal Probate Registry on April 6, 2003 to her daughter, Miss Catherine Testor.

By her will Mrs Testor left £2,500 to each of her two grandchildren, Mr David Kay and Mrs Elizabeth Forbes. The residue was given after payment of debts, funeral, testamentary and other expenses and legacies to Mrs Briony Kay and Miss Catherine Testor. The will excluded the need to apportion income. The personal effects have been taken by Miss Catherine Testor in partial satisfaction of her entitlement at an agreed valuation of £410. Mrs Testor had made chargeable *inter vivos* transfers in the seven years before her death.

Capital Account

	£	£
Investwell Building Society account		181,500
Northern Crest Unit Trust		88,520
Current account		950
Cash in Hand		70
Personal effects—estimated value		410
GROSS ESTATE		271,450
Less debts and other expenses		
Funeral Expenses	1,450	
Solicitors' fees	520	
Arrears at Nursing Home	760	
Inheritance tax	8,000	
		(10,730)
NET ESTATE		260,720
Less Legacies		
Mr D. Kay	2,500	
Mrs E. Forbes	2,500	(5,000)
Residue available to beneficiaries		255,720
½ Mrs B. Kay	127,860	
½ Miss C. Testor	127,860	255,720

Income Account

	£	£
Income received since death		
Investwell Building Society	1,100	
Northern Crest Unit Trust	1,400	
		2,500
Less: Interest on bank loan taken		
out to pay inheritance tax		(100)
Income available to beneficiaries		2,400
½ Mrs B. Kay	1,200	
½ Miss C. Testor	1,200	
		2,400

Note:

Having calculated the entitlement of the two residuary beneficiaries to capital and income it would then, strictly speaking, be necessary to produce an account for each showing how their entitlement is to be made up. However, on these facts each will receive her entitlement in cash (apart from the personal effects valued at £410 which are to go to Catherine Testor) so that the preparation of additional accounts is not essential.

3. SIGNATURE OF THE ACCOUNTS

18.023 A receipt of a residuary beneficiary is normally given by signing the accounts. Such a receipt normally includes an indemnity, for example "I agree to accept the assets shown in full satisfaction of my entitlement and hereby discharge X as executor and indemnify him against all claims and demands". However, such a release and indemnity is only effective if the beneficiary had full knowledge of all the assets, accounts and dealings.

If a beneficiary persists in a refusal to approve accounts he may commence an administration action for examination of the accounts. If he does not, the personal representatives may pay the outstanding funds into court under the Trustee Act 1925, s.63 as amended by s.36(4), Sch. III of the Administration of Justice Act 1965. However, this involves the estate in extra expense and should not be done unless there is no satisfactory alternative. It will rarely be necessary since a recalcitrant beneficiary will not wish to be deprived of the estate assets indefinitely and will usually either approve the accounts or commence proceedings relatively quickly. If the reason that approval is not forthcoming is that a beneficiary is missing, the personal representatives may have taken steps earlier in the administration to obtain a "*Benjamin Order*"; if they have not they should consider either obtaining an indemnity from the other beneficiaries or obtaining insurance cover or retaining assets.

A residuary beneficiary who lacks mental capacity will be unable to approve the accounts. A receiver may have been appointed by the Court of Protection to deal with that person's affairs. In this case the personal representatives should inform the receiver of the entitlement and act in accordance with the receiver's directions. Provided the personal representatives act in accordance with the court's directions they will obtain a good discharge. If no receiver has been appointed an application should be made to the Court of Protection for the appointment of a receiver. Such an application is normally made by a close relative of the disabled beneficiary. The personal representatives will retain the assets pending the application. However, if the relatives are reluctant to make such application, the personal representatives will have to consider alternative arrangements such as payment into court under the Trustee Act 1925, s.63.

19.   Post-Mortem Alterations

A. Introduction

The persons entitled to a deceased person's property under the terms of **19.001** the will or under the intestacy rules may not need or want the property left to them. It is sometimes possible for the disposition of a deceased person's estate to be altered after the death. An alteration may achieve a more satisfactory disposition of the property of the deceased and in certain cases may result in a saving of tax. There are a number of ways in which alterations after death to the dispositions of a deceased person's property can be achieved. In this chapter we will consider the following methods:

    (a) A "disclaimer"
    (b) A "variation"
    (c) An order made under the Inheritance (Provision for Family and Dependants) Act 1975
    (d) A "two-year discretionary trust"
    (e) A "precatory trust"

In each case we will consider the effect on succession to property and on taxation. We will also look at the right of a surviving spouse under the intestacy rules to elect to capitalise his or her life interest. This is not, strictly speaking, an *alteration* of the intestacy rules merely an application of them. However, the exercise of the right can alter the inheritance tax liability of the estate and it is, therefore, convenient to consider it in this chapter.

B. Disclaimer

1. THE SUCCESSION EFFECT OF DISCLAIMER

It was said as long ago as 1819 that "the law certainly is not so absurd as to **19.002** force a man to take an estate against his will" (*per* Abbot C.J. in *Townson v Tickell* (1819)); the right of disclaimer is long established. The beneficiary is free to disclaim any property. A person entitled on intestacy is also apparently free to disclaim entitlement under the intestacy rules (*Re Scott* (1975)). A disclaimer is simply a refusal to accept property.

Limitations on the right to disclaim
The right to disclaim a gift is lost altogether once any benefit from it has **19.003** been accepted by the beneficiary. This will be the case where, for example, the beneficiary has had the property vested in him or where he has received income from a specific legacy or interest on a pecuniary legacy.

Unless the will provides to the contrary, it is not possible to disclaim part only of a single gift, the entire gift must be given up. If a beneficiary is entitled to two separate gifts, he can disclaim one while accepting the other. Thus a beneficiary given two legacies, one of £1,000, the other of a clock, can disclaim the clock and still accept the money (or *vice versa*).

The effect of disclaiming

19.004 If a beneficiary disclaims a gift in the will or an entitlement under the intestacy rules, the property passes as if the gift to him had failed. The destination of the disclaimed property thereafter depends on the nature of the gift or entitlement that has been given up.

If a non-residuary gift in a will is disclaimed the property will fall into residue. If a residuary gift is disclaimed, the property passes under the intestacy rules, unless the gift is a class gift in which case it passes to the other members of the class. If it is a gift to joint tenants, it passes to the other joint tenant.

If a gift in a will is disclaimed, this does not prevent the beneficiary receiving the property (in whole or in part) under the intestacy rules. Thus, if a deceased died leaving a spouse and children having by will given his entire substantial estate to his wife, she could disclaim her interest under the will and still share in the property with her children under the intestacy rules, if this distribution is acceptable. If it is not, a "variation" might be more appropriate (see below, para.19.011).

Disclaiming an interest on intestacy will either result in the property passing to the other members of the same class of beneficiaries or, if there are none, to the next category of relatives. Thus, if one of a number of children disclaims, the result is that the others enjoy a larger share of the deceased's estate. The child who disclaims is not treated as having predeceased the testator or intestate and so there is no question of his share passing to his own children by substitution unless there is a will which provides that this should happen. If an only child disclaims, the result is that the deceased's parents or brothers and sisters benefit.

It can be seen that a disadvantage of disclaimer is that the original beneficiary has no control over the ultimate destination of the property, which must pass under the terms of the deceased's will or the intestacy rules. This may be acceptable to the beneficiary who merely wants to give up his rights to certain property (perhaps because it carries with it onerous covenants or unacceptable conditions), but it will not be acceptable if he wants to ensure that someone, other than the residuary beneficiary or next of kin, takes in his place. In the latter case a "variation" would ensure he achieves his wishes.

Method of disclaiming

19.005 There are no statutory provisions governing the method of disclaiming a gift in a will or an entitlement under the intestacy rules. It is sufficient for the beneficiary to indicate his intention to the deceased's personal representatives either orally or in writing. Written notice is advisable. A letter stating that the beneficiary does not want the property is sufficient.

2. THE TAXATION EFFECT OF DISCLAIMER

The inheritance tax rules

Under general principles a beneficiary who refuses to accept an entitlement is treated as making a transfer of value for the purposes of inheritance tax. Thus, if the beneficiary were to die within seven years of disclaiming, tax would (subject to any exemptions and reliefs available) be payable. If certain conditions are complied with, a disclaimer will not be treated as a transfer of value. Inheritance tax will, instead, be payable as if the deceased had left his property to the person entitled once the disclaimer takes effect. The conditions are set out in Inheritance Tax Act 1984, s.142:

19.006

    (a) the disclaimer must not be made for consideration in money or money's worth (other than the making of a disclaimer or variation in respect of another disposition),
    (b) the disclaimer must be in writing,
    (c) the disclaimer must be made within two years of the death.

Provided these conditions are complied with, no further formalities are required. The property disclaimed will pass to the person next entitled under the terms of the deceased's will (or on his intestacy). The original beneficiary will not be treated as making a transfer of value. If the change of entitlement results in a change in the amount of inheritance tax payable on the deceased's estate (for example, where the spouse exemption becomes available on more or on less of the estate) the personal representatives will recalculate the tax and submit a corrective account to the Inland Revenue.

In some cases the effect of a disclaimer may be to increase tax unnecessarily. For example the spouse exemption will be lost if the spouse disclaims. In such cases a disclaimer which is not in writing or which is made more than two years after death should be considered. Section 142 will not then apply, the surviving spouse will be treated as making a transfer of value but provided this is potentially exempt and the spouse does survive seven years no tax will be payable.

A disclaimer is unilateral. The consent of the personal representatives is not required to a disclaimer even if its effect is to increase the tax due.

Section 142(1) refers to the disclaimer of property comprised in the deceased's estate immediately before death "whether passing by will, intestacy *or otherwise*". As a result of the reference to property passing "otherwise" than by will or intestacy, it is possible to disclaim an interest in joint property passing by survivorship. (Property in which the deceased had merely an interest in possession is not treated as a part of the deceased's estate for the purposes of disclaimer (s.142(5)).

The capital gains tax rules

Under general capital gains tax principles a disclaimer will amount to a disposal by the original beneficiary for capital gains tax purposes.

19.007

However, the Taxation of Chargeable Gains Act 1992, s.62(6) provides that if certain conditions are complied with a disclaimer will not be treated as a disposal. Instead the property will be treated as if left by the deceased to the person entitled once the disclaimer has taken effect. As death is not a disposal, no capital gains tax will be payable. The conditions are identical with those required for inheritance tax relief. No further formalities are required.

The income tax rules

General principles

19.008   There is no statutory provision which makes a disclaimer retrospective for income tax purposes. Therefore, the position with respect to income from the property disclaimed is governed by the general law.

A disclaimer can only be made where no income or interest has been accepted. Where the gift disclaimed is a pecuniary legacy it carries with it, in certain circumstances, the right to receive interest (see Chapter 16, para.16.054). If such interest is disclaimed, the beneficiary will not be liable to tax on it (*Dewar v I.R.C.* (1935)) unless a fund to meet the legacy has been set aside (*Spens v I.R.C.* (1970)).

The position with regard to disclaimers made by specific and residuary beneficiaries is probably the same as in the case of variations (see para.19.017). Thus, there will be no charge to tax as no income will have been received.

Disclaimer by parents

19.009   A disclaimer is a refusal to accept an entitlement rather than a gift of the entitlement to a new beneficiary. This can have an important and beneficial income tax consequence for parents.

Under the Income and Corporation Taxes Act 1988, Pt XV, a parent who during his lifetime settles income or income producing assets on an infant, or unmarried child will have the income assessed to income tax as part of his own income (unless the settlor makes an irrevocable capital settlement and the income is lawfully accumulated, s.660(B)). "Settlement" is widely defined and includes any disposition, arrangement or transfer of assets.

If a parent *disclaims* an entitlement it may happen that the person next entitled to the disclaimed property under the deceased's will (or under the intestacy rules) is the parent's infant, unmarried child.

Several commentators have said that a disclaimer in these circumstances will not amount to a "settlement" and that a parent would not be assessed to income tax on income produced by the disclaimed property. However, R. T. Oerton and M. D. Wood in *Capital Taxes News and Reports* (November 1989) cast doubt on this and gave the following warning:

> "Enquiry has been made of the Inland Revenue, but they have declined to express any general view, emphasising that each case must depend upon an exhaustive examination of the facts and of any documentation. It would, in these circumstances, be unwise to assume that s.663 will not apply."

The stamp duty rules

19.010   A disclaimer does not attract any form of stamp duty and the instrument giving effect to it does not need to be presented to the Stamp Office.

C. Variations

1. THE SUCCESSION EFFECT OF VARIATION

A variation is a direction from a beneficiary to the personal **19.011** representatives to transfer property to someone other than the original beneficiary. There are no special rules on the form of a variation for succession purposes since it is, in effect, an ordinary *inter vivos* gift. In cases where one or more of the recipients of the property under the variation is providing no consideration, a deed is advisable as the personal representatives may be reluctant to act on the basis of an unenforceable agreement.

For succession purposes, a variation is similar to a disclaimer in that the original beneficiary gives up his rights to receive property under the terms of the will or the intestacy rules but a variation differs from a disclaimer in three material respects:

- (a) A variation is possible even though the original beneficiary has accepted the property, whether by receiving income or by having the property vested in him. It is even possible to vary the deceased's dispositions once the administration of the estate is complete.
- (b) The original beneficiary can make a partial variation of a gift by, for example, giving up part of a gift. (This is not possible in the case of a disclaimer unless the will makes specific provision.)
- (c) The original beneficiary can control the ultimate destination of the property since it passes to whoever he specifies. The property does not have to pass under the terms of the deceased's will or the intestacy rules.

Thus, a variation may provide a solution where a person has inherited property which he does not want but which he does not wish to pass to the person next entitled under the deceased's will or the intestacy rules.

Example
Ann dies leaving her residuary estate to her husband Brian. He has no need of it and wishes to give the property direct to his two grandchildren, rather than to his child Charlotte. A disclaimer will not achieve his aim since if he were to disclaim his interest under the will and his entitlement under the intestacy rules, the property would pass to Charlotte.

Brian could achieve his aim by making an ordinary *inter vivos* gift to the grandchildren without altering the disposition by the deceased at all. However, this would be a potentially exempt transfer for inheritance tax purposes and a disposal for capital gains purposes which might result in unnecessary payments of tax being made. If he complies with the requirements of the Inheritance Tax Act 1984, s.142, he can vary the terms of the will in favour of his grandchildren and can avoid the transaction being treated as his *inter vivos* gift.

When choosing between a variation agreement and an ordinary *inter vivos* gift, tax considerations should be uppermost in the beneficiary's mind since variation is basically a tax concept.

When is an agreement to vary concluded?

19.012 In *Crowden v Aldridge* (1993) the residuary beneficiaries signed a memorandum after the funeral agreeing that the will should be varied in favour of the deceased's housekeeper and stating that each would sign a deed to that effect. When the deed was prepared four of the beneficiaries refused to sign. The court held that the memorandum was a document showing intention to create legal effect and therefore it varied the distribution of the estate as soon as it was communicated to the executors.

2. THE TAXATION EFFECT OF VARIATION

The inheritance tax rules

19.013 If an original beneficiary makes an *inter vivos* gift of all or part of the property this is a transfer of value for inheritance tax purposes. Thus, if he dies within seven years of the gift, inheritance tax will be payable (subject to any exemptions and reliefs which may be available). However, Inheritance Tax Act, s.142(1) provides that if certain conditions are complied with, a variation will not be treated as a transfer of value. Instead, inheritance tax will be payable as if the deceased had left his property to the substituted beneficiary or beneficiaries. The conditions are:

(a) the variation must not be made for consideration in money or money's worth (other than the making of a disclaimer or variation in respect of another disposition);

(b) the variation must be in writing;

(c) the variation must be made within two years of the death;

(d) the instrument in writing which makes the variation must contain a statement by the person or persons making the instrument (and, where the variation results in additional tax being payable also by the personal representatives) to the effect that they intend s.142(1) to apply to the variation. The personal representatives may only refuse to make the statement if no or no sufficient assets are held by them as personal representatives for discharging the additional tax;

(e) where additional tax becomes payable as a result of the instrument the person or persons making the instrument and the personal representatives are under a duty to deliver a copy to the Inland Revenue and notify them of the amount of the additional tax.

Paragraphs (d) and (e) were introduced by the Finance Act 2002, s.120. They apply to all variations made after July 31, 2002. (The previous provisions required notice to the revenue in all cases—even when no extra tax was payable—but did not require the instrument itself to state that s.142(1) was to apply).

As in the case of a disclaimer, any property comprised in the deceased's estate immediately before death, whether passing by will, intestacy or otherwise, can be the subject of a variation (s.142(1)).

Section 142(5) provides expressly that a variation agreement will be effective for inheritance tax purposes whether or not the administration is complete or the property concerned has already been distributed to the original beneficiary.

The Revenue's view is that a variation, once made, is irrevocable and that s.142 will not apply to an instrument redirecting any item that has already been redirected under an earlier instrument. *Russell v I.R.C.* confirms the Revenue's view that it is not possible to redirect any item or any part of an item which has already been redirected under an earlier instrument.

Further variations in respect of different property is possible provided it is made within two years of death and the requirement referred to above are complied with.

Practical considerations

A beneficiary (B) will often wish to make an election since this results in only one possible charge to tax, from the deceased to the new beneficiary; whereas if B makes an *inter vivos* gift there is one charge to B and a risk of a second charge if B dies within seven years of the gift. If B is the spouse of the deceased it may be beneficial not to elect since the initial transfer to B is exempt; there is still the risk of a charge if B dies within seven years but this will be at B's rates and tapering relief may be available. **19.014**

The capital gains tax rules

Under general principles a variation will amount to a disposal by the original beneficiaries for capital gains tax purposes. However, the Taxation of Chargeable Gains Act 1992, s.62(6) provides that if certain conditions are complied with a variation will not be treated as a disposal. Instead, the property will be treated as if the deceased had left it to the substituted beneficiary or beneficiaries. The conditions are identical to those required for inheritance tax purposes. **19.015**

Although the inheritance tax and capital gains tax rules are basically the same, there is no need to elect the same way for both taxes. The original beneficiary is free to choose for each tax the method which is most beneficial in order to achieve his ends.

Note the House of Lord's decision in *Marshall v Kerr* (1994). If a variation establishes a UK settlement, the original beneficiary is treated as the settlor for the purposes of TCGA 1992, s.77 and will be treated as having retained an interest. Similarly if the variation creates an offshore settlement, the original beneficiary will be treated as the settlor for the purposes of TCGA 1992, s.86. In all other cases the deceased is treated as leaving the property to the new beneficiary for capital gains tax purposes.

Practical considerations

Each case depends on its own facts but three points should be borne in mind. **19.016**

   (a) If a loss has arisen since the date of death the original beneficiary may wish to set the loss off against his own gains and so will choose to make an *inter vivos* gift.
   (b) It is preferable to treat the gift as an *inter vivos* disposition if the property has *increased* in value by an amount not exceeding the

annual exemption from capital gains tax since the beneficiary can take the benefit of the increased acquisition value.

(c) The indexation allowance and taper relief may mean that there is no chargeable gain, in which case it is immaterial whether the disposition is treated as a variation or as an *inter vivos* gift.

Apart from these circumstances, the election will normally be made since no capital gains tax liability arises on death.

The income tax rules

19.017 A variation raises problems with regard to income tax liability since (like disclaimer) there are no statutory provisions making the variation retrospective for income tax purposes.

Thus, income arising between the date of death and the date of the variation will be taxed in accordance with the terms of the will (if any) and the rules on the taxation of the income of estates. Since residuary income is taxed only when it is paid to beneficiaries, there will only be a charge to tax on the original beneficiary to the extent that income has been paid to that beneficiary. Hence, if the variation is made before any income has been paid over there can be no charge on the original beneficiary.

A specific legatee is only assessed to income tax on income once the asset is vested in him so, if the variation is entered into before that point, the original legatee will never be liable to income tax. If the variation is entered into afterwards the legatee should consider whether or not he wishes to retain the income since he will be assessed to tax on it.

The Inland Revenue regards a variation as a "settlement" for the purposes of Pt XV of the Income and Corporation Taxes Act 1988. If a parent varies in favour of a minor, unmarried child any resulting income will, while the child remains a minor and unmarried be assessed to income tax as part of the parent's income (unless the income is lawfully accumulated under an irrevocable capital settlement). As stated earlier it is preferable for a parent, who wishes to benefit his child, to use a disclaimer rather than a variation wherever this is possible.

The stamp duty rules

19.018 In respect of instruments executed after May 1, 1987 the Stamp Duty (Exempt Instruments) Regulations 1987 exempt from duty instruments certified as falling into any of the categories listed in the Schedule. Variations fall into category or M. Instruments falling within the Regulations do not need to be presented to the Stamp Office.

D. Inheritance (Provision for Family and Dependants) Act 1975

19.019 The position in relation to orders made under this Act is governed by s.146 of the Inheritance Tax Act 1984 which provides that for inheritance tax purposes the provision ordered by the court is treated as if it were the disposition of the deceased.

The new beneficiary is liable to income tax on income arising after the date of death from property awarded to him.

E. Settlements Without an Interest in Possession—Property Vested Within Two Years of Death

Some testators wish to leave the ultimate destination of their property **19.020** flexible so that their personal representatives can look at the circumstances existing at the date of the testators's death and made a distribution which is suitable in the light of those circumstances. This flexibility can be achieved by leaving property on discretionary trusts. It is usual for a testator to leave a letter of intent explaining the person(s) the testator would like to receive a benefit.

Where a deceased creates a settlement without an interest in possession in his will and property is vested in any person within two years of the death (but not within the first three months after death—see *Frankland v I.R.C.* (1997)), the inheritance tax payable on the death estate is calculated as if the will left the property to the beneficiary who receives the property once the trustees exercise their discretion. This rule applies to cases where the discretion is actually exercised within two years of death as well as to those where the will requires it to be exercised within that period. Because of the relatively low rate of tax on property leaving a discretionary trust (as to which see para.7.016 above) it will often be appropriate for trustees to make appointments more than two years after death.

There are no special capital gains tax rules applicable in these circumstances so that the exercise of the trustees' discretion is a deemed disposal and re-acquisition by them (see para.7.035). The recipient acquires the asset at its market value when the discretion is exercised and not the value at death. As the appointment from the trust is not a transfer chargeable to inheritance tax no holdover relief is available to the trustees. There will, therefore, be some cases where an exercise of the discretion more than two years after death is advantageous. An IHT charge cannot then be avoided (although the amount of the tax may be small) but holdover relief will be available for CGT.

The normal income tax rules for settlements where no beneficiary has a right to income will apply (see paras 7.040 and 7.044).

F. Precatory Words

Where a testator expresses a wish that property left in his will to a **19.021** beneficiary should be transferred by that beneficiary to someone else, and that beneficiary complies with the wish within two years of the death, inheritance tax is payable as if the deceased had left the property to the eventual recipient.

There are no special capital gains tax rules so the transfer will be treated as a disposal by the original beneficiary.

There are no special income tax rules so income receivable up to the date of transfer will be assessed to tax as part of the original beneficiary's income.

G. Capitalisation of Life Interest by Surviving Spouse

19.022   If a surviving spouse capitalises the life interest received under the intestacy rules (see above para.3.010) this is not a transfer of value for inheritance tax purposes and the spouse is treated as entitled to the capitalised amount. The capitalisation may, however, lead to more inheritance tax being paid since the spouse exemption will be lost on that part of the capital in which the spouse no longer has any interest.

There are no special capital gains tax or income tax rules.

20. The Inheritance (Provision for Family and Dependants) Act 1975

A. Introduction

A testator is free to leave his property in whatever way he pleases; no **20.001** relative has a *right* to receive property under the will. However, this principle of testamentary freedom is to some extent eroded by the Inheritance (Provision for Family and Dependants) Act 1975. This Act gives the court limited powers to order financial provision to be made from the net estate of a deceased person for the benefit of certain categories of applicant. Applications under the Act can also be made where a person dies intestate.

If an application is to be successful the following matters must be established:

(a) that certain preliminary requirements are satisfied;
(b) that the application is made within the time limit;
(c) that the applicant falls into one of the five possible categories of applicant;
(d) that the will or intestacy rules have not made reasonable provision for the applicant.

If these matters are established the court must then decide whether and in what manner to order financial provision for the applicant from the net estate of the deceased (to help the court in its decision there are certain statutory guidelines to be taken into account).

The Act contains certain anti-avoidance provisions under which orders may, in limited circumstances, be made against people who have received property from the deceased before death (see below, para.20.027).

B. Preliminary Requirements

The Act applies only in the case of a deceased who dies domiciled in **20.002** England and Wales after March 31, 1976 (s.1(1)); earlier legislation (which was narrower in its scope) applies to deaths before that date.

There is no equivalent statute applying to persons who die domiciled in Scotland. (However, under Scots law if a person dies domiciled in Scotland leaving a spouse and issue the spouse is entitled to a one-third share in the whole of the moveable estate of the deceased and the children are entitled to another one-third share. If there is a spouse and no children the spouse's share is increased to one-half. The deceased is free to dispose only of the remaining portion).

C. Time Limits

1. NORMAL PERIOD

20.003   Application must normally be made within six months of the date of the first effective grant of representation (s.4). If a grant is revoked because it was wrongly made, the application must be made within six months of the subsequent valid grant (*Re Freeman* (1984)). However, where a limited grant is made time runs only from the making of a full grant. This was decided in the case of *Re Paul Anthony Johnson, (Deceased)* (1987) where a grant limited to pursuing negligence claims was made in 1983. The full grant of probate was made in 1987 and it was held that time ran from the date of the full grant. The court does, however, have a discretion to extend the time limit. This discretion is unfettered and the Act itself contains no guidance as to how the court should exercise it. However, in *Re Salmon (Deceased)* (1980) Megarry V.C. suggested six guidelines. These were concisely summarised in *Re Dennis* (1981) as follows:

> "First, the discretion of the court, though judicial, is unfettered. Second, the onus is on the applicant to show special reasons for taking the matter out of the general six month time limit; ... this is not a mere triviality but a substantial requirement. Third, the court has to consider how promptly and in what circumstances the application has been made after the time has expired; one has to look at all the circumstances surrounding the delay. Fourth, the court has to see whether negotiations has started within the six month period. Fifth, one has to consider whether or not the estate has been distributed before the claim has been notified. Sixth, the court has to consider whether refusal of leave to bring proceedings out of time will leave the applicant without recourse against anyone else, ..."
> (An example of such a person would be a negligent solicitor.)

The list was not intended to be exhaustive and *Re Dennis* itself added a further guideline, by analogy with applications for leave to defend in Order 14 proceedings, the applicant must show that he has "an arguable case, a case fit to go to trial".

In *Re C* (1995) a claim made 18 months after the date of the grant and three years six months after the death was allowed. However, the circumstances were unusual. The applicant was an eight-year-old illegitimate child. The delay was not hers but her mother's. The estate was large so that prejudice to others would be not too great, and finally the chances of a successful claim were high. The *Salmon* guidelines were approved.

In *McNulty v McNulty* (2002) a widow brought a claim four years after death. The reason for the late application was that an asset of the estate which had been valued at £175,000 for probate purposes, was subsequently sold to a building developer for £1,600,000.

She had first discovered the increase in value in June 1998 but proceedings were not issued until April 1999. The court said that she could not be criticised for not bringing the claim before June 1998 but that "the matter was treated with inexcusable tardiness between June 1998 and April 1999". However, permission was given for the following reasons:

- she had a strong case on the merits;
- the estate had not been distributed and as a result there would be no prejudice to the beneficiaries of the will in granting the application;

2. PRACTICAL CONSIDERATIONS

The reason for having such a short time limit is to enable personal **20.004** representatives to distribute assets without fear of personal liability if a successful application is later made. The Act provides therefore that a personal representative can distribute after the expiry of six months from the date of grant without personal liability even if the court does later extend the time limit (s.20). Where an out of time application is allowed there is power to recover any part of the estate already distributed to the beneficiaries by the personal representatives.

Obviously a cautious personal representative would wait six months before distributing assets; yet in most cases such caution will be unnecessary and may even cause hardship if a beneficiary is in urgent need of finance. A personal representative must therefore carefully consider the circumstances before deciding whether or not to wait for the expiry of the six month period. The following matters are relevant:

(a) Since an order for financial provision is made against the *net* estate of the deceased (see below, para.20.025) there can be no objection to paying funeral, testamentary and administration expenses, debts and liabilities before the expiry of the six month period.

(b) It will normally be safe to pay a legacy to a beneficiary who is intending to make an application to obtain more (unless there is a risk of applications from other people).

(c) Since it is unlikely that the court would order provision to be financed out of a very small legacy when the estate is large such a legacy can safely be paid.

(d) Similarly it will often be safe to distribute assets to a beneficiary who has a strong moral claim particularly if in urgent need.

D. The Categories of Applicant

1. SECTION 1(1)

The following persons may apply to the court for an order in their favour **20.005** on the ground that the deceased's will or the intestacy rules have not made reasonable provision for them.

(a) *The spouse of the deceased.* The applicant must show that there was a subsisting marriage at the time of the deceased's death. This category includes a judicially separated spouse and a party to a voidable marriage which has not been annulled prior to death. Unusually a person will be regarded as a surviving spouse even though the marriage was *void*, provided the applicant entered into the marriage in good faith, unless in the lifetime of the deceased:

(a) the marriage has been dissolved or annulled; or

(b) the applicant entered into a later marriage.

The Act provides that a decree of judicial separation may contain a term barring the spouses from making an application for financial provision (s.15).

(b) *A former spouse.* A former spouse is a person whose marriage with the deceased was dissolved or annulled during the deceased's lifetime by a decree made under the law of any part of the British Islands or in any country or territory outside the British Islands by a divorce or annulment "which is entitled to be recognised as valid by the law of England and Wales" (s.25). The Act provides, however, in the interests of finality that a former spouse may be barred from applying for financial provision by a court order on the granting of a decree of divorce or nullity (ss.15 and 15A). Moreover, the Court of Appeal observed in *Re Fullard* (1981) that in view of the wide powers of the court to make financial arrangements on divorce, the number of cases in which it would be appropriate for a former spouse to apply under the family provision legislation would be small; an example of such a case might be where the deceased's estate receives the proceeds of a large insurance policy on the deceased's death or where the applicant had been provided for in the divorce proceedings by means of periodical payments rather than by a lump sum.

20.006   In *Barrass v Harding* (2001) and in *Cameron v Treasury Solicitor* (1996) the Court of Appeal emphasised that, where the parties regard themselves as having settled accounts with the divorce settlement, it will be inappropriate to make a family provision award unless there is some special circumstance. An example would be an assumption of responsibility by one party for the other after the divorce. The following have been held to be insufficient:

- the applicant's "parlous financial circumstances" and poor health in a case where the estate was *bona vacantia* (*Re Cameron*);
- the substantial value of the deceased's estate (*Barrass v Harding*); and
- the fact that the divorce was pre-1970 at a time when the court had much less extensive powers to redistribute property than it now has (*Barrass v Harding*).

(ba) *A person who has cohabited with the deceased for two years.* This is a new category introduced by the Law Reform Succession Act 1995. To be eligible the applicant must not be included in either of the two preceding categories. The deceased must have died on or after January 1, 1996 and during the whole of the period of two years ending immediately before the death of the deceased the applicant must have been living:

(a) in the same household as the deceased, and

(b) as the husband or wife of the deceased.

The Act was not intended to apply to same sex partners. When Mackay L.C. introduced the Bill, he said: "Living as husband and wife appears to us, as the law stands, to apply to partners of opposite sexes and not to partners of the same sex". *Hansard*, February 13, 1995.

It is doubtful whether the present interpretation is consistent with the Human Rights Act. It is likely that there will be a challenge in the relatively near future. *Mendoza v Ghaidan* (2002) allowed a same sex cohabitee to claim a secured tenancy under the Rent Act on similar wording.

Notice that as a result of the wording of the new subsection an application is bound to fail if there is any interruption in the two year period of cohabitation prior to death. For example, where an applicant cease living with the deceased, then resume but fail to "clock up" a full two year period before the death. However, separations brought about by external circumstances *e.g.* illness necessitating a stay in hospital or hospice care are irrelevant. In *Re Watson, (Deceased)* (1999) exactly this situation arose. The deceased was hospitalised for three weeks prior to death. All parties accepted that the deceased had not ceased to be part of the household.

Re Watson, (Deceased) (1999) is the leading case on this subsection. The applicant and the deceased had known each other since 1964. She moved into the deceased's house in 1985. They had no sexual relationship after she had moved in although they had had one earlier. Mr Watson worked and provided most of the funds for the household. The applicant paid her share of the cost of utilities and would be responsible for shopping, cooking and gardening.

The court decided that they had lived together as husband and wife. When making that decision, the court should ask whether, in the opinion of a reasonable person with normal perceptions, it could be said that the two people in question were living together as husband and wife. However, "one should not ignore the multifarious nature of marital relationships".

The fact that the couple had an agreement as to who paid for what and who did which jobs did not prevent the arrangement being a marital one. It was also irrelevant that the claimant had another property available to her.

(c) *A child of the deceased.* This category includes a child of a non-marital relationship, a legitimated or adopted child and a child *en ventre sa mere.* A child who has been adopted is no longer eligible to make a claim as a child of the *natural* parent (*Re Collins, (Deceased)* (1991)).

There is no distinction between sons and daughters and neither age nor marriage are automatic disqualifications. However, the courts do not look sympathetically at applications by able-bodied adults capable of earning their own living.

In *Re Coventry* (1980) for example, the Court of Appeal quoted with approval the statement by Oliver J. at first instance that "applications under the Act of 1975 for maintenance by able-bodied and comparatively young men in employment and able to maintain themselves must be relatively rare and need to be approached ... with a degree of circumspection".

In *Williams v Johns* (1988) the court said that the approach to an   **20.007** application by an adult daughter should be the same as that for an application by an adult son.

It used to be said that adult able-bodied children had to show an additional "threshold" requirement of a special obligation owed to them by the deceased (see *Goodchild v Goodchild* (1997)).

The Court of Appeal has expressly rejected this in a number of recent cases (*Re Hancock* (1998), *Re Pearce* (1998), *Espinosa v Bourke* (1999)).

The approach now is that the court will consider all the circumstances in reaching its decision and try to balance all factors. An adult able-bodied child who cannot produce any argument to buttress a claim beyond being badly off is still unlikely to be successful. In *Espinosa v Bourke* the applicant (the deceased's daughter) had behaved badly and had already received some benefit form the deceased during his lifetime. However, this did not outweigh the factors in her favour. These included:

- her poor financial position;
- the substantial size of the estate;
- the fact that the only beneficiary of the will was her son who was at university starting his career without compelling needs;
- the applicant had taken her father into her home and cared for him, at least to a degree, for seven years, thus providing some return for the financial provision he made for her during his lifetime;
- the deceased had an obligation to the applicant in that he had promised her mother to pass on the mother's share of the paternal grandmother's portfolio of shares to her.

(d) *A person (not being a child of the deceased) who is treated by the deceased as a child of the family in connection with a marriage to which the deceased was a party.* The concept of "a child of the family" is imported from family law (Matrimonial Causes Act 1973, s.52(1) although under that Act the child must have been treated as a child of the family by *both* parties to the marriage). In *Re Callaghan* (1984) and in *Re Leach, (Deceased)* (1985) it was held that a person was a child of the family even though he was an adult when the deceased married his parent.

20.008 (e) *Any person (not being a person included in the foregoing paragraphs) who immediately before the death of the deceased was being maintained wholly or partly by the deceased.* It is often difficult to decide whether a person is within this category but certain points have been decided in recent cases:

(i) *The meaning of "maintained"*
The starting point is s.1(3) which provides that "a person shall be treated as being maintained by the deceased, either wholly or partly, ... if the deceased otherwise than for full valuable consideration, was making a substantial contribution in money or money's worth towards the reasonable needs of that person". It has been held that a person is to be regarded as maintained by the deceased *only* if he can bring himself within s.1(3) (*Re Beaumont* (1980); *Jelley v Iliffe* (1981)). It is obviously difficult to state definitely what amounts to "a

substantial contribution" but in *Jelley v Iliffe* the Court of Appeal regarded the provision of rent free accommodation as substantial.

In *Re Watson* (1999) the cohabitee applicant had also applied as a person maintained by the deceased on the basis that the deceased had provided her with rent free accommodation. She was not successful in this category. The court found that at the time she lived with the deceased, she had no housing "need" because she had a property of her own available to her. It was irrelevant that by the time of the application the property had become unsuitable for her future needs because she was unable to manage stairs. The question of maintenance has to be determined by reference to the situation prevailing during the life of the deceased.

Once it is established that the deceased was making a substantial contribution, the next problem for a would-be applicant is to show that it was not made for full valuable consideration. It is accepted that consideration may be full and valuable even though not provided under a contract (*Re Beaumont*; *Jelley v Iliffe*).

(ii) *The provision of services can amount to valuable consideration*
The court sometimes has to balance imponderables like companionship and other services provided by an applicant against contributions of cash or accommodation provided by the deceased. The court accepts that such services are *capable* of amounting to full valuable consideration (*Re Wilkinson* (1978); *Re Beaumont*; *Jelley v Iliffe*). However, it is a question of fact in each case. The court will normally allow an application to proceed to the later stages of trial unless it is absolutely clear that the services made by the applicant outweigh the contributions made by the deceased to the applicant's maintenance. If, however, it is *clear* that the services amounted to full valuable consideration the application should be struck out at a preliminary stage in order to avoid the costs of further proceedings. In *Bishop v Plumley* (1990) the Court of Appeal stated that a commonsense approach should be adopted "avoiding fine balancing computations involving the value of normal exchanges of support in the domestic sense". The court held that the devoted care and nursing provided by the applicant did not amount to full valuable consideration for the rent-free accommodation of the deceased. The applicant was, therefore, eligible to apply.

In *Re Watson* (1999) the court declined to consider whether or not the applicant's contribution to household expenses and the work she did in the house would have amounted to valuable consideration as it had already found that she had not been maintained. However, it said that it was a difficult point.

(iii) *The meaning of "immediately before the death"*
Section 1(1)(e) expressly states that the applicant must have been maintained "immediately before the death" of the deceased. Problems have arisen in connection with this phrase. For example, in *Re Beaumont* the deceased had habitually maintained the applicant but had been unable to do so in the few weeks immediately before her death, when she was ill in hospital. Megarry V.C. accepted that

the court must look at "the settled basis or ... general arrangement between the parties" not at "the actual, perhaps fluctuating, variation of it which exists immediately before ... death".

E. Reasonable Provision

1. TWO STANDARDS

20.009   The Act sets out two standards for judging whether or not provision is reasonable, one to be applied in the case of a surviving spouse and one to be applied in other cases.

2. THE SURVIVING SPOUSE STANDARD

20.010   This is such financial provision as it would be reasonable in all the circumstances for a spouse (not including a judicially separated spouse) to receive "whether or not that provision is required for his or her maintenance" (s.1(2)(a)). This standard was introduced so that the claim of a surviving spouse to matrimonial assets should be equal to that of a divorced spouse and the court's powers to order financial provision as extensive as in a divorce application.

The court has a discretion to apply this standard where a decree of judicial separation, nullity or divorce has been made within 12 months of death and no order for financial provision has been made (or refused) in the matrimonial proceedings (s.14). The reason is that the applicant would otherwise have no opportunity to obtain a fair share of the matrimonial assets.

3. THE ORDINARY STANDARD

20.011   This is "such financial provision as it would be reasonable in all the circumstances of the case for the applicant to receive for his *maintenance*" (s.1(2)(b)). It is difficult to give a precise meaning to the word "maintenance" in this context. It does not mean just enough to enable a person to get by (*i.e.* mere subsistence) but on the other hand it does not extend to everything which may be regarded as reasonably desirable for their general benefit or welfare. Buckley L.J. suggested in *Re Coventry* (1980) that it could be regarded as "such financial provision as would be reasonable in all the circumstances of the case to enable the applicant to maintain himself in a manner suitable to these circumstances."

The restriction of provision to that required for maintenance is often fatal to applications by non-spouses.

In *Re Jennings, (Deceased)* (1994) the applicant was an adult son. At first instance the trial judge found that the applicant had a comfortable standard of living and was unlikely to encounter financial difficulties in the future, providing he maintained his health and his capacity to work. However, he made an award on the basis that the plaintiff reasonably required an amount which would enable him to pay off his mortgage. He identified as a need the fact that the applicant had made no real provision for his pension and observed that the reduction in the mortgage would allow him to provide for his future security.

On appeal Nourse L.J. pointed out that the applicant currently paid the mortgage from his income and had not said that he could not pay his mortgage without further help. "No further financial provision is necessary to enable the plaintiff to discharge the cost of his daily living at the standard appropriate to him".

It is not the purpose of the Act to provide legacies for disappointed beneficiaries but this does not mean that provision for maintenance is limited to income payments. Provision could be by way of a lump sum, for example, to buy a house in which the applicant could be housed, thereby removing one expense from the applicant (*Re Dennis* (1981)).

4. AN OBJECTIVE STANDARD

The court is to decide whether the provision made for an applicant *is* reasonable. This is an entirely objective question (*Moody v Stevenson* (1992)). The court is concerned therefore with the facts of the case rather than merely with the facts known to the deceased. If a testator has reasons for making no provision for a relative or dependant it is desirable that he should leave a record of those reasons with the will. The court will consider the reasons given by the testator and in so far as the reasons are good will take them into account; if, however, the testator was mistaken or motivated by malice the reasons will be ignored. It is not advisable to include the reasons in the will itself as a will is a document of public record.

20.012

Under s.3(5) the court will consider changes in the position of beneficiaries and applicants arising after the death of the deceased. In both *Re Hancock* (1999) and *McNulty v McNulty* (2000) the court took into account increases in the value of assets occurring after the death of the deceased. The court will not consider facts which arise between the hearing of the application and an appeal to the Court of Appeal (*Re Coventry*), nor will it consider legally unenforceable assurances given by beneficiaries to an applicant (*Rajabally v Rajabally* (1987)).

It may be reasonable for the deceased to have made no financial provision at all for an applicant; this was so in *Re Coventry* and in *Williams v Johns*. In both of these cases the court refused to order any provision for adult children of the deceased.

In *Rhodes v Dean* (1996) it was held that it was not unreasonable for the deceased to have made no provision for his cohabitee. In *Parish v Sharman* (2001) it was held not unreasonable for the deceased to have made no provision for his spouse.

F. The Court Must Decide Whether and in What Manner to Make an Order (s.3(1))

1. THIS IS A DISCRETIONARY MATTER

If the court decides that the provision made for the applicant is not reasonable it must then go on to consider whether to exercise its

20.013

discretion to make an order (and what type of order to make). At both stages the court is directed to consider various guidelines. Some guidelines are common to all applicants while some are limited to a particular category.

2. THE COMMON GUIDELINES

20.014   Under s.3(1) the court will have regard to the following matters:

(a) *The financial resources and needs of the applicant, any other applicant and any beneficiary.* Earning capacity and social security benefits would be relevant here (*Re E* (1966)). The court must balance the resources and needs of all the persons with a claim on the estate.

(b) *Any obligations and responsibilities of the deceased towards the applicant or any beneficiary.*
The Court of Appeal made it clear in *Re Jennings* (1994) that the obligations and responsibilities must still be operating on the deceased at the date of death. The deceased had abandoned his wife and son (the claimant) when the son was two. He had had no further contact with him and made no provision for him. When the father died, he left nothing to the son, the bulk of the estate going to charity. At first instance the judge construed s.3(1)(d) so as to include legal obligations and responsibilities which the deceased had, but had failed to discharge during the child's minority even though they were long spent and would have been incapable of founding a claim against him immediately before his death. The Court of Appeal said that was a wrong approach. The Act does not "revive defunct obligations and responsibilities".

(c) *The size and nature of the estate.* If an estate is large it is frequently relatively easy for the court to make adequate provision for applicants; where the estate is very small, however, it is often impossible to provide adequately for all beneficiaries and applicants. Moreover since the costs of an action normally come out of the estate the action may exhaust a large part of the assets. The courts, therefore, discourage applications in such cases (*Re Coventry*; *Jelley v Iliffe*). In *Re Fullard* (1981) Ormrod L.J. suggested that judges might reconsider the practice of ordering the costs of both sides to be paid out of the estate and look very closely indeed at the merits of an unsuccessful application before ordering the estate to bear the costs. Solicitors should always bear in mind the question of costs when advising clients who wish to make a claim, especially one against a small estate. The Court of Appeal have also exhorted practitioners to inform the legal aid authorities of the likely effects of an application and (*a fortiori*) an appeal on an estate in cases where legal aid is applied for.
The source of the deceased's assets is often an important consideration. For example, the court is likely to be sympathetic to an application by a child when the deceased parent inherited a large part of his/her estate from the other parent (as in *Espinosa v Bourke* (1999)).

(d) *Any physical or mental disability of any applicant or any beneficiary.*

The availability of state aid, hospital accommodation and social security benefits may be considered (*Re Watkins* (1949)).

(e) *Any other matter*, including the conduct of the applicant or any other person which the court may consider relevant. This obviously gives the court a great deal of freedom. In *Re Snoek, (Deceased)* (1983) an award to a spouse was set at a much lower amount than it would otherwise have been as a result of a history of assaults and other abuses in the years before the deceased's death. In *Espinosa v Bourke* (1999) the applicant's conduct in abandoning her father while she went on extended holidays counted against her. In *Re Goodchild* (1997) the applicant's mother had died believing that there was an agreement between herself and her husband to leave their combined estates to their son after the death. The agreement was not enforceable but was regarded as relevant to the Inheritance Act application.

3. THE PARTICULAR GUIDELINES

Under s.3(2) without prejudice to the common guidelines the court will also consider additional guidelines in relation to each category.   **20.015**

(a) *The surviving spouse.* The court will consider:
  (a) the age of the applicant and the duration of the marriage; and
  (b) the contribution made by the applicant to the welfare of the family of the deceased, including any contribution made by looking after the home or caring for the family; and
  (c) the provision the applicant might reasonably have expected to receive if on the day on which the deceased died the marriage (instead of being terminated by death) had been terminated by a decree of divorce. In *Re Besterman, (Deceased)* (1984) the Court of Appeal held that this did not mean that the same provision should be made as if there were a divorce on the day of the death. The other guidelines must also be taken into account and, in any case, further applications to the court if circumstances change may be made following a divorce whereas this is not possible in the case of a family provision application.

In *Moody v Stevenson* (1992) the Court of Appeal had seemed to suggest that the court should *only* consider the amount a spouse would have been entitled to on divorce. However, the Court of Appeal in *Re Krubert* (1996) stated that this approach was confusing when applied to a small estate. On divorce there were two parties to be considered whereas in a family provision case there was only one and, thus, it might well be reasonable to award the whole estate to a surviving spouse.

Inevitably changes in divorce law will affect the amount available to spouses under the Inheritance Act. The recent House of Lords decision in *White v White* (2001) has already resulted in a change in approach to applications by spouses. In *White* the House of Lords said there should be no bias in favour of the money earner and that a judge would always be well-advised to "check his tentative views against the yardstick of equality   **20.016** of division". As a general guide, equality should be departed from only if, and to the extent that, there was good reason for doing so.

In *Re Adams* (2001) Behrens J. said there was no reason to depart from the *White v White* principle of equality. In this case the deceased had been married to the claimant for 54 years and they had had 12 children. The deceased left her the household goods, his personal effects and a legacy of £10,000. The claimant contended that this was not reasonable and wanted to receive the family home. Three of her daughters opposed this. They accepted that the provision made was not reasonable but argued that the house was too large for her. The court held that the question of her needs was irrelevant. She was entitled to receive the family home.

In *Stephanides v Cohen and Stephanides* (2002) the deceased had left the bulk of his estate to his son and little to his second wife. The court made a substantial award in her favour. The deceased had a legal obligation to provide for his wife, whereas he had only a moral obligation towards his son. The applicant had been a good and loyal wife to the deceased whereas the son, as a consequence of drug addiction, had been dependent on the deceased for support for much longer than he should have been. In addition the applicant had managed the family business since her marriage to the deceased and had transformed and revitalised it.

In *Parish v Sharman* (2001) the applicant had separated from her husband in 1985 and applied for a divorce. She obtained the decree nisi in 1985 but never applied for the decree absolute. The parties had simply decided to go their own ways. There was a suggestion that the applicant may have been advised at the time to make no application for maintenance in order to prevent the deceased making an application for part of her capital. The applicant had to be treated as still married to the deceased at the date of his death. However, her conduct counted against her as she had left the deceased under the misapprehension that he was free to marry. Moreover, had the marriage ended in divorce on the date of the deceased's death, it was unlikely in view of their respective circumstances that the court would have ordered the transfer of any capital to her. The application failed.

In *Grattan v McNaughton* (2001) a husband left his whole estate to his two children subject to the right of his second wife to occupy the matrimonial home for as long as she remained a widow and did not cohabit. The court found that this was not reasonable provision. It widened the right of occupation by striking out the restrictions on cohabitation and remarriage and permitting her a right of occupation in any substitute property. She also took the residue absolutely subject to legacies of £5,000 to each of the children. In the light of this decision, it is probably necessary to warn a client who wants to include a restriction on cohabitation or remarriage that the restriction may be removed in an Inheritance Act claim.

20.017   (b) *The former spouse.* Guidelines (a) and (b) above also apply in the case of an application by a former spouse. Guideline (c) does not apply unless the court has exercised its limited discretion to apply the surviving spouse standard (see above, para.20.010).

Unless there is some special reason an application by a former spouse who has already received financial provision on the termination of the marriage with a view to a "clean break" will rarely be successful (*Re Fullard* (1981)).

(ba) *A person who has cohabited with the deceased for two years.* The court is directed to consider:

> (a) the age of the applicant and the length of the period during which the applicant lived as the husband or wife of the deceased and in the same household as the deceased;
> (b) the contribution made by the applicant to the welfare of the family of the deceased, including any contribution made by looking after the home or caring for the family.

(c) *A child of the deceased.* The additional guideline here is the manner in which the applicant was being or in which he might expect to be educated or trained.

(d) *A person treated by the deceased as a child of the family.* In addition to the education guideline set out in (c) above the court is also directed to consider:

> (a) whether the deceased had assumed any responsibility for the applicant's maintenance and if so the extent to which and the basis upon which the deceased assumed that responsibility and the length of time for which the deceased discharged that responsibility; and
> (b) whether in assuming and discharging that responsibility the deceased did so knowing that the applicant was not his own child; and
> (c) the liability of any other person to maintain the applicant.

(e) *A person maintained by the deceased.* The court will consider the **20.018** extent to which and the basis upon which the deceased assumed responsibility for the maintenance of the applicant and to the length of time for which the deceased discharged that responsibility.

It will be noticed that while the category (d) guideline directs the court to consider *whether* the deceased assumed responsibility, the category (e) guideline directs the court to consider *the extent to which* responsibility *has been* assumed. This suggests that a category (e) application can be made only if the deceased assumed responsibility for the applicant's maintenance. In *Re Beaumont* Megarry V.C. accepted this and said that the applicant must be able to point to "some act or acts which demonstrates an undertaking of responsibility"; without such an act an application would fail at the outset. However, in *Jelley v Iliffe*, the Court of Appeal expressly disapproved of this view and stated that the mere fact of maintenance generally raises a presumption that there was an assumption of responsibility; in the absence of evidence to rebut this presumption, therefore, the application can proceed to the later stages.

In *Bouette v Rose* (2000) the Court of Appeal found that a mother had been maintained by her brain-damaged daughter.

Robert Walker L.J. then gave a more detailed scrutiny to the question of assuming a moral obligation. He agreed with Megarry V.C. that the contrast in language between the two guidelines was striking. However, he concluded that the category (e) guideline was not adding a new requirement but was merely paraphrasing what is already implicit in s.1(1) (e). In his view *Jelley v Iliffe* makes it clear that the mere fact of one person making a substantial contribution to another person's needs raises a presumption of an assumption of responsibility.

In the end, therefore, the differences in approach are perhaps not that great. All the judges are agreed that an assumption of responsibility is an important element. *Bouette v Rose* and *Jelley v Iliffe* say that it is legitimate to infer such an assumption from the mere fact of maintenance. Megarry V.C. in *Beaumont* said that such an inference might be possible in cases where there was no evidence either way but that the obligation to show the assumption of responsibility would lie on the claimant. If there is no real evidence to suggest that the deceased assumed responsibility for the applicant it is unlikely that the application will be successful. There is nothing to prevent a testator leaving a statement to the effect that he assumed no responsibility for the applicant or did so only during his lifetime and not after death.

G. Types of Order

1. THE TYPES

20.019   Under s.2(1) the court may make one or more of the following orders:

(a) *Periodical payments.* Such an order may provide for:

(a) payments of a specified amount (for example, £25 per week); or
(b) payments equal to the whole or part of the income of the net estate (for example, one-third of the income from the net estate); or
(c) payments equal to the whole of the income of such part of the net estate as the court may direct to be set aside or appropriated (*e.g.* the whole income from the deceased's shares in a named company); or
(d) payments to be determined in any other way the court thinks fit.

Section 2(3) provides that the order for periodical payments may direct that a specified part of the net estate shall be set aside or appropriated for making periodical payments from the income. However, no more may be set aside or appropriated than is sufficient to produce the income at the date of the order.

Periodical payments are for the term specified in the order. In the case of a former spouse the Act provides expressly that an order shall cease to have effect on the remarriage of the former spouse (s.19(2)). In anyother case, however, the court must decide the date of termination when it makes the order. Orders for periodical payments may be varied (see below, para.20.024).

Periodical payments are unpopular because they are expensive to provide (requiring trust machinery to operate them) and lack finality. It is more common for the court to order a lump sum.

(b) *Lump sum payment.* A lump sum may be made payable by **20.020** instalments in which case the number, amounts and dates for payments of the instalments can be varied; apart from that a lump sum order cannot be varied (s.7).

A lump sum is obviously appropriate in the case of an application by a surviving spouse but it can also be ordered in the case of other applicants even though they are only entitled to maintenance.

Where an estate is very small a lump sum order is particularly useful; indeed it may be the only type of provision which can realistically be made.

(c) *Transfer of property.* The court may order the transfer of a particular asset to an applicant. This may be advisable where a lump sum order would require an improvident sale of assets. Such an order once made cannot be varied.

(d) *Settlement of property.* An order for settlement of property is particularly likely in the case of a minor or a person who is in need of protection. Such a settlement must be drafted with an eye to tax and trust law so that, for example, if a settlement on a minor does not give rise to an interest in possession it should comply with the requirements of an accumulation and maintenance settlement. Such an order, once made, cannot be varied.

(e) *Acquisition of property for transfer or settlement.* The court may order that assets from the net estate of the deceased be used to acquire a specified item (for example, a house) which will either be transferred to or settled on an applicant.

Such an order, once made, cannot be varied.

(f) *Variation of marriage settlements.* An ante or post-nuptial settlement may be varied by the court for the benefit of the surviving spouse of the marriage or the children of the marriage or any person who was treated by the deceased as a child of that marriage. Such an order for variation, once made, cannot be varied.

A provision in a pension scheme allowing an employee to direct benefits to a spouse may be a settlement for this purpose *Brooks v Brooks* (1996). Even where not directly available as a settlement, pension benefits may still be important as they may increase the resources of other people interested in the estate.

2. THE BURDEN OF AN ORDER

Any order made by the court may contain such consequential and **20.021** supplemental provisions as the court thinks necessary or expedient for the purpose of securing that the order operates fairly as between one beneficiary of the estate and another. For example, if the court makes a periodical payments order or a lump sum order it may direct which part of the estate is to bear the burden; if the court orders that an asset which had been specifically left to a beneficiary is to be transferred to the applicant the court may vary the disposition of the estate to make alternative provision for the disappointed beneficiary.

"Beneficiary" in this context includes the donee of a statutory nomination or a *donatio mortis causa* or a surviving joint tenant (see para.20.025 below).

3. INHERITANCE TAX

20.022 The court order alters the disposition of the estate of the deceased and is deemed to have done so from the date of death of the deceased for all purposes including the payment of inheritance tax (Inheritance Tax Act 1984, s.146). Thus, for example, if an order increases the amount passing to a surviving spouse the chargeable value of the estate for inheritance tax purposes will be reduced whereas if less property passes to a surviving spouse the chargeable value will be increased.

In *Re Goodchild* (1997) the court used its variation powers to order that the testator's will was to be treated as if it had always left £185,000 to trustees to pay the income to the deceased's second wife until her death or until March 1 1996, whichever was the earlier, and subject thereto for the applicant absolutely. The purpose of the order was to get the benefit of the spouse exemption and avoid the inheritance tax which would have been payable had the property been left directly to the applicant. The parties took the risk of an inheritance tax liability arising on the death of the second wife if she died within seven years of the termination of the interest in possession.

The Court of Appeal expressed some reservations about the use of variation orders under s.2(4) to obtain a tax benefit. However, Morritt L.J. admitted that "if the order made is properly within the jurisdiction of the court the fact that it was sought with the motive of seeking to achieve a better tax position is usually irrelevant". He went on to say that in future, if such an order was sought "the grounds on which it is thought to be authorised by s.2(4) should be clearly demonstrated for the consents and wishes of the parties are not enough".

4. INTERIM PAYMENTS

20.023 The court has power to make an interim order in favour of an applicant if it appears to the court that:

> (a) the applicant is in immediate need of financial assistance but it is not yet possible to determine what order (if any) should be made; and
>
> (b) property forming part of the net estate of the deceased is or can be made available to meet the needs of the applicant.

5. VARIATION OF PERIODICAL PAYMENTS ORDER

20.024 The court has limited power under s.6 to vary a periodical payments order. It has no power to vary other orders (apart from the number, amounts and dates for payment of instalments of a lump sum). This is in the interest of certainty.

An application for variation can be made by the original recipient and also, *inter alia*, by the personal representatives of the deceased, a beneficiary of the estate or a former applicant (s.6(5)). It can be made during the currency of an order or, where the order was to terminate on the occurrence of a specified event, within six months of that event.

Only property already allocated for periodical payments (called "relevant property") can be affected by a variation order. The court cannot order that relevant property be increased (s.6(6)).

The court will consider all the circumstances of the case including any change in matters it considered when making the original order (s.6(7)). It has power to order that periodical payments continue after the occurrence of a terminating event specified in the original order (other than the remarriage of a former spouse where the termination occurs automatically under s.14 and cannot be varied). It can also direct payment of a lump sum or a transfer of property to the applicant from the relevant property.

The variation order can be made in favour of any of the possible applicants. It is not limited to the original recipient (s.6(2)).

H. Property Available for Financial Provision

1. THE NET ESTATE

If the court decides to order provision to be made for an applicant such an **20.025** order is made against the "net estate" of the deceased.

The net estate is defined by s.25 as comprising:

(a) "All property of which the deceased had power to dispose by his will (otherwise than by virtue of a special power of appointment) less the amount of his funeral, testamentary and administration expenses, debts and liabilities including any inheritance tax payable out of his estate on death".

This will obviously not include insurance policies where the proceeds are payable direct to a beneficiary rather than to the estate of the policyholder as the deceased has no power to dispose of such property.

(b) "Any property in respect of which the deceased held a general power of appointment (not being a power exercisable by will) which has not been exercised".

If the power was exercisable by will the property subject to the power falls into (a) above whether or not the deceased actually exercised it.

(c) Any property nominated by the deceased to any person under a statutory nomination (see Chapter 21) or received by any person as a result of a *donatio mortis causa* (see Chapter 21) less any inheritance tax payable in respect of such property and borne by the nominee or donee (s.8).

(d) The deceased's severable share of a joint tenancy, but only if the court so orders (see s.9 and para.20.026 below).

(e) Any property which the court orders shall be available as a result of its anti-avoidance powers (see para.20.027 below).

Lump sums payable under discretionary pension schemes and policies written in trust for others are not part of the net estate (though the writing in trust may amount to an *inter vivos* gift for the purposes of s.10).

2. JOINT PROPERTY

20.026 As a result of the right of survivorship a deceased has no power to dispose of his interest under a joint tenancy by will. However, under s.9 where the deceased was a joint tenant of any property immediately before death the court may, for the purpose of facilitating the making of financial provision, order that the deceased's severable share of the property (or the value thereof *immediately before his death*) shall to such extent as appears to the court to be just in all the circumstances (and after allowing for any inheritance tax payable) be treated as part of the net estate. The discretion only exists in respect of applications made within six months from the date of the grant; there is no power to make such an order in connection with an out-of-time application.

Section 9(4) expressly provides for the avoidance of doubt that for the purposes of this section there may be a joint tenancy of a chose in action, for example the asset represented by a credit balance in a joint bank account.

In *Kourkgy v Lusher* (1981)Wood J. said that the discretion to treat the interest as part of the net estate should be exercised before the court considers whether reasonable provision has been made so that the court can take its availability into account. That is sensible in practice but does not sit well with the limitation that the interest is only to be available if it will facilitate the making of the order.

In *Powell v Osbourne* (1993) the deceased had left his wife and bought a house jointly with a cohabitee. There was a mortgage with a life policy on their joint lives. The benefit of the policy was payable on the death of the first. A decree nisi between the deceased and the applicant had been declared at the date of death. At first instance the judge had ordered the applicant the greater part of the equity of redemption on the house but had said that the policy was not available because the deceased had no beneficial interest, there being no surrender value.

The Court of Appeal said that under s.9 assets had to be valued immediately before death which was the last moment the deceased could have severed. At that moment the policy had a value. This was because it depended for its value on his death. The imminence of his death meant that the value of the policy was the same as on death. The applicant was therefore entitled to a half share of the policy money.

3. ANTI-AVOIDANCE PROVISIONS

Introduction

20.027 A deceased might attempt to evade the Act either by giving away property *inter vivos* so that the net estate on death is substantially reduced or by entering into a binding contract to leave property by will; the effect of such a contract would be to give the other party to the contract a right to enforce it against the personal representatives, thus reducing the net estate available for family provision. Sections 10 and 11 of the Act enable the court to prevent such evasion; they give power to order a person to satisfy a claim for family provision if he has benefited under an *inter vivos* disposition or a contract to provide money or other property.

Inter vivos dispositions

A disposition is covered by s.10 if it was made: **20.028**

    (a) after March 31, 1976 and less than six years before the date of death of the deceased; and

    (b) with the intention of defeating an application under the Act; and

    (c) for less than full valuable consideration.

A "disposition" for this purpose includes any payment of money (including insurance premiums) and any conveyance of property whether or not made by instrument. It does not, however, include any statutory nomination, *donatio mortis causa* or appointment of property under a special power of appointment.

Contracts

A contract is covered by s.11 of the Act if: **20.029**

    (a) entered into after March 31, 1976; and

    (b) the deceased agreed to leave money or other property by will or agreed that money or other property would be paid or transferred to any person from this estate; and

    (c) the deceased made the contract with the intention of defeating an application under the Act; and

    (d) when the contract was made full valuable consideration was not given or promised.

In the case of a contract there is no time limit as there is in the case of *inter vivos* dispositions.

The intention of defeating an application

The deceased must have made a disposition or contract with the intention **20.030** of defeating an application. Section 12 provides that this requirement is satisfied if the court is of the opinion on a balance of probabilities that the deceased's intention (though not necessarily his sole intention) in making the disposition or contract was to prevent an order for financial provision being made or to reduce the amount of the provision which might otherwise be ordered.

In the case of a contract, s.12(2) provides that, if a contract is made for no valuable consideration at all (that is, by way of a deed), there will be a presumption that the deceased's intention was to defeat the application.

The facilitating of financial provision for the applicant

Even if a disposition is covered by s.10 or a contract is covered by s.11 the **20.031** court will not use its anti-avoidance powers unless satisfied that to do so will facilitate the making of financial provision.

The powers of the court are discretionary

20.032   If the court is satisfied of the above requirements it may make an order against a donee. However, this is a discretionary matter and in deciding what order (if any) to make the court is directed to consider the circumstances in which the disposition or contract was made, any valuable consideration that was given, the relationship (if any) of the donee to the deceased, the conduct and financial resources of the donee and all the other circumstances of the case (s.10(6) and s.11(4)).

Orders against a donee of a disposition

20.033   The court may order a donee to provide such sum of money or other property as it may specify (s.10(2)). However, there are two limitations:

   (a) if the donee was given money he cannot be ordered to provide more than the money paid to him by the deceased less any inheritance tax borne by the donee in respect of the payment (s.10(3));
   (b) if the donee was given property he cannot be ordered to provide more than the value of the property at the date of death of the deceased less any inheritance tax borne by the donee in respect of the payment (s.10(4)). (If he has disposed of the property prior to the deceased's death the limit is the value of the property at the date of disposal).

Order against a "donee" under a contract

20.034   If the personal representatives of the deceased have not transferred money or other property to the donee in accordance with the provisions of the contract, before the date of the application, the court may order them not to make such payment or transfer, or to make no further payment or transfer or to make only a reduced payment or transfer (s.11(2)(ii)). The effect of such an order is to increase the net estate of the deceased available for financial provision.

   If the personal representatives of the deceased have already transferred money or property to the donee before the date of the application in accordance with the provisions of the contract, the court may order the donee to provide such sum of money or other property as it may specify (s.11(2)(i)).

   The court may only make such orders to the extent that the property transferred under the contract exceeds the value of any consideration given (the property to be valued at the date of the hearing) (s.11(3)).

Order against donee's personal representatives

20.035   If a donee has died the court has the same powers against the donee's personal representatives under ss.10 and 11 as it would have had against the donee. However, once property has been distributed by the personal representatives the powers of the court cease with regard to that property. The personal representatives will not be liable if they distribute the donee's property without notice of the making of an application under ss.10 and 11 (s.12(4)).

Order against a trustee of the donee
If the deceased transferred property to a trustee or contracted to have **20.036**
property transferred to a trustee with the intention of defeating an
application the trustee can be ordered to provide property (s.13(1) and
(3)). Section 13 also provides limits on the amount that the trustee can be
ordered to repay.

Illustration of use of power
Hanbury v Hanbury (1999) is a good illustration of the court using its
anti-avoidance powers. The deceased had had no contact with his
mentally and physically disabled daughter from the date of the
breakdown of his marriage to her mother save that he paid £900 per
annum for her maintenance. After legal advice and with the intention of
defeating any claim brought on behalf of the daughter he transferred
assets into either the joint names of himself and his wife or into her name
alone. When he died he left his daughter £10,000 from his estate of
£11,981 (apparently calculating that this would be sufficient to prevent a
claim).

Sections 9 and 10 were used to recover more than £50,000 of assets from
the second wife. Shares in investment trusts (worth £100,000 at the date of
death) had been bought in the second wife's name from a joint bank
account fed by both parties.

See *Re Dawkins, (Deceased)* (1986) for another example of s.10 in
operation.

I. The Choice of Court

1. THE COUNTY COURT

As a result of the Courts and Legal Services Act 1990, the county court **20.037**
has unlimited jurisdiction (see County Courts Act 1984, s.25 inserted by
the High Court and County Court Jurisdiction Order 1991 (SI 91/724)).
This is in marked contrast to the jurisdiction in normal probate and equity
cases which is limited to £30,000.

Proceedings can issue in any county court. London based practitioners
may wish to have proceedings heard in the Central London County Court
which has a Chancery Users list. The judges here have a great deal of
expertise. However, it is necessary to ask expressly to be put in the
Chancery Users list. The matter will not be allocated automatically just
because of its nature.

2. THE FAMILY OR CHANCERY DIVISION OF THE HIGH COURT

An application for an order may be made either in the Chancery Division **20.038**
or in the Family Division. There are no rules limiting the applicant's
freedom of choice and a practitioner is therefore free to choose whichever
seems the more appropriate. Frequently they will be equally suitable so
that the practitioner's choice may be governed by personal preference
and experience; on occasion, however, one Division may have a particular
advantage. For example, it is appropriate to use the Family Division in a

case involving the determination of the award a spouse would have got on divorce. The Chancery Division is more suitable where there is a dispute as to the validity of a will which is alleged not to make reasonable financial provision for the applicant (in such a case the probate action can be heard immediately before the family provision application by the same judge with a consequent saving of time and expense), where the true meaning of the will must first be determined under a construction summons or where complicated accounts have to be taken.

21. Disposing of Property otherwise than by Will

A. Introduction

It is generally considered to be a "good thing" to make a will. In this **21.001** chapter we will consider, firstly, to what extent it is possible to dispose of property on death without a will and, secondly, why solicitors advise clients to make wills.

B. Disposition of Property Without a Will

It is important to remember that making a will is not the only means of **21.002** disposing of property after death. Solicitors advising intending testators should ensure their clients are aware of the other possibilities.

1. STATUTORY NOMINATIONS

Where a person is entitled to certain types of investments he can **21.003** nominate a third party to receive them on his death. In such cases the property will not vest in the nominator's personal representatives on death but will be paid directly to the nominee. The payer will, therefore, want to see the death certificate of the deceased but will not require production of the grant of representation. The nominated property does, however, form part of the deceased's estate for inheritance tax purposes.

Nominations were originally designed to allow the poorer members of society to dispose of small amounts of money without the necessity of making a will or of their representatives obtaining a grant. They can be made in respect of deposits in certain Trustee Savings Banks, Friendly Societies and Industrial and Provident Societies up to a limit of £5,000 each. It used to be possible to nominate National Savings Certificates and deposits in National Savings Banks and Trustee Savings Banks but this power was withdrawn as from May 1, 1979 in respect of the latter and May 1, 1981 in respect of the two former (nominations of such property *made* before those dates remain effective).

To be valid, a nomination must be:

(a) in writing;
(b) made by a person who is 16 or over; and
(c) attested by one witness.

Since a will cannot be made by a person who is under the age of 18, a nomination is the only way in which a minor can dispose of property (unless he has privileged status) after death.

A nomination is revoked by subsequent marriage, a later nomination or the death of the nominee before the nominator but it is *not* revoked by a subsequent will. It is therefore important when drafting a will for a client to ascertain whether or not any nominations have previously been made. They are easily overlooked as the paying authority normally holds the nomination form.

2. Discretionary pension schemes

21.004 Many pension schemes allow contributors to "nominate" a third party to receive benefits after the contributors' death either in the form of a lump sum or a pension. Where a lump sum is paid it is often the most substantial single asset passing on death and may be used to make a substantial gift to a beneficiary. However, such lump sums are normally only paid when the contributor dies "in service" and therefore the provision for the beneficiary may have to be reconsidered when the contributor ceases to contribute to the scheme (whether on retirement or as a result of changing jobs).

Such a "nomination" is not binding on the trustees of the pension fund being merely an indication of the deceased's wishes, although, naturally, they will usually abide by the expressed wishes of the deceased. This procedure is sometimes referred to as a "nomination" but it is obviously different from the type of nomination referred to in para.21.003 above where the deceased has an absolute right to the property and is free to deal with it as he likes whether after his death or during his lifetime.

These benefits do not form part of the deceased's estate for inheritance tax purposes.

3. Donatio mortis causa

The requirements for a donatio mortis causa
21.005 A *donatio mortis causa* is an *inter vivos* gift which is conditional on death. It has some of the attributes of a legacy and some of an *inter vivos* gift. There are four requirements which must be satisfied if a *donatio mortis causa* is to be valid:

(a) *The gift must be made in contemplation of death.* The death need not be imminent so it is, for example, sufficient that a person knows he has a serious illness and cannot live for long. It is irrelevant that death occurs from a supervening cause (such as an accident or a sudden second illness—*Wilkes v Allington* (1931)) but the gift fails if the donor recovers from the contemplated cause of death. The cause of death need not be an illness as such, contemplation of a dangerous operation is enough.

(b) *The gift must be conditional on death.* If the donor recovers from the contemplated cause of death, the gift will not take effect and the donor will be entitled to regain possession of the property. If, however, the donor dies then the gift to the donee becomes absolute. If there are formal requirements for transfer which need to be complied with in order to complete title then the donee can compel the deceased's personal representatives to complete the transfer.

(c) *The donor must part with dominion over the property before death.* Delivery must be made to the donee (or his agent) of the subject-matter of the gift or the means of obtaining it. In the case of chattels it is usually readily apparent whether or not this has taken place but in the case of choses in action it is a little more difficult. Since choses in action cannot be physically delivered there must be delivery of the essential evidence of title which will entitle the possessor to the property given (for example, delivery of National Savings Certificates or bills of exchange).

In both *Sen v Headley* and *Woodard v Woodard* (1991) the deceased **21.006** delivered a set of keys (in the first case of a house and in the second case of a car) but retained a set himself. In both cases the Court of Appeal held that the retention of the keys did not prevent the donor parting with dominion. In both cases, however, the donor was terminally ill in hospital and could not have made use of the second set of keys unless there had been an unexpected recovery which in any event would have revoked the gift. In *Woodard* it was also argued that the deceased should have handed over the registration document (and possibly the insurance certificate and servicing log book). The Court of Appeal rejected this argument. These items were not documents of title, nor was it essential to hand them over to give the defendant dominion over the car. The handing over would merely have been evidence of the intention to make a gift.

(d) *The subject-matter of the gift must be capable of passing as a valid donatio mortis causa.* Most personalty is so capable (for example, chattels, bonds, insurance policies or National Savings Certificates). A cheque drawn by a third party can be the subject of a valid donation but a cheque drawn by the deceased cannot since it is merely an order to the deceased's bank to pay which will be automatically revoked by death.

It has been suggested that shares cannot be the subject of a valid *donatio mortis causa* (*Re Weston* (1902)) but there seems to be no reason in principle why this should be so and indeed the possibility of a *donatio mortis causa* of company shares was accepted in *Staniland v Willott* (1852), although on the facts it was held to have been revoked by the donor's recovery from his illness.

The Court of Appeal held in *Sen v Headley* that, contrary to previous thinking, land is capable of passing by *donatio mortis causa*.

Comparison with legacies
It is worth noting the more important similarities and differences between **21.007** legacies and *donationes mortis causa*.

(a) *Similarities*

(a) *Lapse.* A *donatio mortis causa* lapses if the donee predeceases the donor. The subject-matter will then form part of the donor's estate on death.
(b) *Tax.* Inheritance tax is payable on the property which is the subject-matter of the *donatio mortis causa* as it is part of the donor's estate on death.

(c) *Liability for debts*. If the estate of the deceased proves insufficient to pay the deceased's debts then the subject-matter of a *donatio mortis causa* may be taken (see para.15.018).

(b) *Differences*

(a) *No assent*. Normally the personal representatives of the deceased transfer title to beneficiaries by means of an assent. However, since death makes a *donatio mortis causa* absolute, the personal representatives need do nothing unless there are formal requirements which need to be complied with in order to complete the title.

(b) *Revocation*. A *donatio mortis causa* is revoked if the donor recovers from the contemplated cause of death or if the donor resumes possession and dominion of the property. It cannot be revoked by a subsequent will.

4. JOINT TENANCIES

21.008 Joint tenancies are extremely important in practice since they are the most common way for property to be transferred without a will.

Where the deceased was a joint tenant in equity of any property, on his death his interest will pass automatically to the surviving joint tenant(s). It will not devolve on the deceased's personal representatives and cannot pass under the terms of his will. This is because it is not possible to sever a joint tenancy by will. However, a joint tenant is free to sever the joint tenancy *inter vivos* in which case the deceased and the co-owners will hold as tenants-in-common in equity. Such an interest *will* devolve on the deceased's personal representatives and *will* pass under the deceased's will or on intestacy.

Solicitors who are preparing wills for clients should explain to them that jointly owned property will pass to the survivor no matter how short the period of survivorship may be, despite anything said in the will. For this reason it may be appropriate for a client to sever a joint tenancy *inter vivos*. The client is then free to leave the beneficial tenancy-in-common to the survivor *provided the survivor survives* for a stated period.

In *Carr-Glynn v Frearsons* (1998) a solicitor was held to have been negligent for allowing a testatrix to execute a will not knowing whether or not it would be effective and without explaining that it was possible to serve a precautionary notice of severance.

It is also important to remember that joint tenancies can be severed without serving a notice of severance. Section 36(2) of the Law of Property Act 1925 introduced the notice of severance but expressly preserved all the existing methods of severing a beneficial joint tenancy. According to *Williams v Hensman* (1861) 1 John & H at 558 there are three methods:

(1) an act of any one of the persons interested operating upon his own share may create a severance as to that share;
(2) mutual agreement;

(3) any course of dealing sufficient to intimate that the interests of all were mutually treated as constituting a tenancy in common.

In *Re Woolnough, Perkins v Borden* (2002) a brother and sister, Len and Emmy, owned a property as beneficial joint tenants. They went together to see a solicitor and each made wills leaving the house to the survivor for life and then to their niece, Dorothy, with a substitutional gift to her children. In 1989 Dorothy died and Len made a new will picking out one of Dorothy's three children as his residuary beneficiary. Emmy left her will unchanged. After Emmy's death, Len made a new will leaving everything to charity.

21.009

The issue was whether or not the joint tenancy had been severed by mutual consent before Emmy's death. If it had, only half of the value of the house was in Len's estate. If it had not, he had the whole value of the house.

The court found that the making of the two wills was inconsistent with the continuance of the joint tenancy and amounted to an agreement.

It would not, of course, have amounted to severance had one joint tenant alone made a will dealing with the half share. This is because a will is ambulatory in form and has no effect until death.

Where, as in *Re Woolnough* clients want to make wills which are inconsistent with a continuing joint tenancy, it is important that there is clarity as to when the severance takes place. Solicitors should consider preparing a signed agreement or notice of severance without delay.

It may be necessary to establish whether there has already been a severance by mutual agreement:

- when taking instructions for a will from a client who appears to hold the beneficial interest in the whole of an asset as a result of survivorship (like Len in *Re Woolnough*); or
- when administering an estate for a deceased who appears to be a sole surviving joint tenant.

5. INSURANCE POLICIES

Where a person takes out life assurance, on his death the insurance company will pay the assured amount to the deceased's personal representatives. This sum will form part of the death estate and so can potentially attract inheritance tax.

21.010

Inheritance tax will not be payable if the death estate falls within the nil rate band or an exemption (such as the spouse exemption) applies. However, even if the property is to be paid to a spouse, the personal representatives will have to wait until a grant is obtained before the insurance company will hand over the money. This delay may be inconvenient at best or financially disastrous for the spouse, at worst.

Rather than have the money channelled through the estate (which will be ill-advised for inheritance tax purposes if the sum is large and the intended beneficiary is not a spouse or a charity), it is better to have the money paid direct to the intended beneficiary.

This can be achieved in one of two ways. First, the assured can make use of the Married Woman's Property Act 1882, s.11. Under this section a policy of life assurance effected by a person on his own life can be expressed to be for the benefit of his spouse and/or children (which includes children of a non-marital relationship). This creates a trust in their favour and on the death, the sum assured is paid direct to the trustees of the policy for the benefit of the named beneficiaries. No inheritance tax charge will arise in respect of the assured's estate where policies are written in trust in this way since he has no beneficial interest. However, provided the gift is not subject to a contingency, the named beneficiary receives an immediate absolute interest. Therefore, should the beneficiary predecease the assured, the beneficiary's estate suffers tax on the appropriate proportion of the value of the policy. Since the beneficiary has an immediate absolute interest in the policy the assured is no longer free to surrender or assign the policy.

Since s.11 permits the assured to name his children as beneficiaries it is advisable to appoint trustees to hold the money until the children reach a suitable age. If such trustees are not appointed, the assured's personal representatives will hold the money as trustees, on trust for the children. Should this situation arise, the sum is still not taxed as part of the assured's estate since the sum does not belong to the estate, it is merely administratively convenient for the personal representatives to hold the property in this way.

If the assured wants to benefit someone other than a spouse or children (such as a friend or grandchildren) the policy must be expressly written in trust for them. The trust has the same effect as a s.11 policy. The same result will be achieved by assigning the policy to the named beneficiary.

6. ENDURING POWERS OF ATTORNEY

21.011 Any person may appoint an attorney to deal with his property. However, the power of attorney will automatically end if the person who made the appointment (the donor of the power) becomes mentally incapable. However, the Enduring Power of Attorney Act 1985 provides for the appointment of an attorney whose powers will survive the incapacity of the donor. A solicitor who is advising a person making a will should consider advising the appointment of an attorney with an enduring power. Where such an appointment is made the attorney may be given power to sell the donor's property, and to a limited extent to give it away, notwithstanding the donor's incapacity.

An attorney acting under such a power should try to avoid acting in such a way as may cause ademption of testamentary gifts. (See *Re Dorman* and para.16.054 above).

C. Lifetime Planning

1. GIFTS

21.012 As an alternative to leaving property to an intended beneficiary by will, a client can consider making a lifetime gift.

Such a gift has the advantage of giving the beneficiary the immediate use of the asset but it has the corresponding disadvantage that the donor will lose the benefit of the property (unless, for example, the gift is to a spouse).

Therefore, it is important to ensure that the donor has no need of the property to be given away. A gift of money that will leave the donor with financial problems is pointless as is the gift of an asset that the donor still wants to use. It is quite common for testators to want to leave books, jewellery, fishing tackle, golf clubs and similar items to friends or relatives but they would obviously not wish to make such gifts during their lifetime.

While lifetime gifts should always be considered, they are usually only practicable where the donor is fairly wealthy. An additional advantage is that a lifetime gift may be useful in saving tax.

Tax considerations

Although tax should never be the first consideration, since lifetime **21.013** transfers to individuals do not attract an immediate inheritance tax liability a lifetime gift will prima facie produce a saving. There is a danger that the donor will die within seven years of the transfer in which case inheritance tax will be charged (subject to tapering relief). It may be wise to insure against the risk of death in this period. The advantage of saving inheritance tax may be outweighed by capital gains tax considerations.

Inheritance tax

In deciding when a lifetime gift is advantageous for inheritance tax **21.014** purposes the donor should remember that because of the existence of the nil rate band, one large estate attracts a greater liability to tax than two small ones. For example, in tax year 2003/04 an estate of £605,000 will attract £140,000 in tax on death (assuming no chargeable *inter vivos* transfers have been made within seven years). However, two estates of £302,500 will attract only £19,000 each (again assuming nil lifetime cumulative totals).

Where one party to a marriage owns substantially more property than the other, it may be advisable for that party to consider making lifetime gifts to the other. Then in the event of both parties to the marriage dying at or about the same time they can each leave their estates to their children obtaining the benefit of two nil rate bands. There will not be any tax saving if the spouses equalise their estates but the first to die leaves his or her entire property to the other. However, it may be that one spouse *needs* to leave his or her estate to the surviving spouse to ensure that the survivor has sufficient funds.

There is an advantage in making potentially exempt transfers of assets which are likely to increase in value over the next few years. Inheritance tax in the event of the transferor's death is calculated on the value of the property at the time the gift is made, not on its value at the time of death. Thus, the value of the property is effectively "frozen" and less inheritance tax will be payable. This value "freezing" will not occur if the donor continues to derive a benefit from the property given away. In such a case the reservation of benefit rules will apply and the property will be treated for inheritance tax purposes as part of the deceased's estate on death (see para.4.011).

Capital gains tax

21.015 In view of the fact that capital gains tax is not paid on death and the donor acquires the property at its market value at death, lifetime gifts are apparently less advantageous. However, the exemptions or reliefs (such as the annual exemption, the spouse relief, retirement relief, taper relief and indexation allowance) may in many circumstances mean that no capital gains tax is actually payable, so that the gift can be made if other considerations make the disposition advisable.

2. BUSINESS PROPERTY

21.016 The proprietor of a business should give careful consideration to what provisions he wishes to make for the continuation of the business after his death. It will often be necessary to make provision *inter vivos* and not by will. For example, if the business is run through a company consideration should be given to the possible alteration of the articles so as to provide for the company purchasing its own shares and/or for rights of pre-emption in respect of these shares. If the business is a partnership some provision should be made for succession to the deceased partner's interest by the remaining partners or by the deceased partner's relatives or for the realisation of the value of the interest when the partner dies or retires.

In making such arrangements taxation must be taken into account. It is important to realise, however, that a tax effective disposition should not be made if it conflicts with more general commercial considerations.

Business property is favourably treated for tax purposes. A gift of a business or an interest in a business is eligible for inheritance tax business property relief (see para.4.034) which may in itself produce a large saving in the tax payable. However, planning in advance may produce further savings. Provision may be made in a partnership agreement for automatic accrual of goodwill. This means that when a partner dies his interest in the goodwill passes automatically to the other partners. Clearly this automatic accrual reduces the partner's interest in the goodwill and the value of his estate on death. To the extent that consideration in money or money's worth was given for the accrual clause, the entry into the clause will not be a transfer of value for inheritance tax purposes. There may be some difficulty in showing that consideration was given for such an accrual clause in the case of a family partnership. However, an estate duty case (*Attorney General v Boden* (1912)), which is generally considered still to be relevant, held that an agreement to work for the business is consideration in money or money's worth.

An option granted (for money or money's worth) to purchase goodwill at a fixed price may also give rise to a tax saving. The value of the goodwill to the partner on death is the price that his estate will be paid on the exercise of the option. An agreement that a partner's share *must* be purchased on his death is not advisable as the Inland Revenue argues that this contract of sale may disentitle the deceased partner to the business property relief (Statement of Practice 12/80, October 13, 1980).

The Revenue now accepts that automatic accruer clauses (where the share of a deceased partner passes automatically to the surviving partners in return for a payment either on valuation or in accordance with a formula) do not constitute binding contracts for sale and that neither do option arrangements (see *Law Society Gazette* September 4, 1996, p.35).

If a business is to be run as a company then, when the company is formed consideration should be given to the possibility of providing pre-emption rights. These are rights whereby when one shareholder disposes of his shares, or dies owning these shares, the other shareholders are given a right to buy at a price fixed by or to be fixed in accordance with the company's articles of association. Such a pre-emption right is an option so that the same considerations apply as in the case of a partner's option to purchase goodwill.

D. Why Make a Will?

There are a number of reasons why solicitors often advise clients to make wills.

1. To avoid the application of the intestacy rules

As was explained in Chapter 3, the property of a person who dies without **21.017** making a will, passes according to a strict legal order. A person who dies intestate, therefore, has no control over who are to be the recipients of his estate and so cannot benefit friends or charities without making a will. Persons who are married will usually want their property to pass to their spouses but it is only in the case of small estates that the whole of the property will pass to the surviving spouse under the intestacy rules. If the estate is larger and the deceased is survived by a spouse and issue, the intestacy rules which leave the spouse personal chattels, a statutory legacy of £125,000 and only a life interest in one half of the residue may be unacceptable. Although the spouse may be able to capitalise the life interest, a portion of the estate will still go to the children and the spouse may have insufficient funds to maintain an existing standard of living. While a variation (see Chapter 19) may in some cases provide a solution it is clearly more desirable to prevent the problem ever arising. A beneficiary who is under 18 cannot give up an interest in an estate; a parent or guardian cannot do so on behalf of a minor.

The solicitor should, therefore, suggest making a will since otherwise clients cannot ensure that their wishes as to the disposition of their property will be respected. (A solicitor should inform a client that in certain circumstances a relative or other dependant might be able to claim under the Inheritance (Provision for Family and Dependants) Act 1975).

Even though a client is satisfied with the general disposition of property under the intestacy rules, if he wants to ensure that a particular item is to pass to one of the people specified in the intestacy rules, this can be only done by will.

Furthermore, clients may wish to demonstrate expressly that they are happy for their property to pass to the persons who would be entitled under the intestacy rules by making a will in their favour.

2. APPOINTMENT OF PERSONAL REPRESENTATIVES AND TRUSTEES

21.018 In a will, a testator can make a choice of executors and trustees, whereas on intestacy the personal representatives are determined by r.22 of the Non-Contentious Probate Rules 1987 (see para.8.016). If a will is made, it is possible for the testator to choose persons who are suitable and who are likely to be willing to act.

Since an executor's authority dates from death, whereas an administrator's dates only from the grant of representation, the appointment of an executor may facilitate the administration of the estate.

3. APPOINTMENT OF GUARDIANS

21.019 Testators are often concerned to provide appropriate care for their children. A solicitor should explain that guardians can be appointed in the will. These guardians will normally act after the death of the surviving spouse but can act jointly with the spouse in certain circumstances. It is advisable to include an express appointment since this will ensure that the testator gives thought to whom to appoint. A solicitor should advise a client who proposes to appoint a guardian to consult the prospective guardian as to whether or not he or she is willing to act. The question of finance for the guardian should be considered. Guardians are dealt with more fully in para.22.018.

It is not necessary to make a will to appoint a guardian but it is a convenient place to do it.

4. EXTENSION OF STATUTORY POWERS

21.020 If a will is made, additional powers can be conferred on personal representatives and trustees which will facilitate the administration. These powers are considered in Chapter 22.

5. DIRECTIONS AS TO BURIAL AND DISPOSAL OF BODY

21.021 If the testator has special wishes as to burial or cremation these can be included in the will.

The wishes are not binding as people have no property in their bodies after their death *Williams v Williams* (1882). Although personal representatives will normally want to give effect to the deceased's wishes, they can ignore directions for a lavish or unconventional funeral.

Some people consider "alternative burials" in woods, fields or gardens. They must obtain the consent of the relevant local authority. This is because a body is treated as clinical waste and can, therefore, only be disposed of by a licensed operator in accordance with the Control of Pollution Act 1974 and the Environmental Protection Act 1990.

If relatives want to bury the body in the garden, they will have to take advice from the Environment Agency which has a list of minimum distances from the site of a grave to water, cabling and wells or boreholes. The Department of the Environment, Transport and the Regions says that it is not necessary to apply for planning permission to bury up to two people in a back garden. Permission would be required to bury any more. It is possible to apply for a certificate of lawfulness as regards planning law. The result of the application is recorded on a public register. If the application is refused, there is a right of free appeal.

The British Humanist Association website at *www.humanism.org.uk* has publications on secular funerals and provides advice on non-religious funerals. See also *www.funeralsuk.com.*

Testators may want their organs to be available for donation. A person can give written consent at any time or oral consent during his or her last illness to the use of organs for therapeutic purposes or for the purposes of medical education or research. (Even without that consent the persons lawfully in possession of the body can authorise the use of organs so long as after making reasonable enquiries, they have no reason to believe the deceased had expressed any objection and have no reason to believe that any surviving spouse or surviving relative will object).

Such directions can be included in the will but it is better for the client to carry a donor card and make sure that family members are aware of his or her wishes. A mere statement in the will may not be discovered in time to be useful.

6. "LIVING WILLS"

It is never lawful to take active steps to cause or accelerate death. Even where a person wishes to die, anyone offering assistance will be guilty of complicity in suicide under the Suicide Act 1961, s.2 (see *R. (on the application of Pretty) v DPP* (2002)). **21.022**

However, in certain circumstances it is lawful to withhold life-sustaining treatment such as artificial feeding and ventilation without which the patient will die (see *Airedale Trust v Bland* (1993)). There is a Practice Note, *Official Solicitor: Vegetative State* (1996), which deals with the procedure to be followed in applications for the withdrawal of artificial feeding and hydration. The official solicitor acts on behalf of the patient. Previously expressed advance directives of the patient, in writing or otherwise, will be an important factor.

It is becoming increasingly common for people to want to make advance directives (commonly referred to as "living wills") stating that in the event of a loss of mental capacity they do not wish to be given medical treatment for any life-threatening illness. Such a statement should not be incorporated into a will but should be kept separately. Close relatives should be informed of the existence and whereabouts of the statement.

Many organisations have produced living wills. A good example is that produced by the Terrence Higgins Trust (Gray's Inn Road, London WC1). This declares that a testator should not be kept alive by artificial means where the testator suffers from illnesses from which he or she is unlikely to recover, or from mental impairment or permanent unconsciousness.

There are no statutory provisions dealing with living wills and their legal status is uncertain.

Even though there is uncertainty as to the extent to which the medical profession will feel able to comply with the expressed wishes of patients, it is likely that increasing numbers of clients will wish to have such living wills.

It is necessary to be very specific in the terms of such a document. In *Re B: Consent to Treatment: Capacity* (2002) Ms B wrote a living will which stated that should the time come when she was unable to give instructions, she wished for treatment to be withdrawn if she was suffering from a life-threatening condition, permanent mental impairment or permanent unconsciousness. As a result of a ruptured blood vessel in her neck she was left paralysed from the neck down.

Her living will was not appropriate to the circumstances of her illness and the medical staff refused to withdraw treatment. She was able to give instructions that she did not wish treatment to continue but the medical staff questioned her mental capacity. The Court of Appeal found that Ms B had possessed the requisite mental capacity to make decisions regarding her treatment and, thus, the administration of artificial respiration by the trust against her wishes had amounted to an unlawful trespass. She was to withdraw consent to future treatment.

7. Tax considerations

21.023   The possible dispositions that can be made are considered in detail in Chapter 22 but the tax advantages to be gained from a carefully drafted will should be drawn to the testator's attention.

The particular circumstances and wishes of the testator must, of course, be paramount in the mind of the solicitor who must not suggest a disposition that is tax-efficient but leaves a beneficiary destitute or that is directly contrary to the desires of the testator.

Assuming the estate is large enough to make tax planning a worthwhile exercise, the solicitor should advise on matters such as the use of the inheritance tax nil rate band to give legacies to non-exempt beneficiaries and the use of survivorship clauses. A survivorship clause will only save tax where the deaths occur within a short space of time. If the survivor outlives the first to die by the period specified in the clause, the property will belong to the survivor and any tax saving may be lost.

22. Planning and Drafting a Will

A. Introduction

1. TAKING INSTRUCTIONS

A solicitor who is asked to prepare a will for a client will usually find that a **22.001** personal interview is necessary. The object of the interview is to obtain, in as short a time as possible, all the information which the solicitor needs in order to prepare the will.

It is often helpful to have a "checklist" for taking instructions so that none of the information required is forgotten and no further correspondence or meetings are required. If the checklist is in the form of a questionnaire it may be possible for some other member of the firm to use it to draft the will if necessary.

In appropriate circumstances the solicitor should discuss with the client possible action that can be taken during the client's lifetime to arrange financial and business affairs sensibly. In order that advice can be given on taxation and on the suitability of the proposed dispositions the solicitor should find out what property the client owns and whether there is any property (such as joint property or insurance policies) which will pass independently of the will. The client should also be advised on the effect of any proposed dispositions.

If the testator is married, the solicitor should point out that it is advisable for the testator's spouse to make a will at the same time. The reason for this is that thought can then be given to the ultimate destination of their respective estates.

The solicitor who takes instructions from the client should make a written note (on the questionnaire, if used) of the details of the name and address of the testator, the executor(s), and the beneficiaries and where relevant of any testamentary guardian(s) or trustee(s). He should make sure that he has the correct names of the various people mentioned in the will—this is particularly important in the case of institutions, such as charities.

Where specific items of property are dealt with in the will, a sufficient description is required so that they can be identified. A draftsman should be careful to avoid errors in description which may cause a gift to fail.

2. TYPES OF DISPOSITION

Dispositions of property in a will are basically of three types—specific **22.002** gifts, general legacies and gifts of residue. The testator should be encouraged to think carefully about the purpose of each intended gift. If he wants a particular person to have a particular asset, then a specific gift is likely to be suitable (although he should be warned that the gift will be adeemed if the property is sold or changed in nature). If he wants a particular person to have a fixed amount of money, then a general (pecuniary) legacy is suitable. A residuary gift is likely to be most suitable for the major beneficiary or beneficiaries of the estate. A residuary gift should always be included in a will so as to avoid the possibility of a partial intestacy. For the same reason the testator should consider the possibility that the residuary beneficiary may predecease him and should consider whether he wishes to include a substitutional beneficiary.

The choice of dispositions will largely depend on the testator's family circumstances. The following are among the most common dispositions where a will is made by a married person with children:

(a) *All to spouse.* A will which leaves everything to the testator's spouse will ensure that the surviving spouse is provided for as far as possible. However, the testator has no control over the ultimate destination of the property and must trust the spouse to make appropriate dispositions. There is a danger of accidental disinheritance of children where a surviving spouse remarries without realising that marriage automatically revokes an earlier will. If, because of the size of the estate, inheritance tax is a consideration the following points should be borne in mind:

(a) No tax will be payable on the testator's death (since the spouse exemption is available);

(b) If the entire estate is given to the surviving spouse the testator will die without having made use of the nil rate band;

(c) Inheritance tax will be payable on the surviving spouse's death on the whole of the property owned at that time (unless an exemption is available). A relatively large amount of tax may be payable on the surviving spouse's estate since it is likely to include much of the property inherited from the first spouse and yet there will be only one nil rate band available. This problem can be mitigated if the surviving spouse makes *inter vivos* gifts, taking advantage of lifetime exemptions;

22.003   (b) *Spouse for life remainder to children.* With this type of disposition the testator retains control over the ultimate destination of the property. However, since the spouse is entitled only to the income from the property, he or she may have insufficient funds available—this problem can be alleviated if the trustees are given power to advance or lend capital to the surviving spouse.

The inheritance tax consequences are virtually the same as in the case of an outright gift (since the surviving spouse has an interest in possession in the settled property and the spouse exemption is therefore available).

(c) *Legacy to spouse, residue to children.* This type of disposition may be appropriate where the testator's spouse is independently wealthy but should always be viewed with a certain amount of caution. Changed circumstances and/or inflation may make the provision for the surviving spouse by means of a legacy quite inadequate in the future. The spouse exemption for inheritance tax is lost, except to the extent of the legacy, but in the long run there may be a tax saving because of the effect of equalising estates.

(d) *Legacy to children, residue to spouse.* This type of disposition has the advantage of making some provision for the children immediately. The legacy should not, of course, be so large as to leave the surviving spouse with insufficient funds.

There may be inheritance tax advantages with this type of gift. The spouse exemption is lost to the extent of the legacy. However, there will be no tax payable until the nil rate band is exhausted. Some provision can, thus, be made for the children immediately without an inheritance tax liability.

It is fairly common to give a legacy of "Such amount as can pass at the date of my death without payment of inheritance tax". This is often referred to as a nil rate band legacy. It is worded as it is, so that if the deceased has used up some of his nil rate band by the time of death only an amount equivalent to the unused portion will pass.

There are two dangers with such a gift:

(a) The size of the nil rate band is likely to fluctuate with successive governments. The gift may turn out to be much larger or smaller by the time the testator dies than was envisaged at the time the will was made.

(b) If the estate contains property which attracts 100 per cent business or agricultural property relief, it can pass without payment of inheritance tax. The gift may turn out to be very much larger than was originally envisaged. It may be desirable to impose a maximum limit on the size of the gift. For example,
"... or an amount equivalent to the nil rate band whichever is the lesser".

(e) *Nil rate band discretionary trust, residue to spouse.* This is becoming increasingly popular. The beneficiaries will include the spouse and issue of the testator. So long as the amount passing away from the spouse does not exceed the testator's unused nil rate band at the date of death, there will be no tax to pay on creation and no periodic or proportionate periodic charges. It allows the testator to build into his will a large element of flexibility.

3. USE OF PRECEDENTS

Precedents are an invaluable aid to good will drafting. Sometimes a **22.004** precedent may be available which is almost exactly what is required but this is unusual. In all but the simplest cases it is likely that the precedent will have to be substantially amended. Before a precedent can be adapted for use in a particular case the draftsman must ensure that he understands what the precedent was intended to do. For example, if a precedent was designed for use where a complicated settlement is being created it is unlikely to be of much use in drafting a will which makes a straightforward absolute gift of residue. Old precedents should be viewed with some caution since they may deal with problems which are no longer relevant (such as capital transfer tax rules) and may not deal with problems resulting from new law (such as those arising from the introduction of inheritance tax). So that the terminology used in different parts of the will is consistent it is best to use precedents from one particular source as far as possible and to take care when combining two or more precedents.

Wills are traditionally drafted without punctuation. To make reading a little easier it is usual to divide the will into numbered clauses and to capitalise the words which explain what the clause is for (so that clauses making gifts usually contain words such as "I GIVE", clauses appointing an executor usually contains the words, "I APPOINT" and clauses containing trusts usually contain the words "UPON TRUST"). Definitions are sometimes very helpful. In particular where several executors or executors and trustees are appointed the words "hereinafter together called 'my Executors' " (or "my Trustees") can be included so that references later in the will can be made to those persons without setting out their names again. Where there is such a definition, it is good practice to capitalise the first letter of the word defined so that the reader can see more readily that the word has been defined (for example, "my Trustee" not "my trustee").

4. STRUCTURE OF A WILL

22.005 A will usually includes the following:

(1) Words of commencement,
(2) Revocation clause,
(3) Appointment of executors (and trustees and guardians if appropriate),
(4) Specific gifts (if any),
(5) General legacies (if any),
(6) A gift of residue,
(7) Extension of executors' and trustees' powers and Declarations,
(8) Attestation clause,
(9) A date.

In the rest of this chapter we will consider the drafting of the various parts of the will.

B. The Formal Parts

22.006 Every professionally drafted will should have the words of commencement, a revocation clause, a date clause and an attestation clause. For the sake of convenience these "formal parts" are dealt with together in this section.

1. COMMENCEMENT

22.007 The commencement of the will is intended to identify the person making the will. The testator's full name and address should be included. If the testator is known to own property in a name which is different from his full name or to use a name which is not his true and proper name, it is advisable to refer to this fact in the opening words of the will. The reason for this is that after the testator's death it will be clear that the grant of representation should refer to both names.

A commonly used form of wording for the commencement of the will is "This is the Last Will and Testament of me [AB] [(also known as [CD])] of [address] [occupation]". If the will is made in expectation of the testator's marriage, it is necessary to incorporate suitable words (see para.2.046).

2. REVOCATION CLAUSE

In Chapter 2 we explained that a later will revokes an earlier will to the extent that it is inconsistent. If the later will deals with the testator's entire estate, all earlier wills and codicils are revoked. Nevertheless, for the avoidance of any possible doubt, a revocation clause should be included in all professionally drafted wills, even if the solicitor believes the present will to be the only will the testator has ever made. **22.008**

The revocation clause can be included in the commencement of the will but it is often set out as a separate clause. (See Wills 1, 2 and 3 in the Appendix.)

An appropriate form of wording is "I hereby REVOKE all former wills and testamentary dispositions made by me".

3. THE DATE CLAUSE

The date can be included in the commencement of the will, or at the end immediately before the attestation clause. It is more common to include the date at the end. **22.009**

The date clause may be important in identifying which of a number of wills was the last or in identifying the subject-matter of a gift. The usual form of words is "IN WITNESS whereof I have hereunto set my hand this   day of   200   ".

4. THE ATTESTATION CLAUSE

The presence of a correctly drafted attestation clause will in most cases satisfy the registrar that the requirements of Wills Act 1837, s.9 as amended by the Administration of Justice Act 1982 have been complied with. (As was explained in paragraph 10.044 the absence of an attestation clause will lead the registrar to require affidavit evidence to prove due execution under the Non-Contentious Probate Rules 1987, r.12.) **22.010**

The two most common forms of attestation are as follows:

(a) The Short Form.

"Signed by the above [AB] in our joint presence and then by us in [his/hers]."

(b) The Long Form.

> "Signed by the above-named [AB] as [his/her] last will in the presence of us both present at the same time who at [his/her] request in [his/her] presence and in the presence of each other have hereunto subscribed our names as witnesses."

These clauses, implying as they do that the witnesses signed in each other's presence as well as in the presence of the testator, go beyond the strict wording of s.9 as amended but may reduce the possibility of the attestation being challenged after the death.

Where the testator suffers from some disability which would cast doubt on the validity of the will due to the suspected absence of knowledge and approval of the wording of the will, the forms of attestation clause set out above should be amended. The purpose of the amendment is to indicate that the testator did in fact know and approve of the contents of the will.

Thus, if the testator is blind or illiterate or seriously ill the attestation clause should state that the will was read over to him and that he appeared thoroughly to understand and approve its contents.

If someone signs on the testator's behalf, this fact should be stated in the clause together with a confirmation that the will was signed in the presence of, and at the direction of, the testator. The person signing may sign in his or her own name or that of the testator.

22.011 Whenever the circumstances are such that, after the testator's death, there may be doubt as to his capacity or as to his knowledge and approval of the contents of the will the solicitor should try to be present and should make a full and careful file note. It is desirable that a medical practitioner be asked to prepare a note of the testator's mental and physical state.

Illustrations of such clauses appear below.

(i) ATTESTATION CLAUSE WHERE SOMEONE SIGNS ON BEHALF OF THE TESTATOR

Signed by [AB] with the name of the above-named [testator] as [his/her] last will in [his/her] presence and by [his/her] direction in the presence of us present at the same time who at [his/her] request in [his/her] presence and in the presence of each other have written our names as witnesses.

(ii) ATTESTATION CLAUSE WHERE THE TESTATOR IS BLIND (AND SOMEONE SIGNS ON BEHALF OF THE TESTATOR)

Signed by [AB] with the name of the above-named [testator] as [his/her] last will (the will having been first read over to [him/her] when the said [testator] appeared thoroughly to understand and approve the contents thereof) in [his/her] presence and by [his/her] direction in the presence of us present at the same time who at [his/her] request in [his/her] presence and in the presence of each other have written our names as witnesses.

(iii) ATTESTATION CLAUSE WHERE THE TESTATOR IS ILLITERATE AND SIGNS HIS OR HER MARK

Signed by the above-named [testator] as [his/her] last will with [his/her] mark (the will having been first read over to [him/her] when the said [testator] appeared thoroughly to understand and approve the contents thereof) in [his/her] presence and by [his/her] direction in the presence of us present at the same time who at [his/her] request in [his/her] presence and in the presence of each other have written our names as witnesses.

C. Executors and Trustees

When taking instructions for the drafting of the will, the testator's wishes must be ascertained as to the persons who will administer the estate (the executors) and who will act as trustees of any trust created under the will.   **22.012**

It is often administratively convenient to appoint the same people to hold both offices, a common form of wording being "I APPOINT [AB] of [address and occupation] and [CD] of [address and occupation] to be the executors and trustees of this my will (hereinafter called 'my Trustees' which expression shall where the context so admits include the trustees for the time being)". The final words are required to make it clear that any powers conferred on the trustees are not personal to the original trustees.

1. NUMBER OF EXECUTORS AND TRUSTEES

Any number of executors may be appointed but no more than four may take out the grant in respect of the same property. One executor will always suffice. However, two are often appointed in case one predeceases the testator or dies before completing the administration. Moreover, if the executors are also to be trustees, it is desirable to appoint two since two trustees (or a trust corporation) are required to give a good receipt for capital money.   **22.013**

2. THE CHOICE OF APPOINTEES

A testator may appoint an individual, a firm of solicitors, a bank or trust corporation. The testator must consider the relative merits of such appointees.   **22.014**

Individuals
Testators frequently appoint friends or relatives to act as executors. Such an appointment has the advantage of ensuring the administration is completed by someone of whom the testator has personal knowledge and who will not charge for the work done. A disadvantage may be that the appointee lacks expertise but there is nothing to prevent the appointee taking professional advice. However, the need for such advice may mean that the supposed advantage of cheapness is more apparent than real.   **22.015**

The testator has freedom of choice and so can appoint any person to act, including a bankrupt, a criminal, an infant or a person suffering from a mental or physical disability but there are limitations on who can actually take a grant (see para.8.002).

Further points must be considered when choosing individuals. The most important points are the appointee's ability to cope with the burdens of the office and his willingness to act. A commercially inexperienced person may find the problems of dealing with a complicated estate excessively onerous.

It may be appropriate to appoint a beneficiary as an executor. The beneficiary will have a personal interest in ensuring the estate is properly administered. However, the possibility of a conflict of interest may arise. If the only executor is a specific legatee, there may be a danger that the interests of the residuary beneficiary will be disregarded. Appointing several individuals may lead to disputes if they are unable to agree on the appropriate steps to be taken when dealing with the assets.

No matter how suitable the appointee may seem to be, if he is older than the testator, there is the probability of the executor predeceasing the testator. In this circumstance a substitutional appointment should be included in the will.

Professional advisers

22.016 The appointment of professional advisers, such as solicitors or accountants, has the advantage of ensuring that the administration is dealt with by experts who, frequently, will have a detailed knowledge of the estate and its assets. Such knowledge, together with their knowledge of estate administration and probate practice, may be invaluable when the estate is complex. The disadvantage of appointing professionals, as compared with individuals, is that the executors will have no personal interest in the estate and will charge for their services.

When appointing solicitors or accountants as executors, although the testator may wish to appoint a particular person to act, problems will arise if that person dies, retires or leaves the firm. For this reason it is usual (subject to the testator's wishes) to appoint the firm to act rather than named individuals.

Unless the will says otherwise, an appointment of a firm of solicitors is construed as an appointment of the partners in the firm at the date the will is made. Since partners may die, retire or leave the firm, it is advisable to provide expressly that appointment is of the partners in the firm at the date of death. It is possible that the firm may change its name or amalgamate with another firm and the testator may wish to consider making provision to cover this possibility. It is usual to express the wish that only two of the partners should take the grant but this is not essential.

In the case of a Solicitors' Incorporated Practice (under the Solicitors' Incorporated Practice Rules 2001) care should be taken in drafting to ensure that the individual solicitors who are directors or members of the practice at the time of death are appointed. The practice itself cannot be appointed as it is not a trust corporation.

A suggested wording for such an appointment is to be found in Will 2, clause 2 and Will 3, clause 2 in the Appendix.

Since executors and trustees (as holders of fiduciary positions) are unable to make a profit from their offices unless expressly authorised, a charging clause must be included in the will.

Trust corporations—banks
Instead of or in addition to individuals and professional advisers it is possible to appoint corporations sole or trust corporations, such as the trustee department of one of the leading banks.   **22.017**

Banks generally insist that their own standard appointment clause (which incorporates a charging clause) be inserted in the will otherwise they will refuse to act. Such clauses can be readily obtained from any branch. Furthermore, where banks are appointed they often require a sight of the draft will before it is signed.

The banks have scales of charges which the testator may wish to compare with solicitors' fees. The appointment of a corporation may prove expensive since if difficulties arise the corporation may instruct solicitors to act on its behalf with the result that there may be an element of double charging.

The Public Trustee
The testator can appoint the Public Trustee but the circumstances when the appointment will be appropriate may be limited.   **22.018**

The office was created (by the Public Trustee Act 1906) to meet the difficulty of finding someone willing and able to act as a trustee. He can refuse to accept any trust (except on the ground that it is too small) and he cannot accept the appointment if the trust is solely for religious or charitable purposes. He will not normally accept an appointment which would involve the management of a business.

The Public Trustee can act either alone or jointly with others. (If sole trustee, he is empowered to deal with land).

The appointment has some advantages:

(1) The Public Trustee is a corporation sole and so has a permanent existence independent of the office holder.
(2) The State is liable for loss caused by breach.

A fee will be charged for the service and this will have to be compared with the fees a solicitor would charge.

The disadvantage of the appointment is that the Public Trustee will know nothing of the estate or its beneficiaries prior to the appointment and the fees may be higher than those of a solicitor.

D. Guardians

Testators with minor children should consider who will have the care of any minor children who survive them. The relevant law is contained in the Children Act 1989.   **22.019**

A parent with parental responsibility may appoint a guardian. Broadly speaking, a mother has parental responsibility irrespective of her marital status. A father has automatic parental responsibility if he has been married to the mother at any time later than the date of conception. An unmarried father may acquire parental responsibility by court order or agreement with the child's mother. An appointment may be made by will or in writing (s.5(5)).

Under s.5(7) and (8) of the Children Act, an appointment by one spouse where the other spouse survives will now not normally take effect until the death of the surviving spouse. If the surviving spouse also appoints a guardian, the two guardians will act together after the death of the surviving spouse.

There is one case where an appointment would take effect immediately despite the existence of a surviving spouse. This is where there is a residence order in force in favour of the existing parent.

For example, H and W have been divorced for five years and there is a custody order in force by which the children live with W; W dies and appoints X as guardian. X will become guardian on W's death and will share parental responsibility with H.

A disgruntled surviving parent in such circumstances could apply to the court to have the guardianship terminated (s.6(7)).

An appropriate form of words for an appointment under the Children Act in normal circumstances is "I APPOINT [AB] of [address] and [CD] of [address] to be the guardians after the death of my [husband/wife] of any of my children who may then be minors". (See Will 2, Clause 3 in the Appendix). If a residence order was in force in favour of the deceased spouse the appointment would be "to act jointly with [my husband/wife]".

When a testator is considering appointing guardians, the appointees should be consulted to ensure that they are willing to act.

Where guardians are appointed consideration should be given to the additional expense the guardians will incur. It is common to make them trustees (either alone or jointly with the professional executors) of a trust fund for the benefit of the children. In such a case the powers of trustees may have to be amended to suit the circumstances.

Although ss.31 and 32 of the Trustee Act 1925 permit the income and capital of a trust fund to be made available for the benefit of the children, testators might wish to make express provision in the will. For example, power could be given to the trustees to allow the trust's capital to be used for the purchase of a larger house for the guardians and the children to live in. The capital could be lent to the guardians at a low rate of interest; alternatively the money could be used to help fund a purchase of the property in the joint names of the guardians and the trust fund.

E. Specific Gifts and General Legacies

1. INTRODUCTION

22.020 When drafting specific gifts and general legacies, the draftsman must consider both the nature of the legacy and the status of the beneficiary (for example, particular problems may arise where the beneficiary is a charity or a minor).

2. SPECIFIC GIFTS

A specific gift is one the wording of which distinguishes the gifted **22.021** property from all other property belonging to the testator at the date of death.

Section 24 of the Wills Act 1837

Section 24 provides that, as regards property, the will "speaks from **22.022** death" unless it expresses a contrary intention. The use of the word "my" coupled with a specific item (for example "my piano") is often construed as showing such a contrary intention. However, if the word "my" is followed by a description of property capable of increase or decrease, this is not usually construed as contrary intention so that, for example, a gift of "my collection of Dresden china" would be construed as a gift of the whole collection at the date of death.

Drafting specific gifts

The solicitor should take great care to ascertain the testator's wishes. The **22.023** testator may wish to give a particular item owned at the date the will is made or may wish to give any item which corresponds to a particular description owned at the date of death.

If the testator wishes to give a particular item owned at the date of the will, the property must be carefully identified.

This may be relatively easy where, for example, shares are involved but difficulties can arise where the gift is of personal chattels. Thus, a gift of "my gold ring" may give rise to problems if the testator owned several gold rings. A reference to an insurance valuation may be helpful in identifying the particular ring given.

When taking instructions, the solicitor should explain to the client that a gift of a particular item owned at the date of the will suffers ademption if the item is sold, destroyed or changed in substance. The result of such ademption is that the beneficiary will get nothing. This may or may not be what the testator wishes.

If the testator wants the beneficiary to receive any item owned at the death corresponding to a particular description, suitable wording should be used. An example of such wording is "I give to [AB] any motor car which I own at the date of my death".

In some cases, the testator may wish to give a particular item with a provision for a substitutional gift if that item is sold, destroyed or changed in substance. A suggested wording is "I GIVE to [AB] absolutely my grand piano or any other piano which has replaced it and which I own at the date of my death". Such wording is not desirable where there may be several changes between the making of the will and the death (for example, where a testator makes a gift of shares) as it may prove difficult to identify the replacement assets accurately. In such a case it may be preferable for the testator to include a pecuniary legacy to be given in substitution of the original property, if that property is not owned at the date of death.

Power to select

22.024 Specific legacies are often made as a way of passing a "keepsake" to a friend or relative. An outright gift of items of property causes no difficulty but if the testator wishes property to be shared between beneficiaries as they choose various matters should be considered:

(a) the order of selection;

(b) the insertion of a time limit to avoid the executors' having to wait an unspecified length of time before the beneficiary or beneficiaries make up their minds;

(c) a procedure for resolution of disputes (for example by the executors);

(d) a gift over to a substitutional beneficiary in the event of a beneficiary pre-deceasing or the beneficiaries failing to choose all the items, as the case may be;

(e) a limit on the value of items selected.

Selection clauses are included in Will 1, clause 6 and Will 2, clause 5 in the Appendix. The latter clause avoids problems by giving the personal representative an overriding discretion as to the distribution.

The testator may give to *one* beneficiary the right to select such items as he chooses. In this case para.(a) above will not be relevant.

22.025 *Mortgage, expenses and inheritance tax*

(a) *Mortgage.* Where a gift is made of property which was charged during the testator's lifetime with a mortgage or other debt the Administration of Estates Act 1925, s.35 provides that the property passes to the beneficiary subject to that debt unless the will provides otherwise. The effect of s.35 should, therefore, be explained to the testator so that if he wishes the beneficiary to take the property free of the debt suitable wording can be included. An example of such wording is given in Will 1, clause 4 in the Appendix. The solicitor should remember that in the case of a mortgage, a mortgage protection policy may have been taken out by the testator. The solicitor should, therefore, enquire whether or not such a policy exists so that the testator can give thought to the destination of the estate bearing in mind the existence of the policy (see para.15.010).

(b) *Expenses.* Unless the will provides otherwise specific beneficiaries bear any costs of insuring, packing and transporting of property left to them in a will from the time that the assent is made in their favour. This should be explained to the testator who may not wish a specific beneficiary to bear the costs. This is especially likely where the nature of the gift or the circumstances of the beneficiary would result in high insurance or transportation costs being incurred, which the beneficiary might have difficulty meeting.

If contrary provision is made in the will the costs are borne by residue. An example of such wording is given in Will 1, clause 5 in the Appendix.

(c) *"Free of tax."* Whenever the disposition of an estate may give rise to an inheritance tax liability, the testator should consider which beneficiaries should bear the burden. Inheritance tax on United Kingdom free estate which vests in the personal representatives is usually a testamentary expense borne by undisposed of property or residue unless the will provides otherwise. The draftsman may consider providing expressly that non-residuary gifts are to be "free of tax" so that the question of burden is brought to the testator's attention. The testator can then consider whether the disposition of the estate is suitable having regard to the burden of inheritance tax.

3. GENERAL LEGACIES

A general legacy is a gift of property which is not in any way distinguished from property of the same kind (for example, a gift of "100 shares in ABC Ltd"). If the testator does not own such property at death, the personal representatives will purchase property fulfilling the description. Unless there are special reasons for such a gift, a gift of money is usually more appropriate.

22.026

4. PARTICULAR PROBLEMS ARISING FROM PECUNIARY LEGACIES

Particular problems arise where a pecuniary legacy is given to a minor as, in the absence of an express direction, a minor cannot give a good receipt. (This problem was discussed in para.18.017).

22.027

Problems also arise where a pecuniary legacy is given to an unincorporated association. Such an association has no legal identity separate from its individual members. Therefore, a legacy to such an association is construed as a gift to all the individual members. In the absence of an express provision in the will the personal representative would have to obtain a receipt from each individual member of the association. This would be an onerous and time consuming task and, therefore, it is advisable to provide that the receipt of the person appearing to be the treasurer, bursar or other appropriate officer will be sufficient to give the personal representatives a good discharge.

The words "appearing to be" are used so that the personal representatives do not have to enquire whether the appointment of the treasurer etc. was properly made. (See Will 3, clause 8 in the Appendix).

When drafting a gift to an unincorporated association, the draftsman, having taken appropriate instructions from the testator, should ensure that:

(a) the association is in existence;
(b) the association is correctly identified;
(c) provision is included to cover a change of name, change of objects, the amalgamation of the association with another similar body or the dissolution of the association prior to the testator's death.

Where a gift is left to a charity which ceases to exist during the lifetime of the testator, the gift will not lapse but will be applied *cy-près* provided the testator showed a general charitable intention. If this is in accordance with the testator's wishes it may be desirable to include words clearly showing a general charitable intent, for example, "To X association for its general charitable purposes". It is important to check whether any particular institution has charitable status.

F. Gifts of Residue

22.028 Once the formal parts of the will and any specific or pecuniary legacies have been drafted, it is necessary to consider the drafting of the clause or clauses disposing of residue. The main objective of the draftsman in drafting such clauses is to ensure that the residue of the estate goes to the testator's intended beneficiaries. This will include consideration of whether substitutional beneficiaries should be included in case a primary beneficiary fails to achieve a vested interest and whether a survivorship provision is required. The draftsman should also consider how best to deal with the payment of debts and expenses (which will usually be paid out of residue).

1. PAYMENT OF DEBTS

22.029 The rules as to payment of debts of the estate were considered in Chapter 15 where we saw that, unless there is undisposed of property, unsecured debts are, in most circumstances, payable out of residue. This will usually comply with the testator's wishes but, even so, it is usual to make express provision in a professionally drawn will. One way in which this is commonly done is by making the residuary gift subject to the payment of debts and other expenses.

For example, "I GIVE all the rest and residue of my estate both real and personal SUBJECT TO the payment of my debts, funeral expenses and testamentary expenses unto [AB] of [address]".

Another way in which payment of debts can be provided for is by creating a trust for sale, the first object of which is the payment of debts (there are a number of other reasons why a trust for sale may be desirable—see below).

For example, "I GIVE all the rest and residue of my estate both real and personal unto my Trustee UPON TRUST for sale with full power to postpone sale and after payment thereout of my debts funeral expenses and testamentary expenses to hold the balance (and any parts of my estate for the time being unsold) UPON the following TRUSTS ..."

Where a debt of the estate is charged during the deceased's lifetime on specific property it will be payable out of that property unless the will shows a contrary intention (Administration of Estates Act 1925, s.35). Clauses, such as those above which deal with the payment of debts generally, are not sufficient to require charged debts to be paid out of residue. If the intention is that charged debts should be paid out of residue then words such as "including any debts charged on specific property" should be added after the word "debts" in the clauses above.

2. PAYMENT OF PECUNIARY LEGACIES

The rules as to property available for payment of pecuniary legacies are considered in Chapter 16. They are complicated and, in order to avoid possible problems, it is desirable to direct that residue be held on trust for sale and proceeds used to pay debts *and legacies*. This has the effect of making realty available proportionately with personalty under the rule in *Roberts v Walker*. It also ensures that, in cases where residue has been left to two or more persons equally and one has predeceased (with the result that part of the residue is undisposed of), it is clear that legacies are to be paid before the residue is divided into shares. This avoids the possibility of costly disputes between residuary beneficiaries and the persons entitled to the testator's undisposed of property.

22.030

3. INCLUSION OF A TRUST

In some cases a trust of residue should be included. A trust is advisable where the residue is to be divided between two or more beneficiaries or where minors may be entitled to residue. Before the Trusts of Land and Appointment of Trustees Act 1996 an express trust for sale (with power to postpone sale) was generally employed so as to avoid the complication so the Settled Land Act 1925. The trustees of a "trust of land" as defined by the 1996 Act have all the powers of an absolute owner, including sale, so an express trust for sale is no longer necessary. However, if there is no land in the residuary estate, any trust created will fall outside the definition of a "trust of land" with the consequence that the statutory powers will not be available to the trustees. An express trust for sale may, therefore, be considered despite the 1996 Act. If such a trust is included it should include a power to postpone sale. If an express trust for sale is included and the residuary estate does in fact contain land the trust will be a "trust of land" under the 1996 Act. An alternative approach is to create a trust of residue without a trust for sale but with a power of sale. Again this will be a "trust of land" if there is any land included in the residue. If there is no land then the trustees will be able to exercise their power of sale under the express power of sale in the will.

22.031

Personal representatives also have a power to sell the assets of the estate for purposes of administration under the Administration of Estates Act, 1925, s.39.

4. ABSOLUTE GIFT OF RESIDUE TO ONE PERSON

Where the residue is to be given to one person absolutely, the drafting of the will is quite straightforward. It is usual to describe the gift as a gift of "all my real and personal property whatsoever and wheresoever not by my will or by any codicil to it specifically disposed of" or of "subject to the above gifts all the rest and residue of my estate". The draftsman should consider whether to make a substitutional gift so as to prevent an intestacy if the intended residuary beneficiary predeceases and whether to include a survivorship clause (see para.22.037 below).

22.032

5. ABSOLUTE GIFT OF RESIDUE TO MORE THAN ONE PERSON

Named beneficiaries

22.033   If the residue is to be divided between two or more persons in equal shares the following form may be used "My Trustee shall hold all the rest and residue of my estate UPON TRUST for [names] in equal shares". If the shares are to be unequal the simplest technique is to divide the residue into a suitable number of equal parts and to say how many parts each beneficiary is to get.

Where residue is given "equally" or "in equal shares" and any of the residuary beneficiaries predecease, there will be a partial intestacy. It is, therefore, desirable to add words giving the lapsed share to the surviving beneficiaries or words making a substitutional gift of that share (for example, to the children of the deceased beneficiary). If it is intended that the surviving beneficiaries are to take a larger share suitable wording of the whole clause would be "My Trustee shall hold all the rest and residue of my estate for such of [names] as survive me and if more than one in equal shares".

Class gifts

22.034   Many gifts of residue to more than one person are gifts to a class of beneficiaries rather than to several named individuals. Most class gifts are gifts to a particular class of relative. The draftsman should explain the class closing rules to the testator and explain that they may artificially exclude certain unborn persons. He should also explain that the exclusion of the class closing rules is possible but may delay final distribution of the estate.

A draftsman should consider carefully whether or not it is desirable to include words expressly limiting class gifts to persons *living at the testator's death*. Where there is an immediate gift to a class (for example, "to my grandchildren") the class closing rules apply (unless excluded). Their effect is that the class will close at the date of the testator's death and will include only those class members living or *en ventre sa mere* at that date (if there are no members living or *en ventre sa mere* at that date the class remains open indefinitely). This is likely to accord with the wishes of most testators since, although it will exclude any later born class members, it does allow the benefits of early distribution. Many precedents state expressly that such gifts are to be limited to persons *living at the testator's death*. These words merely restate the relevant class closing rule but it is probably desirable to include them to ensure that the testator is aware of the position.

Where a gift to a class is contingent (for example, "to those of my grandchildren who reach 18") or deferred (for example, "to X for life and then to my grandchildren") the class closing rules apply (unless excluded). Their effect is, broadly speaking (but see Chapter 16 for a fuller discussion), that such a class will remain open until the first class member fulfils the contingency or until the life tenant dies and will include any persons born after the date of the testator's death and before the date of which the class closes. This is likely to accord with the wishes of most testators. Since any distribution is impossible until one person fulfils the contingency or until any life tenant dies there is no point in closing the class until distribution is possible. If the words *living at my death* are included they limit the gift to persons alive or *en ventre sa mere* at the testator's death and exclude any born thereafter. Unless this is an accurate reflection of the testator's wishes it is desirable not to include the words.

Care should also be taken with the definition of the class so as to avoid any ambiguity and so as to comply with the testator's wishes. If the testator says that he wishes to benefit his "cousins", further instructions are needed to establish what degree of relationship is intended. A reference to any class of relative is construed as a reference to the testator's blood relatives only and not to relatives by marriage. Thus, a testator who wishes to benefit "nephews and nieces" should be asked whether the nephews and nieces of his spouse are to be included or only his own nephews and nieces (if the spouse's nephews and nieces are to be included in the gift suitable words must be inserted in the will). Unless contrary provision is made a reference to any class of relative is deemed to include adopted relatives of the testator but not, for example, step-children who have not been adopted. The fact that a person's parents were not married to each other at the time of his birth is irrelevant for the purposes of succession to property unless a contrary intention is expressed in the will.

As with gifts to named beneficiaries the will should make it clear what is to happen to the share of a member of the class who predeceases. A class gift (for example, "to my nieces") is normally construed as a gift to those nieces who survive the testator. There will, therefore, be no question of lapse unless all the members of the class predecease the testator. The testator may wish to include a substitutional clause providing that, if any member of the class predeceases the testator leaving issue who survive the testator, the issue will take *per stirpes* the share which their parent would have taken. In the case of a class gift to *children or issue of a testator* s.33(2) of the Wills Act 1837, as substituted by the Administration of Justice Act 1982, s.19, provides that such a substitution shall take place unless a contrary intention appears by the will. Despite this provision, it is probably desirable to include express words of substitution so that the matter is brought to the testator's attention and so that there can be no doubt as to his wishes. Suitable wording is given in para.22.038.

6. Successive Interests in Residue

The testator may wish to create a life or other limited interest in the residue of his estate. In such a case it is best to include an express trust, the first object of which is to pay debts and legacies. The trustees are then directed to pay income to the life tenant and, subject thereto, to hold the balance of the remainderman. For example "UPON TRUST to pay the income thereof to [name of life tenant] during his lifetime and subject thereto UPON TRUST for [name of remainderman] absolutely". **22.035**

The life tenant will frequently be the testator's spouse, in which case the testator may wish to ensure that the spouse is entitled to occupy the matrimonial home for life. This can be achieved by making a specific devise of the matrimonial home (so that it is not part of residue). If the matrimonial home is part of residue it will be a trust of land. Section 12 of the Trusts of Land and Appointment of Trustees Act 1996 then gives the beneficiary a right of occupation (see para.22.055 below).

A testator may wish to give the trustees power to advance or lend capital to the life tenant.

7. CONTINGENT INTERESTS IN RESIDUE

22.036 A gift of residue, whether to a named beneficiary, a number of named beneficiaries or a class and whether immediate or in remainder, may be contingent on the happening of some event or the satisfaction of some condition. (For example, "To such of my children as survive me and reach 18 or marry under that age".) Wherever the gift is contingent the testator should be asked to decide what is to happen to the income pending the satisfaction of the contingency and what is to happen if the contingency is never satisfied. In the absence of any direction to the contrary the provisions of the Trustee Act, s.31 (as to which see paras 11.015–11.017) will apply in respect of the income. If the contingency is never satisfied the capital and any income which has been added to it will pass as on an intestacy unless there is a substitutional gift.

The effect of the rule against perpetuities should be considered whenever a contingent gift is made. A gift which would vest outside the perpetuity period (a life or lives in being plus 21 years or the statutory period of 80 years) is void. However, the Perpetuity and Accumulations Act 1964 introduced various provisions which mitigate the severity of the rule against perpetuities. Thus, a gift which *might* vest outside the perpetuity period will not fail at the outset as it is possible to "wait and see"; it is possible, where necessary to save a gift, to reduce the age at which a gift will vest and/or to exclude members of a class from benefit where otherwise the whole gift would fail. As a result of these provisions problems of perpetuity are much less likely to lead to failure of benefit.

It is always worth remembering that a gift to the testator's *children* contingent on reaching any specified age can never present a perpetuity problem as the children are all lives in being. A gift to a testator's *grandchildren* contingent on reaching a specified age can only present a perpetuity problem if the specified age is greater than 21.

8. SURVIVORSHIP CLAUSES

22.037 A beneficiary who survives a testator by a very short time or who is deemed to survive (under s.184 of the Law of Property Act 1925) will obtain a vested interest in any unconditional gift made to him. Often a testator will want to provide that a beneficiary is not to benefit unless he survives for a reasonable period. This can be achieved by means of a "survivorship clause" which provides that the beneficiary is only to take if he survives the testator for a specified period, if he does not so survive, then a substitutional gift takes effect. Such clauses are particularly common in the case of gifts to spouses (this is because the possibility of death in a common accident is greatest in the case of spouses).

The advantages of a survivorship clause in such a case are:

(a) the testator retains control of the ultimate destination of the property—if there were no such clause the property would pass on the death of the surviving spouse according to the terms of the survivor's will or of the intestacy rules;

(b) the property of the testator passes to the other beneficiaries rather than to the surviving spouse. This means that the spouse exemption is lost but it also means that there are two estates rather than one for inheritance tax purposes. The rate of tax will, therefore, be reduced overall where each spouse owns a substantial amount of property.

A survivorship clause should never be for more than six months since, if it is for longer, a settlement will be created for inheritance tax purposes and there may as a result be an unnecessary charge to tax. However, the spouse exemption is not lost if the survivorship clause does not exceed 12 months and the spouse does in fact survive to achieve a vested interest.

If there is a survivorship clause in a will, distribution of the estate cannot begin until the primary beneficiary dies (when the substitutional gift takes effect) or until the end of the period (when the primary beneficiary achieves a vested interest). Because of the inconvenience of a long delay, it is usual for survivorship clauses to specify a period of 28 days or one month. (See Will 2, clause 7 in the Appendix).

9. SUBSTITUTIONAL GIFTS

When a specific or general legacy lapses the subject-matter "falls into residue" and goes to the residuary beneficiary. When a residuary gift fails, there is, prima facie, a partial intestacy. The draftsman should ascertain the testator's wishes as to the disposition of property in the event of a beneficiary predeceasing or failing to survive for a specified period. The testator may decide that he would rather make a substitutional gift than have the property pass on intestacy. A suitable clause substituting one beneficiary for another if that other predeceases or fails to survive for a specified period is "I GIVE all the rest and residue of my estate to [AB] or if [he/she] shall predecease me or fail to survive for 28 days then to [C/D]". **22.038**

Where the primary beneficiary is the spouse of the testator the effect of the Administration of Justice Act 1982, s.18A, must be remembered. In the case of deaths occurring after December 31, 1982, a divorce causes a gift to a spouse to fail. If the will gives residue to the spouse, the residue will pass as undisposed of property unless a substitutional gift can take effect. Section 18A has been amended by s.3 of the Law Reform (Succession) Act 1995. Any property which is given by the will to the former spouse passes as if the former spouse had died on the date of the divorce or annulment. A substitutional gift will therefore take effect even though it is expressed to be contingent on the spouse having predeceased or failed to survive for a specified period. This amendment applies to deaths on or after January 1, 1996.

Often the most appropriate substitutional beneficiaries are the children of the primary beneficiary. If the gift of residue is to the *testator's* children, the testator may decide that the property be divided amongst the surviving children or he may decide that the share of a deceased child should go to that child's children or remoter issue. If the will is silent, then the Wills Act 1837, s.33 (as substituted) provides that, if a child of the testator predeceases leaving issue who survive the testator, the issue take the share that their parent would have taken.

Despite s.33 it is advisable to include an express substitutional gift so that the testator is given an opportunity to consider whether or not the clause accords with his wishes. (An *express* substitutional gift is always required if the original gift is to anyone other than a child or issue of the testator). A suitable clause for a substitution of a child by his own issue on the assumption that there is a trust for sale of residue is "My Trustee shall hold the proceeds thereof UPON TRUST for such of my children as are living at my death in equal shares PROVIDED THAT if any child of mine shall predecease me leaving issue living at my death such issue shall take by substitution and if more than one in equal shares per stirpes the share of the said proceeds which such deceased child of mine would have taken if he or she had survived me". (Note that, under this clause issue of a non-marital relationship will take. If the testator wishes to exclude them, express provision must be made.) If desired a further substitution providing for the possibility of the testator dying without any living issue may be included. However, in drafting a substitutional clause unnecessary complications arising from the remote possibility of a large number of potential beneficiaries predeceasing the testator should be avoided by advising the testator of the need to make a new will if circumstances change.

G. Administrative Powers

1. INTRODUCTION

22.039   As we saw in Chapter 11 personal representatives and trustees have various powers conferred on them by statute which can be excluded, restricted or extended by the will. It is also possible for the will to confer *additional* powers on the personal representatives. We will now list and consider some of the more common extensions and additions. The purpose of including such clauses is to facilitate the administration of the estate and of any trust which may arise under the will.

2. COMMON EXTENSIONS TO POWERS OF PERSONAL REPRESENTATIVES

Power to appropriate assets without consent of beneficiary

22.040   (a) The personal representatives have a power under s.41 of the Administration of Estates Act to appropriate assets in or towards satisfaction of a legacy bequeathed by the deceased or interest under the intestacy rules but must obtain the consent of the beneficiary (or other specified persons as set out in para.11.018).

It is administratively convenient for personal representatives to be excused from the necessity of obtaining formal consent (even though they would, no doubt, informally consult with the beneficiaries and would be under an obligation to exercise their powers in good faith).

A further reason for continuing to give the personal representatives a power to appropriate without consent is that the Revenue may view an appropriation *with* consent as a sale for a variety of tax purposes. It is, therefore, desirable to ensure that the personal representatives have both a power to appropriate with consent and without consent enabling them to choose the most tax effective method. A suitable form of wording would be "This power is exercisable in addition to the power conferred by Administration of Estates Act 1925, s.41".

(b) Since an appropriation is in effect a sale of assets to the beneficiary any personal representative who is beneficially entitled to a part of the estate and who makes an appropriation in his own favour will be purchasing estate property. There is authority that this is permissible (*Re Richardson* (1896)) but such a purchase might be attacked subsequently as a breach of the equitable rule that a trustee must not profit from his trust (see for example *Kane v Radley-Kane* (1999)). Where personal representatives are beneficially entitled it is, therefore, common to authorise such personal representatives to exercise the power to appropriate in their own favour. (See Will 1, clause 8 in the Appendix).

The power to insure contained in Trustee Act 1925, s.19 (as amended by Trustee Act 2000) gives personal representatives and trustees power to insure as if they were absolute owners. Express power is therefore no longer needed.

Power to accept the receipt of parent or guardian on behalf of a minor or of the minor at a specified age

(a) An unmarried minor has no statutory power to give a good receipt   **22.041** for capital or income. A married minor can give a good receipt for income only. The minor's parent, guardian or spouse has power under the Children Act to give a good receipt on the minor's behalf (see Chapter 18). A testator should consider whether it is appropriate to allow the legacy to pass into the hands of the parent or guardian (or spouse). If not, the legacy can be left to trustees to hold until the child reaches a suitable age. It is probably good drafting to include a clause in the will authorising the personal representatives to accept the receipt of parent or guardian so that the testator is aware that this will happen. (See Will 1, clause 7 in the Appendix).

(b) There is a statutory power under s.42 of the Administration of Estates Act for the personal representatives to appoint trustees to hold a legacy for a minor who is *absolutely* entitled but this does not apply if the minor has only a contingent interest. There is no reason why the testator should not expressly authorise the personal representatives to appoint trustees in such a case.

(c) The testator may authorise the minor to give a good receipt at a specified age, for example 16.

(d) Alternatively, the will may direct the personal representatives to purchase a suitable investment (perhaps National Savings Certificates) in the name of the minor.

Exclusion of the Apportionment Act 1870 and the common law rules on apportionment

22.042 As we saw in Chapters 16 and 18, the Apportionment Act 1870 requires that "rents, annuities, dividends and other periodical payments in the nature of income ... shall, like interest on money lent, be considered as accruing from day to day" and shall be apportioned accordingly. Interest has to be apportioned under the common law rules. The trouble and expense involved in the calculations is usually thought to outweigh any benefits to the beneficiaries. As a result, in cases where the apportionment of income would otherwise be necessary (that is, where a will gives an income-producing asset to one person, residue to another) the Act and the common law rules are frequently excluded. The effect of exclusion is that all income paid to the personal representatives after death is treated as income of the estate for *distribution* purposes even though some or all of it may be attributable to the period before death. (See Will 2, clause 8(5) in the Appendix).

Power to carry on a business of the deceased

22.043 As we saw in Chapter 11 the powers of personal representatives to run a business carried on by the deceased as a sole trader are limited. It is, therefore, usual in cases where a testator is a sole trader to provide that personal representatives may:

    (a) continue to run the business for as long as they see fit,
    (b) use such assets of the estate as they see fit.

(A specimen clause is set out below.)

> "I DIRECT that my Trustees shall have power to carry on my business of [nature of business] for so long as they shall in their absolute discretion think fit and they shall have power to use any assets employed in the said business at the date of my death together with any assets comprised in my Residuary Estate I DECLARE that my Trustees shall have the same powers to carry on the said business as if they were absolute owners thereof without being personally liable for any loss that may arise I FURTHER DECLARE that in the event of my business being carried on at a loss my Trustees shall be reimbursed for any loss they suffer from my Residuary Estate."

It is most desirable that a sole trader should consider and make provision for the running of a business after his death, perhaps by taking in partners or by incorporation of the business during his lifetime. Such matters should certainly be discussed when drafting a will for a sole trader. The question of personal representatives should also be carefully considered. It is usually difficult to find a professional person who is willing to accept the office of personal representative where this would involve the running or supervision of a business. Where the business is to be transferred to a beneficiary it may be helpful to appoint that beneficiary either as a general personal representative or as a special personal representative to deal only with the business.

Where a client is a partner in a business or runs a business through the medium of a limited company it is desirable to discuss with the client what provisions if any have been included in the partnership agreement or Articles of Association to deal with death. Matters which should be considered are whether persons surviving the deceased should have options to purchase the interest of a deceased partner/shareholder and what financial arrangements should be made for the dependants of the deceased.

3. COMMON EXTENSIONS TO POWERS OF TRUSTEES

These extensions should be considered where a will creates a trust **22.044** initially (for example by leaving property to a spouse for life) or where a trust may arise if a beneficiary predeceases the testator (for example "to my spouse absolutely but if he does not survive me by 28 days for such of our children as may reach the age of 25"; even if all the testator's children are over 25 at the time the will is drafted a trust may still arise if a child predeceases and is replaced by issue).

Power to invest

As we saw in Chapter 11 trustees and personal representatives are now **22.045** given very wide powers of investment. No express power is needed. In rare cases a testator may wish to restrict the power of investment for which purpose a clause could be included in the will.

Power to purchase a house as a residence for a beneficiary

The Trustee Act 2000, s.8 gives trustees and personal representatives **22.046** power to buy freehold or leasehold land in the United Kingdom including the power to do so "for occupation by a beneficiary" (s.8(1)(b)). An express power would be needed if the personal representatives were to be able to buy a house outside the United Kingdom for a beneficiary or an interest in land.

Power to advance capital to beneficiaries with a vested or contingent interest in capital

We saw in Chapter 11 that trustees have a statutory power under s.32 of **22.047** the Trustee Act 1925 to advance capital to beneficiaries with a vested or contingent interest *in capital*, but that it is subject to the following three limitations:

(a) No more than one half of the beneficiary's vested or presumptive interest can be advanced.
(b) Any advances must be brought into account when and if the beneficiary becomes absolutely entitled.
(c) Any person with a prior interest (for example the right to receive income from the trust property) must be in existence, of full age and must consent in writing to the advance.

It is common to give the trustees wider powers of advancement by excluding some or all of the limitations listed above and giving them power to advance in their absolute discretion. (See Will 2, clause 8(4) in the Appendix.) The case of *Henley v Wardell* (1989) illustrates the need for careful drafting. A will enlarged the powers conferred by s.32 "so as to permit my trustees in their absolute and uncontrolled discretion to advance ... the whole ... of any ...share...." The trustees made advances without the consent of the life tenant arguing that as they had an "absolute" and "uncontrolled" discretion such consent was unnecessary. It was held that the only purpose of the enlargement of trustees' powers was to permit the advancement of "the whole" of a share and that the wording was not sufficient to do away with the need for consents. It is important, therefore, in cases where there is a prior interest and reference is made to enlarging the statutory power expressly to exclude the need for consent. For example, in such a case the clause should include the words:

"... without the need to secure the consent of any person with a prior interest."

Such an advance will not attract inheritance tax if the settlement is a qualifying accumulation and maintenance settlement under the Inheritance Tax Act 1984, s.71 although it may do so if the settlement is not. There will be a disposal for capital gains tax purposes if assets are advanced *in specie* or if assets are sold to raise cash for the advancement.

A testator may also wish to include an express power authorising trustees to *lend* money to beneficiaries on whatever terms they think fit.

Power to advance capital and make loans to life tenants

22.048   The statutory power to advance capital to beneficiaries is only available where beneficiaries have an interest in capital. There is no statutory power to advance capital to a life tenant. Neither is there a statutory power to *lend* capital to a life tenant. A testator, who is proposing to leave property to a person for life, may wish to give the trustees a power to advance or lend capital to the life tenant in case the life tenant finds the income insufficient. (See Will 3, clause 7(4) in the Appendix.) This is particularly likely where a testator proposes to leave a life interest to a spouse.

Advances and loans to a life tenant will have no inheritance tax effect since the life tenant is already treated as the owner of the underlying trust assets. Such payments may, however, amount to disposals for capital gains tax purposes (as in para.22.047).

If advances are made regularly to a life tenant for the purposes of supplementing income there is a danger that they will be regarded as "annual payments" for the purposes of income tax and will have to be grossed up and included on the life tenant's income tax returns as part of total *income*. This danger can be avoided to some extent if the advances are made irregularly. Alternatively, there will be no danger if the payments are treated as loans repayable on death.

Power to apply income for maintenance, education or benefit of minor beneficiaries

22.049   We saw in Chapter 11 that trustees have power under the Trustee Act 1925, s.31 to apply available income to the maintenance, education or benefit of minor beneficiaries and that to the extent that they do not, such income must be accumulated. If the beneficiary reaches the age of 18 and his interest is still contingent the discretion ceases and the trustees must pay the income to the beneficiary until the interest vests or fails.

(a) Section 31(1) provides that the trustees may apply the whole of the income or such part as may in all the circumstances be reasonable; they are required to have regard to the age of the minor and his requirements and generally the circumstances of the case and in particular to what other income, if any, is applicable for the same purpose; where trustees have notice that the income of more than one fund is applicable for these purposes, then so far as practicable unless the entire income of the funds is paid or applied as aforesaid or the court otherwise directs, a proportionate part only of the income of each fund shall be so paid or applied. These provisions are sometimes varied to give the trustees an unfettered discretion to apply income as they see fit. A specimen clause is included in Will 3, clause 8(7) in the Appendix.

(b) The provision that a beneficiary who attains the age of 18 is to be **22.050** *entitled* to income at 18 even though his interest in capital is still contingent is sometimes excluded or postponed to a later age. One reason for this is that once a beneficiary becomes entitled to income the beneficiary is treated for inheritance tax purposes as the owner of the underlying trust assets even if his interest in capital is merely contingent. Thus, should the beneficiary die after becoming entitled to income an appropriate portion of the trust assets will be included in his estate for the purposes of calculating inheritance tax. The inheritance tax attributable to the trust fund will be borne by the trust fund and will reduce the trust assets available to surviving beneficiaries of the trust; the inclusion of the trust property in the estate of the deceased beneficiary will increase the *rate* of inheritance tax payable on the deceased beneficiary's estate and will reduce the assets of the estate of the deceased beneficiary available for distribution.

When excluding the proviso to s.31 the draftsman must remember that if the trust is to be a qualifying accumulation and maintenance settlement under s.71 of the Inheritance Tax Act 1984 he must ensure that the beneficiaries will become entitled to the capital or income before reaching age 25. (A suitable specimen clause is shown below.)

Section 31 of the Trustee Act 1925 will have effect as regards the income arising from my Residuary Estate as if:

(a) the words in subsection 1(i) "as may, in all the circumstances, be reasonable" were deleted and in their place the words "as my Trustees shall in their absolute discretion think fit" were substituted.

(b) the words from "Provided that" to the end of subsection 1 were deleted.

I FURTHER DIRECT that during the period of twenty-one years from my death the statutory powers of maintenance and accumulation continue to be exercisable by my Trustees in favour of any child or remoter issue of mine who has reached the age of 18 but not yet attained a vested interest in the capital of my Residuary Estate.

The draftsman should also be aware of the capital gains tax implications of removing the right to income at 18. If the beneficiary becomes entitled to both income and capital at 25 the settlement continues as an accumulation and maintenance trust until the end of its life; thus, holdover relief will be available when the beneficiary becomes absolutely entitled to the capital assets. This would normally be regarded as an advantage. However, so far as the beneficiary has no right to receive income, the trust income will be subject to the additional rate of income tax and therefore all gains realised by the trustees will be taxed at 35 per cent, rather than 25 per cent.

Exclusion of the Apportionment Act 1870 and the common law rules on apportionment

22.051   We have already explained in para.22.042 above that it is usual to exclude the need to apportion for the purposes of distribution of the estate on the death of a testator. However, the duty to apportion does not arise only on the death of a testator. If a trust is created in favour of a person for life, the duty arises on the death of the life tenant. Similarly, if there is a trust in favour of those members of a class who fulfil a contingency, a need to apportion arises whenever an additional member joins the class (for example, by birth or whenever an existing member leaves the class either by attaining a vested interest or by dying before reaching a specified age (*Re Joel's Will Trusts* (1967)). It is, therefore, most important that any clause intended to exclude the duty to apportion is drafted sufficiently widely to exclude it not merely on the death of the testator but on any other occasion where it would otherwise apply. The specimen clause contained in Will 2, clause 8(5) in the Appendix is intended to have this effect.

Exclusion of the equitable rules as to apportionment

22.052   We saw in Chapter 18 that where residuary personalty is left to persons in succession there is an obligation under the rule in *Howe v Lord Dartmouth* (1802) to sell wasting, hazardous and unauthorised assets together with reversionary interests and non-income producing assets; where such an obligation arises the personal representatives will be under a duty to apportion between life tenant and remainderman any income received pending sale from assets in the first category and to apportion the proceeds of the sale of assets in the second category between life tenant and remainderman. Similarly under the rule in *Allhusen v Whittell* (1867) where residue (real or personal) is left to persons in succession outgoings must be treated as paid partly from capital and partly from the income accruing from that portion of capital from the testator's death to the date of payment of the outgoings. It is extremely common to exclude these rules so as to avoid the need for complex calculations. The rules do not apply on the death of a life tenant and it is, therefore, unnecessary to exclude them on the death of the life tenant. No similar calculations are required for inheritance tax or income tax purposes. (See Will 3, clause 7(5) in the Appendix.)

4. POWER TO CHARGE

22.053   The general rule is that personal representatives and trustees may not charge for their services in the absence of express provision to the contrary. However, the Trustee Act 2000, s.29 provides an important exception to this rule. Under this section a trust corporation or a person acting in a professional capacity as a personal representative or trustee is entitled to "reasonable remuneration" for any services that he provides to or on behalf of the trust provided each other personal representative or trustee (as the case may be) gives written agreement to this. If the will itself makes "any provision about the personal representative or trustee's entitlement to remuneration" s.29 does not apply—the terms of the will take priority.

Despite the statutory provisions, charging clauses should be included in a will which appoints a professional person to be a personal representative both because the approval of other personal representatives will not then be needed and because it will make the position clear to the beneficiaries.

Where provision is made in the will for remuneration to a trust corporation or person acting in a professional capacity, the Trustee Act 2000, s.28 provides that this is not to be regarded as a gift. Consequently the entitlement to the remuneration will not be void if the professional personal representative witnessed the will nor will it abate if the estate is insufficient to pay legacies. There is now a presumption that provision for payment for services is to include payment in respect of services even if they are services which a lay personal representative could perform personally.

5. INDEMNITY

Personal representatives and trustees have a statutory power to indemnify themselves for expenses incurred in carrying out their powers and duties (Trustee Act 2000, s.31). A testator may wish to extend this to provide that they shall not be liable for any loss resulting from improper investment or from any mistake or omission made in good faith. However, it may be thought inappropriate to include such a clause particularly in the case of professional trustees. **22.054**

6. WILL DRAFTING IMPLICATIONS OF THE TRUSTS OF LAND AND APPOINTMENT OF TRUSTEES ACT 1996

This Act imposes certain terms into trusts of which practitioners should be aware. **22.055**

Section 11 requires trustees of land, so far as is practicable, to consult beneficiaries of full age with an interest in possession when exercising any function in respect of land and so far as it is consistent with the general interest of the trust to give effect to their wishes. The section does not apply if the trust instrument includes a declaration that it should not. It seems desirable to relieve the trustees from *the obligation* to consult by including such a declaration.

Section 12 gives a beneficiary who is beneficially entitled to an interest in possession in land a right to occupy the land if either:

(a) the purposes of the trust include making the land available for his occupation, or

(b) the land is held by the trustees so as to be so available.

"Interest in possession" is not defined in the Act. It has the same meaning as for inheritance tax.*

Section 13 goes on to provide that where there is more than one beneficiary entitled to occupy land the trustees may exclude or restrict the entitlement of one or more (but not all) of the beneficiaries. The trustees may impose conditions on the occupying beneficiary (for example, payment of expenses) and may require the occupying beneficiary to make compensation payments to any excluded beneficiaries or forgo benefits to which he would otherwise be entitled.

These provisions seem unduly complex and to be avoided if at all possible. When drafting a will it may be desirable to state that "the purposes of the trust do not include making land available for occupation by beneficiaries". The problem is that the testator may wish to give the trustees power to buy land as a residence for a beneficiary. The mere inclusion of such a power might suggest that, despite the declaration, the purposes of the trust did include making land available for occupation (and once the land is purchased it will be "so available" under s.12(1)(b)). (There is of course an arguable distinction between a power and a purpose.)

A further problem is that if the trustees decide to buy land as an investment for the trust, a beneficiary might be able to insist on occupying it under s.12(1)(b) if the property was vacant. The inclusion of a declaration as to the purposes of the trust would then be of no relevance.

However, even though a declaration as to purpose will not always be of any help in escaping ss.12 and 13, it may help sometimes and it is difficult to see that it can ever do any harm.

Section 19 allows beneficiaries who are of full age and capacity (*i.e. sui juris*) and between them absolutely entitled to the trust property to require the trustees to retire and to appoint replacements specified by the beneficiaries. This provision will not apply if the trust instrument says that it should not.

While the prospect of beneficiaries arbitrarily removing and replacing trustees may seem alarming, it is important to look at the matter in context. Beneficiaries who are *sui juris* can in any event always bring a trust to an end and resettle the property with trustees of their choice. The drawback of so doing is that the termination of the trust will give rise to a potential capital gains tax liability. The s.19 power prevents there being a charge to capital gains tax.

It is likely that for most people the tax advantage will outweigh the concern over the arbitrary replacement of trustees so only rarely will it be appropriate to exclude the s.19 power.

---

* Land held by trustees "so as to be available" for occupation by the beneficiary includes land which is suitable for this occupation and is not occupied by someone else (such as a tenant under a lease).

Appendix

Introduction

In this appendix we have included various blank forms and specimen wills. We have prepared three relatively straightforward wills each illustrating common types of disposition. In order that the reader may consider what clauses should be included in each will, we have listed full details of three imaginary testators, including their names, details of their property, their intended beneficiaries and their executors.

Any resemblance to real persons, alive or dead, is purely accidental.

Oath for executor(s)   Extracted by:[1]

IN THE HIGH COURT OF JUSTICE

FAMILY DIVISION

[PRINCIPAL] [**DISTRICT PROBATE] REGISTRY**[2]

IN THE ESTATE OF   **DECEASED**

I/We[3][4]

make oath and say that:

1. [5]
   of[6]   deceased
   was born on   and died on[7]
   aged[8]   domiciled in England and Wales.
2. I/We believe the paper writings now produced to and marked by me/us to contain the true and original
   last will and testament[9]   of the deceased.
3. To the best of my/our knowledge information and belief there was no land vested in the deceased
   which was settled previously to the death (and not by the will[9]   ) of
   the deceased and which remained settled land notwithstanding such death.
4. I am/We are[10]   executor(s) named in the said will[9]
5. I/We will
   (i) collect, get in and administer according to law the real and personal estate of the said
       deceased;
   (ii) when required to do so by the Court, exhibit in the Court a full inventory of the said estate and
        render an account thereof to the Court; and
   (iii) when required to do so by the High Court, deliver up to that Court the grant of probate.
6. To the best of my/our knowledge information and belief the gross estate passing under the grant
   [does not exceed] [amounts to] [11]£
   and the net estate [does not exceed] [amounts to] [11]£
   [and that this is not a case in which an Inland Revenue Account is required to be delivered].[2]
7. That notice of this application has been given to[12]
                                                                          the executor(s)
   to whom power is to be reserved.
8. [3][5]

Sworn by the said   ⎫

at   ⎪

this   day of   ⎬

before me   ⎭

Commissioner for Oaths/Solicitor

Sworn by the said   ⎫

at   ⎪

this   day of   ⎬

before me   ⎭

Commissioner for Oaths/Solicitor

Notes

(1) Insert name, address, postcode and DX number (if any) of the solicitors extracting the grant and any reference required.

(2) Delete as appropriate.

(3) Full true name(s) of the executor(s) applying: any difference between this/these names and those appearing in the will (codicil(s)) may be explained by separate statement at the end of the oath or by separate affidavit of identity.

(4) Full permanent address: any executor(s) acting in their professional capacity may use their business address.

(5) Full true name of the deceased appearing in the death certificate. If there is any other name by which the deceased was known or in which he/she held any asset this must be given and the reason why it should appear in the grant stated.

(6) Last permanent address of the deceased. If any former address is required to appear in the grant this must be inserted and the reason for its inclusion given.

(7) Insert dates of birth and death as they appear in the death certificate.

(8) Insert age or if not precisely known as approximation e.g. "over 65".

(9) Insert, if appropriate, "and (one) (two) (or as the case may be) codicil(s)".

(10) Insert "the sole" "the surviving" "two of" "three of" or as the case may be.

(11) Insert the gross and net figures from the Inland Revenue Account or where there is no Account to be delivered the figures the estate does not exceed those figures prescribed by the Inheritance Tax (Delivery of Accounts) Regulations, set out in the PREP Form supplied by Laserform.

(12) Insert the name(s) of any executor(s) having power reserved.

Oath for administrators
(with will annexed)

Extracted by:[1]

IN THE HIGH COURT OF JUSTICE

FAMILY DIVISION

[PRINCIPAL] [DISTRICT PROBATE] REGISTRY[2]

IN THE ESTATE OF   DECEASED

I/We[3][4]

make oath and say that:

1. [5][6]

                                            deceased

was born on   and died on[7]
aged[8]   domiciled in England and Wales.
2. I/We believe the paper writings now produced to and marked by me/us to contain the true and original last will and testament[9]   of the deceased.
3. [A][No] minority and [a][no][2] life interest arises in the estate.[10]
4 To the best of my/our knowledge information and belief there was no land vested in the deceased which was settled previously to the death (and not by the will[9]   ) of the deceased and which remained settled land notwithstanding such death.
5.[11]
6. I am/We are[12]
7. I/We will
   (i) collect, get in and administer according to law the real and personal estate of the said deceased;
   (ii) when required to do so by the Court, exhibit in the Court a full inventory of the said estate and render an account thereof to the Court; and
   (iii) when required to do so by the High Court, deliver up to that Court the grant of letters of administration (with will).
8. To the best of my/our knowledge information and belief the gross estate passing under the grant [does not exceed] [amounts to] [13]£
and the net estate [does not exceed] [amounts to] [13]£
[and that this is not a case in which an Inland Revenue Account is required to be delivered].[2]

Sworn by the said

at

this   day of

before me

Commissioner for Oaths/Solicitor

Sworn by the said

at

this   day of

before me

Commissioner for Oaths/Solicitor

Notes
(1) Insert name, address, postcode and DX number (if any) of the solicitors extracting the grant and any reference required.
(2) Delete as appropriate.
(3) Full true name(s) of the applicant(s).
(4) Full permanent address.
(5) Full true name of the deceased appearing in the death certificate. If there is any other name by which the deceased was known or in which he/she held any asset must be inserted and the reason for its inclusion in the grant given.
(6) Last permanent address of the deceased. If any former address is required to appear in the grant this must be inserted and the reason for its inclusion given.
(7) Insert dates of birth and death as they appear in the death certificate.
(8) Insert age or if not precisely known as approximation e.g. "over 65".
(9) Insert, if appropriate, "and (one) (two) (or as the case may be) codicil(s)".
(10) If either or both such interests arise at least two applicants are required.
(11) Here set out the "clearing off" of the executor(s) by reciting their pre-decease or renunciation.
(12) Here set out the applicant(s) title to apply e.g. "the residuary legatee(s) and devisee(s)". See Rule 20 N.C.P.R. 1987.
(13) Insert the gross and net figures from the Inland Revenue Account or where there is no Account to be delivered the figures the estate does not exceed those figures prescribed by the Inheritance Tax (Delivery of Accounts) Regulations, set out in the PREP Form supplied by Laserform.

Oath for administrators

IN THE HIGH COURT OF JUSTICE

FAMILY DIVISION

[PRINCIPAL] [**DISTRICT PROBATE] REGISTRY[2]**

IN THE ESTATE OF   **DECEASED**

I/We[3][4]

make oath and say that:

1. [5]
   2. of[6]   deceased
   3. was born on   and died on[7]
      aged[8]   domiciled in England and Wales intestate[9]
      [and without any other person entitled in priority to shate in the estate by virtue of any enactment].[10]
4. [A][No] minority and [a][no][2] life interest arises in the estate.[11]
5. To the best of my/our knowledge information and belief there was no land vested in the said deceased which was settled previously to the death of the said deceased and which remained settled notwithstanding such death.
6. I am/We are the [lawful][12]
   and [one of] the [only] person[s] [now][2] entitled to share in the estate of the said deceased.
7. I/We will
   (i) collect, get in and administer according to law the real and personal estate of the said deceased;
   (ii) when required to do so by the Court, exhibit in the Court a full inventory of the said estate and render an account thereof to the Court; and
   (iii) when required to do so by the High Court, deliver up to that Court the grant of letters of administration.
8. To the best of my/our knowledge information and belief the gross estate passing under the grant [does not exceed] [amounts to] [13]£
   and the net estate [does not exceed] [amounts to] [13]£
   [and that this is not a case in which an Inland Revenue Account is required to be delivered].[2]
9. [5]

Sworn by the said

at

this   day of

before me

Commissioner for Oaths/Solicitor

Sworn by the said

at

this   day of

before me

Commissioner for Oaths/Solicitor

Notes

(1) Insert name, address, postcode and DX number (if any) of the solicitors extracting the grant and any reference required.
(2) Delete as appropriate.
(3) Full true name(s) of the applicant(s).
(4) Full permanent address.
(5) Full true name of the deceased appearing in the death certificate. If there is any other name by which the deceased was known or in which he/she held any asset must be inserted and the reason for its inclusion in the grant given.
(6) Last permanent address of the deceased. If any former address is required to appear in the grant this must be inserted and the reason for its inclusion given.
(7) Insert dates of birth and death as they appear in the death certificate.
(8) Insert age or if not precisely known as approximation e.g. "over 65".
(9) Insert the deceased's status at death, e.g. "a widow", "a bachelor" and the necessary clearings in accordance with Rule 22 N.C.P.R. 1987 e.g. "without issue or parent or brother or sister of the whole blood".
(10) Delete words in square brackets where the applicant is the surviving spouse or issue of the deceased.
(11) If either or both such interests arise two applicants for the grant are required.
(12) Delete "lawful" except where application is by the surviving spouse e.g. "lawful widow"; insert the relationship to the deceased e.g. "nephew and niece of the whole blood".
(13) Insert the gross and net figures from the Inland Revenue Account or where there is no Account to be delivered the figures the estate does not exceed those figures prescribed by the Inheritance Tax (Delivery of Accounts) Regulations, set out in the PREP Form supplied by Laserform.

A2.1   Instruction sheet for Will of Evelyn Worth (Will No. 1)

This is the will of an unmarried person with a small to medium estate. The executors appointed are individuals. Apart from some minor gifts the estate is given to the testatrix's parents with a substitutional gift to a sister.

DETAILS OF TESTATRIX

name:	Evelyn Worth
address:	Flat 8,
	33 Woodland Gardens,
	London, SW6
occupation:	Civil Servant.
date of birth:	3rd March, 1962.

INTENDED BENEFICIARIES

sister:	Dr Annabel Worth
	12 Arundel Street, London, SW3
parents:	Colonel Stephen Worth
	Doctor Moira Worth
	both of 'The Blue House',
	Hazlemere, Sussex.
godchild:	William Nicholls,
	Garden Cottage, Long Wootton,
	Lincs.
	(age 6).
friend:	Philip Markham,
	16 Glebe Street, London, SW6

DETAILS OF ESTATE

flat:	33 Woodland Gardens (see above) £110,000 (less mortgage £46,000).
chattels:	£5,000 (includes a car (£2,000), a pair of candlesticks (worth £1,000 see below), books (£800) and various items of furniture, other household effects and clothing (£1,200)).
money:	£13,000 (in a Building Society Account).
pension:	£92,000 is payable at the discretion of trustees (*i.e.* it will not form part of the deceased's estate).

	Evelyn Worth has informed the trustees that they should pay the money to her parents.
debts:	Mortgage (see above). Other debts—£750.

PROPOSED TESTAMENTARY DISPOSITIONS

minor gifts:	Flat (free of mortgage) to sister. Candlesticks (inherited from grandmother, Lorna Worth) to Philip Markham. Books—to be shared between sister and Markham as they choose. £1,000 to Godchild.
residue:	Residue to parents (or survivor if one predeceases), substitutional gift to sister.
direction as to body:	Deceased's body is to be available for organ transplants and/or medical research.
executors:	Sister and Philip Markham.

A draft will is shown below.

A2.2

WILL NO. 1

THIS IS THE LAST WILL AND TESTAMENT of me EVELYN WORTH of Flat 8 33 Woodland Gardens London SW6

1. I HEREBY REVOKE all former wills and testamentary dispositions made by me.

2. I APPOINT my sister Doctor Annabel Worth of 12 Arundel Street London SW3 and Philip Markham of 16 Glebe Street London SW6 to be my executors.

3. I REQUEST that my body or any part thereof may be used for medical purposes including corneal grafting organ transplantation and medical education or research in accordance with the provisions of the Human Tissue Act 1961.

4. I GIVE to the said Annabel Worth absolutely my leasehold property known as Flat 8 Woodland Gardens free of all taxes[1] and from any mortgage debt or other charge affecting the same which I direct shall be paid out of my residuary estate.

5. I GIVE the pair of Georgian silver candlesticks which I inherited from my grandmother Lorna Worth to the said Philip Markham free of all taxes[1] and all costs of package carriage and insurance incurred for the purposes of giving effect to this gift.

6. I GIVE all the books which I own at the date of my death free of all

taxes[1] to the said Annabel Worth and the said Philip Markham equally as they shall choose within three months of my death choosing turn and turn about in the order in which their names appear in this clause each choosing five volumes on each turn.

7. I GIVE to my godchild William Nicholls of Garden Cottage Long Wooton Lincolnshire one thousand pounds (£1,000) absolutely and free of all taxes[1] and I DIRECT that if he has not attained the age of 18 years at the time when the said legacy is payable my executors may pay the said legacy to his parent or guardian whose receipt shall be a full discharge to them.

8. I GIVE all the rest and residue of my estate both real and personal whatsoever and wheresoever SUBJECT TO the payment of my debts, funeral and testamentary expenses and legacies (hereinafter called my 'Residuary Estate') unto my parents Colonel Stephen Worth and Doctor Moira Worth of The Blue House Hazlemere Sussex in equal shares absolutely PROVIDED THAT they survive me by 28 days. In the event that either of my parents shall predecease me or fail to survive me by 28 days I GIVE the whole of my Residuary Estate to the survivor absolutely.

If both my parents predecease me or fail to survive me by 28 days but not otherwise than I GIVE my Residuary Estate to the said Annabel Worth absolutely.

9. I GIVE my executors the powers to exercise the powers of appropriation conferred by section 41 of the Administration of Estates Act 1925 without obtaining any of the consents required by that section and even though one or more of them may be beneficially interested.[2]

IN WITNESS whereof I have hereunto set my hand this   day of   20

| Signed by the said Evelyn Worth in our joint presence and then by us in hers |)))) |

Note:

(1) It is not necessary to provide that specific and pecuniary legacies should be free of inheritance tax since under Inheritance Tax Act 1984, s.211 inheritance tax on such gifts will be a testamentary expense (unless the will provides otherwise). However, it is desirable to state that such gifts are to be free of tax to ensure that the testator and beneficiaries are aware of the position.

(2) This clause is included for administrative convenience.

A3.1 Instruction sheet for Will of Susan Webster (Will No. 2)

INTRODUCTION

This is the will of a married person with a medium sized estate. A firm of solicitors is appointed as executors. The estate is given to the testatrix's husband with a substitutional gift to their children.

TESTATRIX
   name: Susan Ann Webster
   address: 13 Norwich Way, Wanstead
                       London, E11 4XJ
   occupation: School teacher
   date of birth: 13th February, 1957

INTENDED BENEFICIARIES
   husband: Peter Webster
                       13 Norwich Way, Wanstead
                       London, E11 4XJ

   children: David Webster (aged 14) and Karen
                       Webster (aged 12).

DETAILS OF ESTATE
   house: 13 Norwich Way, Wanstead,
                       London, E11 4XJ, in joint names with
                       husband. Value £165,000 (net of mortgage
                       £29,000).

   chattels: A car (£7,200), jewellery (£800) and various
                       items of furniture, other household effects
                       and clothing (£1,000).

   money: £500 (approx.) in a building society.

   pension: £69,000 is payable at the discretion of
                       trustees (*i.e.* not part of the deceased's
                       estate).
                       Susan Webster has asked the trustees to
                       pay the money to her husband.

PROPOSED TESTAMENTARY DISPOSITIONS
   minor gifts: Personal chattels to son and daughter in
                       equal shares subject to husband's power to
                       select such chattels as he wishes.

   residue: Residue to husband absolutely provided he
                       survives by 28 days otherwise to be held on
trust for sale for such of
the children as they reach
the age of 21.

   executors: Green & Co., Solicitors of 13, High Street,
                       Wanstead, London, E11 4PP.

   trustees: Green & Co., Solicitors (as above) and
                       Testatrix's Brother, Eric Jameson of
                       18, Norwich Way, Wanstead, London,

E11 4XJ.

guardians:	Eric Jameson and his wife, Mary Jameson both of 18, Norwich Way, Wanstead, London, E11 4XJ.
funeral:	Cremation desired.

A draft will is shown below.

A3.2

WILL NO. 2

THIS IS THE LAST WILL AND TESTAMENT of me SUSAN ANN WEBSTER of 13 Norwich Way Wanstead London E11.

1. I HEREBY REVOKE all wills and testamentary dispositions heretofore made by me.

2. (a) I APPOINT the partners at the date of my death in the firm of Green & Co. Solicitors of 13 High Street Wanstead London E11 or the firm which at that date has succeeded to and carries on its practice (hereinafter called 'my Executors') to be the executors of this my will. I express the wish that two and only two of them shall prove my will in the first instance.

(b) I APPOINT my proving Executors and my brother Eric Jameson of 18 Norwich Way Wanstead London E11 (hereinafter together called 'my Trustees' which expression shall include my Trustees for the time being of this will) to be the trustees of this my will.

3. I APPOINT my brother Eric Jameson and his wife Mary Jameson to be the guardians after the death of my husband of any of my children who may then be minors.

4. I DECLARE that any of my Executors or Trustees who are solicitors shall be entitled to charge and be paid without abatement all usual professional or other charges for business done services rendered or time spent by them or their firm in the administration of my estate or the trusts hereof including acts which a trustee who was not a solicitor could have done personally.

5. I GIVE to my husband Peter Webster of 13 Norwich Way aforesaid absolutely such of my personal chattels as defined by section 55(1)(x) of the Administration of Estates Act 1925 as he may within three months after my death select and subject thereto I give the same to my children David and Karen to be divided between them equally as my Executors shall in their absolute discretion determine.

6. If my said husband is living at my death and survives me by 28 days (but not otherwise) I GIVE to him absolutely but subject to the payment of debts funeral and testamentary expenses all the rest and residue of my estate both real and personal whatsoever and wheresoever not hereby or by any codicil hereto more specifically disposed of (hereinafter called my 'Residuary Estate').

7. If my husband is not living at my death or does not survive me by

28 days or if the gift to my husband fails for any other reason[1] (but not otherwise) I GIVE my Residuary Estate unto my Trustees TO HOLD the same on trust to sell and convert the same into money with power to postpone the sale and conversion thereof so long as they shall in their absolute discretion think fit without being liable for any loss UPON TRUST TO HOLD the proceeds of the said sale and conversion and any property for the time being remaining unsold and unconverted for such of my children as attain the age of 21 and if more than one in equal shares PROVIDED THAT if any of my children shall die before attaining a vested interest in my Residuary Estate leaving issue who attain the age of 21 years such issue shall take by substitution and if more than one in equal shares per stirpes the share of my Residuary Estate which such deceased child of mine would have taken if he or she had survived me to attain a vested interest.

8. I DIRECT that my Executors and Trustees shall have the following powers in addition to the powers given to them by the general law:

(1) To advance any capital money from my Residuary Estate in such manner as they in their absolute discretion think fit to or for the benefit of any of the beneficiaries for the time being hereof provided that the money so advanced to or for the benefit of any beneficiary shall not exceed in amount the presumptive or vested share in my Residuary Estate of that beneficiary.[2]

(2) To treat as income all the income from my Residuary Estate whatever the period in respect of which it accrues and to disregard in this respect the legal rules of apportionment.[2]

(3) In any case where my Trustees have power to apply income or capital to or for the benefit of any person who is a minor to accept the receipt of the parent or guardian of such a person or of the minor personally if of the age of 16 years in full discharge and my Trustees shall not be required to see the application of any income or capital so paid.[2]

(4) Section 31 Trustee Act 1925 will have effect as regards the income arising from my Residuary Estate as if:

(a) the words in subsection 1(i) "as may, in all the circumstances, be reasonable" were deleted and in their place the words "as my Trustees shall in their absolute discretion think fit" were substituted.

(b) the words from "Provided that" to the end of subsection 1 were deleted.

I FURTHER DIRECT that during the period of twenty-one years from my death the statutory powers of maintenance and accumulation shall continue to be exercisable by my Trustees in favour of any child or remoter issue of mine who has reached the age of 18 but not yet attained a vested interest in the capital of my Residuary Estate.[2]

8. I DESIRE that my body shall be cremated.

IN WITNESS whereof I have hereunto set my hand this   day of
       200 .

Signed by   )
Susan Ann Webster   )
in our joint presence   )
and then by us in hers   )

Note:

(1) These words are included to cover the possibility of the gift to the spouse failing for reasons other than divorce (*e.g.* forfeiture)

(2) These clauses are included because there is a possibility that a trust may arise in the event of the spouse predeceasing and a minor taking under the substitutional gift.

(3) These clauses are included in case there is no land comprised in the estate at the date of death. (Remember the statutory powers under the Trusts of Land and Appointment of Trustees Act 1996 do not apply in such a case.)

A4.1   Instruction sheet for Will of Thomas Shaw (Will No. 3)

INTRODUCTION

This will is a will of a widower with a relatively large estate. The executors appointed are the members of a firm of solicitors. Apart from some minor gifts including one to a University College the estate is given to the testator's sister for life remainder to a charity.

DETAILS OF TESTATOR

name:	Thomas Shaw
address:	3, Normandy Street, Hastings, Sussex, HA2 3SS.
occupation:	Retired company director.
date of birth:	12th May, 1916.

INTENDED BENEFICIARIES

sister:	Miss Edith Shaw, 16, Gray Square, Eastbourne, Sussex.
college:	St. Michael's, University of Camford.
cousin:	Frederick Roberts, 3, Castle View, Dorking, Surrey.
charity:	Hastings Society for the Relief of Poverty.

DETAILS OF ESTATE

house:	3, Normandy Street as above value £261,000.
shares:	(a) Minority shareholding in Hastings Holdings (Manufacturing) Ltd. value £5,000 (20% of share capital in Company). (b) Quoted shares in various companies total value £55,428.
money:	Building Society Account £10,527. (South Coast Building Society Ordinary A/C No. 1234567) Bank Account current (at Bartholomew's Bank Hastings) £583.
money:	Cash £37.
stamp collection:	Value £12,700.

household goods,
etc.:   Value £5,000.

PROPOSED TESTAMENTARY DISPOSITIONS
minor gifts: Stamp collection to sister
                               £1,000 to St Michael's College Camford.
                               £5,000 to Frederick Roberts.

residue: To sister for life remainder to Hastings
                               Society for the Relief of Poverty.

executors and   Messrs French and Co. (Solicitors)
trustees: Bank Chambers, 27 South Street, Hastings
                               HA1 4SJ.

A draft will is shown below.

A4.2

WILL NO. 3

THIS IS THE LAST WILL AND TESTAMENT of me THOMAS SHAW of 3 Normandy Street, Hastings, Sussex.

1. I HEREBY REVOKE all former wills and testamentary dispositions made by me.

2. I APPOINT the partners at the date of my death in the firm of French and Co. Solicitors or the firm which at that date has succeeded to and carries on its practice (hereinafter called 'my Trustees' which expression shall where the context so permits include any trustee for the time being of this will) of Bank Chambers 27 South Street Hastings to be the executors and trustees of this will and I express the wish that two and only two of them shall prove my will I DECLARE that my Trustees shall be entitled to charge and be paid without abatement all usual professional or other charges for services rendered and time spent by them or their firm connected with the administration of my estate or the trusts of this will including anything which a trustee not engaged in any profession could have done personally.

3 I GIVE to my sister Edith Shaw of 16 Gray Square Eastbourne Sussex absolutely and free of all taxes and all costs of package carriage and insurance incurred for the purposes of giving effect to this gift, my collection of postage stamps together with all albums catalogues and other materials relating thereto.

4. I GIVE to the Master Fellows and Scholars of the College of St Michael in the University of Camford the sum of £1,000.

5. I GIVE to my cousin Frederick Roberts of 3 Castle View Dorking Surrey the sum of £5,000 absolutely and free of all taxes.

6. I GIVE all the rest and residue of my estate both real and personal whatsoever and wheresoever not more specifically disposed of hereby or by any codicil hereto to my Trustees TO HOLD the same on trust for sale with full power to postpone the sale thereof without being liable for loss

and after payment thereout of all my debts and funeral and testamentary expenses and all legacies given hereby or by any codicil hereto TO HOLD the balance and any property for the time being remaining unsold (hereinafter called my 'Residuary Estate') UPON TRUST to pay the income therefrom to my said sister Edith Shaw during her lifetime and subject thereto UPON TRUST after the death of my said sister to pay and transfer the same to the Hastings Society for the Relief of Poverty for its general purposes.

7. I DIRECT that my Trustees shall have the following powers in addition to the powers given to them by the general law:

(1) Power to exercise the power of appropriation conferred by section 41 of the Administration of Estates Act 1925 without obtaining any of the consents required by that section.

(2) Power in their absolute discretion to pay to my sister for her sole benefit or to lend to my sister with or without security and on such terms as to repayment and as to the payment of interest as they see fit the whole or any part or parts of the capital of my Residuary Estate.

(3) Power to treat as income all the income from my Residuary Estate whatever the period in respect of which it accrues and to disregard in this respect the rules of equity known as the rules in Howe v. Lord Dartmouth and Allhusen v. Whittell in all their branches and the legal rules of apportionment.

8. I DIRECT that if before my Trustees have given effect to any gift contained herein any charitable or other body to which such gift is made has changed its name or has amalgamated with or transferred its assets to any other body my Trustees shall give effect to such gift as if it had been made as a gift to the body in its changed name or to the body with which it had amalgamated or to which it had transferred its assets as the case may be and I FURTHER DIRECT that the receipt of the person who appears to my Trustees to be the bursar treasurer or other proper officer for the time being of any charitable or other body to which any gift contained herein is made shall be a sufficient discharge to my Trustees.

IN WITNESS whereof (etc. as in Will No. 1).

A5.1 Wills Instructions Checklist

1. *Details of testator*
   (a) Testator's full name
   (b) Any former name(s) or alias(es)
   (c) Address/occupation
   (d) Age (for purposes of tax advice)
   (e) Previous will? If so, what arrangements for revocation?

2. *Value of estate*
   (a) Property owned in testator's sole name
   (b) Property owned with another as beneficial tenants in common
   (c) Property owned with another as beneficial joint tenants

(d) Nominations
(e) Superannuation benefits—nominated?
(f) Insurance policies—MWPA
                    written in trust
                    payable to estate
(g) Trust property
(h) Foreign property
(i) Inter vivos gifts to date
(j) Property likely to be inherited
(k) Debts charged on property?
(l) Mortgage protection policy
(m) Business and Agricultural property

3. *Intended beneficiaries*
      (a) Spouse—full name/size of spouse's personal estate
      (b) Children—names/ages
      (c) Others—names/addresses
N.B. Explain Family Provision legislation particularly if disposition is away from immediate family.

4. *Disposition of property*
      (a) Legacies
            (i) specific
            (ii) general
            (iii) free of tax/expenses/mortgage?
N.B. Explain possibility of ademption of specific gifts.
      (b) Residue
      (c) Trust for sale
      (d) Directions as to substitutional gift where beneficiary predeceases.
          In case of gift to institution directions as to possible change of name, amalgamation, dissolution.
      (e) Provision for payment of debts? Secured debts?

5. *Extension of statutory powers*
      (a) No trust created (remember that a trust may arise where minor beneficiaries take by substitution the share of a deceased parent)
            (i) insurance
            (ii) appropriation
            (iii) receipt clause—infant—unincorporated association
            (iv) exclude Apportionment Act
      (b) Trust created
          as above *plus*
            (i) investment
            (ii) power to buy land
            (iii) maintenance
            (iv) advancement
            (v) loans to beneficiaries
            (vi) exclude legal and equitable apportionments if appropriate

N.B. Although powers are implied in "trust of land" consider possibility that land will not be included in estate.

6. *Executors/Trustees*
    (a) Choice—explain merits of individuals, solicitors' firms, banks
    (b) Charging clause if appropriate
    (c) Special PR's to deal with special parts of estate, *e.g.* literary executors.

7. *Guardians*
    (a) Names and addresses
    (b) Willing to act?
    (c) Finance?

8. *Special problems*
    (a) Testator suffering from disability—capacity? Special attestation clause?
    (b) Testator sole trader—special provisions to deal with business?

9. *Directions as to body, funeral, etc.*

Inland Revenue Account for Inheritance Tax

Inland Revenue
Capital Taxes

Fill in this account for the estate of a person who died on or after 18 March 1986.
You should read the related guidance note(s) before filling in any particular box(es).
The notes follow the same numbering as this form, so section headings are shown
by capital letters and the items in each section are on a dark background.

A   Probate Registry, Commissary Court or Sheriff Court District

Name A1 [   ]   Date of Grant [   ]

B   About the person who has died

Title B1 [   ]   Surname B2 [   ]

First name(s) B3 [   ]

Date of birth B4 [/ /]   Date of death B5 [/ /]

Marital status B6 [   ]   Last known usual address

Surviving relatives   B7 [   ]

Husband/Wife B8 [   ]

Brother(s)/Sister(s) B9 [   ]

Parent(s) B10 [   ]   Postcode

Number of   Nursing /
                   Residential home B13 [   ]

Children B11 [   ]   Domicile B14 [   ]

Grandchildren B12 [   ]   Occupation B15 [   ]

National Insurance number B16 [| | | | |]

Income tax district B17 [   ]

Income tax reference or self assessment reference B18 [   ]

C   Solicitor or other person to contact

Name and address of firm or person
dealing with the estate   Telephone number
C1 [   ]   C4 [   ]

                                           Fax number
                                           C5 [   ]

              Postcode   For IR CT use

DX number and town
C2 [DX   ]

Contact name and reference
C3 [   ]

IHT 200 (PDF)
Version 2.0.0.1

Ⓓ Supplementary pages

You must answer all of the questions in this section. You should read the notes starting at page 10 of form IHT 210 before answering the questions.

If you answer "Yes" to a question you will need to fill in the supplementary page shown. If you do not have all the supplementary pages you need you should telephone our Orderline on 0845 2341000

		No	Yes	Page
• The Will	Did the deceased leave a Will?	☐	☐	⟫ D1
• Domicile outside the United Kingdom	Was the deceased domiciled outside the UK at the date of death?	☐	☐	⟫ D2
• Gifts and other transfers of value	Did the deceased make any gift or any other transfer of value on or after 18 March 1986?	☐	☐	⟫ D3
• Joint assets	Did the deceased hold any asset(s) in joint names with another person?	☐	☐	⟫ D4
• Nominated assets	Did the deceased, at any time during their lifetime, give written instructions (usually called a "nomination") that any asset was to pass to a particular person on their death?	☐	☐	⟫ D4
• Assets held in trust	Did the deceased have any right to any benefit from any assets held in trust or in a settlement at the date of death?	☐	☐	D5
• Pensions	Did the deceased have provision for a pension from employers, a personal pension policy or other provisions made for retirement other than the State Pension?	☐	☐	⟫ D6
• Stocks and shares	Did the deceased own any stocks or shares?	☐	☐	⟫ D7
• Debts due to the estate	Did the deceased lend any money, either on mortgage or by personal loan, that had not been repaid by the date of death?	☐	☐	⟫ D8
• Life insurance and annuities	Did the deceased pay any premiums on any life insurance policies or annuities which are payable to either the estate or to someone else or which continue after death?	☐	☐	⟫ D9
• Household and personal goods	Did the deceased own any household goods or other personal possessions?	☐	☐	⟫ D10
• Interest in another estate	Did the deceased have a right to a legacy or a share of an estate of someone who died before them, but which they had not received before they died?	☐	☐	⟫ D11
• Land, buildings and interests in land	Did the deceased own any land or buildings in the UK?	☐	☐	⟫ D12
• Agricultural relief	Are you deducting agricultural relief?	☐	☐	⟫ D13
• Business interests	Did the deceased own all or part of a business or were they a partner in a business?	☐	☐	⟫ D14
• Business relief	Are you deducting business relief?	☐	☐	⟫ D14
• Foreign assets	Did the deceased own any assets outside the UK?	☐	☐	D15
• Debts owed by the estate	Are you claiming a deduction against the estate for any money that the deceased had borrowed from relatives, close friends, or trustees, or other loans, overdrafts or guarantee debts?	☐	☐	⟫ D16

2

E **Domicile in Scotland**

- Has any claim for legal rights been made or discharged?   No [ ]   Yes [ ]

- How many children are under 18 [ ]   or 18 and over [ ]

F **Estate in the UK where tax may not be paid by instalments**

- Quoted stocks, shares and investments *(box SS1, form D7)*   **F1** £ _____

- UK Government and municipal securities *(box SS2, form D7)*   **F2** £ _____

- Unquoted stocks, shares and investments   **F3** £ _____

- Traded unquoted stocks and shares   **F4** £ _____

- Dividends or interest   **F5** £ _____

- Premium Bonds   **F6** £ _____

- National Savings investments *(show details on form D17)*   **F7** £ _____

- Bank and building society accounts *(show details on form D17)*   **F8** £ _____

- Cash   **F9** £ _____

- Debts due to the deceased and secured by mortgage *(box DD1, form D8)*   **F10** £ _____

- Other debts due to the deceased *(box DD1, form D8)*   **F11** £ _____

- Rents due to the deceased   **F12** £ _____

- Accrued income   **F13** £ _____

- Apportioned income   **F14** £ _____

- Other income due to the deceased *(box IP4, form D9, box PA1 form D6)*   **F15** £ _____

- Life insurance policies *(box IP3, form D9)*   **F16** £ _____

- Private health schemes   **F17** £ _____

- Income tax or capital gains tax repayment   **F18** £ _____

- Household and personal goods *(sold, box HG1, form D10)*   **F19** £ _____

- Household and personal goods *(unsold, box HG2, form D10)*   **F20** £ _____

- Interest in another estate *(box UE1, form D11)*   **F21** £ _____

- Interest in expectancy *(reversionary interest)*   **F22** £ _____

- Other personal assets in the UK *(show details on form D17)*   **F23** £ _____

Total assets *(sum of boxes F1 to F23)*   **F24** £ _____

Liabilities, funeral expenses, exemptions and reliefs

- Liabilities

Name	Description of liability	

Total liabilities F25 £

- Funeral expenses

Total of funeral expenses F26 £

Total liabilities and funeral expenses *(box F25 plus box F26)* F27 £

Net total of assets less liabilities *(box F24 less box F27)* F28 £

- Exemptions and reliefs

Total exemptions and reliefs F29 £

Chargeable value of assets in the UK where tax may not
be paid by instalments *(box F28 less box F29)* F30 £

4

G **Estate in the UK where tax may be paid by instalments**

Do you wish to pay the tax on these assets by instalments?   No ☐   Yes ☐

- Deceased's residence — **G1** £
- Other residential property — **G2** £
- Farms — **G3** £
- Business property — **G4** £
- Timber and woodland — **G5** £
- Other land and buildings — **G6** £

- Farming business   *Interest in a business* **G7.1** £   *Interest in a partnership* **G7.2** £   **G7** £
- Other business interests   *Interest in a business* **G8.1** £   *Interest in a partnership* **G8.2** £   **G8** £
- Business assets   *Farm trade assets* **G9.1** £   *Other business assets* **G9.2** £   **G9** £
- Quoted shares and securities, control holding only   **G10** £
- Unquoted shares   *Control holding* **G11.1** £   *Non-control holding* **G11.2** £   **G11** £
- Traded unquoted shares   *Control holding* **G12.1** £   *Non-control holding* **G12.2** £   **G12** £

Total assets *(sum of boxes G1 to G12)*   **G13** £

Liabilities, exemptions and reliefs

- Name and address of mortgagee

  G14 £

- Other liabilities

  Total of other liabilities   **G15** £

Net total of assets less liabilities *(box G13 less boxes G14 and G15)*   **G16** £

- Exemptions and reliefs

  Total exemptions and reliefs   **G17** £

Chargeable value of assets in the UK where tax may be paid by instalments *(box G16 less box G17)*   **G18** £

(H) **Summary of the chargeable estate**

You should fill in form IHT(WS) so that you can copy the figures to this section and to section J.
If you are applying for a grant without the help of a solicitor or other agent and you do not wish to
work out the tax yourself, leave this section and section J blank. Go on to section K.

Assets where tax may not be paid by instalments

- Estate in the UK *(box WS1)* — H1 £
- Joint property *(box WS2)* — H2 £
- Foreign property *(box WS3)* — H3 £
- Settled property on which the trustees would like to pay tax now *(box WS4)* — H4 £

Total of assets where tax may not be paid by instalments *(box WS5)* — H5 £

Assets where tax may be paid by instalments

- Estate in the UK *(box WS6)* — H6 £
- Joint property *(box WS7)* — H7 £
- Foreign property *(box WS8)* — H8 £
- Settled property on which the trustees would like to pay tax now *(box WS9)* — H9 £

Total of assets where tax may be paid by instalments *(box WS10)* — H10 £

Other property taken into account to calculate the total tax

- Settled property *(box WS11)* — H11 £
- Gift with reservation *(box WS12)* — H12 £

Chargeable estate *(box WS13)* — H13 £

Cumulative total of lifetime transfers *(box WS14)* — H14 £

Aggregate chargeable transfer *(box WS15)* — H15 £

J Calculating the tax liability

Calculating the total tax that is payable

- Aggregate chargeable transfer *(box WS16)* — J1 £
- Tax threshold *(box WS17)* — J2 £
- Value chargeable to tax *(box WS18)* — J3 £

Tax payable *(box WS19)* — J4 £

- Tax (if any) payable on lifetime transfers *(box WS20)* — J5 £
- Relief for successive charges *(box WS21)* — J6 £

Tax payable on total of assets liable to tax *(box WS22)* — J7 £

Calculating the tax payable on delivery of this account

- Tax which may not be paid by instalments *(box TX4)* — J8 £
- Double taxation relief *(box TX5)* — J9 £
- Interest to be added *(box TX7)* — J10 £

Tax and interest being paid now which may not be paid by instalments *(box TX8)* — J11 £

- Tax which may be paid by instalments *(box TX12)* — J12 £
- Double taxation relief *(box TX13)* — J13 £
- Number of instalments being paid now J14 ___ / 10 *(box TX15)*
- Tax now payable *(box TX16)* — J15 £
- Interest on instalments to be added *(box TX17)* — J16 £
- Additional interest to be added *(box TX18)* — J17 £

Tax and interest being paid now which may be paid by instalments *(box TX19)* J18 £

Total tax and interest being paid now on this account *(box TX20)* J19 £

K Authority for repayment of inheritance tax

In the event of any inheritance tax being overpaid the payable order for overpaid tax and interest in connection with this estate should be made out to

L Declaration

I/We wish to apply for a **L1**

To the best of my/our knowledge and belief, the information I/we have given and the statements I/we have made in this account and in supplementary pages **L2** attached (together called "this account") are correct and complete.

I/We have made the fullest enquiries that are reasonably practicable in the circumstances to find out the open market value of all the items shown in this account. The value of items in box(es) **L3** are provisional estimates which are based an all the information available to me/us at this time. I/We will tell IR Capital Taxes the exact value(s) as soon as I/we know it and I/we will pay any additional tax and interest that may be due.

I/We understand that I/we may be liable to prosecution if I/we deliberately conceal any information that affects the liability to inheritance tax arising on the deceased's death, OR if I/we deliberately include information in this account which I/we know to be false.

I/We understand that I/we may have to pay financial penalties if this account is incorrect by reason of my/our fraud or negligence, OR if I/we fail to remedy anything in this account which is incorrect in any material respect within a reasonable time of it coming to my/our notice.

I/We understand that the issue of the grant does not mean that

- I/we have paid all the inheritance tax and interest that may be due on the estate, or

- the statements made and the values included in this account are accepted by IR Capital Taxes.

I/We understand that IR Capital Taxes

- will only look at this account in detail after the grant has been issued

- may need to ask further questions and discuss the value of items shown in this account

- may make further calculations of tax and interest payable to help the persons liable for the tax make provision to meet the tax liability.

I/We understand that where we have elected to pay tax by instalments that I/we may have to pay interest on any unpaid tax according to the law.

Each person delivering this account, whether as executor, intending administrator or otherwise must sign below to indicate that they have read and agreed the statements above.

Full name and address	Full name and address
Signature Date	Signature Date
Full name and address	Full name and address
Signature Date	Signature Date

8

Inland Revenue
Capital Taxes

Inheritance tax worksheet

Working out the value of the estate

Assets where tax may not be paid by instalments

- Estate in the UK *(box F30, form IHT200)*

  WS1 £
  Copy to box H1 on IHT200

- Joint property – *passing by survivorship*. Copy the figure from box JP5 on form D4. If you have filled in more than one form D4, there is space here to copy the figure off each form.

  Total £

  WS2 £
  Copy to box H2 on IHT200

- Foreign assets – copy the figure from box FP7 on form D15. If you have filled in more than one form D15, there is space here to copy the figure off each form.

  Total £

  WS3 £
  Copy to box H3 on IHT200

- Settled property – *on which the trustees would like to pay tax now*. Copy the figure from box SP5 on form D5. If you have filled in more than one form D5, there is space here to copy the figure off each form.

  Total £

  WS4 £
  Copy to box H4 on IHT200

  Total of assets where tax may not be paid by instalments
  (WS1 + WS2 + WS3 + WS4)

  WS5 £
  Copy to box H5 on IHT200

Assets where tax may be paid by instalments

- Estate in the UK *(box G18, form IHT200)*

  WS6 £
  Copy to box H6 on IHT200

- Joint property – *passing by survivorship.* Copy the figure from box JP10 on form D4. If you have filled in more than one form D4, there is space here to copy the figure off each form.

  Total £

  WS7 £
  Copy to box H7 on IHT200

- Foreign assets – copy the figure from box FP12 on form D15. If you have filled in more than one form D15, there is space here to copy the figure off each form

  Total £

  WS8 £
  Copy to box H8 on IHT200

- Settled property – *on which the trustees would like to pay tax now.* Copy the figure from box SP10 on form D5. If you have filled in more than one form D5, there is space here to copy the figure off each form.

  Total £

  WS9 £
  Copy to box H9 on IHT200

  Total of assets where tax may be paid by instalments
  (WS6 + WS7 + WS8 + WS9)

  WS10 £
  Copy to box H10 on IHT200

IHT(WS)
(PDF) Version 2.0.0.1

ROH4262 IRCT9/01

Other property taken into account to calculate the total tax

- Settled property – copy the figure from boxes SP5 and SP10 on form D5. If you have filled in more than one form D5, there is space here to copy the figures off each form

Total £

WS11 £
Copy to box H11 on IHT200

- Gift with reservation *(box LT2, form D3)*

WS12 £
Copy to box H12 on IHT200

Chargeable estate *(WS5 + WS10 + WS11 + WS12)*

WS13 £
Copy to box H13 on IHT200

Cumulative total of lifetime transfers *(box LT1, form D3)*

WS14 £
Copy to box H14 on IHT200

Aggregate chargeable transfer *(WS13 + WS14)*

WS15 £
Copy to box H15 on IHT200

Working out the total tax that is payable

- Aggregate chargeable transfer *(WS15)*

WS16 £
Copy to box J1 on IHT200

- Tax threshold

WS17 £
Copy to box J2 on IHT200

- Value chargeable to tax *(WS16 – WS17)*

WS18 £
Copy to box J3 on IHT200

Tax due *(WS18 @ 40%)*

WS19 £
Copy to box J4 on IHT200

- Tax (if any) on lifetime transfers *(box LT6)*

WS20 £
Copy to box J5 on IHT200

Total of lifetime transfers

LT3 £
Copy from box WS14

Tax threshold

LT4 £
Copy from box WS17

Lifetime transfers chargeable to tax
(LT3 – LT4)

LT5 £

Tax on lifetime transfers *(LT5 @40%)*

LT6 £
Copy to box WS20

- Relief for successive charges

WS21 £
Copy to box J6 on IHT200

Tax payable on chargeable estate *(WS19 – WS20 – WS21)*

WS22 £
Copy to box J7 on IHT200

Working out the tax that is payable on this account

Tax which may not be paid by instalments

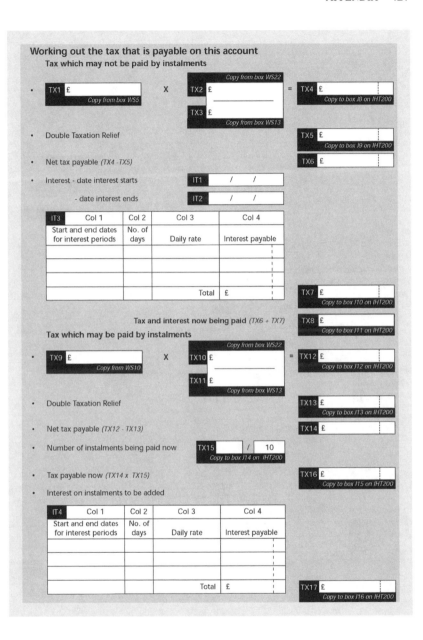

- TX1 £ _Copy from box WS5_ **X** TX2 £ _Copy from box WS22_

  TX3 £ _Copy from box WS13_ **=** TX4 £ _Copy to box J8 on IHT200_

- Double Taxation Relief TX5 £ _Copy to box J9 on IHT200_

- Net tax payable *(TX4 -TX5)* TX6 £

- Interest - date interest starts IT1 / /

  - date interest ends IT2 / /

IT3	Col 1	Col 2	Col 3	Col 4
	Start and end dates for interest periods	No. of days	Daily rate	Interest payable
			Total	£

TX7 £ _Copy to box J10 on IHT200_

Tax and interest now being paid *(TX6 + TX7)* TX8 £ _Copy to box J11 on IHT200_

Tax which may be paid by instalments

- TX9 £ _Copy from WS10_ **X** TX10 £ _Copy from box WS22_

  TX11 £ _Copy from box WS13_ **=** TX12 £ _Copy to box J12 on IHT200_

- Double Taxation Relief TX13 £ _Copy to box J13 on IHT200_

- Net tax payable *(TX12 - TX13)* TX14 £

- Number of instalments being paid now TX15 [   ] / 10 _Copy to box J14 on IHT200_

- Tax payable now *(TX14 x TX15)* TX16 £ _Copy to box J15 on IHT200_

- Interest on instalments to be added

IT4	Col 1	Col 2	Col 3	Col 4
	Start and end dates for interest periods	No. of days	Daily rate	Interest payable
			Total	£

TX17 £ _Copy to box J16 on IHT200_

• Additional interest to be added

IT5	Col 1	Col 2	Col 3	Col 4
	Start and end dates for interest periods	No. of days	Daily rate	Interest payable
		Total	£	

TX18 £
Copy to box J17 on IHT200

Tax and interest now being paid *(TX16 + TX17 + TX18)*

TX19 £
Copy to box J18 on IHT200

Total tax and interest now being paid on this account *(TX8 + TX19)*

TX20 £
Copy to box J19 on IHT200

Working out Successive Charges Relief
Estate of first person to die

Net value of estate for inheritance tax   SC1 £

Legacies paid out from estate   SC2 £

Inheritance Tax paid on estate   SC3 £

Deceased's entitlement from estate   SC4 £

Rate of relief   SC5 %

Formula for relief

$$\frac{\text{SC3 £}}{\text{SC1 £}} \times \text{SC4 £} \times \text{SC5 \%} = \text{SC6 £}$$

Working out Double Taxation Relief

Value of foreign property included in form IHT200 on which foreign tax has been paid (figure in sterling)   DT1 £

Foreign tax paid (in sterling)   DT2 £

Formula for relief

$$\frac{\text{WS22 £}}{\text{WS13 £}} \times \text{DT1 £} = \text{DT3 £}$$

The relief is the **lower** of boxes DT2 and DT3.

Inland Revenue
Capital Taxes

The Will

Name

Date of death
/ /

Give details about the latest Will made by the deceased. If a Deed of Variation has been signed before applying for a grant, fill in the form to show the effect of the Will and the Deed together. You should read form D1(Notes) before filling in this form.

1 Is the address for the deceased as shown in the Will the same as the address on page 1 of form IHT200?

No ☐ Yes ☐

If the answer is "No", say below what happened to the property shown in the Will.

2 Are all items referred to in the Will, for example, legacies referring to personal possessions, stocks and shares, loans or gifts made by the deceased, included in form IHT200?

N/A ☐ No ☐ Yes ☐

If the answer is "No", say below why these items are not included.

3 Does the whole estate pass to beneficiaries who are chargeable to inheritance tax?

No ☐ Yes ☐

If the answer is "No", deduct the exemption on form IHT200.

D1 (PDF) Version 2.0.0.1

R0G4113CTO11/99

Inland Revenue
Capital Taxes

Probate summary

Fill in this form to give details of the estate that becomes the property of the personal representatives of the deceased. It is this property for which the grant of representation is to be made. You should read form D18(Notes) before filling in this form.

A Name and address

Probate registry

Date of grant
(for probate registry use)

B About the person who has died

Title

Surname

First name(s)

Last known usual address

Date of death   /   /

Domicile

Postcode

C Summary from IHT200

Add the value of any general power property on form D5 to boxes PS1-PS5

Gross assets, section F, box 24	PS1	£
Gross assets, section G, box 13	PS2	£
Gross value to be carried to Probate papers *(box PS1 plus box PS2)*	PS3	£
Liabilities, section F, box F27	PS4	£
Liabilities, section G, boxes G14 plus G15	PS5	£
Net value to be carried to Probate papers *(box PS3 less box PS4 less box PS5)*	PS6	£
Tax and interest paid on this account, section J, box J19	PS7	£

                /   /

Signature of person or firm calculating the amount due   Contact name and /or reference   Date

(For IR CT use only)

IR CT reference

EDP

Cashier's reference

IR CT Cashiers

D18 (PDF) Version 2.0.0.2

ROG4138 IRCT7/01

Index